Adventures of a Jelly Baby

ALSO BY JUDY CORNWELL

~

Cow and Cow Parsley

Fishcakes at the Ritz

The Seventh Sunrise

Fear and Favour

Adventures of a Jelly Baby

A memoir

~

JUDY CORNWELL

SIDGWICK & JACKSON

First published 2005 by Sidgwick & Jackson
an imprint of Pan Macmillan Ltd
Pan Macmillan, 20 New Wharf Road, London N1 9RR
Basingstoke and Oxford
Associated companies throughout the world
www.panmacmillan.com

ISBN 0 283 07001 3

1 3 5 7 9 8 6 4 2

A CIP catalogue record for this book is available from
the British Library.

Typeset by SetSystems Ltd, SaffronWalden, Essex
Printed and bound in Great Britain by
Mackays of Chatham plc, Chatham, Kent

For all those who urged me to tell my story,
especially my husband, John, and my son, Edward,
who lived it with me.

~

Part One

Chapter One

1940–1947

~

ACCORDING TO MY mother, in one of her more waspish moods, I was the result of a Volpar Gel contraceptive that did not work. A moment of madness in May, a determined sperm living up to my father's family's motto – 'Perseverance and Faith' – and bingo, I was created, the unplanned, unexpected jelly baby.

All because a young colonial called Barry Cornwell arrived in England in 1939. He had just finished a tour of Europe with his fiancée and her mother, and having become aware of a possible war with Germany he had joined the RAF ready to fight the Hun. On a weekend leave in London he had wandered into a tobacconist shop just off Trafalgar Square where he was served by the twenty-two-year-old Irene McCullen. He found her slight Wearside accent fascinating and her beauty irresistible; and she reminded him of Vivien Leigh. She said she would not go out with him unless he shaved off his beard. Later, she found him waiting on her doorstep, clean-shaven and clutching a bunch of roses.

My conception caused a broken engagement and a hasty marriage, and by September, when I began kicking in the safety of Mother's womb, war was declared. I was born at 55 Wendell Road, Hammersmith, on 22 February 1940, my mother's twenty-third birthday, in time for tea. One of the Queen Charlotte's nurses delivered me into a world where bombs were dropping and I spent most of the first months of my life in air-raid shelters.

My father was one of those brave young pilots on coastal command, starting the war as a flight lieutenant and quickly becoming a squadron leader. After I was born he was sent down to Plymouth and my mother, deciding it was getting too dangerous in London, made plans to join him – a good decision as our house was bombed while we were in a shelter. I was baptized quickly in case we were killed and then we moved into a house in Plymouth. That was fire-bombed while Mum was taking me for an outing in my pram. I had obviously been allotted a rather conscientious guardian angel.

But it was across the Bristol Channel, at a house in Pembroke-shire, where my memories begin in December 1940. I was ten months old and I remember feeling curious about a dangling, glittering ball reflecting light from the fire. I was sitting on the hearthrug in a dark room and was aware that my mother and another woman were peeping round some blackout curtains and whispering together. I reached for this glittering orb dangling from the branch of a small tree and took it down to examine it. It was white and soft with bits of crusted silver reflecting the light. I wanted to know what was inside it, so felt round the soft ball until I found a loose bit of cotton wool that slowly unwound. I was enraged to find there was nothing inside and yelled with frustra-tion. The women came hurrying over, thinking I had hurt myself. It was my first lesson in understanding that just because something glitters this does not mean it contains anything of substance – prob-ably the best lesson I could have for my future as an actress.

As the bombing increased in the South-West of England, Mum decided she would go back up to Sunderland, in the North-East. Although both her parents were dead, her elder brothers and Hilda, her eldest sister, still lived there. We were going to stay with Hilda, a warm jolly woman who was always baking, so I called her 'Cookie'.

On our way north the train compartment was full of soldiers. They looked after me whenever the train stopped and my mother got out and tried to get me some milk. I was fifteen months old and I remember sitting on the soldiers' knees and feeling sorry for them because their uniforms were made of such rough material. The sol-diers and Mum talked and laughed a lot as we travelled, and even at that age I was aware they thought my mother was very pretty.

~

BY THE TIME I was two, we had crossed Scotland and sailed to Benbecula in the Hebrides. We lived in an isolated crofter's cottage and Dad made Mum carry a revolver in her pocket at all times, in case the Germans landed. He gave her shooting lessons and I'd hear dreadful banging sounds when the birds would screech and my mother would yell with fright, while Dad was shouting, 'Shoot from the hip! Shoot from the hip!' She would walk around with this big hard lump on her hip and if ever my father sent anyone over with a message they would shout out loudly, 'Don't shoot, Mrs Cornwell – I've got a message from your husband.'

One night there was the thundering sound of marching outside the cottage. My father was at the airbase on the other side of the island and my mother was terrified. So was I. I wanted a cuddle but was told to hang on tightly to the back of her dressing gown, do everything she told me to do, and keep quiet. Mum had the gun in her hand ready to blast the first Hun setting foot over the threshold. I was trying to suck my thumb and hold on to her dressing gown at the same time. The marching went on for about an hour and then stopped. Mum was shaking with fright and waving the gun around. We waited to see what would happen next. There were a lot of snorting sounds, not usually associated with marching soldiers. Gradually Mum realized it was a herd of Shetland ponies wandering round the cottage, trying to keep warm. I was allowed to sleep in her bed that night.

I loved Benbecula – the cries of the peewits on a clear sunny morning, the smell of peat burning on the fire and the howling of strong winds that would bump and shake the cottage.

I remember one sunny day sitting on the grass outside the house with some older children and watching one of them take out of her mouth what I thought was one of her teeth. She put it back in again, then took it out and put it back in. She kept doing this and it worried me. Only years later did I realize that what I mistook for her tooth was in fact chewing gum.

At two and a half I was very ill with measles. Mother took me to hospital and I went to sleep with her sitting by my cot. When I woke, I was all alone in a strange, green-coloured room. I remember standing up in the cot and wondering how to get out. The floor was a long way down if I fell climbing over the bars, but I reckoned I could try. Though, even if I could get down from the cot, I would not be able to reach the door handle, and I didn't know where I was or how to get home. So I yowled at the top of my voice. Two nurses came rushing in, one of whom called me a bad-tempered child and told me to stop all the noise. I have always found the presumption that all nurses are tender hearted and kind quite wrong. Some of them can be utterly callous. This nurse was one of them. I felt lost, unable to communicate and frightened. My mind went to sleep for the rest of the hospital stay and I remember nothing more of it.

WHEN I WAS three, my father was transferred to an airbase in Norfolk and we moved into a house in New Hunstanton, not far from the sea. To make sure we had a supply of fresh eggs, he had bought some ducks and chickens. Most of the back garden was used for growing vegetables. I loved watching the ducks marching in single file back to their roosting boxes at night and listening to the clucking sounds of the chickens as they scratched the earth. Behind our garden was a field where the man who ran the donkey rides on the beach kept his donkeys. I would climb the fence and watch them as they grazed and moved about. The beach, too, was another wonderful place, especially for sandhoppers.

Then there were the night-time air-raid warning sirens, when mother and I, clutching our gas masks, would rush to hide under the dining-room table. We crouched there for what seemed like hours, until the all-clear sirens told us we could go back to the warmth of our beds.

Because my father was away at the airbase so often, my mother's older unmarried sister, who was a school cook in south London, came to visit us. Although Aunty Gladys had the same clear complexion as my mother, she was smaller with a square-shaped body and tiny feet. She wore a leopard-skin coat and a matching hat, and I was fascinated by her coat and the smell of her perfumed hair. She helped Mum by taking me for walks and by doing a lot of the cooking. Aunty Gladys also loved telling me stories, especially the one about Cinderella. Her favourite part of the story was when the prince rode up on his white horse to look for Cinderella. She would make her trumpet sound, 'Toot-toot-to-too', and triumphantly shout, 'And in he rode!'

Mother was a little odd at this time. She seemed to need to rest a lot, so I was happy to be with Aunty Gladys, especially as she gave me all her sweet coupons. One day my father took us to the airbase and there was a march-past of all the airmen. Mother, Aunty Gladys and I were in the stands. I was excited by the brass band and was fascinated by what my father did when he was away from us. When the marching airmen all turned to what seemed my direction and saluted, I returned the salute, much to my mother's amusement.

That day my father lifted me into the inside of a bomber and let me wear his RAF cap as I walked around inside. Then he explained how he also flew another kind of plane, a smaller one so he could be quick when chasing the enemy. It was called a Spitfire. The name made me laugh because it sounded like spitting, which I was not supposed to do.

Mother started to get fatter and rest a lot and I continued to make friends with the donkeys in the field at the back of our garden. A boy who was a year older than me moved into the house next door and so I had someone to play with and someone with whom I could share my sandhoppers.

In April 1944, when I was four, my mother disappeared one morning. Father and Aunty Gladys told me that I was going to have a brother and I was thrilled. I had seen a photograph of my cousin Barry who lived in America, and I knew the boy next door, so I thought my new brother would be like them. I hurried down to the beach and collected a lot of sandhoppers in a tin for him. That afternoon, when we reached the nursing home, I was shown a scrunched-up baby and told this was my brother. I was appalled but I still gave him the sandhoppers, emptying the tin into his cot. I was led out of the place in disgrace with the grown-ups saying things like 'She's obviously jealous' or 'You see, she's had all the attention so far, you'll have to watch her'. What were they going on about? They promised me a brother and gave me this pink and wrinkly thing in a cot.

Now there was the baby to join us under the table when the air-raid sirens went off at night. Mother was totally busy with him. In the mornings, after breakfast, she would sit on the front porch while he slept in a pram. One day, while she was sitting there with him, I climbed over the fence and somehow scrambled on to the back of one of the donkeys in the field. The man who took them down to the beach did not notice me and the herd started moving off while I was hanging on to the donkey's mane. They were driven past our house on their way down to the beach. I could see my mother and I shouted out to her and waved as the donkeys picked up speed. The faster they went the harder my bottom bounced and slid on the donkey's hairy back. My head felt as if it was going to be shaken off my shoulders and my teeth were rattling, but apart from sliding perilously far down the donkey's ribs, I managed to hang on to its mane all the way down to the beach, when the man in charge spotted me and came to help me down. I hung around the donkeys for a while, watching the man saddle them up. When I saw Mum and the pram in the distance. There was a great shout of 'You stay there' and she arrived a bit later, breathless, yelling, 'You could have been killed'. Then I was led home.

As a result of my adventure with the donkeys a young woman called Pauline was hired to look after me and help in the house. One day she took me to the swimming pool. I was bored in the small children's paddling pool. I could see all the grown-ups climbing to the top of a wonderfully long slide and shooting down into the water in the bigger pool, where Pauline was practising her breast stroke. So I joined the queue for the slide. I had just reached the top when there was a shriek of 'Judy, you stay where you are' from my mother. Her sixth sense, or my guardian angel, had warned her to take the pram down to the swimming pool to check up on Pauline. I was holding up the queue, but Mother was telling me not to move. Some men in the pool pacified her and swam over to the bottom of the slide. They called out to me, beckoning me to come down and promising they would catch me. I yelled with glee as I came shooting down the slide into the water. I loved it, but Pauline was in deep trouble.

After Pauline left, my father's youngest sister, Deirdre, came to stay with us. She was very pretty and when she took me for walks or to the beach men would turn to look at her. One afternoon she took me to a small lagoon, where a young serviceman started talking to her. They sat on a bench chatting while I tried to join in the conversation. The serviceman told me that if I could run round the lagoon he would give me a threepenny bit. I did very well that afternoon and went home with three threepenny bits. While Aunt Deirdre stayed with us I developed quite sturdy legs from running round the lagoon and collected a pile of coins.

~

THERE WAS GREAT excitement on the day before my fifth birthday. Mother told me I was going to have a party to celebrate and it meant I was big enough to go to school. When I woke the next morning I was so excited. I ran to the dressing-table mirror in my parents' bedroom to see how much taller I had grown and was disappointed to find that I was still the same size as the day before. All day I ran backwards and forwards from our front gate to announce to anyone who would listen that this was the way to the party. Mum and Dad came, so did Aunt Deirdre and the boy next door with his mother. I was given a coloured picture book with each page showing what a five-year-old should take to school and what happened there. There were pictures of a pencil box, a satchel, a peg to hang your coat on and a desk; also of a toothbrush and mug, soap and a towel, and all the things that should be familiar to a five-year-old. I do not remember much about what we ate or what other presents I received. The book was the most important thing to me that day and the most beautiful book I had ever seen. It had a hard cover, the pages were glossy, brightly coloured photographs with bold print, and the paper had a special clean smell. It made me really look forward to going to school.

I started at the state primary in the spring of 1945 and was lucky enough to have a wonderful teacher, Miss Scaler, a tall old lady who wore her grey hair in a bun at the nape of her neck. She was a clever ventriloquist who kept a puppet called Joey in a cupboard. Once a day Joey would come out of the cupboard and talk to us. Miss Scaler introduced us to a magical world of letters that became words, sentences and finally stories. I could read by the end of the term. She taught us numbers with a brightly coloured abacus and baskets of smooth shells. We learnt our two times table by rote and went out on nature walks. Our classroom was a world of discovery but out in the playground there were bigger children who shouted, sometimes fought each other, made a lot of noise, and used words I had not heard before.

On the last day of term before the summer holidays, Aunt Deirdre picked me up from school and took me home, where my mother was entertaining other officers' wives for tea. One of the guests asked me what I had been doing at school, and I replied, 'We've been cleaning the flies' shit off the windows.' My mother was horrified at my language. And that was the end of my time at the state primary school.

~

IN MAY THE war in Europe was over. There were no more air-raid sirens, the grown-ups seemed happier and there was lots of laughter. There were flags and brightly coloured bunting hanging in the street and my father was at home much more. During the summer holidays in 1945 lots of exciting things happened. We moved to a bigger house, in Old Hunstanton, a village a few miles away. I had a freshly painted pink bedroom and my baby brother had one in blue. The house had about an acre of land made up of rockeries and lawn, a vegetable garden, an orchard, and a large wild field which led down to the beach road, the sand dunes and the sea. The ducks and the chickens came with us and someone called Sylvia, who was Irish, arrived to help in the house. Although my brother and I, like all British children, were taking cod liver oil and orange juice provided by the government, my father decided goat's milk would be healthier for us than any powdered milk. A nanny goat arrived and Dad showed Sylvia how to sit astride her, holding her horns, while my mother milked into a pail. Soon the larder was full of dripping goat's cheese. I quite liked it, but then a piece of yellow Cheddar was always a welcome luxury.

As I could now read, my father took me to join the Boots children's library in New Hunstanton. I was told I could change my book every week and the first book I chose was *The White Snake* because the design of the snake on the front cover fascinated me. He also enrolled me at Miss Barcombe's dancing school. Miss Barcombe wore a black, pleated, silky skirt and a white frilly blouse. She wore her fair hair in plaits wound across her head. Her friend Miss Godfrey, who played the piano, also wore a black pleated skirt with a more tailored blouse; her hair was short and dark and she wore glasses. I loved the dancing classes with the chalk circles on the floor, representing our own space to dance in, and the cross where we placed our feet for the basic ballet positions. When it was hot we would dance in the garden to the sound of crashing chords coming through the French windows.

After collecting me from dancing class one afternoon Dad told me I was to be a bridesmaid for one of his friends. So I was taken to the dressmaker where they made me a pink nylon bridesmaid dress that crackled when I moved. Father told me that nylon was made from coal but I wondered how the black stuff that burned in the fire could turn into this crackly dress. I was allowed to keep the dress and it became my first party dress. As there was such a shortage of clothes and materials after the war, and of course everything was rationed through coupons, Mother was thrilled that I was given it.

The grown-ups talked a lot about the war, and about the rationing. Some of Dad's friends talked about being taken prisoner. Whenever I was caught lurking and listening, I would be sent off to play. When Dad arranged for two Italian prisoners of war to come and cut the wild field at the bottom of the garden, I used to watch them scything the grass in the heat and I felt sorry for them being prisoners. So I raided my money box for threepenny pieces, cut two slices of Swiss roll, wrapped it all in a handkerchief, took the bundle to them and told them to escape. They ate the Swiss roll but refused the money, saying they were quite happy, and then taught me to count in Italian.

Dad got Mum a bicycle, with a basket on the handlebars, so she could ride to the village shops. He also bought a three-wheeler Morgan and took us for drives when he could get petrol. That summer I tasted my first ice cream. It was Walls strawberry ice cream in a tub. It was watery and horrible and I could not understand why the grown-ups were so excited about the sudden availability of ice cream. Then, a week later, I was given an oblong white vanilla ice cream between two wafers. You had to lick the sides quickly or it would drip down your frock. Now I understood!

At the end of the summer holidays, as a special treat, I was taken to the cinema for the first time to see *Bambi*. I cried when his mother died but Mum reassured me that Bambi would be all right so I was able to see the rest of the film.

~

WHEN THE NEXT autumn school term started, I was put in a green uniform and sent to Ingoldsthorpe Preparatory School, run by the Reverend Potts. A special school bus stopped at the top of our road and collected pupils on the way to school, and then returned us in the evening to where a parent would be waiting. It was a really good school with dedicated teachers and I thrived there. We learned French, Roman numerals and tables by rote. I also took piano lessons, and when I told Dad how much I enjoyed them, he went straight out and found a piano for me, so I could practise.

After lunch, we would all get our blankets and rest while the teacher read us a story, and then we were allowed to play before the next lessons. It was a mixed school and my special friend was a boy called Bertram, who always seemed to be in my team during games.

We went to school on Saturday mornings and had a special lunch of rolls and Cheddar cheese, a welcome change from goat's cheese, before leaving for home on the bus. My mother would meet me at the New Hunstanton bus stop, and we would go to Boots to change my library book, buy a quarter of sweets with a coupon, and then go to a place called Woodcock's for tea. There they served buns with icing on top and jam inside, and something that looked like a blob of cream, except it dissolved as soon as it went into your mouth. Once we went to the cinema after tea, and saw a Lassie film, but I cried so much for the dog that I was not taken to the cinema again for a long while.

Because of the rationing, grown-ups seemed preoccupied with food and coupons. Poachers regularly came to the kitchen door at night, with rabbits, hare or other game, and the kitchen would be filled with fur or feathers. Nothing was wasted. My brother and I both had rabbit-fur hoods and mittens.

One Sunday, when I was wandering along our unadopted road, I noticed that one of the houses seemed empty. I let myself into the garden through a wooden gate and explored the place. It had the most abundant vegetable garden. I looked through the windows and the letter box – not a sign of life. It seemed to me that it was such a waste of vegetables if nobody lived there. The next Sunday, I went back to look again. Still no one had picked any vegetables. So I went home, found the biggest shopping basket in the cupboard and set off down the road, feeling sure that my contribution to the family food shortage would be very welcome. As I heaved cabbages, sprouts and swedes into the basket I felt so proud – I was doing my bit to help. I dragged the basket all the way home and proudly showed my spoils to my parents. They were horrified that I had gone into someone's garden. My father went along the road to see if the house really was empty and found out that I had been telling the truth. We kept the vegetables but I was told not to go there again because it was stealing, and the following Sunday I was enrolled at the local Sunday School.

~

WITH CHRISTMAS APPROACHING, two of us in my class at school were chosen to be the narrators of the school nativity story. A vicar's daughter was playing Mary and I, in my first term there, had been chosen for my reading ability. This, of course, was due to the wonderful Miss Scaler and the endless number of books I read after school.

Now that father was home, Christmas became a full-scale production. My brother, Brian, by now resembled the child in the advert for Pears Soap. He had copper curls and long, sweeping dark eye lashes. My eye lashes, on the other hand, were fair and straight; so was my long hair, which I wore in plaits. Before Christmas Eve, we both sent a letter up the chimney to Santa Claus. I was worried that Santa might have seen me taking the vegetables and not bring me my presents, but I was assured that he would know my intentions had been honourable. So I asked for a toffee hammer, not a doll as my mother wanted me to have. I had heard someone mention the name 'toffee hammer' and though I did not know what it was I liked the sound of it.

On Christmas Eve we were told that we had to be very quiet in case Santa found out we were not in bed yet, and if we were very good we could see the Christmas tree. The sitting room had an alcove with a door that led out on to a verandah. My father went behind the long curtains drawn across the alcove, saying that he was just getting the tree ready. Then we heard the front door knocker. My brother and I clutched each other and waited to see whether it was Santa Claus, when we heard a booming voice asking Mum whether Judy and Brian had been good children. 'Yes,' she replied, and I felt so grateful. Then the voice said, 'Goodnight Mrs Cornwell,' and the door shut. Mummy came back into the sitting room and whispered conspiratorially, as if we had not heard, 'I told him you'd been good.' The swishing sound of the alcove curtains being drawn by Dad revealed the Christmas tree in full splendour, with lit candles on the window sills and paper chains draped across the alcove walls. A large silver star glittered at the top of the tree, and lots of pretty coloured balls dangled from the branches. It was a magical moment for us, but because we knew Santa was still in the area, my parents had no difficulty getting us into bed.

The next morning Brian and I found our presents all wrapped up and laid out in front of the tree. I had a tricycle and a toffee hammer, my brother a teddy bear and a spinning top. There was another big parcel for me which Dad said came from my godmother, Musi – his nickname for Lydia Craven, his ex-fiancée's mother. Musi had a bookshop in Tunbridge Wells, and when she heard I loved reading, she insisted on beginning a tradition of supplying me with books. In the parcel were a set of Beatrix Potter books, a set of Flower Fairy books, a beautifully coloured copy of *The Little Fir Tree, The Water Babies, Just So Stories* and a large coloured shiny book of Robert Louis Stevenson's *A Child's Garden of Verses*. I was in heaven. Christmas lunch was roast chicken, an incredible luxury, followed by Christmas pudding with custard. We had to be careful with the pudding because there might be sixpences inside. I saw Dad slip one on to the edge of my brother's plate and I found one too. Another coin for my money box.

On Boxing Day, Mum took me to my first pantomime. Brian was too young to go. We went by bus, all the way to King's Lynn, to see *Dick Whittington*. The old gag, Busy Bee, Busy Bee, give me some honey, when the comedian blows water over the stooge, had me in hysterics.

During the holidays I was out pedalling my tricycle all over the village. One day I ran into some bigger boys who taught me a new word. When I asked what it meant, they sniggered and told me to ask my mother. I went home trying to remember what the word was – it rhymed with duck. I sat on the stairs silently going through the alphabet, and then I remembered. 'Mummy, what does —— mean?' I asked. There was a clatter and a crash and Mum came out of the kitchen with that 'war is declared' look. Such a reaction to one word! She sat beside me on the stairs and, after establishing who had told me and where, she explained it was the king of the swear words and I was made to promise never to use it again.

'What is the queen of the swear words?' I asked.

'You'll be told when you're older,' was the reply.

～

THE NEXT TERM at school was taken by a Mrs Crocker and she introduced us to *The Pilgrim's Progress*, which John Bunyan wrote when he was in prison. The book had a profound effect on me and made me realize that good people often suffer for trying to do good. Also Musi's present of *The Water Babies* gave me a great feeling of sadness that little children who were poor could be treated so badly. As a sixth birthday treat, I was taken to the cinema one Saturday to see *Robin Hood*, played by Errol Flynn, who looked a bit like my father. I immediately identified with all Robin's rebels and vowed that if ever there was a wicked king, I would fight on the rebel side.

During this time, one cold morning, waiting for the school bus, the vicar's wife whose daughter had played Mary in the school nativity play snubbed my mother. Why? I have no idea. Unless my mother's slight Wearside accent offended her sensibilities. When Mum had greeted the other mothers waiting at the bus stop they had smiled, but this snob of a woman had turned her back on her. I was aware of the woman's coldness towards my mother and felt my mother wince with embarrassment. I also felt a rage I had never felt before and wanted to use the king of the swear words, hit this po-faced vicar's wife as Robin Hood would have done. Instead, I gave my mother a special cuddle goodbye as I stepped on to the bus, and I fixed my gaze on the rude woman and swore vengeance. Revenge is a dish best served cold. It took me thirty-five years to appease my six-year-old child's wish for vengeance. But more of that later.

Miss Barcombe was putting on a dance for a boys' orphanage and I was given a solo as a witch, dancing with a broomstick and wearing a black velvet dress with rhinestones round the collar and a tall pointed hat. The large public-room floor, where we were to perform to rows of bored-looking boys sitting cross-legged on it, had been highly polished, and we were warned to take care. I started my dance and was doing wonderfully well until a large spider dropped out of my broomstick. With a yell of fright I slipped on to my bottom. The boys roared with laughter. That was my first public comedy appearance – very humiliating.

During the Easter holidays I caught whooping cough and became very ill and Doctor Marshall came to see me. I spent a lot of time with a towel over my head breathing in the steam from a basin of hot water. The whooping cough became worse and I developed pleurisy. My parents cosseted me while my father ranted about the vagaries of English weather. I read my books, listened occasionally to *Mrs Dale's Diary* on the radio and got better. While I recuperated Dad used to play me a lot of his records. One piece of music was the *Rustle of Spring* by Christian Sinding. We improvised and combined a nature discussion with ballet. He told me about a caterpillar turning into a butterfly inside a chrysalis, and arranged flower pots all over the sitting room for me to dance around. I loved these times with my father and all the music in his precious collection of His Master's Voice records which he kept in large record books.

~

I ALWAYS KNEW when my parents were going out for the evening as I could hear them creeping over the gravel in the front of the house. They looked beautiful together. I remember two of my mother's evening dresses. One was made of a dark green jersey wool material with padded shoulders and a crisscross V pattern across her bosom, and the other was a dark red taffeta with a halter neckline.

Among the grown-ups, there was a brisk trade in children's clothes. Because of rationing, outgrown children's clothes were quickly sold or traded for other clothes. One day, my mother arrived home triumphantly carrying a pile of dresses she thought would fit me. They had been given to her by a Canadian friend, about to return to Toronto. Mother's friend's daughter had curly hair and looked a bit like Shirley Temple. She was called Candy, and when she wore her pretty dresses, she flounced about in them, showing her matching frilly knickers. I was not like Candy, did not want to wear her dresses, and hated her frilly knickers. Mother was determined that I should wear these beautiful outfits, and I was equally determined that I would not. As fast as she dressed me in them, I would take them off. She would scream at me and I would scream back. There was a trail of frilly dresses right across the lawn. Dad intervened and we compromised. I would wear one of the reasonably plain sun-suits, and the rest of the clothes went back into the trading pool.

Meanwhile my father's family had arrived back from overseas and settled in Sussex so I was able to meet my grandmother at last. My grandfather did not come with her the first time she visited us – as a Colonel in the army he was too busy. It was also the first time Mum had met Dad's mother, and I could sense she did not feel at ease with her. My grandmother was much taller than my mother, had dark auburn hair, wore tinted glasses and was softly spoken. She did not want to be called grandma or granny, but Dearie. I heard my mother muttering under her breath that it was a stupid name. The first night 'Dearie' stayed, she told me I should not suck my thumb or it would be bad for my teeth. I agreed, waited until she had kissed me goodnight, then returned to my thumb and fluffy blanket.

During the few days of my grandmother's visit, she wanted to hear me read to her. She also wanted to see me dance and listened while I played the piano; my brother Brian was asked questions about his toys. Mother walked about with pursed lips most of this time. When Brian and I were sent out to play, we went to the small lane by the side of the house, where I could whiz downhill on my tricycle with Brian hanging on to the back. I sensed something was wrong when I saw Mum standing at the top of the hill watching us, not warning us to be careful but just staring into the distance and smoking a cigarette. She had never behaved like that before.

When Dearie left, she said she would see us again soon. Sylvia left shortly afterwards and returned to Ireland. Then Aunty Gladys came to stay and slept in Sylvia's old room, and while cycling along the road, I saw my first banana. I knew it was a banana as I had seen them in books and on a picture hanging on the greengrocer's wall. A boy from the village was walking along eating one. I rushed back home and told Mum. She and Aunty Gladys ran down to the village and came back with a bunch of bananas. I was praised for recognizing one, and we were fed bananas until I was sick of them.

~

AS THE SUMMER term started I noticed that there were a lot of arguments at home. Once I heard the back door slam. Mother had gone out and did not come back for hours. When Aunty Gladys began shouting at Dad I became worried and wanted to know what was wrong. Aunty Gladys' face was flushed and her eyes glittered. 'Never you mind,' she said. But I did mind and decided to run away. So the following Sunday, after Sunday School, I went down to the orchard, climbed the cherry tree and hid among the cherries. I stayed there until well after dark, watching the grown-ups running around shouting my name. I ate a few cherries while I was up the tree, and thought about life and my parents. Then, when I began to feel really stiff and cold, I came down and went to the back door. I was hugged and kissed and asked where I had been, and I told them I had run away because they were all shouting at each other. That's when I was told we were going to Australia. Aunty Gladys said nothing but looked very sad.

On the large globe in the sitting room, Dad had shown me how the moon moved round the earth by using an orange, and he had used my beach ball to show me how the world moved round the sun. He now showed me where Australia was, right down the bottom part of the globe, and how a ship would travel there. We were going to live on a farm in Queensland, but while we were waiting for a ship, we would be moving down to Sussex, near Dearie. When I told my best friend, Bertram, that we were going to Australia, he was very sad. I told him he was my best friend and I would miss him, and at the end of the term he gave me a letter. In it he asked me to marry him if I came back from Australia.

During the summer holidays, Aunty Gladys would take Brian and me down to the beach, while my parents filled huge black trunks with everything we were taking to Australia. She would sometimes make tomato sandwiches, a great luxury. More often it was egg, and she would wrap them in a damp tea towel to keep them moist. Sometimes we would have butterfly cakes afterwards.

The Morgan went, then the goat and the chickens and ducks. By the end of the summer holidays, we had moved to Seaford in Sussex. My grandmother had found us a furnished flat while we waited for a ship, and I went to school at the Annecy Convent. I wore a navy uniform with a navy hat and tassel. When I was taken to meet the Mother Superior of the French order, she suggested that a girl who was a little older than me, a very responsible girl, who lived in the same road, would walk me to school so I would not get lost. She was a sweet-natured, neatly turned-out girl called Jane Simmons, who called on the first day of term and looked after me, taking me all the time I attended the convent. I liked Jane and felt safe on our journeys to school together. She was one of nature's natural carers and I respected her enormously.

On one of our journeys coming home from school, Jane and I found a shop where you did not need coupons for something sweet. For a penny, you could buy liquorice bark wrapped up in newspaper, or a small bagful of lemon sherbet. We told all the other children of our find, and felt very proud of our discovery.

I was in Sister Carmelita's class. In another class was a bigger girl called Penelope Hatfield. Years later we would work together, when she was known as Penelope Keith. I was very happy at the Annecy Convent. The nuns were kind and good teachers. There was one special teacher who was not a nun called Miss McHugh, who was elegant, gentle and, I thought, beautiful.

On Sundays, we went round to my father's cousin, Aunt Phyllis' place. There were always lots of people in her house, and one of Dad's other cousins played the guitar and Dad played the violin. My brother Brian blossomed with all the music and attention, and we found he had the most beautiful singing voice. Every Sunday, he would sing and I would dance. There was always lots of laughter and plenty of sandwiches and sweet cakes to eat. Sometimes, we would go to my grandmother's, where we would see Aunt Deirdre and her two sons, who were younger than my brother. I was a bit scared of my grandfather, who was very stern and did not seem too comfortable with children around. Although he and Dad used to talk a lot, my mother also seemed very wary of him. My grandparents would discuss Dad's plans for farming in Australia and enquired whether he had thought of returning to Canada, where they had all lived for a while. They were disappointed that he had left the RAF, where they thought he had an excellent future, but Dad convinced them that Australia was the country of tomorrow. They would also talk approvingly about the assisted-passage scheme to Australia. For a contribution of ten pounds per person, the Australian government would pay the rest of the passenger's fare on the understanding that the immigrant would work for a minimum of two years there. The Australians called these immigrants 'ten-pound poms'.

Mother took us into Brighton one Saturday. We went on the Palace Pier and had a ride on the ghost train and the merry-go-round. I wanted to see What the Butler Saw, but mother said it was not suitable for children. After we had visited the Pier, we went to the Aquarium and saw all the exotic fish. We then had some afternoon tea, and on our way to Pool Valley to catch the bus back to Seaford, we passed a toy shop. Sitting in the window was a small doll, dressed in a pale blue knitted outfit. There was a placard in front of the doll saying, 'Please will you give me a home'. 'Oh,' I said, 'I love that doll.' Mum was so thrilled that there was a doll I liked, that she told me she was sure I could have it for Christmas. She told us to stand where we were and not to move, while she went inside. The doll was taken out of the window. When she came out of the shop, she was carrying an extra carrier bag in her hand, but said, 'I've asked them to put the doll aside for Santa Claus.'

The week before Christmas many children were going carol-singing. My little brother wanted to go too, like the children he had seen outside our front door. He had learnt the words of the carols and was desperate to go. There were strict instructions from Mummy not to go into anyone's house, and to sing only in the street where we lived. We were wrapped up warmly and sent off with a torch and a pouch for the money. Brian was beside himself with excitement. At each house we visited, he sang with all his heart. We went all the way along the street, receiving a couple of apples and biscuits, and lots of sixpences. His little face was flushed, and every time someone gave us something, he would squeak with pleasure. Even though my brother wanted to go on for ever, I went to a few houses close to where we lived, as it was getting colder, so that we ended up outside our own house. We sang again and Dad answered the door. Brian had such an expression of disappointment when he realized it was the end of the carol-singing that I felt ashamed for tricking him. It was at that moment I saw him, not as the baby that was always hanging around me, but as a very special little person whom I loved very much. I made a pact with myself that night, that I would always protect my brother.

Christmas 1946 was full of family visits. We also went to the local Ritz cinema to see *Snow White and the Seven Dwarfs*. My brother yelled with fright, much louder than me, when the wicked queen became a witch, but we both loved the dwarfs and we sang 'heigh ho' for the rest of the holidays.

I had one more term at the Annecy Convent and was doing really well in my French lessons. In February 1947, when I celebrated my seventh birthday, and mother celebrated her birthday too, I had a party with lots of friends, and Dad had a date for the ship sailing to Australia.

Chapter Two

1947–1952

~

AUNTY GLADYS CAME with us to Tilbury docks. She and Mum clung together and cried a lot. She squeezed my brother and me until we were overwhelmed by leopard skin, but just pecked Dad on the cheek.

The SS *Ormonde* was the biggest ship I had ever seen, and there was so much noise and confusion as people milled about on the decks and on the dockside. Like Aunty Gladys, other relatives and friends of passengers were shouting and waving their goodbyes to those leaning against the ship's railings.

Walking up the gangplank felt very strange, and when we were aboard, we walked down corridor after corridor until we came to our cabin. A steward helped us by showing us where the bathrooms were, then we were up on deck again waiting for the ship to sail. We shouted down to Aunty Gladys, who shouted back and waved. Then the ship's horn blasted and we started to move away from the wharf, and Aunty Gladys became smaller and smaller on the quayside.

Our family did not suffer from sea sickness and quickly adapted to life on board ship. I was fascinated by the salt-water baths and the special soap we had to use to make a lather. Staying up late to see a film on the big screen outside on deck was a great treat and I looked forward to the formal meals with the same group of people each day, when we children could listen to the grown-ups' conversations. Many of the men were ex-servicemen like my father.

Then Brian and I developed mumps and were put in quarantine. We were only allowed on deck at the stern of the ship, close to the laundry. I did not mind as I had an endless supply of books from the library. Mother read to my brother or he would play with some Dinky toys. Sometimes I used to watch the sea being churned up, creating a foamy path trailing behind the ship, hoping to spot birds or fish. I also used to test my memory while watching the foam, tracing time back through all the places where we had lived and people I had known.

When the ship reached Port Said, the quarantine flag was on the mast and no one was allowed ashore. They were all angry and disappointed. We had not only seriously embarrassed our parents, but also compromised the plans of everyone on board.

By the time we had travelled through the Suez Canal into the Red Sea and reached Aden, our period of quarantine was over, and we were allowed to join the rest of the ships' passengers. Small boats came alongside the ship and the passengers all leaned over the railings to see what the boat people were selling. I wanted to barter like the grown-ups, so Dad let me negotiate for a coconut. A couple of men further along the deck were also bartering for some pretty boxes but when they got them they did not send the money agreed back down to the man in the boat. 'That's cheating,' I said to my father. He agreed, and then admitted, 'Sometimes, Judy, you will find that the British are not always popular in other countries, and it is usually because of people like them.'

On crossing the equator all the children were initiated into the Solemn Mysteries of the Ancient Order of the Deep, promising to be a trusty shellback in the domain of Neptunus Rex, ruler of the raging main. We were also issued with salt pills to take once a day.

When we reached the port of Fremantle, in Perth, Western Australia, some of the people were disembarking with all their trunks. We went ashore with some other families and I listened to all the women gasp and crow with excitement as they crowded round the butchers and the grocers. They had not seen such an abundance of food for years. I too felt excited about being in Australia, the place at the bottom of Dad's globe, so different from the England I knew.

At each port we watched more of the passengers disembark but we stayed on board until we reached Brisbane, in Queensland, where Dad's friend Bob Wenbourne came to the docks to meet us.

Mr Wenbourne lived in a house on stilts with a verandah all the way round it. We had never seen houses made like this before. And trees, flowers and birds were quite different from the ones I knew in England. We had lunch with the Wenbournes and they served huge steaks. Brian and I could not cope with them. Mum and Dad told them all about the rationing in England and why we were overwhelmed by the amount of meat on our plates. Dad also told them about the shares he had bought in a farm further north and they all agreed that Mum, Brian and I should stay with them until Dad had got the place sorted out. Bob took Dad and a lot of our trunks to the station the following day.

In Brisbane we found out that sweets were not rationed and my pennies could buy any sweet without coupons. I was also introduced to Captain Marvel and Superman comics. Bob warned Mum that this lovely sunny weather we were having was the Australian winter and it would get a lot hotter where we were going. However, the day we set off for Dagun on the train, it was raining.

~

DAGUN STATION WAS the length of a British bus shelter. Dad was there to meet us and we were bundled quickly into a car while his friend, another farmer, loaded up the rest of the suitcases and trunks. From the station road, passing one general store and a church, we motored along muddy tracks, climbing steadily up hills until we came to our farm house. Like the Brisbane house where we had stayed, this house was on stilts, but in the middle of acres and acres of pineapple plants. The rain thundered down on the corrugated iron roof, and my mother's face matched the weather. My brother and I were ushered into our newly decorated bedrooms to unpack our toys, while all hell broke loose in the sitting room – Mum was obviously not impressed with our new home. Our beds had swathes of mosquito netting supported by a frame so that the beds resembled the four-posters I had seen in story books. There was no electricity and when daylight faded paraffin lamps were lit. Dad told us that one light always had to be placed in a certain window so that if anyone was lost in the bush they could get their bearings.

The next day the rain stopped and we were shown how everything worked. The water we used was rainwater and very precious so was never to be wasted. There was a huge tank by the side of the house. The lavatory was outside and because Dad knew Mum would never go out to it at night he had also bought a commode. Under the house was the washing area with huge sinks for soaking and washing clothes, and some sort of contraption for boiling up the water. One of my daily jobs would be to fetch some milk in a billycan from a dairy farm a few miles away.

We walked together all the way down the hills, past the station and past a school on stilts until we came to the dairy farm. I was introduced to the farmer, who said he would expect to see me every day. He filled up the billycan and I carried it all the way home without spilling a drop. On our walk back home Dad said we should be proud to be Australian citizens, because he believed this was the country of the future. He also warned me to be careful when walking on my own that I did not tread on a snake thinking it was a twig. When we reached home we found Mother and my brother in hysterics. She insisted that there was a lunatic running round the pineapple fields laughing madly. After calming her down Dad assured her it was just a kookaburra.

As some farmers near by had asked us over for the evening, Mum dressed us up and we were all picked up in a truck. They had a house on stilts too, but something far more exciting for me was the pianola they had in the sitting room. The most wonderful tinkling music came from this strange piano. All you had to do was to press the pedals and a cylindrical thing went round, pressing the piano keys down automatically. While the grown-ups talked, two boys a few years older than me asked me about England.

Because they had been told that most of the farmers' children went to school in Lagoon Pocket, my parents arranged for me to go there too. This meant walking in the opposite direction from the dairy farm, across a citrus farmer's land where there was a small halt where the train stopped. All the children caught the train there and travelled two stops up the track to Lagoon Pocket.

My first day at the new school arrived and I was sent off with my lunch packed into my satchel, to walk across the fields to the train. I arrived safely at the school to find it was one big school-room with one teacher for all the different age groups. We had slates to write on and strange pencils that squeaked against the slates. The trouble was you could only write two pages at a time. To write page three you had to rub out page one on the first side of the slate. I could cope easily with the work, except for the history, which was Australian history, about which I was ignorant.

Playtimes were more worrying as I stood out dreadfully with my polished shoes and English accent. Some of the children did not wear shoes, arrived at school on horseback, and soon saw that the meat ants which scurried about in the dry dust scared me. They were such big ants and there were so many of them that I was frightened of being bitten. So naturally it became a sport to shove them down the 'pommy's' neck. In order to survive each playtime I deflected their natural savagery by showing them games they did not know, from Oranges and Lemons to the Big Ship Sails Down the Illy Ally Oo. As I ran out of games to entertain them with, I would start on stories that I knew, from *Cinderella* to Enid Blyton. Soon, Mum and Dad realized this was not the school for me, so it was all change and I was sent to another school in Dagun. It was just as well, as I was fast running out of stories.

Dagun was a very orderly school with a much bigger, airier schoolroom and the children were more friendly. There was one teacher for the different age groups but we were divided up with more space between us. A Methodist minister took us for religious knowledge and there were no slates and squeaky pencils but proper exercise books to write in. We would start every morning singing in front of the Australian flag then march proudly into school. As Dad said, I was now an Australian citizen, so I looked forward to learning about Australian history.

All community life in Dagun took place round the general store and the church. The general store was run by Mrs Duckworth, a large lady with strong pink arms and lots of chins. She was a friendly soul who could sell you everything from screws and bacon to vegetables and knitting wool.

On Sundays our faces were washed until the skin shone and I had to wear a straw bonnet like the other girls. We would all dutifully turn up for church, and after singing lustily and listening to the sermon, we would gather outside, where the grown-ups would talk and gossip and the children would play. Any other socializing was in people's homes. On Friday nights there was the special treat of listening to the battery radio: Bob Dior's *Pick a Box* and the *Gracie Fields Show*. Mum always got weepy when the *Gracie Fields Show* finished. She hated life on the farm, although she did her best to hide it from my brother and me. To her the whole country was full of things that slithered or crawled.

Most of the farmers near by had sons, a little older than me. Soon my brother and I were adept at dried cow pat wars, so that we often arrived home covered in manure. But you should have seen the other kids. One day I found a wild cotton plant and tried to open it. One of the boys said it looked like a —. This was a new word. I asked what it meant, thinking it was something to do with cotton, and they rolled around with laughter and said, 'Ask your Mum.' I'd heard that line before, so cautiously I asked Mum about it. She huffed and puffed, then came the question, 'Who told you that?' I knew if I told her there would be a row and the boys would get into trouble, so I said, 'I just heard it around . . .' I was then told that was the queen of the swear words and I was never to use it. Now I knew the king and the queen of swear words!

As the weather got hotter, Mum became more irritable, complaining about the humidity and 'this dreadful place'. Whenever she got into a mood, which usually meant a lot crashing about in the kitchen and nagging me about tidying my room, I would sit on the back steps of the house and whisper the king and queen of swear words to myself.

By November the pineapples were beginning to turn yellow gold and Mum was going mad with prickly heat. She had grown her hair and wore it plaited over her head to keep her neck cool. When we ate the first ripened pineapple, and experienced the sharp, sweet juiciness, even she joined in with praise for Dad's efforts.

At school I had one embarrassing moment when helping to

butter bread for sandwiches for the cricket match. One of the older girls asked, 'Who's being mean with the butter?' I felt my face going very red. 'Me,' I said, and I explained how in England we had very little butter and it had to go a long way, so we were taught to spread it thinly. 'Well you're in Australia now,' she replied. So I slapped the butter on to the bread with the best of them.

I enjoyed the heat and loved the rainwater we drank from the big tanks at home and school. It was sweet water and the most thirst-quenching I have ever drunk. At the dairy farm where I collected my billycan of milk, the mandarin orchard was full of plump orange fruit. One day I asked the farmer if I could try one. He told me to help myself, so I filled my school shirt and took some home. The delicious juiciness of a mandarin picked from the tree was just the thing to help me walk the long distance up the hills to our farm on a hot afternoon.

With all the fresh fruit and meat available, my brother and I began to put on weight. Our clothes became too tight and were now unsuitable for the hotter weather. So a trip to the nearest town, Gympie, was arranged. We took the train from Dagun in a state of great excitement. As we walked from the station to the main high street we passed the Olympia cinema and saw all the forthcoming attractions advertised. In the main street, Mary Street, we saw an Italian milk bar so we stopped for huge coconut milkshakes before heading towards Rankins, the big store. On the way to the clothing store my mother suddenly screeched and danced on the pavement. We did not know what was happening but it turned out that a lone praying mantis had dropped down from one of the shop's awnings straight on to her head. Passers-by were amused at her antics but I was mortified by my mother's hysterics. Dad tried to pacify her, while my brother and I walked a couple of steps behind our parents, pretending we were not with them. We bought new clothes and sandals but by now Mum's head was darting about like a nervous chicken's wherever we went and it was not until we caught the train home, carrying lots of parcels, that she recovered.

At school we had survival classes and health and safety lessons. We had been taught what to do if bitten by a snake and how important it was to sterilize with boiling water or by fire anything to be

used for removing a splinter or anything coming in contact with a
wound. So one night, when Dad was away and Mum was moaning with pain from a toothache – we had tried using cloves and she
had taken some aspirin but she was getting more and more upset
by the pain; and there was no telephone and I was not allowed to
walk in the dark to try and get help for her – I offered to pull the
offending tooth out. It was an upper left-hand molar and much
more difficult to pull than my milk teeth from my earlier years. So
I went to Dad's tool box and fetched some pliers. Then I sterilized
them as I had been taught, and having made my mother rinse her
mouth with salt water, I began to pull the tooth. My mother was
yelling, my brother was wailing but I knew I was right to take
charge and I yanked it out. Next morning the pain had gone and
she was calm again.

As the heat grew more intense it was arranged between a few
farmers that we would all take a trip to the beach. We set off early
in the morning in one of the farm trucks, children in the back of
the truck with the baskets of food and drink and the grown-ups
squeezed into the front. We arrived in Noosa in the morning and
found a shady place under a tree at the edge of the sands. Mother
said she could breathe again and was happy to stay in the shade,
while we raced across the sands looking for the blue crabs that
marched along the wet surf line. I was scared of the big rolling
waves which occasionally pulled me down a sand hole but the joy
of being by the sea counteracted all my fears. What surprised me,
as it reached midday, was the boiling heat of the sand burning the
soles of my feet when coming out of the water. I had to run as fast
as I could to the less hot sand in the shade.

Mum was reluctant to leave the coast and the breezes but the
journey back home was full of laughter and singing and most of us
in the back of the truck were nearly asleep when we reached home.
We made quite a few trips to the seaside that hot summer, occasionally to Tewantin and also Tin Can Bay. At Tin Can Bay Dad had
a near miss with a shark. Mum, Brian and I were sitting on the
beach eating some sandwiches while Dad was up to his waist
fishing. We spotted the fin coming towards him and Dad said, 'Just
keep absolutely quiet.' We froze, clutching each other in panic. Dad

kept still in the water. The shark headed towards him, circled round him and then went back out to sea. Dad moved pretty quickly back out of the water after that and we all yelled and shrieked with relief.

Occasionally a woman called Betty Shepherd, the wife of a friend of Dad's who was in the Forestry Commission, babysat while Mum and Dad went to the cinema in Gympie. Getting out more made Mum a little happier. Also, there was a new arrival at home – a small, mewling bundle of fluff Dad had found in the bush. The mother cat had been killed defending her kittens from a snake, leaving two orphans, a tom and a female. Another farmer took the tom and we had Sooty. Once the kitten knew her place to drink milk and her place to sleep, she adapted to the family very quickly. I had always loved Kipling's *Just So Stories* and my favourite story was 'The Cat that Walked by Himself'. Sooty was just like the cat in the story, especially when it came to approaching my mother. She entertained, amused and was careful not to overstep the boundaries of Mother's rules about keeping animals outside; she would creep up the stairs as far as she could until catching Mum's eye, then mince down the steps again as if playing.

By the time Brian started school and was able to come with me to collect the billycan of milk, Sooty had grown into a beautiful young cat, who hunted everything that ran, crawled or hopped. When we set off to school, she followed us, leaving us at the entrance, where she would turn round and make for home. One morning, she lingered a little behind us, and we soon saw why. We had just passed the general store when there was a crashing and shouting and out flew Sooty with a piece of meat in her mouth. Brian and I disowned Sooty and ran for the school as soon as we saw Mrs Duckworth appear at the shop door, and Sooty at least had the grace to flee in the other direction.

By now I had developed a bit of an Australian twang, which I had to lose as soon as I crossed the threshold at home. So I had one accent for school and one for home. But Mum was more worried about my father, who was looking more and more tired. There were long discussions about his suitability for farming work or manual work of any kind. His war years had weakened him and Mum nagged him about giving up the farm and moving to somewhere more suitable. She found an advert in one of the newspapers for a job at 4GY, a radio station in Gympie, and forced him to go for an interview. He got the job, and even though he regretted leaving the farm, common sense told him that Mum was right.

~

So we were on the move again. The town of Gympie was founded on gold discovered by James Nash in 1867. His discovery saved the fledgling colony of Queensland from near bankruptcy. The name came from the local Kabi aboriginal tribe's name for local stinging nettles, *gimpi gimpi*, which lined the banks of the Mary river. The river winds past the town and through a lush pasture-land so when the gold ran out there was rich agriculture, timber, dairy and beef cattle to keep the town thriving.

Dad had found a house with a lavatory that flushed and Mum was ecstatic. No more traipsing down to the pineapple patch. The drinking water still came from a rainwater tank, but the Mary river, which was not far from the house, supplied our kitchen, toilet and bathroom. We also had electricity so were civilized again. Dad had even managed to find an ice box to keep the food cool.

Our house was number 24, in Wickham Street, a wide palm tree-lined road with mostly big Queenslander houses. Ours was more modern, with a lawn running right up to the road, a vegetable garden and mulberry tree by the side of the house, and a paddock behind the back lawn. From the paddock, the wild bush country-side ran downhill to the Mary river.

After we had settled in and Dad had put his swords, paintings and various ornaments up on the wall, he checked in to 4GY to meet all the people he would be working with and also found out about schools in the area. The main town-hall clock was at the bottom of two hills, Carlton and Caledonian. At the top of Carlton Hill stood Saint Patrick's Church with the Christian Brothers one side and the Sisters of Mercy the other. My parents decided it would be best for me to attend the convent and they took Brian and me to meet the Mother Superior, Sister Mary Helen. It was agreed that I should start school the following Monday. Then the nun looked at my brother, who seemed extremely agitated. 'And will little Brian be starting in our primary class?' she enquired. Brian's reaction was immediate. 'No,' he yelled, 'she's a witch,' and he buried his face in Mum's skirts and would not be pacified. What good instincts my baby brother possessed. My parents said they would think about it and assured her that I would be there the following Monday. My lucky little brother began at the state primary the day I began school in the convent.

The girls at Saint Patrick's Convent were curious about the new English child and I spent most of my early days talking during the lunch break to a crowd of them because they wanted to hear my English accent. The day began quite differently from those at the Dagun State School. We would file into class, all face Sister Mary Helen and then it was down on your knees for an Act of Faith, an Act of Hope and an Act of Charity, the Lord's Prayer, a couple of Hail Marys and a couple of Glory be to the Fathers. If your knee was on a crack in the floor, your leg ached to be moved but no one dared to shift. There was a reading and Sister Mary Helen's interpretation, and we, being suitably and seriously inspired, would then begin our lessons.

The schoolroom was on the first floor and was large and airy with different classes being taught by individual nuns. The other buildings were for the boarders and the nuns. We kept our satchels and coats on the ground floor and carried our books and pencil boxes up to the classroom. I enjoyed the lessons and the nun teaching us was pleasant but firm and a good teacher. We would hear a lot of shouting and smacking sounds from Sister Mary Helen's class but we were safe in ours.

Saint Patrick's night was not too far away and everyone was learning the Irish jig. I picked it up pretty quickly and Mum arranged for someone to make me the right costume for the march down Mary Street with the statue of the Holy Virgin following us on wheels. When the night came we danced the jig to music while the statue of Saint Mary, following us, was all lit up by candles. Dad, Mum and Brian joined the crowded main street to see us and I went home with them, exhausted but happy. I was also put into the school choir, which was made up with some of the boys from the Christian Brothers. I was close to the boys, being a contralto, and a lot of flirting went on out of view of the priests and nuns who were watching us like hawks.

Dad had decided that, as I was developing breasts and becoming a bit self-conscious so I was walking with rounded shoulders, he would send me to club-swinging classes where it was impossible to do anything but keep your shoulders back. I was enlisted with Miss Gladys Hughes, a wiry old Scottish lady. Dad got me a pair of blue clubs and I would swing them in the evening down in the park. For a little woman Miss Hughes had a powerful voice, and the park would ring out with the sounds of 'eee wunn, eee tu, ee thrrreee . . .' and we would swing our clubs so that the spangled glitter of red, white and blue dazzled any passers-by. Dad was right, it did straighten my shoulders. It also strengthened my arm muscles.

During the holidays, the rodeo came to Gympie and all the girls I knew had a new dress. We wore our Sunday straw bonnets and took our pocket money we had saved to spend there. Dad, Mum, Brian and I spent a whole day watching tree-felling races, wild horse riding and my favourite, Paula, Queen of the Snakes. Paula wore a bathing suit and worked in a pit full of snakes – huge ones and little ones. She would let us touch the big ones, emphasizing that the little, fast-moving snakes were far more deadly than the big ones. Mum would not come in to the tent so Dad took us. There were all sorts of amusements and candy floss and toffee apples to buy. After a day at the rodeo I would sleep contentedly, dreaming of being Judy, Queen of the Snakes.

On Saturday afternoons, the Olympia cinema had a children's programme and after lunch we would all queue up to get in. Armed with popcorn, we would sit through Roy Rogers, Hopalong Cassidy or Tom Mix, cheering our heroes against the baddies. Sometimes we would see a Walt Disney film, or a film about Huckleberry Finn or Tom Sawyer, or a film with Abbot and Costello or Laurel and Hardy. Occasionally there was one with Chips Rafferty, a famous Australian actor. Whatever the main film, there was always a second feature, a cowboy story, included in the programme, where the hero upheld the law and justice. As well as being devoted to cowboy films, I was also passionate about Superman and Captain Marvel, who again fought against bullies and baddies.

During the following term another English girl, Patsy, joined the convent. Although she was younger, I made friends with her and told Mum there was another English girl in the school. Mum immediately gave me a letter inviting Patsy and her mother to tea. When they arrived after school and my mother opened the door, the two women hugged each other, cried and laughed. It turned out that they had shared a flat in London before Mum had met Dad. So Mum had a friend now and was happy. Dad too was happy at 4GY and had made lots of friends. He was now writing and producing programmes he created as well as presenting and reporting. Life was good. Even when the hot weather came Mother was all right. She did not like the heat or humidity but there were trips to the beach with Dad's friend at work, Herb Lister, and his family, and a more social life for her.

Dad often befriended new immigrants, bringing them home and helping them in any way he could. One was a Hungarian who had managed to escape from a concentration camp. I remember his pastel drawings of the barbed wire and the yellow lights through the camp windows, of haunted expressions on the faces he had drawn, and the intense loneliness the pictures conveyed.

Whenever my parents had people over for the evening I always preferred to listen to the men talking. The women jawed on about clothes and female things which I found boring. It was far better to listen to the men and the tales they told.

As the weather grew hotter, on Sundays, after church, some of my school friends would take sandwiches down to the river and sit in the shade. Once, for a dare, I stripped off and jumped into the water nude, then dried myself on the tablecloth. One of my friends took it upon herself to confess this on my behalf, during her own weekly confession, as I did not consider swimming in the nude a sin. The result was, I was up before Sister Mary Helen for behaving in an unseemly way and caned across the palm of my right hand. I was shocked by the stinging pain and amazed that she knew about my swim. I did not discover until thirty-five years later how she had found out, when my friend wrote and owned up to what she had done.

A pie van used to come outside the school each lunchtime. Those who had not brought lunch could buy a freshly made, hot meat or apple pie. One Friday I went out and bought a meat pie. Some others had bought apple and when they saw I had a meat pie they said, 'but it is a sin to eat meat on a Friday'. I decided that this was stupid, arguing that God would not be so petty as to judge a person as a sinner for eating a meat pie. 'You'll be punished,' some of them said. 'Watch me. Nothing is going to happen,' I assured them. I ate the meat pie and a bell started ringing and I was up before Sister Mary Helen again. When I argued my case, she called me a heathen and I was caned again. When I returned to my friends I told them that this was not God hitting me but Sister Mary Helen. I think that particular sin has now been dropped by the Catholic Church.

A few weeks later, I had a quarrel in the playground with a girl from a class above me, Margaret Sharman. We were fighting each other when the familiar bell went and we were both up before Sister Mary Helen and told to put our hands out ready for the cane. Margaret (who is really a good friend) was very brave and just put her hand out obediently. I kept putting mine up and taking it away again. The nun really walloped us and I could hardly use my hand for days.

After the holidays I was put up a class and felt quite proud that I had been considered ready to go up one, until I realized I would be in Sister Mary Helen's class. She did not believe in sparing the rod and spoiling a child, but ruled and taught by fear, and possessed a Gestapo-like talent for inflicting pain. The side of her wooden ruler was her instrument of torture for knuckles and shins. The sign of impending violence was a flushing of her face until she turned bright red. I used to watch her very carefully as I knew she already considered me a heathen. Anyone getting a sum wrong was ordered up on to the bench and she would hit the girl's shin with the side of the ruler. It made me feel sick to hear the victim's cry. We would walk to the verandah for reading and those she disliked always seemed to have to sit with their backs to the sun, which made the pages glare and the print jump before the eyes. Even I, who read easily, would stumble over words with the print dancing about and my eyes watering with the glare from the blinding white pages. One of my friends was given a shove by the nun when she stumbled over a word. When I heard her head thud against the brick wall and saw a small trickle of blood oozing from her hair, I felt really angry about the nun's brutality.

Sister Mary Helen kept her most vicious bullying for a child who had obviously been seriously ill. The girl was taller than us but had thin legs and arms. She reminded me of the pictures of the survivors from Belsen. Her face was permanently red and flushed and her hair was matted. The poor creature was a boarder. One day she got something wrong and the nun charged at her and threw her across the floor. She slid along on her bottom, her skinny arms and legs crashing into chairs and desks, and she wept pitifully. Not content with what she had done, Sister Mary Helen then grabbed her by her scant hair and dragged her back to our class. The other nuns said nothing, but I wanted to pick the girl up and rescue her from this horrible bully. I felt tears welling up in my eyes at the wickedness of this woman who was supposed to be a bride of Christ. I have since found out that the girl grew up to be quite beautiful and clever enough to get to university and held a very responsible job. But the hell she went through at the hands of the nuns, I doubt would ever have been forgotten.

There was one story that Sister Mary Helen told us while we were on our knees. She said, 'Once two people wanted to do wrong. So they went to a field. And he said, "Let's do wrong here." But she said "No, someone might see." So they went to a very dark cave, and he said, "Let's do wrong here." But she said, "No someone might see." "Who could possibly see us here?" he said. "God can see us," she replied.' That story probably screwed up a lot of women's sex lives. And I had begun to loathe Sister Mary Helen.

The crunch came when we were being shouted at for our test results. The back row of girls were already standing on the bench ready to be hit on the shins with the ruler. I could hear the staccato sounds of wood against skin, the cries of pain, and I remember thinking, 'This is stupid.' I was ten years old and waiting to be hit

like the others. This woman was mad and unjust and someone had
to stand up to her, so I decided to leave. I emptied my desk, turned
and yelled across the room, 'You're a cruel bugger, and I've had
enough.' Then I walked out of the class and downstairs to my
satchel, and placed my books inside. I heard the swishing of her
skirts and the speed of her feet.

'How dare you speak like that,' she yelled. 'Get back upstairs at
once.'

'No', I replied, 'I'm leaving, and you're a bully.'

She grabbed my left hand and tried to twist my arm behind my
back.

All those cowboy films now came to my rescue. What would
Roy Rogers have done? Why of course, he would fight. I dropped
my satchel, made a fist and with all my strength I hit her. She
caught the punch right on the jaw, reeling back and falling among
the coats and satchels. I grabbed my satchel and ran like hell.

When I got home Mum was out. I sat on the steps wondering
what was going to happen to me. Sooty came and sat next to me
while I waited. When she came home and I told her what had happened Mum was ready to kill the nun. Dad decided it was best that
he should see Sister Mary Helen and tell her that I would not be
returning to the convent. I was officially expelled that day and I
have been told since that, every few months or so, one of my convent friends would stand up to Sister Mary Helen and get expelled.
Out of our original class only one girl became a nun. She was sent
to the Philippines where she met a Polish priest and ran off with
him. People are like a good wine, there are good years and bad
ones. Our year was a good year for rebels, and I like to think that
I was 'the little boy who said the Emperor has no clothes on' helping the rebels to find a voice – even if I did swear.

~

AFTER I WAS expelled, I was enrolled into the state junior school,
where the teacher approached me with caution. She had no need
to worry. I was happy there and enjoyed the new sporting activi-
ties, especially the game of vigaro, an Australian women's cricket.
I also took part in the school sports and could run one hundred

yards in thirteen seconds so I was put in the relay team in third position. Our team beat all the other schools and I felt so proud.

Like the school in Dagun we started every morning with the flag and a school song, then marched in ready for lessons. No more aching knees and no one seemed to get smacked. When I was moved up to Mr Spillane's class I really blossomed. He was a wonderful teacher and strict but absolutely fair. He loved teaching and pushed those he knew were capable of better work, but was patient with strugglers. Never would he let any clever dick make fun of someone who found learning difficult. I loved everything Mr Spillane taught us: history, geography, nature, English, Latin roots, maths and general knowledge. While in his class I began to write poetry at home. Dad loved poetry and it became a ritual to compare our work at the end of the week. Whenever he returned home he would ask, 'What poem do you have for me today?' and I would present him with one. Australia inspires the muses for poetry, with its abundant life and space. I loved the sounds of the bush, the cackles of the kookaburras and the parrots' screeches, but most of all the magpie calls in the morning at sunrise.

Sometimes Dad would take me fishing during a school holiday. We would read poetry and he would tell me family stories and share his thoughts and hopes. I told him the difficulty I had accepting the Genesis story, and asked him whether it was possible that at one time all the land on the planet was joined together. He said it was possible, and told me there was no religion greater than truth, and emphasized the importance of noble thinking, loyalty, the need to question all propaganda and never to follow the crowd but to be true to myself.

He told me of the two great-aunts from Tasmania, 'the Cornwell Girls', who had been sent to London for the season and then been sent back in disgrace for behaving badly. And there were stories about our ancestry from my grandmother's family, which reached back to the twelfth century in England, starting with Sir Michael Carrington who was Standard Bearer to Richard I, the Lion Heart, and died in the Holy Land. Dad also told me how the family changed their name to Smyth during the conflicts between the houses of York and Lancaster, and how they moved in and out of Europe reclaiming their lands when it was safe to return to England.

I learned how he was sent away to an English boarding school when he was a small boy because his parents were in India, and how he joined the Foreign Legion – against his parents' advice – and then had to be bought out because he found it too tough. He told me about studying in Heidelberg, and how although Grandfather could speak six languages, he could speak only four. I heard stories of how he went to flying school in Egypt where he met the Cravens, whose daughter Suzanne became his fiancée. Lydia Craven (Musi) later became my godmother. It was while he was in Egypt that he crashed a plane when caught in a *khamseen*, a sandstorm. After recovering in hospital he still suffered from the occasional blackout. All these stories I stored in my memory and they emerged many years later in my novel, *The Seventh Sunrise*.

At this time, in 1951, my life was full of interesting things to do. A ballet teacher had begun teaching in Gympie so Dad had booked private lessons for me. I had joined the Girl Guides and started to collect silkworms. Dad made me a wooden spinner so that when a caterpillar became a chrysalis, I could spin the silk, and at the end of the cycle I had enough yellow silk to make Dad a bookmark for Christmas.

Laddie arrived just before Christmas. He was a black horse that Dad kept in the paddock behind the back garden. Dad was a good horse rider, skilled enough to break in a wild horse. He trained Laddie and when he thought he was docile enough, he wanted me to learn to ride. But Laddie was cunning. While Dad was around he behaved beautifully but as soon as I was alone with him he would move to the fence and squeeze my leg until I jumped off. I persevered, however, always riding bareback because Dad thought it the best way to learn. Brian was more cautious with the horse, so Dad always stayed with him. I got a purple-coloured bicycle that Christmas which gave me the freedom to hurtle across the bridge over the Mary river with my friends and head out to the bush. We felt like cowboys galloping across the plains.

During the holidays I was sent off with the Young Women's Christian Association to a summer camp in Cairns. The train crowded with Brisbane girls pulled into Gympie station and I was shown to my compartment and given a top bunk by one of the chaperones who accompanied us. It was a three-day journey, stopping for meals at different stations on the way. One night the chaperones came running to our compartments telling us to be alert, not open any windows and sit still. We were about to go through a bush fire. We all sat up and held each other's hands while the train sped through swathes of swirling flames. The smoke crept through the corridors and we were all quite scared but it soon passed. Afterwards we did not go back to sleep for quite a while.

At Cairns we spent our days exploring the coral reefs and different islands, and going up the mountain to the Baron Falls. We sang songs around campfires and enjoyed delicious barbeques. Some of the older girls got some records and taught us all how to jive. It was a wonderful holiday which I shall always remember.

When I returned home there was a drive by the authorities to encourage all children to play tennis. On Saturday mornings the top Queensland coaches would give lessons at the Gympie tennis courts. For sixpence we would play tennis all morning and eventually we took part in tournaments. With the club swinging, tennis playing, Guides and Saturday afternoon cinema, there was no time to get up to naughtiness.

Mum got herself a job working in a dry-cleaner's shop, which surprised me, as it was not usual for mothers to work unless it was on a farm. Dad did not seem too happy about it either. She was still complaining about the heat and humidity and that year there was a drought. The Mary river level dropped and our bathwater came out of the tap quite brown, adding to Mum's discomfort. A long period of humidity led up to the rains. When the rain came there was thunder, lightning and then a torrential, non-stop downpour. People ran out to feel the rain on their faces. Men coming home from work rolled up their trousers and walked home in bare feet.

Then the Mary river began to swell, and the water ran over the banks and started creeping up the bush land near us. The high street was flooded and Brian and I watched with glee as thousands of cockroaches streamed out of the drains and as carcasses of drowned cattle, dead snakes and branches began to float down a surging river. The Gympie people coped, taking nature's happenings in their stride as flooding was a common event to them. They told Dad about the 'Big Fella' floods of the past, but all these stories did nothing to reassure my mother; they merely confirmed to her that life in England was so much better.

After the floods abated and life got back to normal, I was invited to a fancy dress party. Mum managed to get me a Hawaiian raffia skirt and a coloured halter-neck top. On the day of the party, Dad disappeared early in the morning, arriving back home at midday with fresh flowers, which he sewed together. He brushed my hair like he brushed the horse, gave me a little rouge and lipstick, and placed the garland of flowers round my neck. I think it was the first time Dad had seen me as a girl, instead of just me, and he was trying to make sure I looked as beautiful as he thought I should. As he put flowers in my hair he said, 'Never be one of those women who wear false flowers, always wear fresh blooms.'

On our way back from the party, later in the evening, I think he tried to tell me the facts of life when he said, 'You know, in order to make a beautiful sentence, you have to take one beautiful phrase and another beautiful phrase, but you do have to have a conjunction.' But it was Sooty who really enlightened me. A Manx tom cat started prowling about the place. He was a horrible-looking old cat and the two of them made a terrible noise at night. I thought they were fighting but a few weeks later Sooty swelled up and started to hang around outside my bedroom window. I knew she was banned from coming into the house, but she kept looking up at me in the most beseeching way, so I opened the window and she jumped in. As she padded round my room purring loudly, I was terrified that Mum would hear her. Then she disappeared inside my wardrobe and the next day I found the kittens.

She was a very protective mother and wanted to move them first thing in the morning. So very quietly, I opened the front door, and she picked the kittens up one at a time by the scruff of their necks and hid them outside. I cleaned up inside my wardrobe and told Mum that Sooty had three kittens. Brian wanted to see them but we did not want to worry the cat, so I said I would look for them. I searched the garden and under the house, listened for their squeaks and tried to catch sight of her black fur, but could not see a thing.

Then, just inside the paddock, I saw some grass moving. I was about to put my hand into the foliage when Sooty appeared from nowhere. She flew at me, hissing and spitting, her fur standing on end, and driving me away from where I thought the kittens were hidden. I was shocked that she was so angry but then I saw the snake slide out of the grass. Sooty had saved my life. It was not her hiding place for the kittens but a nest of snakes. Dad got rid of them later, while Mum was hysterical that there had been a nest so close to the garden. Eventually we found the kittens. They were hidden in a warm place, under the house, and we found good homes for them when they were old enough to leave.

A few months later, while Brian, Mum and I were talking in the sitting room, we heard a scratching sound behind the sofa on which Mum was sitting and some big hairy legs appeared over the back. To this day I do not know how my mother managed the long jump from a sitting position, but I am not too keen on spiders either, and certainly not tarantulas. I do not know who was the more scared, we screaming and yelling humans or the spider. It scuttled across the room, up a piece of furniture, and when Brian hit it with a fishing rod it dropped into Dad's fishing hat. We took it in turn to stand guard over the hat until Dad came home and dumped the still squirming tarantula at the end of the paddock.

~

IN THE MIDDLE of February 1952, Mum triumphantly announced that we were going for a holiday to England. Dad was very silent. She told us the ship, called the *Oronsay*, was a sister ship to the *Ormonde* and would leave from Sydney, and we would be getting a plane from Brisbane to Sydney. She said we could go to Lunar Park, which was like a great big fair, when the ship docked in Melbourne. I was suspicious. 'Is Dad coming too?' I asked. 'Not this time,' she replied. She seemed too bright and cheerful. It turned out that, knowing Dad would never return to England, she had worked out the cost of the fare and saved every penny from her wages. Although she told us all it was going to be a holiday, she knew she was never returning to Australia and I think my father suspected it too. Perhaps she thought that Dad would follow her to England.

Despite my suspicions, I could not help getting caught up with the excitement of Mum's plans. Her friend, Mrs Mahr, was given lots of patterns to make outfits for the voyage, and the three of us discussed what Brian and I could wear for the ship's fancy dress party. Mrs Mahr and Mum settled on a cowboy suit for Brian, and then, giggling about the latest exploits of King Farouk of Egypt, they decided I could wear salmon-pink, chiffon billowy trousers with a lime-green sequined top and headgear, and go as King Farouk's Latest.

Mum also decided that my hair was too heavy for me and that it took too long to dry, so she made an appointment with the hairdresser, and it was cut from waist length to just above my shoulders. She also had her own hair cut to a short bob. Dad was distraught. He loved women to have long hair, and was disappointed that she had not consulted him first.

Sooty was now as skilled as a mongoose at killing snakes. Every time she killed one she would drag it across the lawn and lay it underneath my bedroom window. So I would go out and praise her, and tell her she was a clever cat. Only kookaburras were better than Sooty at killing snakes. I would watch them dive for the snake, grab it by the tail, and smack its head against a telegraph pole. Then they would drop it and laugh like mad, swoop again, and pick it up and thrash it against the pole again and again, until it was dead.

I wanted to know who was going to look after the cat while we were away as I always bought her meat on the way back from school. Dad told me not to worry, he could look after Sooty. But who would look after him? Surely he would be lonely without us? I was also worried about school. I was doing well in Mr Spillane's class and I didn't want to have to catch up with the others when I returned after the holiday, but I was told not to worry.

Mum used all her guile to make sure I looked forward to going on the ship. When the day arrived for us to take the train to Brisbane, Brian and I were too excited about travelling to notice that the suitcases we were carrying were only a small proportion of the luggage already sent on ahead. Dad travelled with us to Brisbane and Sydney. Brian, Mother and I had never been on a plane before. The whole experience was exhilarating and terrifying at the same time.

After Dad had settled us on to the ship, it was time to say good-bye. Mum kissed him and then turned away quickly, and I saw his lips tremble and his voice sounded as if he had a cold. Brian gave him a big hug and then I clung to him, smelling his jacket and squeezing him as hard as I could. I told him how much I would miss him. Then Mum interrupted and told me to let go of Dad so we could throw some streamers down to him before the ship sailed.

Brian and I had three streamers each to throw. I threw the first, which caught on the wind and went in the wrong direction. The second one got caught up with other people's streamers. Dad caught the third, and one of Brian's, and hung on to them. I felt hot tears run down my cheeks. He looked so alone on the wharf. As the ship moved away from the dockside, the paper streamer broke and twisted in the wind. Slowly Dad raised his hand and saluted us, and I saluted back. The picture of him standing on the dockside, saluting, is an image burned into my memory. It was the last time I ever saw my father.

Chapter Three

1952–1955

~

UNLIKE THE SS *Ormonde* carrying mostly British passengers to Australia, the SS *Oronsay*, a much bigger ship, had many Americans and a larger number of Australians aboard, all heading for the great European experience. There were also those disillusioned British immigrants who, like my mother, wanted to return home.

Among the Americans were twelve Mormon missionaries, picked, I am sure, because of their handsome faces and tall athletic bodies. I should think there were a lot of women converts when they landed in England. When they strode along the deck, the married women all gazed wistfully after them. Even I, as a twelve-year-old, thought they were wonderful. The only way I knew of showing my appreciation of their handsomeness was to push two of them into the swimming pool. They did not believe in turning the other cheek, and took their revenge by chucking me in, so I came out of the water in the most ungainly way. It certainly dampened my puberty-stricken ardour.

When we docked at Melbourne, Mum took us to Lunar Park. From the moment we walked through the great yawning mouth of the place we were overwhelmed by the choice of so many exciting things – a Ferris wheel, a big dipper, a hurdy gurdy, all sorts of rides, stalls and entertainment. We returned to the ship exhausted with our heads spinning from all the excitement.

Several Australian ice skaters boarded the ship at Melbourne. I discovered that, early in the morning, they limbered up on the sports deck. So I got up earlier than Mum and Brian and joined them, holding on to the rails and working on my ballet exercises. One of the ice skaters was called John Smith. He was a lovely man who did not mind the collection of teenagers, plus me, hanging round him.

Somehow, my mother became a changed person during the voyage. She danced a lot, made friends easily, and never seemed to be cross or angry with us. We were allowed to stay up later than usual. We went to all the film shows on deck. As a special treat, she let me put on my best blue taffeta dress – the one usually worn to go to concerts with Dad in Gympie – to go with her twice to a grown-up dance. She had taught me how to waltz and quickstep in the cabin, so these were the dances I hoped people would ask me for and I was thrilled when they did. On the night of the fancy dress party, I wore my 'King Farouk's Latest' costume and won a prize in my age group. Brother Brian also strutted around as a cowboy and won a prize in his group. Mum was thrilled with us and her own ideas.

Until then, Dad had been the sun around whom we orbited. Mum had always been there, in the kitchen, telling us what to do, tucking us into bed, complaining about Australia. During the voyage, Mum's personality rose like a harvest moon, filling us with the lightness of laughter and fun. She was witty and joked a lot. Some of her wit was cruelly observant of other passengers' failings, and although her wit made me laugh, I felt guilty that sometimes the joke was at the expense of another's vulnerability.

She began to tell me stories about her own childhood. Her mother, Sarah Bonnaire, had been a music-hall singer and dancer. Mum had been hiding under the table in the family sitting room when the doctor had diagnosed her mother's cancer, and she had counted every day on the calendar during the remaining six months before she died. Mum was only sixteen at the time. I enjoyed the new role of being mother's confidante as she had never told me anything about her childhood or my other grandmother before.

The first port of call was Aden, where I was groped. I was not emotionally scarred – just surprised by the furtiveness of the little man selling trinkets. I decided not to tell Mother as she would have been enraged – she was already stepping over each stone on the road as if she expected it to be a turd. But once we were safely on board and relaxing in the cabin, I told her. There followed a diatribe of expletives, a veritable aristocracy of swear words. Not the king and queen, but a lot of dukes, princes and barons. I decided I was right not to have told her while we were in Aden. I am sure there would have been an international incident. I stored up the new words in my memory, however, to be savoured and mulled over in a quieter moment.

The Suez Canal was lined with soldiers carrying guns. We were told not to take photographs or to offend them in any way. Mum made sure that my Bilora box camera Dad had given me for the journey stayed in the cabin that day. She did not want me causing any trouble on board. We did not get off at Port Said but sailed straight on to Naples, where I tasted my first coffee. I had not been allowed to drink coffee or tea before then as Mum did not think it was good for children. I felt so grown up sipping a cup of coffee while Brian had hot chocolate. And we needed the hot drinks as we were beginning to feel the cold. All the other Australians were now wearing jumpers on board the ship, and life on the sports deck was distinctly subdued, although I still went up each morning to join the ice skaters for their morning exercises.

Mum and I practised our French when we docked at Marseilles, and we bought some *bon-bons* and *chocolat*, and when we stopped at Gibraltar Mum bought me a beautiful Spanish fan. Then we were in the Bay of Biscay, and the ship began to roll. At one point, the ship was nearly on its side. I saw one woman, who was playing cards, slide off her chair and across the deck to the other side of the room, while remaining in a sitting position. With great determination she managed to hold on to her hand of cards.

~

AUNTY GLADYS WAS waiting to meet us at the docks, to take us by train to her home in Brentwood, in Essex. We had crumpets and tea in front of a warm fire, and we were introduced to a small box in the sitting room called a television set. Brian and I thought it the most magical apparatus. While Mum and Aunty Gladys gossiped in the kitchen, we watched *Muffin the Mule*.

Leaving the warmth of the sitting room for the hallway was a chilling experience. The bathroom was icy. I had forgotten how cold it could be in England. Mum and Aunty Gladys were talking about getting 'our ration books' and joining the 'National Health Service'. I was amazed that there was still rationing in England and wondered how the Australian ice skaters would cope being unable to buy sweets. I told Aunty Gladys that I was very glad we had bought sweets and chocolate in Marseilles. It should be enough to last the holiday. She said nothing but gave my mother a tight-lipped look.

After supper, and clutching a hot-water bottle in bed, I watched my breath forming in the air and remembered Aunty Gladys' look at Mum. Something was going on and they were not telling me. When I had complained earlier that the taste of the tap water was bitter compared to the beautiful rainwater we drank in Australia, Aunty Gladys had replied defensively, 'At least there are no poisonous snakes or spiders under your bed.' Yes, something was definitely going on.

We spent a day in London, where we visited Madame Tussaud's and the Zoo, as one would on holiday. Then we travelled down to Seaford in Sussex. Dearie had arranged for us to stay in a furnished flat. It was on the top floor of a large house in Cricklewood Road, within walking distance of her place and close to the sea. I was glad to be in Sussex, away from London and the smog that made me cough and caused Brian to snuffle.

When we were settled in the flat and visited Dearie, the atmosphere between my mother and my grandmother was icy. Mum did not have a bank account so each week Dad was going to send cheques to his mother who would cash them. I could see that Mum did not like the arrangement, but I thought it would not be for too long because we would be returning to Australia.

Then the subject of school came up. Why were they talking about school when we were on holiday? When I challenged Mum about this later she replied that Dad would probably be joining us and we would be staying in England now, so we had to go to school. I was horrified. I wanted to go back to Australia, to my friends and Sooty, but Mum was adamant, saying England was now going to be our home. I wanted to know when Dad was arriving. 'Soon,' she replied, 'soon.' That was all I could get out of her. And I learned that I was not returning to the Annecy Convent, but was to start at the local secondary modern.

~

I WAS PUT in Mr Day's class and found the work very easy. Because I was tanned from all the years in Australia, I was a bit of a curiosity at the school. I was also good at sport so got on well with everyone, especially one group of older boys. They belonged to a small select gang, the leader being a boy about to go into the RAF. At weekends they would play adventure games on the downs. There were no girl members but I really wanted to join the gang and was determined to pass their tests to get in. These involved dangling from some very high scaffolding and pulling ourselves across from one side to the other, jumping from an old army building on the downs and rolling as if landing with a parachute, and the most scary one was running as fast as possible round a curved part of the cliffs while not falling to your death. I passed all the tests and it was decided I would be useful to be lowered down on the end of a rope to collect seagulls' eggs, to sell to the local hotels. So I was accepted and I was thrilled.

Each weekend we would be given a time and meeting place and we would have to find it. I learned how to make a sling like the one David had when he slew Goliath. We would practise our sling shots at various targets across the downs, and one day we discovered a mortar bomb embedded in the earth. Carefully we dug it out and carried it to the edge of the cliffs, then threw it over whooping with glee. It exploded. We ran like bats out of hell back to our respective homes and lay low for the rest of the weekend.

Dearie told me off for running around with a group of boys. It was causing gossip, she said. 'Why?' I demanded to know.

'It's not nice for a girl to be seen with so many boys.'

I argued that it was fun.

'It will give you a bad reputation.'

'Why?'

'Because it will.'

Mr Day gave me a letter for Mum. I wondered whether the letter contained something about what Dearie had said, that my membership of the gang was being talked about. Thankfully it was not. Mr Day had written that in his opinion, and the opinion of the other teachers, I was not suitable for the secondary modern school, but was grammar school material. Although I had missed sitting the eleven-plus exam, there was a twelve-plus exam I could take.

While waiting for the results of the exam Dad stopped sending money. According to Dearie he was ill and could no longer support two homes. She suggested we should go back to Australia but Mum refused. When she wrote to Dad asking how she would survive, he wrote back and told her God would provide. Suddenly we were very poor. Thanks to school dinners at the secondary modern and Brian's junior school we had one good meal a day and free school milk. Apart from that it was tighten your belts and drink lots of water. I hated feeling poor. I was also worried about Dad and wanted to go back to Australia to look after him. Although I felt very angry with Mum for placing us in this dreadful position, I also felt sorry for her, especially when she began to sell her jewellery to buy us food.

After realizing that her bluff had been called, and Dad had no intention of returning to England, Mum found a job as the manageress of a sweet and tobacconist shop which also provided a flat above. Not only was she now independent but we were given the occasional coupon-free chocolate bar too.

I passed the exam, which thrilled Mr Day, and then I had to have an interview with Miss Moss, the headmistress, to see if I was acceptable. Mum bought me a new dress for the interview, a green and white spotted one. I knew both Mum and Mr Day thought it important that I was successful at the interview, so I was polite and when asked what I wanted as a career I said I wanted to be a missionary. Miss Moss seemed to approve of my choice. A letter arrived a couple of weeks later accepting me, and I was told that the next term I would be attending Lewes Grammar School for Girls.

Mum also found out about a dancing school held every Saturday at the Old Barn. The dancing teacher, Mrs Neale, agreed to take me as a pupil. My membership of the gang was finished as Mum also made sure that I joined a tennis club, so my weekends were booked up. Even Saturday evenings were taken up with the Children's Theatre Club which was held in the room over the Ritz cinema. Two ladies, Mrs Marsh and Mrs Beale, ran the Children's Theatre. They were wonderful women, inspiring us with fun and a sense of belonging to a group. We danced and sang, worked on routines and sometimes there were parties and games like musical chairs, biting the bobbing apple, musical bumps and old-time dancing such as the Gay Gordons.

At the tennis club the first game fixed for me was with Deirdre Catt, who also went to Lewes Grammar. Because her parents knew I had been playing in Australia, they wanted to see how she could cope with me. She was smaller than me but had a powerful forehand and service. I played hard but I could not beat her. She eventually made it to Wimbledon.

During the summer holidays, the Caryl Jenner players put on a series of plays at the drill hall in Seaford. The programme changed on Thursday, so you could see two plays a week. Because Mum was working all day she arranged for Brian and me to have our lunches at the Belmont café and made sure our days were filled so we could not get up to any mischief. So once a week we attended the theatre matinee, seeing everything from the Browning Story to Agatha Christie. The young male juvenile lead in the company was Harold Snoad, who was later to become one of the finest directors of comedy at the BBC, and who directed me in *Keeping Up Appearances*.

Another excitement in Seaford that year was some night-filming on the seafront. A very handsome actor called David Knight was making a love story with a beautiful French actress. We kids all hung around watching in awe while the actors performed. A small yearning began to take hold of me. I wanted to be part of this world of theatre and films, but it seemed impossible. After all, I was not in charge of my life. But I found out about a theatre group called Peacehaven Varieties run by a producer called Kathleen Tayler.

They produced a lot of music-hall productions. I got in touch with them and joined the group early enough to take part in their next pantomime, *Red Riding Hood*, to be put on at Telscombe Hall, Telscombe Cliffs, early in January 1953.

Towards the end of the summer holidays we heard that Aunty Gladys had been taken to hospital after suffering a stroke. Mum was distraught and insisted that she come to stay with us to recuperate. My Aunt had changed towards me, often muttering disapprovingly that I was just like my father. However, she doted on my brother. I kept out of her way while she stayed with us and was very glad when I started school again in the autumn of 1952.

∿

I HAD TO travel by train with lots of other girls to Lewes. With new hat and uniform I began the term in the third form. They were starting a choice of German or Latin. As I chose German – I had studied Latin roots in Australia and knew Dad spoke German – I was put into Miss Shearer's class. She was a wonderful old Scottish lady, an aunt to Moira Shearer, who I had seen in the film *The Red Shoes*. She loved her subject but insisted that the English were useless when it came to using consonants. 'Only the Scottish can really speak good German,' she said. I was determined to prove her wrong and worked very hard for her. We learned our declensions by rote; I can still remember them now. Miss Warner was another wonderful teacher with a great sense of humour. She taught us English and religious knowledge. A very serious Miss Caine took us for science, which I loved; Mrs France, with rosy-red cheeks, took us for history. She was a fascinating teacher, who stopped me from being lazy and pushed me into a very good position in class. All the teachers loved their chosen subjects and were strict but we respected them – with the exception of the art teacher, who was a skittish, fluttery creature.

I teamed up with two girls, Janet Mortimer and Jenny Winwood. We sat together, were occasionally separated for bringing out the worst in each other, and are still friends. All of us meet regularly as members of the Headstrong Club, a political debating society in Lewes.

In 1952, many girls were in the same position as myself: father-less. Except their fathers had been killed in the war while mine was in Australia. Many of the girls' mothers worked, which made me feel a lot better.

In the summer term 1953, the Coronation was set for 2 June and we were all given special mugs. Anyone who had a television set was suddenly terribly popular. The only other way of seeing it was to wait for the film to come out in the cinemas. I was lucky. One of the boys at the Children's Theatre had television and asked a few of us over for the Coronation. It was a lovely day. I was sent over in a clean dress, hair brushed, to Ken Green's house. There was a table full of sandwiches, trifles, Tizer and Dandelion Burdock, and we all waited for the great moment to begin. It helped if you had good eyes as the black and white picture was tiny, but we all oohed and aahed and felt part of the making of history. Later, when the film came out in colour, I went with Mum and Brian to see it again.

Just before Guy Fawkes night Jenny asked me to stay at her house in Lewes and go to the town's famous bonfire. Her mother wrote to my mother and I was allowed to go. Wrapped up warmly, we joined the march down the High Street, dodging the occasional squib thrown in our direction. If ever Sister Mary Helen thought I was a heathen she was now proved right. It was like being caught up in a pagan festival, with torches burning and everyone chant-ing as we followed the figure of the guy held aloft, which was then placed on the bonfire. The rockets and screaming bangers, Catherine-wheels and bright colours bursting into the sky created a frenzy of excitement and awe. Two Plumpton agricultural stu-dents flirted with us, which reduced us to uncontrollable giggles. We returned to Jenny's house elated and calmed down only when her mother made us some cocoa.

During the Christmas holidays Mum's youngest brother, Uncle Ron, came down from London to visit us. He had been in the navy during the war and after being torpedoed and washed up on an Italian beach, he had met an Italian girl while sheltering with a family, and married her. However, when he brought her back to England she became homesick and left him. My uncle loved opera and at a drop of a hat would launch into song. When he knew I loved ballet he promised he would take me. All I had to do was get on the train and he would meet me at Victoria.

One Saturday afternoon in February 1954, dressed in my best coat, I was put on the train for London. I was beside myself with excitement. Uncle Ron met me at Victoria station and we went to the Royal Opera House to see *The Sleeping Beauty* with Leslie Caron and Roland Petit. We were up in the circle of the vast, packed theatre, with chandeliers and ornaments everywhere. It was like being in heaven. Then the overture began and the lights went down and magic was created on the stage. Travelling back on the train, watching all the passing lights, remembering Henri Dutilleux's beautiful music, I floated home in a state of wonderment.

On 22 February, when I reached fourteen, Mum gave me a wonderful party. It was our joint birthday. It was held in a private room over a restaurant. My friends from Lewes and some of my friends from the Children's Theatre came. How Mum could afford such an extravagance I did not know, but I suspected Uncle Ron had contributed to it. She also asked whether I wanted to try and catch up with my class in French as I was a year behind after returning from Australia. So I began lessons with Mr Nicholson, a tutor living in Seaford, who smoked a pipe and had a motorbike. If I did well in the lesson, he would give me a ride on the back all the way home. He taught me some French swear words first, 'Oh la barbe', and 'merde alors', and I made progress. By Easter I was able to join the lower stream of my year in French lessons.

Mum filled our time with lessons and treats but it did not stop me pining for my father. I started visiting my grandmother regularly to find out whatever I could about Dad. I was always told that he had not been very well, which was why he had not replied to my letters. She in turn asked me about my mother. I was cautious. Neither woman liked the other and I was not going to let myself get caught like piggy in the middle. On one visit I met my grandmother's cousin, Freddy, an Austrian, and I was able to practise my German during his stay.

Mrs Neale, my dancing teacher, told Mum I would make a good teacher and that if I could demonstrate in front of the younger pupils I could have my lessons free. She was getting older and it was difficult for her now to execute the steps. Mum worried about me doing too much but I said I could cope. I knew she was finding it difficult paying the fees and it made me feel I was contributing if I could be responsible for my own lessons. So I joined Mrs Neale at her school above the Winter Gardens in Eastbourne early on Tuesday and Friday evenings and had my own lessons on Saturday morning in Seaford. By the time I reached fifteen I had my teacher's certificates in tap-dancing and had reached elementary in the RAD exams in ballet. I also had studied Greek dancing and musical comedy. I joined the Seaford Dramatic Society. They were casting their next play, a comedy called *Mrs Inspector Jones* by James Parish. A Mr Bacon was producing it and he thought I could play the part of a vamp. I worked very hard learning the lines and played Earl Bostic's 'Jungle Drums' at home to try and get into the character. My hair was piled up to make me look older and I was poured into a very sexy dress with a fox fur wrap. Being in the play was exciting and when the audience laughed at the lines it was exhilarating. The local paper called me a 'find' and also mentioned that I went to Lewes Grammar School.

I was summoned to Miss Moss's study the following day. She was surprised that I had not shown any interest in the drama productions at school but I said I had taken part in one which I found boring. It had been about Welsh women baking bread and gossiping in a kitchen, full of 'look yous' and 'indeed to goodnesses'.

~

IN 1955, AT the age of fifteen, I felt more confident, more in control of my own life because I knew that officially I could now leave school. One of my school friends suddenly upped and left to be a nurse. Then Miss Shearer, my German teacher, died. I felt lost. Her replacement sweated a lot and tried to be popular but I did not like her. Another teacher I respected, Mrs France, left. And the skittish art teacher suggested I give up art when, after being asked to design a future product, I drew a bottle of green nail varnish and called it Grünex. 'Who on earth would wear green nail varnish?' she twittered. It was on the market two years later.

Mrs Neale offered me a permanent position as one of her student dancing teachers but I knew I had to find a better teacher for myself and I did not want a career working for someone else. I had heard of a really good teacher in Brighton called Molly Ball whom I hoped I could join as a pupil.

I read in the *Evening Argus* that on Saturday, 2 April, at the Bedford Hotel in Brighton, Mr Wills, a top model agent, was holding auditions for new young models. I decided to catch the train to Brighton after my morning ballet class. At the hotel I was ushered into a room with lots of older girls and given a pair of shorts with a zip to put on. I put them on the wrong way round, with the zip at the front like a man would wear it, but the older girls showed me how they were supposed to be worn, with the zip at the back. We then had to walk up and down in front of Mr Wills and his training staff who were sitting at a table and taking notes. Someone then took our details and we left.

There were three fifteen-year-olds who passed the audition that day: Mandy Morris from Rottingdean, who went on to become a top mannequin, Christina Gregg from Brighton, who became a famous photographic model, and me.

Mum was worried about me not finishing my schooling and travelling up to London every day for the course, but I was adamant about leaving school and taking advantage of the opportunity. At the same time brother Brian passed his eleven-plus exam so he would be accepted into a grammar school. The three of us celebrated by taking a bus to Eastbourne where Mum took us to Chez Maurice, a very posh French restaurant. But Miss Moss was disappointed that I had decided to leave. 'I had high hopes for you, Judy. I think you would have made an excellent civil servant,' she said.

I began the course in May. We were taught to walk on the catwalk by an extremely elegant ex-model who always had the straightest of seams in her stockings. She taught us how to show clothes in every detail. There were fencing classes, which I loved, and photographic classes, learning how to love the camera. We learned about make-up from a woman who said she trained as a beautician with Vivien Leigh's mother, and we exercised strenuously every day. For two months we studied the art of being a model. I often travelled down on the train with Christina and Mandy to Brighton, taking the train to Seaford from there. I also enrolled with Molly Ball as a student two evenings a week and worked harder in her class than I had ever worked before.

At the end of the modelling course we were all put on a contact list. I was offered the job of teenage model at Harrods but it would have meant living in London so I decided to take my chances of getting photographic work and to concentrate on my dancing classes instead.

~

THEN JANICE GITTINGS, a seventeen-year-old ex-Annecy girl from Newhaven, got in touch with me. She was opening her own dress shop and wanted to have Newhaven's first fashion show, so I agreed to model all her teenage clothes. The event was a great success with hundreds of people turning up. While in Newhaven I also found out about Jean Cantell, a young woman who was running a dancing school and teaching ballroom classes as well. So I enrolled with her for ballroom dancing, eventually getting my bronze medal.

Christina, Mandy and I often met at a coffee bar in Brighton to exchange information about modelling work and I had also discovered jazz. There were several jazz clubs in Brighton. For two shillings and ninepence (approximately 14p) I could get a bowl of spaghetti bolognese, an espresso coffee and entrance to a traditional jazz club before rushing for my last train back to Seaford.

Whether it was my influence or not I do not know, but Mum suddenly decided she would be happier in Brighton. She managed to get a job there and found a house in Westway, Hove, and as she did not want to disrupt my brother's schoolwork, we moved during the summer holidays.

We had a telephone in the new house. Suddenly I could phone and make arrangements without running to a telephone box. Mum also rented a television set. Life was really looking up. Brian was enrolled at Hove Grammar to start in September. I managed to get quite a few modelling jobs, especially for action shots, leaping in the air and looking carefree. One of my favourite jobs was working all day at the Guildford School of Photography with the students. There were so many different styles and ways of working that it never bored me. I used the money I earned to pay for my dancing classes and singing lessons with a Madame de Monci who had a studio in Hove.

Molly Ball was putting on a show called *Kaleidoscope* at the Dome and wanted me to be in it. Janet Ball, her niece and a brilliant professional dancer, was a soloist. I loved watching Janet at rehearsals. She was tall and beautiful and always wore the most exotic dance gear; we younger ones all tried to copy her style. I was put into a Greek dance and a Spanish dance with Diana Pelling, another of Miss Ball's brilliant dancers. When the music started the sound of the packed audience was thrilling, the applause the most wonderful thunderous noise. All I had ever experienced before was the applause at the drill hall in Seaford and the hall in Telscombe Cliffs. Mum and Brian came to see the show and were very proud of my efforts.

Then Mum lost her job and it was poor time again. She applied for National Assistance until she could find another job. Televisions and telephones were considered unnecessary extravagances, so when a man in a grey raincoat turned up to inspect us we hid the telephone and covered the television with a pile of washing. For the next few weeks Mum did some moonlighting, working in the evenings as a barmaid and not declaring her earnings. With my small erratic modelling fees we managed to get Brian his new uniform for school. I knew somehow I had to earn more money if I was to continue my own lessons and contribute to the housekeeping. Seeing how precarious modelling work could be, Mum suggested I should return to school so I could eventually pursue another career but I racked my brains to find another way.

In the local paper was an article about a fête to be held in Portslade, where there was also to be a beauty competition. The prizes were £15, £10 and £5. Each prize seemed a fortune to me. So I put on my best dress and, remembering what Dad had said about wearing fresh flowers, I bought a carnation, pinned it to my hair, and entered the competition. I came third and won £5.

I had noticed that although there were many dancing schools in

Brighton and Hove there was none in Portslade. After the time spent helping Mrs Neale, and remembering the way Miss Barcombe had taught me during my very first lessons, I knew I could teach. So I found out about the rates for Saint Nicholas Church Hall in Portslade and how much it would cost to have some posters printed. I got to know a retired music teacher, Mrs Piper, who wanted a little bit of extra work, and I was all set to start my own school. The posters were printed in bright red on a white background announcing the opening of Saint Nicholas School of Dancing on Saturday, 17 September, with our telephone number on the poster for any enquiries. I walked miles asking shops and schools to put up my posters, which had cost two pounds ten shillings. I worked out that I had enough to pay the hall and Mrs Piper with the remainder of my beauty competition winnings but if I did not get a certain number of pupils the whole idea would have to be scrapped.

∼

THE BIG DAY arrived and I had had only eight enquiries. I wondered if a person could go bankrupt at fifteen. I dressed carefully, wearing my hair in a bun to make me look older, and I booked a taxi so I could arrive with some air of importance. I was hoping to see the eight pupils waiting outside the hall, but as the taxi turned into Abinger Road, I saw a queue stretching from the hall right to the end of the road – my guardian angel had been very busy. I started my school with sixty pupils all wanting to learn how to dance and there was enough money to help Mum and pay for my lessons. But the great bonus was that I loved teaching the children and they enjoyed their classes. Mothers were banned from watching because I had experienced the trouble caused by ambitious, bitchy mothers while demonstrating for Mrs Neale. The children in my classes were allowed to be themselves and to set their own goals. One of the young boys even got into a West End musical before I did.

By November the school was flourishing and I was making strides in my own lessons. I heard from the older girls at Molly Ball's classes that there were auditions for the Hippodrome pantomime, *Cinderella*, and a lot of them were going along. Sherman Fisher was seeing dancers that week, but you had to be seventeen to work. I decided to turn up even though I was too young. I worked on an audition routine with Molly and arrived at the Hippodrome in make-up that was a credit to the modelling school; I also stuffed old nylon stockings into my bra to make me look more curvy.

As I watched from the wings, one dancer after another performed for Sherman Fisher and his choreographer, who was called Bridget. I noticed that tall, really good dancers were sent to one side and the smaller, or not so able, dancers were sent to the other side. I ended up with the smaller dancers, so I belted round the back of the theatre and joined the taller dancers. Sure enough, Sherman Fisher sent the other group off and told my group that he would have a second audition the following week. We were to bring our national insurance cards and he would then select who would be in the pantomime.

All week I worked on my audition dance and found if I stuffed my shoes with cardboard I could make myself seem taller. I got my national insurance card and realized that it was easy to see I wasn't seventeen, so I poured ink over the date-of-birth section.

For the second audition, Sherman Fisher made us all go through our routines again. After I had finished mine, he called me over, wanting to see my national insurance card. My face must have been blushing because he looked at me carefully. 'I see you've had an accident with your card.'

I could feel the heat at boiling point on my cheeks. 'Yes.'

'I'm sure I put you into the too small group last week.'

I said nothing but could feel the heat round my ears. He suddenly chuckled, 'I'm letting you in, my girl, because of your cheek.'

I could have hugged him. Instead I thanked him, promising to work very hard.

It took a bit of doing but I managed to run my dancing school and travel to London for rehearsals. The older girls from Miss Ball's gave me lots of tips, such as the best and cheapest place near the rehearsal rooms to get lunch. This was Lyons Corner House, near Piccadilly Circus. For five shillings you could eat as much as you liked from the salad bar. On pay day, some of us went into the Seven Star Grill and had waitress service. It was there my eyes nearly fell out of my head when I saw Charlie Chaplin at a table near us.

After rehearsals the Brighton contingent would rush to catch the non-stop train back to Brighton. Everyone would pile into the first carriage, which was the noisiest and full of Brighton lads escaping from their various offices. I often saw Christina or Mandy on the train and caught up with their news. That's how I found out that one of the very pretty older girls who had been at the modelling school with us had died following an abortion. She did not want to settle down to marriage before she had enjoyed her career for a while. Her boyfriend was distraught. I was to hear a lot of stories like this over the next few years. Many girls died or were seriously ill after visiting these backstreet abortionists, or 'retired nurses' as they were often called. Mum had told me I was not to go out with anyone in London or Brighton without telling her first. She warned me about white-slave traffickers who could whisk me off to the Middle East where I could be enslaved. She also told me never to sit on public lavatory seats in case I caught something, so I spent many years balancing precariously whenever the need arose.

After two weeks' rehearsal in London we began the final rehearsals with the stars of the pantomime at the Hippodrome. Derek Roy was playing Buttons, Jimmy Wheeler was the baron and Peggy Thompson the prince; Hilda Dixon was Dandini and Susan Swinford Cinderella; Terry and Doric Kendall were the ugly sisters and the broker's men were the Four Jones Boys, who were well-known singers. I spent most of the rehearsals staring at people who I had heard on the radio or seen in the comic *Radio Fun*.

We were given our costumes by a very strict wardrobe lady, who threatened us with death and destruction if we ate anything while wearing them. For the transformation scene ballet, when Cinderella gets her magical ball gown, we were dressed as blue fairies and had to wear blue wigs. At the end of the ballet we formed a circling wheel and, being one of the smallest, I had to run to keep up and grand jeté my way at the furthest point; all that and keep my wig on at the same time. I was terrified of slipping or letting the wheel down.

When the opening night arrived the older girls told me I was to be initiated. I had to strip to my knickers and bra, then they pushed me out of the chorus room into the corridor and told me to turn round three times and swear three times before they would let me back in. I used all the words I knew and was welcomed into the professional theatre. Joyce, another of Miss Ball's pupils, was given the job of head girl and we all had to do what she told us.

The overture and beginners were called and the music wafted up the corridors. We were first on as the villagers dancing in the village square before Dandini comes on. I loved every moment of the show. As I watched the scenes between Buttons and Cinders from the wings I was caught up in the magic of the story myself.

Each day I would come down early to the theatre and work on my dance steps and practise my tap-dancing; each night I would watch the scenes with Cinderella and wonder whether I could ever play a part like Susan Swinford's. One day Terry and Doric came in early to practise their comedy dance throws and asked me if I would like to practise some of their tap routines. Terry had learned the American style of tap and soon I was copying him. When Corky, the assistant stage manager, wanted understudies for the principals, I volunteered for Cinderella. We were called daily to practise the lines and the songs. Early one morning I was telephoned and told to come down to the theatre as Susan Swinford was ill with flu and unable to go on.

'You'll be playing Cinders tonight, Judy,' Corky told me. 'And we want you to try on the costumes.'

I was thrilled and Mum was beside herself with excitement. I also had the divine confidence of the stage-struck innocent and inexperienced beginner and was unaware of anything that could go wrong. It seemed like a miracle that I was going to take part in the magical story I had watched from the wings every night.

At rehearsals the other stars were very kind and patient. Terry and Doric gave me a good-luck gift and Susan had sent me a good-luck telegram. I was moved into her dressing room, which was number seven, and played Cinderella, believing every word I said.

At the end of the performance Derek Roy introduced me to the audience, and I was applauded for my efforts.

Madame de Monci, who had taken me through the songs, came bustling backstage to see me, followed by Mum and Brian. Brian had nearly been strangled by Mum when he developed the giggles over my rendering of 'Wonderful, Wonderful Day'. In those days, apart from a few foot mikes, you had to fill the theatre with your natural voice and, while true, my singing voice was not as mature or strong as Susan's. Today, everyone in pantomime is wired for sound amplification and I doubt if many of these entertainers would be heard without their personal mikes.

I played Cinderella for a week and received my first complimentary letter from a Brighton policeman and his wife, Les and Mabel Killick, who congratulated me on taking over the role of Cinders. I also had a write-up in the local paper. It was a wonderful, magical week for me before Susan recovered and I had to return to being a dancer again. My guardian angel had shoved me into the limelight. It was now up to me to see if I could stay there.

After a week away from the chorus, the perils of the wheel at the end of the transformation scene came back as a shock. I tried to keep up at the end but lost my grip, my blue wig slipped down my neck and I went hurtling off into the wings – Lucille Ball eat your heart out. Ramming the wig back on I managed to catch up for the finish of the ballet and received a well-deserved ticking-off from Joyce, the head girl, for being sloppy and not fixing my wig on properly.

Chapter Four

1956–1957

~

WHEN MUM ANNOUNCED that she had found a new job, again as a manageress of a sweet and tobacconist shop with a flat provided, it was all change again. I was sad about leaving the house in Westway but glad that Mum was now independent of the National Assistance man, who could cause such panic when he arrived unexpectedly. I too was contributing to the household, buying my own clothes and paying for my own lessons. The extra money I had earned during the week I played Cinderella bought me a new amber tweedy skirt and a lime-green jumper with pom-poms.

One morning Terry and Doric asked me to come and have lunch with them in the Seven Stars Pub where they were staying. It was just round the corner from the stage door of the Hippodrome. I was flattered that they were taking me for lunch, especially as I was wearing my new skirt and jumper.

Doric told me she was thinking of retiring from the act and they had both agreed I would be the right person to take over from her. It would mean learning all the routines and working with them in London so I could be ready for the next summer season. I decided that now was the time to admit that I would be only sixteen in February, not seventeen as I had claimed. They were not worried and said they would like to talk to my mother. Later Mum told me they wanted me to travel up to their place in Clapham Common on Sunday evenings, stay there working all week and return on Friday evening so I could keep my dancing school running. They would pay my fare, provide all food and if necessary send me for any dance lessons they thought I needed. I thought hard about the offer. If I lived away from home Mum would have only Brian to look after and if I went to classes in London perhaps it would be a good experience, even if I did not like the air or the water. Also, by being part of an act my theatre wages would be higher than the five pounds ten shillings I was earning as a chorus dancer in Brighton. I agreed to join the act. It was then that I met Kay Kendall, Terry's daughter from his first wife. She would drop into the theatre between shows and I was thrilled to be introduced to this tall and beautiful woman, with short, thick red hair, who was famous for her performance in the film *Genevieve*. She was just about to get married to Rex Harrison and was very much in love. Both she and her sister Kim had started their careers as Sherman Fisher dancers, which gave me a great boost of optimism for my own future. During the rest of the pantomime season not only did I work in the mornings with Terry and Doric but I also had a lot of fun.

One night the rival ice-show pantomime skaters threw a big party after the show and we Hippodrome dancers were invited. We danced until late and didn't realize that snow had fallen heavily with huge drifts stopping all traffic, so we all walked home, shouting and throwing snowballs as we went. Mum was waiting up for me, checking I had eaten something.

Because I had now joined Equity, the actors' trade union, I was also allowed into cinemas and other theatres free during the pantomime season and saw Leslie Caron playing Gigi at the Theatre Royal, the spectacular ice-show pantomime in West Street and the show at the Grand Theatre.

~

THE PANTOMIME SEASON finished just before my birthday. And then I started work with Terry and Doric, who lived with their fourteen-year-old son Cavan in a ground-floor flat at an apartment block called Oakeover Manor, on the edge of Clapham Common. Marie Kendall, Terry's mother, a famous music-hall performer, lived in the flat above. She came down when I arrived and we had a long conversation. Over supper she announced to Terry and Doric, 'This child is not just music hall, she is Cinderella, she is an actress.' I did not know what that meant or whether it was a compliment or not, so I just smiled and said thank you.

Our daily work routine started early in the morning by practising lifts in the garden. Tap-dancing followed, and after a quick lunch of rolls and cheese, we would work on comedic replies to hecklers or on tag lines to jokes. Later in the day we would use a church hall close by to work on the routines. 'Hey there, mister, you'd better watch your sister for the fleet's in, the fleet's in . . .' 'You're the cream in my coffee . . .' and comedic ballroom dancing which began in perfect Victor Sylvester style then slowly became knock-about comedy. I was so glad now that I had invested in Jean Cantell's ballroom classes as I was able to follow perfectly.

Terry announced that he had arranged for me to join Philip Buchel's tap-dancing lessons in Chelsea. I was to remember everything he taught me and show Terry what they were doing. I set off on the bus the following morning with a map and my dance kit in a bag in time for the lesson. When I entered the studio, the first person I spotted was David Knight, whom I had watched filming in Seaford. He was taking the class like me. I was finally with the people I had wished to be with when I had watched the filming, but I didn't say anything to him. I was there to learn the steps for Terry, but inside I was almost bursting with excitement, and made a note to tell Mum at the weekend.

We danced to jazz music. It was the American Negro style. The music and the steps were sensual and soon the whole body was caught up in the rhythm, unlike the more upright tap-dancing taught in the English dancing schools. I bounced back to Terry and showed him the routines and steps, which once developed added another dimension to his routines.

I had also heard about another teacher in London called Anna Northcott, who taught Russian ballet in a studio just off Saint Martin's Lane. As I could not get to Molly Ball's classes I was going to try and attend hers after I had finished the daily work with Terry. Anna worked us even harder than Molly Ball. I began the evening classes with her but could manage only two a week. With the tap classes and the daily work with Terry I was now as thin as a worm.

By the end of June, I was still waiting to hear about the summer show we had talked about when Terry, Doric and I had lunched together in Brighton. They then told me that they had decided to work together again in Jersey but that there was an offer for me to go into the chorus which would pay me eight pounds a week and we could continue our work on the routines there. You should be able to get some good digs for about three pounds a week, they said. I told them I would think about it, but I was disappointed as I was supposed to be in the act by now.

The following Monday, on the way back from Philip Buchel's class, I picked up the *Stage* newspaper and saw that there were auditions for a new non-stop revue at the Irving Theatre Club in Irving Street. The producer was Len Mitelle and the show was going to start early October. That same day I called into the Irving Theatre to find out about the auditions. Len Mitelle was there and told me to come back the following week with a good snappy routine and I might get in as a soubrette; at the moment he was auditioning nudes. He explained they were challenging the Windmill Theatre, known for its non-stop revues. People like Kenneth More and Jean Kent worked in this famous vaudeville, theatre in Windmill Street. Len also told me there would be six shows a day, commencing at one o'clock and finishing at eleven, and the show would change every eight weeks. I went back the following week and after singing one of the numbers I had worked on with Terry and Doric, I performed a hectic tap-dancing routine for him. He then gave me a sketch to read with the stage manager and called me into his office.

'We start rehearsals in September and I can offer you ten pounds a week, Monday to Saturday.'

'I will take it,' I said, and filled in all the forms he wanted and promised to get my mother's signature for him. Ten pounds a week for someone as inexperienced as me was a fortune. I wondered if I could get an agent or other work if someone important spotted me.

I told Terry and Doric that I had auditioned for the Irving and been accepted for the show starting later in the year, so I did not want to go to Jersey and perhaps it would be best if I left that week. They understood and there were no hard feelings. I could now live at home and travel to London on the train. They agreed that it was a good move and I would probably get an agent working in town. So we parted company and I returned to the fresh air of Brighton.

~

I BEGAN MY lessons again with Molly Ball and often met up with Christina and Mandy at the North Street coffee lounge. There we could sit with our ninepenny cups of espresso coffee for hours, gossiping and sharing information. There was a beauty competition coming up for the Queen of Light, to be held at the Brighton Aquarium, and Mandy was going in for it because there were good prizes. So we both entered. She came first and I came second. A friend of mine suggested that I try for the London heat in a different dress, so Mum helped me choose a prettier one. We found a mauve tulle dress with layers of pleating over the bodice which made my bust look a bit more developed. Armed with a pair of high-heel shoes, a carnation for my hair, and my bra stuffed to bursting point with old nylon stockings so I managed a faint cleavage, I entered the London heat at the Lyceum. Among the judges was a famous singer called David Hughes. I did not think I had much chance as all the girls were much older than me and experienced models or beauty queens. One had even been Miss England. I just did my best, smiled at the judges and walked in the best way the modelling school had taught me, and I won. After being crowned Queen of Light I had to dance a waltz with David Hughes. He was charming and told me that all the judges had voted for me. I was enjoying the conversation when I saw the expression on his face change. He was looking straight at my bosom. I glanced down and, horror of horrors, the toe of one of my old nylon stockings had worked its way up and was sticking out of my mauve tulle bodice. I shoved it back down and talked about his singing career and tried to remain as composed as I could. Mum was waiting up for me and my prize money of £25 was laid out on the kitchen table. When I told Mum and Brian about the stocking toe popping out of my dress they screamed with laughter.

The next day my picture was in all the national papers. The Brighton publicity department got in touch with me about a challenge from the Newmark Watch Company of Croydon who were bringing 2,500 of their employees down to the sea for the day. Newmark had stated that the prettiest girls in Britain were to be found at the factory bench and had challenged Brighton to match sixteen of their Newmark girls with sixteen Brighton girls in a beauty contest. Independent judges were brought in and each of the thirty-two contestants was to be identified only by a number so no one would know from which town they came. The judges had to select six winners. The department of publicity wanted their Brighton girls to win. So I agreed to turn up in a new strapless sunsuit I had bought. Thirty-two girls walked across a platform erected down by the beach. We were watched by all the Croydon visitors and Brighton crowds. I was number one, so I could get it over with quickly and watch the others. Then they selected the six winners. I was one of them. All six turned out to be Brighton girls. Croydon had been defeated and the six of us received the kind of cheers usually reserved for footballers.

Another friend of mine told me about a competition to be held at the Bedford Hotel to find Miss Mambo 1956. It was a dancing competition and involved non-stop dancing of the cha-cha-cha and mambo. He said he would enter me and find me a good partner. So again, dressed in my sunsuit, I went in for the competition and we danced and danced. I won and the London judges, mostly musicians, voted for me as Miss Mambo. There was an awful lot of bitching from girls who used the club regularly. But the judges had spoken and that was that. Again there was a lot of publicity both local and national, and I worked with photographers on the beach in one of my old costumes from the Spanish dances in Molly Ball's show *Kaleidoscope*, twirling and dancing. I always had fun on those shoots and slowly got to know quite a lot of newspaper photographers. After so much fun during the summer, it was time to get ready for the revue rehearsals in London.

I would no longer be able to teach as I would be working on Saturdays now. One of the older girls at Miss Ball's classes took over my dancing school gradually, so the children were not thrown by the change. I had loved teaching at Saint Nicholas Church Hall and the money I had earned there had paid for all my classes and given me a lot of confidence, but I knew the children were in good hands with Elizabeth, herself a first-class dancer.

~

BECAUSE I WAS sixteen I could buy a weekly ticket for the train journey between Brighton and Victoria for nineteen shillings (95p in today's money). I set off for rehearsals in September full of excitement and wondering what numbers I was to be given as the youngest in the cast. Another cast member from Brighton was Johnny Webb, a new Columbia recording singer. The choreographer, Ray Lincoln, had been one of the O'Doyle Brothers, and Bryan Blackburn had written the music and lyrics. They were really good numbers and we were fitted for beautiful costumes. I was allowed to do my own choreography for a number with Johnny Webb. He sang 'Seventeen' and I was dressed in a smart pair of jeans with a matching top.

The three other soubrettes I worked with in the production were Sylvia Ellis, Jan Arnold and Rita Cameron, all of them talented singers and dancers. The others were mainly acts like Julie Mendez, an exotic dancer, who looked like a gypsy but was actually from Teeside. She had absolute control over her body and could shake from the ankle upwards, producing a crescendo of tinkling sounds from all the bracelets and bells attached to her ankles and wrists. I used to watch her in amazement as she rehearsed. She could also spin the tassles on her nipple caps clockwise and anticlockwise and was unbelievably supple. There was a great blues singer called Marion Jennings and a comedian called Ken Douglas who worked on all the sketches with us. Then there were the nudes. These were tall beautiful girls and the true stars. They were paid more money than the rest of us, except for Julie, because these were the girls the audiences really came to see, not the comedians, singers or soubrettes. We were just there to fill in when the nudes were changing their positions or drapes. There was Pamela, a tall strawberry blonde with a past in Hong Kong. She was tanned and wore a thin gold chain round her waist and had an infectious, deep throaty laugh. Rita had long red hair and milky-white skin and looked like a figure out of an old painting; Della had the most enormous bosoms and was wonderfully dizzy and funny. In the small shared dressing room, she used to sling her bosoms around as if they were a couple of bean bags.

Mr Chaudhuri owned the theatre and ran an Indian restaurant called The Shalimar next door. He was a very religious man, often returning to India to take part in religious ceremonies, and always extremely courteous to the entertainers.

During rehearsals we used to run across the road for cheese rolls and coffee for our lunch breaks or up to the Quality Inn where we could get lunch and endless coffee for four shillings and sixpence. A public relations man was brought in to take all our details and the press photographers were asked to our final dress rehearsal. Because I was the youngest I attracted a lot of attention which resulted in a huge feature in the *Daily Mirror*. After opening night, the show received good reviews, and I received a lot of praise. At the same time, round the corner from the Irving, at the Palladium, another sixteen-year-old was getting a lot of praise. She was called Shirley Bassey.

Then the talent scouts began to come in to see the shows. Two other men joined the cast: a small man called Ronnie Corbett, who did a mime act of someone sitting on a park bench discovering he had picked up something nasty on his shoe; and Victor Spinetti, who did a wonderfully fast act of brilliant impressions, especially of Danny Kaye. They too received great reviews from the critics. Victor later created the unforgettable drill sergeant addressing a platoon of national service soldiers and was to use this act in the late Joan Littlewood's famous production of *Oh, What a Lovely War*.

Most of the audiences were obviously not there to see the talent but to gawp at the nudes. When the comedians, singers or soubrettes came on, a lot of people would get out their newspapers and read until the nudes returned. The bowler hat brigade had the biggest newspapers, like the *Financial Times*, and it became a challenge to us to make them put down the papers and watch us, if only to raise a smile.

The nudes were on boxes and once the curtain went up they were unable to move. If they did, the show could be closed down. They would rush into the dressing room saying, 'Look out, it's my quick change,' and change their G-string or their nipple caps, which they fixed on to their breasts with Copydex, the carpet adhesive. They were never ever really nude but carefully posed so that a leg or a drape covered the pubic area. Usually the three of them represented a theme or a famous painting, while a compère or singer stood at the side of the stage describing the tableaux to the audience. Occasionally a single nude would stand posed as an artist's model while the comedian talked about the emotional perils of such a relationship.

During the show, we had lunch between appearances. Often it was curry brought upstairs to the dressing rooms by waiters from the restaurant below, who would steal furtive glances at the scantily dressed girls. Julie once found a hole in the dressing-room wall where one of the waiters had poked through to watch the girls changing. Yelling with rage she pounced on the offending waiter and kicked him all the way down the stairs, while all the girls cheered her on.

Sometimes all the curry-eating had repercussions, such as when I was singing in front of the nudes and heard a loud fart from Pamela's direction. I kept singing despite the muffled giggles coming from the boxes. As I turned during the dance, I could see Pamela's tummy shaking with laughter and Della's bosoms swinging like pendulums while Rita's white body was turning a shade of pink. After another elongated rattle of trapped biriani, Pamela let out a snort of suppressed hysteria. I got the giggles and the curtain was pulled down by the stage manager, Mr Freear, who told us off for being unprofessional. The dressing rooms rocked with laughter when the cast heard what had happened.

It was during this time, while performing at the Irving, that I had something in common with Ernest Hemingway. Many of Hemingway's contemporaries thought he was mad when he insisted he was being followed by the CIA. It was because of his Cuba connections, he said. His friends told him he was paranoid. The girls at the Irving thought I was mad when I told them I thought I was being followed. I could sense it, I said. 'Why would anyone want to follow you?' they argued. 'The nudes yes, you, no.'

Well, it has since turned out that Hemingway was right; he *was* being followed by the CIA. And I too was being followed, not by anything as sinister as the British Secret Service, but by the private detective my grandfather had hired after reading the piece about me in the *Daily Mirror*. He was making sure my behaviour did not disgrace the family, as I found out years later when he died and my aunt found the report in his safe.

Then a letter was delivered to me backstage from Lionel Blair, a choreographer and dancer, and Michael Mills, a producer and director. They asked if we could meet, as they had an offer in mind. I telephoned them the following morning and they wanted to know whether I had an agent. When I said I did not know any, they suggested two agents in Charing Cross Road who could arrange things for me if I was interested in working with them.

The following Monday, I came into London early and looked up the two agents. They were both in offices at 26 Charing Cross Road, not far from the Irving. The first was Dorothy MacAusland. I went into her outer office and found a young girl typing. A very warm fur coat was slung over a chair. The agent called me in and I told her where I was working. She did not seem too interested. To fill in the conversation I commented that she must be paying her secretary well for her to be able to afford such a beautiful fur coat. 'Don't you recognize her,' the agent replied, 'that's the new girl who got all the notices at the Palladium, Shirley Bassey.'

The next agent on the list was Joan Wallace, a much older woman who looked as though she had wrapped a sheet round her middle and then covered it with a thick woolly jumper. I introduced myself and she beamed, 'Ah, the child with the great notices. Michael and Lionel are interested in you, dear.' She explained that they were wanting to audition me for the principal girl for a Howard and Wyndham pantomime, *Puss in Boots*, in Aberdeen, but first I would be in a show at the Birmingham Hippodrome for two modern ballets, *Slaughter on Tenth Avenue* and two other big numbers. 'This is a number one company dear,' she said, 'you will probably be asked to be in the *Five Past Eight* show and any other shows they're doing. I can get you about fifteen pounds a week. Are you interested?' Fifteen pounds a week was a fortune. I said that I would most definitely be interested. So a meeting was arranged for an early morning audition at the Howard and Wyndham offices where I sang 'Wonderful, Wonderful Day' and danced for Michael and Lionel.

'You can sing that in the pantomime,' Michael said. 'We'll build the number round it. We're doing *Puss in Boots* and you'll be playing the princess, Rosalind.' Lionel gave me some dance steps and asked me to perform them. 'You're in, Judy,' he said when I had finished. I could not believe my luck.

When I told the girls back at the Irving about the offer, Sylvia said she had just given in her notice because she had been booked for a part in *The Pyjama Game* musical. All the others too were being approached by agents and managers. Len Mitelle was charming when I told him that I had another job offer. 'That's what you all come here for Judy. It's a shop window for talent. If you ever want to come back or fill in I'll be happy to use you again.' So it was time to move on.

~

MUM WAS WORRIED about the work being so far away and that I had lost so much weight. She made me take malt and cod liver oil to build me up, and got me a small case to keep them in, making me promise to keep taking them when I was away. Brother Brian said he would miss me because I would not be with them for Christmas. He was taking music lessons and had joined the Scouts.

Joan Wallace telephoned to say that she had arranged for an older dancer to look after me in Birmingham. She was called Wendy Mclure and I would see her at rehearsals in London. We would be staying at some digs in Pershore Road for four guineas a week all in, and the landlady was called Mrs Crocket. This amused me as a song being played on the radio at the time was called, 'Davy Crockett, King of the Wild Frontier'.

It was a large company of dancers. I was partnered with a boy called Gordon Coster who also attended Anna Northcott's classes. Wendy was a lot older than me and from Glasgow. I could see all the dancers respected her and she dressed impeccably and always wore a lovely perfume, Mitsouka. She was kind and caring, and for someone like me, the perfect role model. The work was hard but I loved working for Lionel. Some of the boys were French dancers, some from Scotland, but most of them were from London. Again I was the youngest but no allowances were made. I had to pull my weight. There was a lot of lifting in the dances and I was glad for the work I had done with Terry Kendall.

Wendy and I travelled by train to Birmingham. From there I was to catch the train to Aberdeen when the Birmingham show finished, so Mum had packed every jumper I possessed and lots of thick vests and warm pyjamas. I had my old school scarf and a spare blanket wrapped in brown paper and tied with string in case of the digs being mean with blankets. I also had my small case with a hot water bottle, Ribena, cod liver oil and malt which Mum insisted I take with me. Poor Wendy, she travelled with such style and elegance. It must have been galling to travel with a girl with a pony tail, school scarf and carrying a wrapped-up blanket. However, Mum was not so stupid. When we reached the digs in Birmingham and I was shown my room, I asked the landlady why there was wet on the walls. She said it was nothing to worry about, it was just condensation. I told Wendy, who immediately opened the windows to let some air in. Then we put my hot water bottle on the sheets and watched steam come out. My blanket was going to be useful.

I arrived at the theatre with my make-up case and my small case with the malt and cod liver oil. We were to rehearse with the musicians. Geraldo and his orchestra were at the back of the stage on a large rostrum. We were to dance in front. When the music started, I felt intoxicated by the sheer power created by the huge number of musicians. It thrilled my whole body. Geraldo was a lovely old man with snowy white hair and a great sense of humour. When he saw how excited I was about his orchestra, he patted me on the head and smiled.

One of the French boys helped me with my hair. 'This is how you should wear it, Judy. It gives you height.' He piled it up on my head and made sure it was secure. 'You should come to Paris to work. They would love you in Paris.' I knew Mum would never let me go to work in Paris. She would be too worried that I might skip off back to Australia.

For 'Steam Heat', a fabulous number where we were all dressed in red, we had the highest heels to work in. And in *Slaughter on Tenth Avenue*, Joanna Rigby was the most beautiful leading dancer. I loved being in that modern ballet. With the theatre packed to capacity. It was a great success.

After the opening night there were lots of men waiting outside the stage door with bouquets.

'I wonder who they're waiting for?' I said to Wendy. 'Joanna do you think?'

'No, Judy, the flowers will be for the boys not the girls,' she replied.

'The boys? But surely you don't give boys flowers.'

'Oh yes they do.' Wendy was emphatic and we rushed to catch our bus back to the digs.

I survived Mrs Crocket's condensation and at the end of the week caught a train to Glasgow, where I was meeting Michael Mills and Daphne Willis, the choreographer, before travelling on with them to Aberdeen. Joan Wallace had arranged digs for three pounds a week with an old lady who lived fifteen minutes' walk from His Majesty's Theatre. Washing all my clothes was included in the deal.

A taxi took me to a block of council flats. The landlady showed me a lovely warm room with spotlessly clean sheets. In her little sitting room she had laid the table close to a fire and she served the most delicious shepherd's pie. I knew I was going to be all right in these digs. The next day, wrapped up warmly, I set off for the theatre. On the way I was appalled to see young children playing in the street with no shoes and holes in their very threadbare jumpers. It was freezing cold and I had never seen such poverty. This was 1956, not war time and rationing. I wondered whether they had enough to eat. I continued walking to the theatre and rehearsals, feeling very distressed at what I had seen.

Mr Freear, who had been the stage director at the Irving, was stage manager for the pantomime. It was lovely to have someone there that I knew. I met Margo Henderson, who was playing the principal boy, and found her a friendly person. However, nothing had prepared me for the resentment some of the other cast members felt towards me. This was because of the publicity that preceded my arrival. A lot was made of my youth and the fact that I had won some beauty competitions. Photographers wanted to take pictures and I was often on the front page in some pose or other, especially as it was near Christmas.

During the three weeks' rehearsal, I often collected the newspapers that had my write-ups or pictures in them and sent them to Mum and Brian. One morning I walked into the rehearsals with some papers under my arm, and it was too much for one comedian, Eddie Reindeer, who was playing the Baroness and topping the bill with Aly Wilson. 'Another picture in the papers dear?' he shouted.

'Yes,' I replied.

'Sending it to Mummy, are we?' he shouted again. I could sense the rage and anger, so I just nodded. 'Isn't that nice!' he said, almost spitting the word 'nice' into the stalls. He and Aly arrived for their first entrance on a motor bike, straight after my opening number, 'Wonderful, Wonderful Day'. The setting was a woodland scene with a bridge over a stream. I had a flowing turquoise-green dress with matching hat, and after singing, I danced, then finished by singing the last chorus again. There was always an attempted applause by the audience which was drowned out by Reindeer starting the motor bike long before I had hit the last note. He did this on purpose, among other things, such as pulling my hair nastily when I, the princess, was supposed to be blindfolded and spun round.

Mr Freear came up to me one day and said, 'You're being upstaged, Judy.' I did not know what being upstaged meant. The actress playing the cat was happily getting further and further upstage of me forcing me to turn away from the audience. That was not how we had rehearsed it but I just followed her. I was playing the part as truthfully as I could, unaware of what she was doing. The audience could not see my face by the time she had crept to the back of the stage. Mr Freear gave me some flowing scarves to take on stage with me. 'Now Judy, when she starts going up stage, just shake the scarf and say your lines straight out to the audience. She'll soon come back down.' So I did what Mr Freear told me and sure enough that cat, in every sense of the word, came rushing down to where she had been originally directed. Mr Freear was a great help to me. He often managed to stop the motor bike from starting too soon so I could get my applause, but mostly he was ignored by Eddie Reindeer.

Although initially I was upset by the few members of the cast who were spiteful to me, I toughened up and soon learned to avoid them. There was plenty of friendship from the dancers, who would include me in their plans. But still, these days if I ever see a comedy actor, or any other actor, being spiteful to a young actress, I usually take them apart by the ears, verbally. I hate bullying, I know how demoralizing it can be, but some actors just cannot bear a pretty young actress getting attention.

Two people in the cast fascinated me. They were actors John Cater and Anthony Carrick, playing the villains. I loved listening to them talking about the different parts they had played in repertory. One day someone missed their entrance to a scene I was playing with them. Being totally wrapped up in my part I just improvised with them until the other entertainer arrived back on stage. Afterwards, John Cater congratulated me on the improvisation, saying that many an experienced actor would not have known what to do. I was thrilled at his praise, and remembering how much I had enjoyed working on the play in Seaford, asked him how one went about getting professional acting parts. He told me the only way in, if one had not been to drama school, was to join a repertory theatre as a student assistant stage manager and that there was a really good repertory in Perth run by a man called David Stuart.

The stars of the show, for me, were the comedy acrobatic team, Warren, Devine and Sparks. They were brilliant and their Australian accents often reminded me just how much I missed Queensland and Dad. I also loved watching the jugglers, Eddie Ross and Marion.

The theatre was owned by Mr Donald. When his son was having a twenty-first birthday party – a Highland party with bagpipes and all – I was invited. Towards the end of the party, young master Donald tried to kiss me and I slapped him hard. We have often laughed about how outraged I was then, whenever I have played at His Majesty's.

At the end of the pantomime I travelled home via Perth, hoping to meet David Stuart. He was happy for me to join the repertory but all he could pay a student a.s.m. was one pound ten shillings a week. I asked him how people lived on thirty shillings a week, and he said a lot of them shared a flat and cooked baked beans. This was not for me, I thought, and after thanking him for seeing me I returned to Brighton.

∼

SOME TIME LATER, Lionel and Michael offered me a job on television, dancing in *Bonanza*, a musical to be performed in the independent television studios in Manchester; and a part in a floor show they were producing for Winston's Night Club. Maggie Fitzgibbon, an Australian singer, Johnny Webb, my old friend from the Irving, and Barbara Windsor were going to be in it.

'You'll have to stay in London, darling,' Lionel said. 'You can't travel home on the train at one o'clock in the morning.' So Mum came up to London and found me a very respectable hotel, Hotel Maurice, next door to a law school, in a small square just off Lancaster Gate. When we started rehearsals, Toni, a fan dancer, who lived with her parents out of London, also booked into the same hotel so we could travel together at night.

I was thrilled to be in a hotel. I was on the top floor next to the bathroom. Although I was coming up to seventeen, I was still the youngest in the company. Bruce Brace, who was the manager of Winston's, used to send Toni and me off in a taxi every night because Bond Street and the Bayswater Road were lined with prostitutes. They could get very nasty if they saw any girls walking along what they considered to be their territory, although I found that the Bond Street lot, once they knew we were dancers, would often just say hello when we walked down the street on our way to the club in the evening.

At Winston's there was one performance at midnight. A stage would slide out over the dance floor, the lights were lowered, and then we would come on. Amanda Barrie and I performed 'Singing in the Rain' with Johnny Webb and two other dancers. We then had a quick change into some Hawaiian skirts for a number with Maggie Fitzgibbon; and another into some billowy Eastern trousers for a number with Barbara, whom I liked. She was very straight-forward, a few years older than me and very streetwise. She advised me on how to survive working in clubs. 'Get in early, girl, and you can get a free meal from chef.' Toni and I had already made friends with the night porter at Hotel Maurice. Because he knew we were coming in late and were ready for a chat, he would make us sandwiches and hot chocolate and never put it on the bill. So Toni and I used to get into Winston's about nine thirty and enjoy steak or whatever we got from the kind Polish chef.

I was able to keep up my classes with Anna Northcott and one day some of the Bolshoi ballet company arrived at her studio for a warm-up class. I watched them with admiration and awe, and it was at that particular class I gave up any dreams of becoming a great dancer. The Russians were brilliant and I knew I could never ever be that good. I was booked for the *Five Past Eight* summer show with all of Lionel's dancers but already I was thinking about how I could get into a repertory company to learn how to be an actress.

One day Barbara came up to me and whispered that she had a boyfriend, Gary Crosby, the son of Bing Crosby, who had just arrived in London and she wanted to spend time with him over the next couple of days. She wanted to know if I could learn her songs quickly so she did not let the show down. I assured her I could and that I could also fit into her costume. She was shorter than me but that was mainly because my legs were longer. I was standing by the day Lionel phoned to say that Barbara was off ill. I rushed in to go through the numbers with the pianist and took over for two nights. It went well, although Amanda, who was older and more experienced than me, was spitting with rage that she had not been asked, but she had got over it by the time we started the next show.

Late one morning, during the last few days of my contract with Winston's, I was taking a bath at the hotel. Because there was never anyone around at that time I had just grabbed my towel and washbag and nipped into the bathroom next to my bedroom.

Unfortunately, my bedroom door had locked and the key was inside. Luckily, I had left my bedroom window open. So, after wrapping my towel round me, I climbed out of the bathroom window and on to the ledge that ran along outside my bedroom. As I edged along, I became aware of pandemonium going on in the law school next door as the boys were all yelling and whistling at this blonde climbing along the ledge. I turned and grinned at them and waved, nearly losing my towel in the effort, then scrambled into my bedroom window. The hotel manager phoned my mother and I was asked to leave as I had disgraced the hotel. That was fine as I was leaving that week anyway.

The *Five Past Eight* show was really hard work. We were in Newcastle at the Theatre Royal, with David Whitfield topping the bill. He was a good-looking blond ex-miner who had the most wonderful voice, and was famous for his record 'Cara Mia Mine', among others. For the opening number, the Five Past Eight girls were all dressed differently, in individually styled white dresses. We then had innumerable quick changes for the various numbers. Most of them we could cope with but one number was a disaster on the opening night. Lionel had choreographed a ballet to 'Pink Champagne'. There would be a huge champagne bottle on stage, and on a certain beat in the music the door in the bottle would open and we would all posé-turn out of the bottle and on to the stage where we began the ballet. The designer then decided to pump bubbles into the bottle before we came out so that bubbles would be floating out with us. Not a good idea. The soap blinded us so we could not see when we came out. Our shoes were soaked and instead of looking like light pretty bubbles we splattered across the stage like wet ducks. Some of us, guess who, landed on our bums most inelegantly. The audience howled with laughter; the bubbles were discontinued.

During the summer show we worked from nine thirty in the morning until five thirty in the evening on the next show, then we went on stage and performed the present show from seven thirty until ten. We were not allowed to turn up at the theatre in trousers and if our hair was not looking immaculate we were fined. We were paid well but we worked hard for it. By the time I finished the *Five*

Past Eight show in early September, I looked like someone just out of Belsen.

When Mum saw how gaunt I looked she forbade me to work again until I had rested and put on some weight. After a week of her cooking, the Sussex air and lying in bed in the mornings, I lost my tiredness and looked much better. With all the money I had saved, I proudly opened a bank account with the Westminster Bank.

~

EVERY SUMMER THERE was a repertory company at the Palace Pier Theatre on the end of the Palace Pier. It was run by a Mr Forbes Russell and usually finished when the weather changed in mid-September. In 1957, however, he was extending the repertory season by moving into the Dolphin Theatre, which was then next door to the Theatre Royal. The producer and director was Alan Hay and I got in touch with him to ask for an interview. When I saw him at the theatre he was very reluctant about offering me a job. He didn't think someone who had mostly singing and dancing experience was right for repertory work. I showed him the write-up I'd had for *Mrs Inspector Jones* in the Seaford theatre, when I was still at school. He was not impressed. Then I remembered what David Stuart in Perth had said and assured Alan Hay that I was not asking to be an actor in his company but a student assistant stage manager. I was prepared to work for thirty shillings a week with the hope of possibly getting a small part. He said he already had two students but I promised to work hard and he capitulated and told me to come in on the Tuesday morning ready for work. He then introduced me to Bill Halls, the stage director, who would be in charge of me.

Bill was a lovely man who looked after his students like a mother hen would take care of her chicks. Thin, dressed in black with a black duffel coat, he moved like a dancer. His face was small and resembled that of a freckled elf. He had a small red moustache and goatee beard. He took me down to the prop room to meet the other students, Elizabeth and Robin, who were about six months older than me. I was told that I would have to keep the stage clean

and set up for morning rehearsals, and after rehearsals everything
had to be put back for the evening performance. Every day I would
be visiting shops to collect borrowed props for the following
week's play. Robin and Elizabeth told me a lot of famous actors
lived in Brighton and they were often guests in the repertory and
were to be looked after at all times.

I reported to the theatre early on Tuesday morning and helped
to set up the stage for the rehearsals. When the resident cast arrived
I was introduced to them. One very haughty leading man told me
that as a student assistant stage manager, the lowest form of life in
the theatre, I should address them not by their Christian names but
by Mr or Miss followed by their surnames. When he then turned
and glided on to the stage, Bill snorted with disgust, 'Don't know
who he thinks he is, the big tart.' However, I did not want to offend
any of the actors so I addressed them formally, unless I was advised
differently.

The guest star arrived in the shape of Binnie Hale, sister of
Sonny Hale, and a lot of fuss was made of her entrance on to the
stage. She was a small, immaculately dressed woman with red hair
pulled back into a bun. She sparkled and loved the attention paid
to her, and as if to emphasize her good mood, performed a high
kick and sank down into the splits. I thought whatever Alan Hay
had said to me, this lady certainly knew about music hall or was
an ex-dancer. I was right – I soon discovered she was a famous
musical star.

After rushing round the various shops to borrow props with
Robin, I was able to watch some of the rehearsal. Elizabeth was on
the book ready to prompt if any of the actors wandered off the
script. The actors were making notes of their moves in their scripts,
just as we had for pantomime. But we had had three weeks'
rehearsal; these actors had only one. They worked until lunchtime
and then Alan Hay went straight to the pub. The actors went back
home or to their digs to learn their lines and to prepare for the
evening's performance in a play which involved a storm at a certain moment in the second act. I was put on the wind machine and
the rain sounds. The wind machine involved winding a handle
either quickly or slowly to get the right moaning sound or banshee-

like screaming wind. The rain machine was like a big washboard that had to be tipped to the side to make the patter of rain sounds. I was terrified of getting it wrong but was conducted from prompt corner by Bill, who artistically waved the noise louder or softer.

The following week, the guest star was Hermione Baddely. She was a famous star of revue, usually working with her friend Hermione Gingold. They were known as The Two Hermiones. I had seen her give a wonderful performance in the film version of Graham Greene's *Brighton Rock*. She was appearing in two one-act plays. Alan told me I had a small part in one of them, as the maid who came on from stage left, put a tray down on the table, then departed downstage right. I then returned from downstage right, picked up the tray and went off stage left. I had two words to say: 'Yes ma'am.'

The first morning of rehearsals I was sent out straight away to 'get Miss Baddely some Alka Seltzer'. She was very hung-over from the 'party last night, dear'. I also had to help her on the opening night by putting make-up on her shoulders and back for a low-cut dress. She had a small, snuffly, Pekinese-come-pug dog called Lotty which she took everywhere with her. On the opening night, I proved I could be trusted with a tray, and Hermione was a huge success. The curtain came down to enormous applause and Hermione sent me to her dressing room to bring 'little Lotty to share the curtain; my friends will want to see Lotty'. They held the curtain and I ran to the number one dressing room to get her dog, only to be confronted by the sight of two identical dogs. One belonged to Hermione's friend Joan. I picked up the nearest dog, rushed back to the stage and handed it over to her. Up went the curtain to more applause and a big bouquet of flowers was handed up for her. Down came the curtain and she turned on me, 'You stupid bitch, you've given me the wrong dog.' She then whacked me over the head with the flowers. The curtain went up again to more applause, revealing Miss Baddely clutching a bunch of stalks, a snarling dog, and one maid covered in flower heads and petals.

Bill leapt out of prompt corner. 'How dare you attack my student,' he yelled at her. She was gracious enough to apologize, and so did I, to her, for picking up the wrong dog, and everyone saved face. During the week she was at the Dolphin she was great fun but I made a resolution never to get involved with actresses' dogs again.

~

WHILE WE WERE performing with Hermione, we also began setting up rehearsals for *I Am a Camera*. I had read Christopher Isherwood's novel *Goodbye to Berlin* and was looking forward to watching the rehearsals with a visiting actress called Frances Cuka. When she arrived, the first thing I noticed was that she was wearing green nail varnish, which she was trying out for the part of Sally Bowles. I remembered the stupid art teacher who had dismissed my design for green nail varnish and felt vindicated.

When Frances began to plot her moves I was entranced. This was nothing like the usual acting in the company, it was a million times more real and I found myself believing totally in everything her character said. I would perform my jobs as quickly as I could so I could hang around and watch Frances working. When there was a moment to catch her on her own I asked her why her acting was so different. 'Probably because I'm with Joan Littlewood at Theatre Workshop,' she replied. I asked if there were any books I could read that would help me understand her method, and she told me to get Stanislavsky's *My Life and Art*, and *An Actor Prepares*. When we opened on the following Monday, I watched Frances give an inspiring, funny and tragic performance as Sally Bowles. I cried and laughed as I watched from the wings and have never since seen an interpretation of Sally Bowles that matched the performance that week given by Frances Cuka. This was great acting. I decided then that somehow I had to work with Theatre Workshop.

The next play was *As Long as They're Happy* and Robin, Elizabeth and I were all going to be in the play. It involved a scene around a table eating supper. The three of us were also in charge of the props, including making the supper with a minimum of float money. We decided to make the meal with sliced bread soaked in gravy browning for the meat dish, mashed potato, and more mashed potato coloured green for the peas. Unfortunately we had to work in very dim light before the meal was served, and the biggest laugh of the evening came when we lifted the cover to the 'peas'. The potato had turned the brightest green. We were mortified and the haughty actor yelled at us when the curtain came down; otherwise, the play went very well. One night, though, Alan Hay decided to stand at the back of the theatre after he had been in the pub. We were into the second act when he decided we were all inaudible so shouted, 'Louder and faster.' We froze with fright but picked up the pace immediately and projected loudly in case he shouted again.

The following Monday, a strange thing happened while travelling on the way home for lunch. I spotted a very bedraggled white rabbit running along the pavement. It was raining, but I was nearly home, so I got off the bus and went over to the rabbit. The poor little thing was shivering. I picked him up, put him inside my jacket and took him home. He was very thin and obviously hungry. After some cabbage and milk, he perked up and scampered all over the flat. He finished up on a rug in my bedroom, having left dozens of pellets on the kitchen floor which I quickly cleared up. Before leaving for the theatre, I left Mum a note telling her about the rabbit and that I intended to get him a hutch.

On Tuesday morning Mum put her foot down and said the rabbit was not roaming round the flat dropping pellets everywhere. Until I had a hutch I was to take him with me to the theatre. So tucking Skimpy, as I called him, into my jacket, I caught the early bus to the theatre and got some left-over carrot and lettuce from the greengrocer near the stage door. I put him into number one dressing room while I tidied up the stage. He was happy enough with all his food, and I reckoned the visiting guest star would not need the dressing room during rehearsals. I was wrong. We were all set up for the rehearsal with Alan Hay waiting and the cast ready for plotting *French Without Tears* with Sybil Wise, an experienced West End actress, when there was a loud scream from number one dressing room. Sybil arrived on stage clutching her chest, gulping for breath.

'There's a rabbit in the dressing room,' she gasped. I apologized immediately and said that I would take it out straight away.

'No,' she wailed, 'I want it to stay there.'

She then told us that early that morning she had been

telephoned with the news that her great friend Jack Buchanan had died. 'The last play I did with my dear Jack was *Harvey, the White Rabbit,*' she whispered, 'and what do I find in my dressing room but a white rabbit.' We were all silent at this strange coincidence.

By lunchtime I managed to find a hutch for Skimpy and carted him, the hutch, some straw and a selection of vegetables on to the bus home. The next day Sybil asked about the rabbit and whether I had managed to get a hutch. She was a lovely, kind woman. I left the rehearsals to clear up the prop room downstairs as I had been told to do. While sorting out the prop room I found a pile of scripts, one of them called *Bachelor's Fling* written by Sybil Wise. I dusted it down and when I returned to the stage to see if there was any-thing else to do, I saw Sybil having some coffee. I showed her the script and asked whether she had written the play. She asked me where I had found it. I told her in the prop room. 'Typical,' she said. I was allowed to read it, so I went home on the bus clutching the play and read it before returning to the theatre in the evening. The next day when I saw her I asked if the play was ever put on in the future, could I try for the part of Bonny. 'Most certainly you can,' she replied and then treated me to afternoon tea at a tearoom by the theatre, where she asked me all about my career so far and what I wanted to do. I told her I really wanted to be an actress, which was why I was working for thirty shillings a week. Soon, though, I would be leaving for a pantomime season for S.H. Newsome, the company that I had first started with at the Hippodrome, when I had understudied and gone on for Cinderella. They had offered me the part of the fairy godmother in the same production. I was start-ing rehearsals for the pantomime early in December, when the repertory season finished. She asked me whether I had any drama training. I told her I'd had lessons only in dancing and singing and she offered to give me the occasional drama lesson, explaining that she had taught at LAMDA after a car crash had ruined her chances of a successful career as a leading lady. She gave me her telephone number and told me to call her if I was cast in anything again that season and she would come to the theatre and give me some notes on my performance.

So began a wonderful friendship with my mentor. It was Sybil who taught me how to break down the text. She told me she did not want to teach me about Acting with a capital A, because I had a natural quality she did not want to destroy. The most important thing Sybil gave me was the confidence to trust my own instincts and how to think one thing and say another, which was important in comedy. As I set off to play fairy in the pantomime in Dudley, armed with the books Frances had recommended and Sybil's notes, I wondered whether my guardian angel had sent me the magic white rabbit.

Chapter Five

1957–1958

~

WE REHEARSED FOR the pantomime at the Max Rivers Studio in London for a week; the dancers and singers had started a week earlier. I had one scene as the old woman in the wood, then the transformation scene where, after a flash of magic, I turned from an old woman into a fairy queen. I then took part in the ballet with Fred and Dorothy, who were the lead dancers. They had found digs in a pub just outside Dudley – three guineas a week for breakfast and an evening meal after the show. The proprietors were a Mr and Mrs Penny who had a dog called Tuppence. We arrived at the weekend, and were told in no uncertain terms that if we came back at night later than expected, the oven would be switched off.

Down at the theatre we rehearsed and tried on costumes. My fairy dress was too big in the bosom for me. Terry Bartlett and Colin Ross who were playing the ugly sisters looked at me in the dress. 'Oh, darling fairy, we can't have you looking like that, can we? Come into our room and we'll juzz it up.' In I went to a room so cosy and homely, with wigs on blocks all around, costumes hanging everywhere, a kettle, bottle of milk, a tin of biscuits and a pile of falsies for their costumes. 'Here, darling, stick those over your boobs.' They gave me two enormous rubber breasts with rigid, pointed nipples. I was embarrassed. 'Now, darling, don't you worry about us,' they said, 'we're not after your body. Now stand up on the chair.' Within minutes they had transformed the outfit by sticking sequins all over the drooping tulle dress and my fairy queen crown. They also sprayed my wand with silver glitter. I left them feeling far cheekier with my much improved dress and enlarged bosoms.

Derek Roy was playing Buttons again and was pleased to see me. So was Peggy Thompson, who was again playing Prince Charming. Cinderella was being played by Shirley Abicaire, whom I had seen on television. She was Australian and known as the Zither Girl, playing the strange instrument and singing with a pure, sweet voice. I liked her a lot. During the week's rehearsal, Sue Crowley, a girl who had been a Sherman Fisher dancer with me in the first pantomime, strode into the rehearsal room dragging a fur coat behind her with one hand, while she carried a baby in a carry cot with the other. I was surprised to see her and wondered what had brought her to Dudley. She told me that she was now married to Derek Roy. I was most surprised. I thought he was already married but decided not to ask any questions. After all it was none of my business.

Back at the digs I was drying my hair with my hairdryer plugged into a light socket when suddenly Mrs Penny leapt through the door. 'Ah, caught you,' she shouted. 'You're using extra electricity. That'll be an extra two and sixpence on your bill.' I could not believe anyone could be so petty-minded and mean so I told her I was leaving.

Sydney Arnold, who was playing the baron, told me there was room in his digs. It was four guineas a week but for three meals a day. It was right opposite the theatre and the landlady was lovely. I moved in straight away and stayed until the end of the run, enjoying endless stories from Sydney about his days as a music-hall comic.

I had a lot of fun during the pantomime season. The male singers and the dancers often got together on a Sunday and went to the country to visit historical places or just to have a party. I always went with them, especially on Christmas Day. However, on New Year's Eve, the male singers planned something evil for me. They knew Terry and Colin had given me rubber falsies for my fairy dress, and when the curtain came down and rose again so we could all cross hands and link up with the audience to sing 'Auld Lang Syne', they got each side of me and pulled with all their might. My rubber falsies made a terrible sucking sound, then flew out of my fairy dress and lay quivering on the stage. There was hysteria all round. I could not feel embarrassed, there was too much laughter from the cast, and the pink falsies did look funny.

After Christmas my mother phoned to tell me that after she and Brian had had a strange sleepless night, they heard the following morning that Aunty Gladys had died. Mum was distraught and I felt very sad for her, knowing how much she loved her older sister. Although Aunty Gladys's hostility towards me had killed the love I once felt for her, her death brought poignant memories of the happy relationship we'd had when I was much younger. When I returned home a month later, my mother was still very subdued and inclined to weep a lot. Then I was contacted by Terry Carney, an agent with Eric L'Epine Smith, who lived near Brighton and who had come to see me when I was at the Dolphin Theatre. He told me the part of a teenage runaway was coming up in the BBC television series *Dixon of Dock Green* and the director would like to meet me. The news cheered Mum and Brian, and Mum was thrilled when I landed the part. The fee too was much bigger than the money I was usually paid in the theatre.

When I told Sybil Wise, she immediately volunteered to work with me on the script. On Sybil's advice I learned the part thoroughly before rehearsals began. The last thing in the world I wanted was to forget my words, or receive a prompt in front of millions of viewers – the dread of all actors. At that time television was live performance and not filmed and edited later as it is now. There was one story of an actor involved in a play set in a mine, who died during transmission. His body was passed along the mineshaft by the other actors who quickly took his lines and continued the play.

I started rehearsals with Patrick Cargill playing my father. The episode was called 'Mr Pettigrew's Bowler'. In the story I had to show teenage rebellion and stamp on his bowler hat with rage, and then run away. Jack Warner, who played PC Dixon, eventually found me, gave me a good talking-to and returned me home. It was a leading part with lots of different scenes and I was often changing my clothes as I crossed from one set to the other or just managed to comb my hair before being waved into the next scene by the floor manager. I did not forget any words and the director was pleased with my work. Terry then sent me a script for a part in two episodes of *Emergency Ward Ten*, playing a schoolgirl who had been bitten by a dog and was very ill. This was much harder because being in bed there were no moves to help remember the words. So, again on Sybil's advice, I learned the words by heart before starting rehearsals. The actor playing my father was nervous but one of the regular members of the cast, who played a nurse, was called Jill Brown. She helped me a lot and realized that being so young and inexperienced I was obviously nervous. She took the time to show me how to stay in the lights focused on me, and how not to put myself into a shadow by moving into the wrong position.

Just before we were due to go on air we had a tea break. I can still remember the sound of my own heartbeat thundering against my chest. When I got into the bed and lay there waiting for my cue I felt sure that someone would come down from the control box and tell me to stop all that thumping. The show went through without a hitch for me and I remembered all my lines. Not so for one of the regulars who played a doctor in the series. He had written a lot of the Latin medical terms round the edge of a wash basin, forgetting that when the show started the basin would be used. When he started to say his lines, performing with that confidence and ease that actors have, knowing their characters, and used to playing in a series, his expression changed as the water poured into the sink. He speeded up his delivery of words, his head getting closer and closer to the sink as the text began to disappear. There was a gargled mumble as the last few words of his script rapidly disappeared down the plughole.

The relief of getting through the show was enormous for all of us. Mum and Brian had been watching with great pride. Sybil too told me I had done well. I was then sent for a film test for a schoolgirl part in Saint Trinian's with Alastair Sims. When I got to the studios there were lots of girls but they were all much older than me and far more experienced actresses. I was eighteen by then but looked a lot younger and was certainly not as well developed as them. Shirley Ann Field was also testing and took me under her wing. I enjoyed the whole day, and though I did not get into the film the experience was invaluable.

~

BY THE SPRING of 1958, I had written to lots of repertory companies but not one of them offered me a season paying enough money to live on. I went up to London to do a round of the agents, who had nothing to offer, when I saw Julie Mendez, the exotic dancer from the Irving, buying some cigarettes from a kiosk in Shaftsbury Avenue. 'Hi ya, Kid,' she shouted. We hugged and went for a coffee to catch up on all our news. She told me she was now working at the Panama Club in Great Windmill Street. Len Mitelle was running it and they were paying really good money. Unlike the Irving, the Panama ran only five shows a day. I went back with her to the club to say hello to Len and he immediately offered me a job at eighteen pounds ten shillings a week. Bryan Blackburn had written the lyrics again and they were funny and topical. Len wanted me to perform a number with Roy Byfield Riches and to work on some sketches with Dickie Arnold, the comedian.

I went and met all the performers backstage. There were two fan dancers with great singing voices, Angela and Peggy, and an opera singer called Shirley, who was only working at the club until she had saved up enough money to carpet her new home. I was to replace her by introducing the nudes when they posed in positions from famous paintings. Rita, who had been in the Irving, was one of the nudes; Anna, who was extremely short-sighted, was another nude, working in the club so that her husband could study at art college; and there was a tall blonde called Paula. She carted a little dog with her everywhere she went. It slept under her dressing table when she was on stage but was occasionally known to start barking and get very snappy if people tried to quieten him down. There was another very bohemian stripper, an Irish girl called Wendy whose husband was an artist. The dressing-room space was a bit bigger than the Irving's and next to it was a large kitchen where the food for the club was prepared.

So I began work at the Panama. I was able to travel up and down easily on the Brighton train and earn enough money to contribute

to Mum's housekeeping and add to my savings. Things were looking up. Mum, Brian and I moved out of the flat over the shop, back
to a rented house in Westway.

I had been working for a few weeks when Len told me a comedian who had been watching the show wanted to talk to me. We
were introduced and he told me that Ross Radio was putting on
a game show for ITV. It was to be shown on a Sunday, so it would
not interfere with my work at the club. He would be hosting it and
they were looking for two girls to be on the show. Was I interested?
I told him I was and he gave me the name and telephone number
of the director, Malcolm Morris. When I met Malcolm a couple of
days later he told me each girl would be tried out on a programme
to see who they would select for the series. I was to get back to him
to find out the first Sunday scheduled.

That evening the comedian came back to the club to ask how I
had got on with Malcolm. I told him everything and then he said,
'Now you have to be nice to me.' Alarm bells went off in my head.
'I wasn't aware I'd been unpleasant to you,' I replied.

He then began to wheedle, offering me my own flat and an
allowance for clothes, if I would be really nice to him. Yuk! The con-
ceit of the man. Not only was he old – he must have been at least
fifty – but he was quite ugly and I loathe wheedling, winging men.
I told him to 'shove it' and called him a dirty old man. I did not
know how much he had to say about employing the girls on the
TV show but mentally I said goodbye to the job and went back to
tell the cast that the TV job was probably not going to happen and
about what he had said. There was a chorus from the girls and the
boys of 'Dirty Old Man'.

The next day I read in the papers that the comedian had
dropped dead the previous night. My guardian angel had obviously called in the soul of a hit man. I waited a day before calling
Malcolm Morris again, who had found a replacement in the shape
of Jon Pertwee. I asked him about the contract for the *Can Do* show
and was told to come round and pick it up for the following
Sunday. He was putting me on an outside broadcast; the other girl,
Lilimore Knudson, would be in the studio. Different celebrities
were to be invited to the studio to guess whether a sporting feat or

some other form of test could be achieved or not. It was 'can do' or 'no can do'. The girls were to be known as the Can Do girls.

I was to travel up to Liverpool after the show on Saturday. On Sunday I would be taken to New Brighton. The idea was for me to stand on a raft out at sea waiting for Anna Gerber to waterski past. As she passed the first time I had to hand her a briefcase, then the second time a bowler hat and finally an umbrella. I was to wear a blue leotard with 'Can Do' embroidered on a pocket over my left breast, with dark blue fishnet stockings and very high-heeled dark blue shoes. The Can Do girls were supposed to be glamorous. With my rather inadequate curves, I packed my old stockings to stuff into my bra.

Everyone on location was friendly. I was given a glamorous make-up, my long hair was curled and I was taken out to the raft. Flags were used to communicate: red for 'stand by' and green for 'on air'. Millions of people would see me standing on the raft in my blue outfit ready and waiting for Anna Gerber to start her skiing run. Back in the studio the celebrities were deciding can do or no can do. The red flag went up and I stuck out my stocking-filled bra and looked as glamorous as I could, teetering on the rocking raft. The green flag waved and Anna started skiing towards me. I leaned forward with the briefcase, and as she grabbed it from me – disaster! The wash from her skis tilted the raft and I went straight into the water. By the time she had circled and was ready to return I had managed to clamber back on to the raft. My hair was hanging like seaweed, my beautifully moulded stocking-filled bra cups were now soggy pouches round my ribs, and my fishnet stockings had split and were creeping down my legs. Nevertheless, I held the bowler hat ready for her to grab as she passed. This is the spirit that won the war, and I was a war baby after all. As she grabbed the bowler hat, the wash sent me into the water again. Looking like an old dishcloth, I managed to scramble back on to the raft just in time to hand her the umbrella. She took it and I hit the raft and held on for dear life. Success! Can Do! The men sent in a boat to rescue me were laughing hilariously as they handed me a big towel. I thought that I was utterly finished with the series until Malcolm came up to me and said, 'I've never heard so much laughter. It was great. You're with us for the series Judy.'

For the next three months I worked a seven-day week. Six days at the Panama, then on Saturday night I would catch the train to Birmingham where a car would collect me and take me to a hotel. On Sunday I would work in the studios until five thirty, after which I would travel home to Brighton. I found it stimulating working with the two different groups of people, and I also liked watching the brilliant Jon Pertwee work. It was amusing that when we were all standing around the studio rehearsing, Jon would carry a shooting stick in order to sit at every opportunity, while Lilimore and I had to balance forever in our high heels. I was also happy to be earning such a lot of money.

~

LEN MITELLE HAD a secretary called Veena Rochforte. I will forever be grateful to Veena, for she persuaded me that I really should have an agent. I told her I had worked through two agents but never signed up with either of them. She arranged a meeting with an old friend of hers, Sonny Zahl at the Kavanagh Agency.

When I walked into Sonny's office I saw this beaming friendly face that wished to know what I wanted from show business. So I told him. I wanted to appear in a musical in the West End, act in the theatre, make a film, perform on television, and make enough money to buy a house. He had seen my work in the club and thought I had a promising future but he wanted me to leave the club so he could send me to meet people. I signed his contract and, as I was still under twenty-one, Mum had to sign as well. It was the law of the land at the time.

While I was working out my notice at the club, Mum decided she wanted to come and see the revue, so she arranged a day off work. I panicked as I had not told her about the nudes. Len told me not to worry, and the day that Mum came to an afternoon show, the nudes had more drapes, the jokes were very clean, and Len made sure Mum was given a tray of tea in the front row. What the usual audience of men thought about the strange watered-down show I have no idea, but Mum thought it was very funny, the people most polite and that I was very good. We all waved to her as she set off back to Brighton.

Cy Laurie's jazz club, where they had the best jazz in London, was in the basement underneath the Panama. As the weather grew hotter the lavatory was often the coolest place to be. The window in there opened on to a well from which the sounds of the jazz music would float upwards. I used to feel quite nostalgic when I heard the music, remembering the wild dancing in Cy Laurie's with my dancing partner Gordon Coster.

Whether it was the heat, the fact that I was waiting to finish my contract or just the monotony of five shows a day that was responsible for my wickedness, I do not know. But some madness made me do something for which I will forever feel ashamed. Short-sighted Anna was on a box, posing centre stage for a sketch with Dickie Arnold, who was delivering a great comedy piece about the temptations of being an artist working with a nude model. I was standing in the wings waiting to go on for the following number and I began to pull faces at Anna. Remember, in those days a nude who moved could close the show. Urged on by some manic bout of mischief, I went on making dreadful faces at her. Then, to my horror, I saw a trickle of pee running down her leg. She had managed to control her facial muscles but lost control of her bladder. The pee started to drip from the box on to the stage. Any pervert in the audience must have thought it was Christmas. Anna's face and body were turning a deep shade of red. Oblivious of what was happening, Dickie droned on until even he heard what sounded like Niagra Falls from the box. After the curtain came down, a distraught Anna groped her way off the stage and I had to dance precariously across a very wet floor. When I came off stage she chased me through the kitchen and hurled a bowl of fruit salad over my hair. I deserved it. I grovelled and tried to make amends for my naughtiness but I do not think she ever forgave me.

Then a letter arrived at the club from my godmother Musi who had seen a picture of me in a newspaper. She wanted to know if I was the same Judy as her god-daughter. I had not been in touch with her since we left Australia, because I did not know her address. The letter was a linking-up with the past for me, bringing back all the memories of my father, his stories, and the wonderful books Musi had sent me as a child. I replied to her letter, telling her all about my career so far, and immediately a wonderful first edition of a book about Anna Pavlova's life arrived in the post. 'The tradition will continue,' she wrote. 'It is my job to feed your mind and your soul.' The way she wrote and the ideas discussed in her letter were a reminder to me of Dad and all the things he discussed with me. I had been so preoccupied with ambition and survival that I had forgotten the inner self. I knew I needed time to read and think about matters other than my career.

By the time I finished working at the Panama I was exhausted from so many months of working seven days a week. At home I slept and slept, resting for a couple of weeks before Sonny telephoned and asked me to go and meet Ben Lyon at Associated Rediffusion.

I was excited about meeting the American who, with his wife Bebe Daniels, was famous from their radio show *Life with the Lyons*. The show was written by Bebe and Bob Block and featured Bebe and Ben's children Richard and Barbara Lyon. I wore a new pink-striped shirtwaister dress with lots of petticoats so the skirt stood out. Ben Lyon was a charming man who told me all about his life in Hollywood and how he discovered many film stars. 'I've got a feeling about you,' he said, 'I'm putting you into the *Dickie Henderson Show*. There's a sketch with Alfred Marks you're just right for.' The show was an extremely popular weekly situation comedy about Dickie's life and because Dickie was a skilled dancer there was always a dancing scene or knockabout routine included.

The following week I began rehearsals for the show. The usual heart-pounding began when the countdown for the show to go on air with a live audience began, but I felt better when I saw Alfred Marks, an experienced comedian, sweating profusely in the make-up room. If such an experienced man felt nervous, there was no reason for me to fear I would let the side down. The show went well and the sketch got a lot of laughs. Sonny phoned me the next day to say he had watched it and thought I had been good in it. He wanted me to go and meet a director called Hugh Goldie who was putting on the pantomime *Puss in Boots* at the Croydon Theatre.

'You'll be able to have Christmas at home,' Sonny said. As I had not been at home for Christmas for two years I was thrilled when I was offered the job.

I had saved quite a lot of money during my short career and felt sure I had enough to put down the deposit on a house, providing I could get a mortgage. Mum and I found a house we liked but it was no use. In 1958, two women buying a house was not on the mortgage people's agenda, especially as I was not in a 'proper' job. So I bought a car instead. It was a second-hand green Morris Minor with only one previous owner and I paid four hundred and fifty pounds for it. The first time I took my driving test I dressed sensibly, with no make-up, and failed. The second time I put on a lot of make-up and wore a shorter skirt with high-heeled shoes and passed. That's life.

I was happy working at the Croydon Theatre. The cast were great and Reg Dixon was a very funny old comic. I had Christmas Day at home with my brother and mother. The house was filled with the rich smells of stuffed turkey and pudding; the tree was dressed and the presents underneath it. I was blissfully happy. There is nothing to replace the warmth and comfort of Christmas with the family.

Chapter Six

1959

∼

UNLIKE THE BIGGER pantomimes produced by S.H. Newsome or Howard and Wyndham which used to run into February, the Croydon pantomime finished at the end of January. For the first time in three years I was not feeling tired at the end of the run. Having cut back on all my dancing I had now put on a little weight and felt a lot healthier.

Sonny called me to tell me that the director Cliff Owen was looking for actors from Australia or New Zealand to appear in a play for ITV called *No Decision*, starring Leo McKern and John Laurie. I went up to meet the director and was offered the part of an Australian barmaid. When rehearsals began I had a ball. With all these Australian or New Zealand actors, the familiar accent soon came back to me. There were a couple of other Australian women in it and the rehearsals were lively and fun. Johnny Meillian was among the familiar Australian faces working in England at the time. The play was about two old boxers who had always hated each other and their attempt to arrange another boxing match to settle an argument. Most of the action took place in an Australian pub. The usual terror arrived when the countdown started for the show to go on air, but everyone pulled together and I did not forget my lines, drop any glasses or spill any beer as I had feared. At home Mum and Brian had watched and enjoyed the play; Sonny was pleased too. The only person who was not pleased was my grandmother, Dearie, who was appalled that I should be playing a barmaid. 'But it was a beautiful part,' I argued when she phoned to complain. This did not mollify her. And in her eyes, things were about to get worse.

Sonny then asked me to go to meet Robert Tronson at Associated Rediffusion. They were about to put on a big production and there were some girls' parts in it. He could not tell me anything about the play.

It was a warm spring day and I put on my lucky pink-striped shirtwaister and a duster coat and went along for an interview. When I got into his office Robert Tronson looked at me and said, 'Oh, I'm sorry. You're just not right, this is supposed to be inside a brothel. The part is of a prostitute who knows the world is coming to an end. You just don't look right.' 'But I can,' I argued, 'with my hair like this and more make-up, I could easily play one. I'll even go and watch them in Soho, I promise.' I talked myself into the part and armed with the script hurried along to Soho where I had a coffee and made plenty of notes from watching the girls on the beat – how they walked, how they paused while looking for any possible clients. Stanislavsky would have approved of my efforts.

Carrying all my notes and the thick script I returned to Brighton on the train. At home I played my Earl Bostic 'Jungle Drums' record again and practised my walk, rehearsing my big speech all the time. When I turned up for rehearsals ready to impress Robert with my walk, I found he wanted us all sitting on chairs, with only the occasional movement. The play was H.G. Wells's *The War of the Worlds*. Originally a science fiction novel, it was adapted in 1938 as a radio play and produced for American radio with Orson Welles. The producers of our adaptation decided to use a well-known announcer to appear on television to announce that the world was about to end before the credits for the play began. After the music and credits the play started. It was a long play and I was on at the beginning. After being cleared by the floor manager, I was able to rush from Wimbledon to Victoria to catch my train. It was a strange feeling knowing the play was still going out while I headed off to Brighton.

On the train I saw some sub-editors I knew from Brighton who worked in Fleet Street. They wanted to know what I was working on at the moment. I told them I had just finished working on the science fiction play which was still being broadcast while we trav-elled. I joked about trying to learn the prostitutes' walk. They were looking at me very seriously. 'You obviously haven't heard then, Judy.' 'Heard what?' They then told me that because the producers had used a well-known announcer to say the world was coming to an end, one man in the East End of London had dropped dead with fright. I was horrified at the news. Not only had the man died but many people had run out into the streets screaming with panic, which had also happened when the radio play was originally pro-duced in America. We all discussed the dangers of a powerful media for the rest of the journey to Brighton.

Mum and Brian thought I had done well, so did Sybil. I did not speak to my grandmother. If she had not approved of me being a barmaid on TV she certainly was not going to approve of me being a prostitute.

~

I WAS RESTLESS. I wanted to be in the theatre but there seemed to be nothing on offer and I needed the practice of breaking down a script and working on it. Then I heard about some amateur actors who worked at the New Venture Theatre Club in Brighton. Some of them had been professional actors in repertory but had been unable to support their families. They were forced to take on 'proper jobs' and satisfied their creativity by being members of the amateur group. I went along to their theatre and asked if I could be in their next production. They rehearsed for six weeks and then played for a week. They made me very welcome and I started rehearsals for their next play. A lot of playwrights were members of the club, and Constance Cox who adapted a lot of books for the BBC often looked in and talked with the other writers. During a rehearsal one of the men told me that the Worthing repertory was going to be doing an Agatha Christie summer season in Llandudno, and there was a chance I might get a part. I phoned Sonny the following morning and asked him to see what he could do to get me into the Connaught Theatre company. He telephoned back to tell me I had an interview with the producer, Melville Gillam, the next day.

I was offered the position of assistant stage manager, playing one part as Mary, the comedy maid in *Murder at the Vicarage*; to be a person sitting in court with my back to the audience in *Witness for the Prosecution*; and nothing in *Alibi*. I said I would take it. Rehearsals were beginning in a couple of weeks at the Connaught Theatre, then we would be rehearsing in Llandudno and playing there for the summer. I was able to finish the play with the New Venture Theatre group before starting at Worthing.

Guy Vaesen was the director. He was quite brilliant and used to working fast in weekly repertory. He obviously did not suffer fools gladly and was inclined to find a whipping boy on each production. I turned up early for rehearsals and was told by the stage director, Arnold Fry, that I was on the book. I sat at the table in front of the rehearsal area with my sharpened pencils, rubber and ruler at the ready. As Guy plotted I had to write down all the moves for the actors, and God help me if I did not keep up with him. I watched very carefully and apart from a few 'tsk-tsks' of irritation and a long drawn-out sigh from Guy, he left me alone to get on with my work. Instead he found his whipping boy in the young leading actor John Laurimore, picking incessantly at everything he did or said.

William Roderick was the older leading man. He was very good-looking and sophisticated. I could tell he was getting concerned at the incessant criticism of the younger actor. Reginald Barratt was the leading character man. He had a face like a wicked pixie and was quite brilliant. Fastidious about plotting his moves and being accurate with every word of script, I watched his work in awe of his perfectionism. Zoe Hicks was the leading lady. A striking-looking woman in her early forties, she had a deep resonant voice and a powerful personality. I learned that she was one of Augustus John's illegitimate children. She was quite open about it, which all added to her mystique for me. Among the other actors was a splendidly zany Zulema Dean, who was the tallest woman in the company, and whose sense of comedy made it difficult for me not to snort with laughter when I was supposed to be watching carefully for any wrong moves.

Arnold Fry's girlfriend Janet was the stage manager. She was a big strong woman who demanded absolute perfection from her assistant stage manager, me. I was to keep the stage cleaner than I would my own home, she told me. Every glass should shine without one fingerprint or smear, and I had to check the actors' personal props at all times and double-check the props on stage. I was determined to earn Janet's approval and did everything she told me to.

I went up to Llandudno a day earlier than the rest of the cast to help Janet and Arnold get into the Palladium theatre with the sets and furniture. I drove to Wales in my Morris and stayed overnight in a seafront hotel, intending to find digs when the sets were up. When the cast arrived the following day, Zoe came up to me and told me that she, Reggie and John were able to rent a cottage and there was room for me if I wanted to share the rent with them. She said that as I was the only one with a car and the cottage was on the Little Orm, I would be a useful member of the household. I was thrilled to be included in their arrangements, and agreed to drive them all from the cottage to the theatre and back every day. The two men had single beds in one bedroom, Zoe had the big double bedroom in the middle and I had the smaller single room by the top of the stairs. It was a beautiful cottage with a lovely garden and view. Zoe said we could all paint while we were there. As there was a small vegetable garden Reggie and Zoe were already planning our suppers. Life was going to be really wonderful, we thought, as we all set off back to the theatre. We then started rehearsals for *Murder at the Vicarage* and Janet took over on the book.

Guy was getting more irritable and picking on John even more. John stood up to it quite well but I could see his confidence beginning to waver. Guy then turned his attention towards me and started pulling me up over everything I tried to do. I began to get very nervous and self-conscious over every move and every line I had. Reggie helped me, by giving me the benefit of his extraordinary talent and timing, so Guy eased off on me but still kept picking on poor John. One morning, during which Guy was being particularly vitriolic, William Roderick exploded with anger and roared out his disapproval of Guy's behaviour. The cast then decided not to work with Guy any more. We were on strike. The whole rehearsal came to a halt and Melville Gillam arrived in

Llandudno that afternoon. Guy went back to Worthing. We continued rehearsals with Melville directing, and he was most inventive. The whole show just came together, everyone relaxed and performed well. With Reggie's help and new direction I found every laugh that my character could possibly get, receiving round after round for my exits on opening night. When all the plays had opened and we were in repertoire, we began to enjoy the summer.

Living with the other three in the cottage was heaven for me. After the show each evening, we would all help to prepare the supper that Zoe or Reggie had planned. After supper we would have lengthy discussions or play music and read. During the day we would take our paints out into the garden and with Zoe's supervision while away the hours, each lost in our own sense of creativity. Mum, who was concerned that I was sharing a cottage with three other actors instead of being in digs, phoned to see how I was and whether I was eating enough. Reggie spoke to her and promised he would stand over me to make sure I finished everything on my plate. I was happy because everything tasted so good and I ate everything we prepared.

Mum and Brian came to Llandudno to see the play I was in and I was praised for my performance. After meeting Reggie and the others and satisfying herself that I was not in any danger, Mum returned home. Shortly after her visit, John and Zoe fell in love, and John moved into Zoe's bedroom, leaving Reggie on his own on one side of Zoe's bedroom and me on my own on the other. Reggie and I accepted the change in arrangements and life went on as usual until one Sunday morning when I woke to the loud cymbal crashing of Sibelius' *Karelia* suite and Zoe and John standing at the bottom of my bed, dressed to the nines, and announcing that they had arranged to get married. A car came for them, and Reggie and I waved them off for their private wedding ceremony. They returned that evening as man and wife. The whole company thought it incredibly romantic.

We were all getting to the mid-season madness by now. One night I took part in some antisocial behaviour. There was a milk machine in the High Street with the milk in bottles and stored on six levels. If one put money into the machine and pressed the top button the milk would come crashing down making the most terrible noise, causing dogs to bark and lights over the shops to be turned on. Zulema, and the other younger members of the cast, including me, did this several times and ran off cackling like lunatics. We also went swimming. One day while horsing around on the beach, Zulema was dropped by one of the actors and she broke her leg. Calamity! She was carted off to hospital and an actress called Eve Pierce arrived to take over from her.

Eve was a beautiful woman, a very experienced actress and a gentle person. Although we all missed Zulema, Eve soon managed to take over and the play went on as before. A friend of Eve's came up to see her in *Murder at the Vicarage*, a TV director called Herbert Wise. The following day Eve told me that he was very impressed with my work and that I should meet him. She was sure that we would get along well. I was to phone her when the season finished and she would arrange a meeting with him.

As the season grew to a close, I began to write again as I had in Australia, mainly short stories, poetry and the outlines of plays. In one romance I imagined a dancer – whom I modelled on Wendy Mclure, the lovely woman who looked after me during *Slaughter on Tenth Avenue* – meeting a romantic man – whom I imagined as David Knight, the handsome actor I had watched filming when I lived in Seaford and who had attended Philip Buchel's tap-dancing classes. They, of course, like John and Zoe, got married and lived happily ever after.

~

ARNOLD FRY CAME up to me the week before we finished the season and said he was directing the Bristol Old Vic pantomime at Middlesbrough and would I be interested in playing Cinderella. I said I would and he got in touch with Sonny about the contract. Some of the other Worthing repertory players were going to be in the show too.

I returned home and was offered some more work with the Worthing repertory. This time, however, not as an assistant stage manager but as an actress. Worthing repertory was one of the most

renowned companies in the country with a pretty impressive cast
list. People like Sarah Miles, Caroline Blakiston, Derek Fowlds,
Gary Bond and a host of visiting celebrities graced their stage. I was
to play a Greek girl partnering a young actor called Robin Phillips,
who was later to become one of the most famous and respected
directors in the theatre. The play was *The Irregular Verb to Love*. All
our scenes were comedic and spoken in Greek, which was going to
be fun. I loved working with Robin. Even Guy was in a good mood
every time it came to our scenes, and working at Worthing meant
I could drive home after the show each night. Bruce Walker and
Sybil came over to see the play and were very complimentary; a
theatre goer spoke to me in Greek believing I was Greek; and
Melville Gillam told me that whenever I wanted to come back I was
just to let him know.

After I had finished the play at Worthing I arranged through Eve
Pierce to meet Herbert Wise at the Granada offices. I went into the
office and we had hardly anything to say to each other except that
he had nothing he could offer me. I reported back to Eve who
thought it was silly, insisting that we should be able to get on really
well together. So I arranged another meeting. This time we talked
for a while and although he had nothing he could offer me at that
moment, we got on well, and he said he would remember me for
the future. On the way out of the Granada offices I ran into Norah
Fielding, a Canadian, who, with her husband Wilf, worked for Ross
Radio. 'Come for coffee, Judy,' she said, 'I've got a lovely young
friend who you'd get on with, I'm meeting her now.' I went with
her and met a young director's assistant called Verity Lambert. We
had coffee and, urged on by Norah, huge portions of chocolate
cake. When Norah found out that neither of us had a boyfriend she
was mortified and decided she would arrange for some 'nice young
Canadian directors' to come to dinner at her house in Haywards
Heath to meet us 'two nice girls'.

Duly, Verity and I turned up at Norah and Wilf's house to meet
these dream boyfriends. The one Norah thought would suit me
nearly knocked himself out on one of the oak beams across her
sitting-room ceiling. The one she had lined up for Verity was

charming company, but as we both agreed later, neither man appealed to us, and Norah gave up her matchmaking.

The rehearsals were beginning for *Cinderella* in the Middlesbrough Civic Theatre. Arnold had arranged a special deal with a hotel close by and all the actors were booked in there. The first person I saw when I arrived was Wendy Mclure, who was playing Prince Charming.

Arnold was a good but very firm director. As mentioned before, apart from popular singers or comedians who used hand-held microphones or one main mike centre stage, in those days we had to fill the theatre with our natural voices. Sometimes there were a couple of mikes in the footlights but all the actors and singers had to be able to project their voices to the back of the circle. It was fine if the theatre had good acoustics but some of the modern theatres had dead areas at the back of the stalls. We would hear Arnold's voice shouting from the depths of the theatre, 'It's all lovely but I can't hear a word you're saying,' and everyone would take a deep breath and project more.

When Cinderella, back in her rags after the ball, tells Buttons what a wonderful night she had with the prince, I was to sing 'I Could Have Danced All Night'. The song needed a lot of breath control and I did well until the last night. Traditionally that's when players are inclined to play jokes on each other, not so that the audience notices, but to reduce the other players to a fit of giggles. At the beginning of the last show, Wendy came up to me and said, 'I hope no one is going to behave unprofessionally tonight, Judy. I do think it is being rude to the paying audience to behave badly, don't you?' I made a note not to play any tricks on Wendy.

When we got to the ballroom scene Wendy, as Prince Charming, asked me for a dance. With a perfectly straight face, she slid a toilet roll down her lacy sleeve straight into my gloved hand. I dexterously managed to hide it behind my large fan, then slipped it with some difficulty down the front of my dress, causing my cleavage to become distinctly lopsided. How we managed to get through our duet I really do not know. I got rid of the toilet roll during the quick change back into my rags and then I had to sing 'I Could Have Danced All Night' to Buttons, played by John Dane. So far, I had sung the number sitting on a still rocking chair. On the last night, still reeling from being presented with the toilet roll, and with John sitting by my feet, I began the song. I had full control until I saw a mad gleam appear in his eye as he began to rock the chair. Grinning faces appeared in the wings. He pushed the chair more and more until I was singing with my feet going up in the air as if I were a child on a swing. I knew the high note was coming up but so was the beginning of hysteria. The dear Buttons stopped the chair a couple of notes from the final high note, and what threatened to sound like a strangled duck seemed to sort itself out into a perfectly respectable top G.

We finished the pantomime at the end of January. I had been home for a week when Wendy phoned and told me that two male friends of hers had tickets for the ballet *Cinderella* with Margot Fonteyn. Would I like to come? With any luck they might take us out for dinner afterwards. 'Put a vest on under your chiffon, Jude, it's pretty freezing up here in London,' she added. Dressed in a black cocktail dress I met up with Wendy and her friends, two very serious men in immaculate suits. Wendy and I were the models of good behaviour, sitting in really good seats, with programmes and a box of very expensive chocolates. While Margot Fonteyn floated across the stage, the devil suddenly got into Wendy. In the middle of the most moving passage of music she leaned towards me and whispered, 'It's all lovely, but I can't hear a word they're saying.' I was shaking with laughter and trying not to laugh resulted in muffled snorts. Wendy was not much better. Needless to say, we were not taken out to dinner afterwards.

It was February 1960 and Mum and I celebrated our birthday. I was now twenty. Next year I would be twenty-one and able to vote, or do anything without having to ask Mum's permission – even go back to Australia. Sybil gave me a woolly white rabbit for my birthday. For lots of luck, she said. Musi sent me a beautiful book about Egypt; and although I still kept writing to him, I heard nothing from my father.

Chapter Seven

1960

~

BRUCE WALKER WANTED to talk to me about a repertory season in Brighton. He was taking over Alan Hay's job as director and he wanted me for the juvenile lead. The thought of staying at home and being able to see many of my friends while working during the summer in Brighton really appealed to me. Mum and Brian were looking forward to me staying at home for the summer too. Brian was now sixteen, about to sit his O-levels. He felt that my presence would help to divert some of Mum's nagging about his studies away from him. I convinced Sonny that people would be more likely to come down from London to Brighton to see me than to travel up to the North of England or anywhere else. He agreed but first booked me on to a television show with Frankie Howerd, a hysterically funny but also very nervous person. It was the first time I had worked with a comedian who worked directly to camera in his asides. The sketch, in which I played a dizzy blonde, also included my friend from the Irving, Ronnie Corbett.

I found out that Ronnie, too, had joined the Kavanagh Agency, so we had a lot to gossip about. One of the joys of being with an agency that also looked after comedy writers like Dennis Norden, Sid Colin or Laurie Wyman, was waiting in the foyer to see Sonny. From out of different office doors, writers would emerge like weathermen. I would be thrown questions, 'Judy, if I saw you in a café and I came up and said — What would you say?' I would respond with an answer immediately and they would disappear into their respective offices again. Or there would be arguments about a line of script and doors would open and other writers would offer their opinions.

I loved working at the Palace Pier Theatre. This beautiful two-tiered Victorian theatre at the end of the pier had wonderful acoustics. Despite the fierce draughts when there was a south-westerly wind, it was a cosy theatre, and the odd creak or groan from the pier gave credence to the stories of a resident ghost. The Forbes Russell company was planning a series of J.B. Priestley plays there, some comedies, including *Is Your Honeymoon Really Necessary?* – with the legendary farce actor, Ralph Lynn – a couple of Agatha Christie's, some modern dramas including *The Five Finger Exercise* and Sybil's play at the end of the season. I liked working with Bruce Walker. He was a roundly built, highly intelligent, witty little man, who smoked a large cigar and looked like Mr Pickwick. He was also an actor and playwright – his play *Cosh Boy* had been made into a celebrated film – and an extremely good director.

Apart from the costume plays, I spent most of the time finding clothes to wear for the modern plays. It was part of one's job as a repertory actor to provide your own modern clothes. I borrowed from Mum, sometimes from friends, and learned to team up my own clothes in different ways to make my wardrobe as varied as possible. The men were much luckier; all they usually had to find were suits and shirts.

Luckily I had no problem with learning lines and was able to keep up the weekly pace. Pamela Green and I played the sisters in *Eden End*. I was the dowdy older one while Pam played the glamorous sister returning home. People in the audience sometimes did not believe that I was the same person who had played the part. The wide range of characters and different ages Bruce cast me to play was the most wonderful experience, from the schoolgirl Pippa in *The Spider's Web* to Lilian in *Eden End*.

The plays worked out well as I was usually given one large part followed by a smaller part the following week so I never felt overloaded with responsibility. While I was performing in the first few plays Sonny had another offer for me and I felt torn between the two jobs. I decided to ask advice from Madame Binnie, the old for-tune-teller whose small office was next door to the stage door.

Madame Binnie was an extraordinary character who kept a fishing line that dropped through a hole in the floor underneath the table on which she kept her crystal ball. A bell was attached to the line and it would ring every time she caught a fish. She would then haul back the damask tablecloth from the table and pull up her catch. Her advice was not to take the other work but to stay with the Palace Pier repertory. 'Something important will happen that will change your life', she told me. Glad that the decision was now made, I let Sonny know I was not interested in leaving Brighton and would stay on the pier for the rest of the summer.

There was one very easy week when I was murdered in the first scene so I could learn the words for the following week's play while waiting for the curtain call. Mum came to every first night. She would make notes and give them to me afterwards. We would drive home together and over supper she would tell me not only what she thought but what she had heard other people saying during the interval.

The Tuesday review in the *Evening Argus* slated the play but said it was worth walking to the end of the pier to see my performance. I was sorry for the company but thrilled with the things written about me, especially as I had been killed off in the first scene. Max Hodges, the man who lived next door, worked as a sports editor for the *Argus*. I asked him to say thank you to the critic, Mr John Parry, for saying such kind things about me. I presumed he must be quite old to be a critic.

The following Monday, after the show, Mum was waiting for me to get dressed for home, having promised me cauliflower cheese for supper. I had put some curlers in my hair ready for the follow-ing day and scrubbed all my make-up off when there was a knock on the dressing-room door. It was John Parry, not quite the old man I thought he would be but about three or four years older than me and very handsome. He also seemed vaguely familiar and asked whether I would like to go for a coffee. I was worried about my mother and the cauliflower cheese but Mum was adamant that I should go with him. I think she was thrilled there was possibly a man in my life who wore a tie and a blazer rather than what she called 'the scruffy chaps' with whom I used to run around the town.

While John went to fetch the coffees I frantically removed all the curlers and shoved them into my shoulder bag. I found out that he was born in Yorkshire and was down in Brighton as a summer relief; and that he used to go to the North Street coffee lounge during the last few months of 1955, the same time that I used to go with all my dancing-school friends. At that time he was stationed at the Maresfield Army Intelligence camp, before leaving for Malaya. I loved the sound of his voice, his straightforwardness and unpatronizing manner.

John had to get back to the *Argus* office to file his copy so I said I would drive him there. When we reached the office he invited me inside. I was very curious to see where he worked. The office had neon strips of light and rows of desks with typewriters. Some other journalists were working at their desks and the sounds of typing reminded me of a record I had once heard. A couple of people looked up at me briefly but were very preoccupied, and I decided to leave John so he could get on with his work, but I gave him my telephone number before I left.

When I reached home I was interrogated by Mum. 'And what did you say?' 'And what did he say?' 'Are you going to see him again?' 'All the best men come from the North.' But the cauliflower cheese was worth going through the endless questions.

A couple of days later he rang and asked me to meet him for a drink after rehearsals at the Colonnade, a bar next to the Theatre Royal. I rushed over and met up with his friends, a very lively bunch. There was Annie Nightingale, a journalist on the *Brighton and Hove Gazette*. She lived with Gordon Thomas who was a senior journalist on the *Argus*. There was the diminutive Jack Tinker, also a journalist on the *Argus*, and Mike Taylor, who was a sub-editor there. Mike and John shared a flat with two other journalists, not far from the pier.

During the following weeks I found out that John loved jazz while I preferred classical music. He loved the modern American writers while I loved the great European writers. In every way we were opposites, except for dancing and then we were both lovers of traditional jazz. We used to go to the Chinese Jazz Club in the Winter Garden opposite the Palace Pier. Bonni Manzi ran it with some of the finest jazz musicians around. There was also the Regent Ballroom where often the *Argus* gang would go dancing to Syd Dean and his orchestra.

Because he was the only journalist who possessed a dinner jacket, the news editor asked John to cover Glyndebourne Opera as a critic as well. One evening he was going to be late returning from the opera and yet we wanted to see each other. I knew Mum would not approve if I went out again after coming back from the theatre so we arranged to meet when he flashed the headlights of the office Ford Popular from the road I could see from my bedroom window. After learning my lines I got into my pyjamas and turned off my bedroom lights and waited. An hour passed before the lights were flashed, and I climbed out of my bedroom window in my dressing gown and ran up the road to meet him. We talked for a good hour that night and I knew I was in love with him. As I crept back into my bedroom window I decided that he was the man I wanted to marry.

~

SONNY WANTED ME to come up to London to meet Joe Collins, Joan and Jackie's father, who was a top variety agent. He was representing Nat Mills, a comedian, famous for working with his wife Bobby in the Nat Mills and Bobby act. Bobby had died while they were working in South Africa and after a couple of years of mourning Nat now wanted to be in a pantomime and needed someone who could do all the things Bobby could. Joe thought I would be the right girl. It involved singing in an opera scene, taking part in knockabout comedy and being shot out of a mock helicopter. More important was being able to feed Nat his lines with perfect comedy timing. We would be the top act on the bill which meant being well paid. The director was Davy Kaye, a small, friendly, easy-going man who said he would leave Nat and me alone to get on with our scenes and then fit us into the show. I liked Nat and knew we could work well together so I agreed to take the offer. Sonny and Joe were pleased. They cared a lot for Nat and wanted to see him recover his confidence again.

The only thing that worried me was leaving John for so long. We spent all our free time together now, having a Sunday lunch with Gordon Thomas and Annie Nightingale, meeting up with Jack Tinker and his wife Mavis, or getting together with Mike Taylor and his friends David and Jane Clymie. David was the editor of *Mad* magazine as well as being an excellent comedy scriptwriter. Occasionally we would all pile into the Harpsichord, a small restaurant opposite the Theatre Royal, run by George Nicholson and Johnny Porterfield. George was an artist and Johnny a singer but they ran a very popular restaurant. People like Brenda Bruce and her husband Roy Rich, Glynis Johns and all the stars who appeared at the Royal would dine there late after the curtain had come down. It was not unusual for the lights and laughter to be still going strong at two or three in the morning. Because the place was so small everyone always ended up talking to the other diners and when we were finally disgorged from the warmth of the restaurant it was as if we had just left a party.

When Mum announced she was going to a party in London on Saturday night and would be returning at lunchtime on Sunday, I told John, 'While the cat's away the mice will play.' After the Saturday night show we rushed back home, where I was going to cook supper and John was going to stay the night. On arriving home I was surprised that my brother was already in his bedroom. I had been planning how to get him upstairs before John and I retired to my room. Then we heard the giggles. Outraged, I stormed his room to find him with his girlfriend. After delivering a lecture about morality I made him empty his money box and send his girlfriend home by taxi. A very sulky baby brother retired to bed early.

At six o'clock in the morning I heard the front door open and Mum's heels clattering around the kitchen. Maniacal laughter came from my brother's bedroom as he knew big sister was about to be caught. I nudged John and whispered that Mum was home. He slithered down the bed and said, 'Do you think she'd notice I'm here?' As he made a huge bump in the bed I assured him she would. We then decided to brazen it out but I wondered whether I would have to leave home. By now my brother was roaring with laughter upstairs.

The bedroom door opened and Mum came in. She saw us both sitting in bed staring at her. Without batting an eyelid she said, 'Tea or coffee?' We mumbled a reply of 'coffee' and she went out again. Clever woman. Although she had pursed lips she never referred to the matter again. I remained at home and John, though embarrassed, did not lose face by having a row.

~

AS THE END of the pier season approached so we began rehearsals for Sybil's play. I worked hard on my American accent, determined to do my best work for Sybil. It was a romantic play and, I suspect, was written with her own past romance as an inspiration. She had met John and was thrilled we were in love but others were not so sure we were right for each other because we were such opposites. John decided that as he was involved with me, and knew Sybil, he should not review the play, which received terrible notices although I had good ones. I was so sad for Sybil, but very glad that John had not reviewed it, although on the first night he couldn't but agree with the critics.

While we were in Sybil's play a friend of John's came down to visit him. She was tall, dark, elegant ex-Cheltenham Ladies College and a journalist on a London magazine. I sensed danger, even though he assured me they were just at college together and he was not interested in her 'that way'. She was charming to me, which made it worse. My hair was practically standing on end every time we met as she was so sophisticated and made me feel like a country bumpkin. No model could have looked better. She stayed only a few days but said she liked Brighton and looked forward to coming down again. I could see the pantomime looming up, taking me away from Brighton for at least four weeks. Anything could happen.

It was a leap year, and remembering my old folklore I knew a woman could propose to a man then, so I did. We were in John's flat playing some jazz when I proposed. He said no, and went and locked himself in the lavatory. 'Women are not supposed to ask men,' he shouted through the door. I assured him it *was* allowed during a leap year. He did not believe me, so I told him to ring the telephone operator and ask them whether it was a leap year. He did and the operator confirmed it. He looked very uncomfortable and sat opposite me saying he had never heard of women proposing to men. I refused to leave the flat until he agreed to marry me. He said he would think about it, and that was good enough for me so I drove home.

I did not hear from him for two days and was regretting my boldness, scared I would never see him again, when he phoned asking me to come down to the newspaper office after the show. He was working late and looked a bit tired. He told me he would marry me but he did not want a lot of fuss, certainly not a great big wedding with all the family. I told him I could not agree more. The last thing I wanted was my family's feuds on my wedding day. We agreed to have a church wedding with very few guests and only our immediate family. Then I remembered that I would have to get permission from Dad as I was not twenty-one yet.

Mum was not surprised when I told her, but wondered what the rush was all about. I explained he was too good-looking to be left alone for four weeks in Brighton, and she understood. So she wrote a letter to Dad. Two weeks went by and we had not heard from him so I telephoned my grandmother and asked her to intervene. Meanwhile, in case no one could contact him, I talked to the vicar of our local church, who turned out to be the brother of Diana Pelling, whom I had danced with at Molly Ball's dancing school. I explained all the problems of reaching my father and he wrote to the Bishop of Chichester. The Bishop gave me special permission to marry on a Sunday when I was not rehearsing for the pantomime.

Mum asked me whether I wanted a big wedding with few presents or a small wedding with lots of cooking equipment and sheets. I told her the latter and John and I booked Saint Helen's Church for 18 December, two days before I was to leave for Gloucester. I would be two weeks at the Gloucester Regal, followed by two weeks at the Dewsbury Pioneer. We found a furnished flat in Marine Square for five pounds a week. Mike Taylor was going to give us one night for our wedding night and then he would move in with us, keeping John company when I was away and also helping with the rent. Mike was also going to be best man and Gordon Thomas was going to stand in for my father and give me away. Sybil was going to come and Dave McEnery, the *Argus* photographer, was going to take all the pictures. I bought my oyster-coloured satin wedding dress off the peg from Richard's Shops in Western Road, and because it was Christmas, I bought a red velvet coat to wear over it. We also ordered a bouquet of red and white carnations.

I was still hopeful that my father's permission to marry would arrive from Australia and I had asked the Brighton post office workers to phone me at any time of the night if they spotted the letter. At three o'clock in the morning about four days before we were to be married someone from the post office phoned me to say there was a letter for me. I was so relieved my father had signed the form, giving his permission.

Davy Kaye came up to me after rehearsals on Saturday. 'I hope getting married isn't going to affect your performance, is it, Judy?' I assured him it would not.

I spent Saturday night with Mum and Brian. I knew Brian was going to miss me and kept reassuring him that he could come over to see me any time he wanted. Mr Harris, the hairdresser, was going to come to the house early to put up my hair. Mum and I had a long chat before I went to bed. Amongst the many things she advised me to do to have a successful marriage was to keep my own bank account.

When I reached the church and went down the aisle on Gordon's arm, I could see John's trouser leg flapping as if a gale was blowing through the church; Mike's legs too were a bit shaky. Sybil was there with Annie Nightingale and John's parents. Mum was wearing a hat that made her look like a small guardsman, and brother Brian's skin shone with all the washing but he looked very uncomfortable in a proper suit. The enormity of the meaning of the marriage sacrament overwhelmed me as we made our vows.

After the ceremony, we signed the legal papers and then headed off to the Imperial Hotel, where Mum had organized a beautiful

lunch. Annie caught my bouquet and then we were off on our own.
John had arranged a special surprise later, supper at Arundel. We
drove all the way there in the Morris. I smiled when I saw the name
of the restaurant. It was called 'The Black Rabbit'.

~

TRAVELLING ON THE train for the last day's rehearsal in London,
I felt sure everyone on the train must see I was newly married. I
kept feeling my wedding ring and grinning to myself. Davy Kaye
watched me closely during the rehearsals and Nat said 'good girl'
several times when all our scenes went well.

We opened at the Gloucester Regal on 22 December. I played
Gretchen and Nat was the Dame in *Mother Goose*. I wore pale make-
up similar to that of a clown, and the character I played was
slow-witted with severe adenoidal problems. My hair was stuck
out in bunches and I had droopy drawers that hung down from my
uneven hem. The show went well and had good reviews, and Nat
was thrilled that we worked so well together. John came up from
Brighton to collect me after seeing the show on Christmas Eve, and
we spent Christmas with his mother and father in Birmingham, but
I had to return to Gloucester for the next day's show.

After the Boxing Day show someone was waiting at the stage
door to see me – a young man who looked very much like John.
'I bet you can't remember me, Judy,' he said.

'I can,' I replied. 'You're Bertram.' I had not seen my best friend
at Ingoldsthorpe Preparatory School since I was six years old.

He smiled. 'Do you remember the letter I wrote you when you
were leaving for Australia?' he said. I remembered the letter my
six-year-old best friend had written, asking me to marry him when
I returned.

'Oh, Bertram. I'm so sorry. I was married a week ago.'

He thought for a while and said, 'Would you like to come for
dinner after the show one night so we can catch up on all our
news?'

We arranged a date for dinner and he left me his telephone
number. I discussed the irony of the situation with one of the other
players in the pantomime, Julia McKenzie, a singer playing the

principal girl. I was not sure whether as a newly married woman I should go for dinner on my own with Bertram. She thought it was a tricky situation but suggested that if I took a chaperone with me no one would be compromised and she volunteered to come. So I phoned Bertram and he agreed it would be the proper thing to do.

While Julia ate heartily, Bertram and I reminisced. How strange life can be. I had married someone I had fallen in love with who looked just like my very first best friend. Now, as I look back, I realize after forty-five years of marriage that my husband too has turned into my best friend.

Part Two

Chapter Eight

1961

~

AFTER THE SHOW finished at Gloucester, I set off in the Morris for the next venue. It was a cold, crisp, January Sunday and there were very few cars on the road – a perfect day for driving. When I reached the beautiful Yorkshire countryside I could see a large dome of grey, dirty air on the horizon. That was Dewsbury, where I was going to be living for the next two weeks.

Jackie, playing the principal boy, Julia, playing principal girl, and I had agreed to stay in the same digs. It was close to the Pioneer Theatre and the landlady had said 'three young ladies could easily share the same large bedroom', which made it cheaper for all of us. We arrived in time for supper and were shown the large bedroom. It had a huge double bed and a small single one. Jackie announced that she was a lesbian, which was a bit of a surprise, so Julia and I decided we would share the double bed which was mined with large stone hot-water bottles and sagged in various places. The hot-water bottles were lethal for chilblains and bruised our toes.

The theatre had good bookings and we were made welcome by the theatre management. However, there were very few dressing rooms. I was lucky to have one next to Nat Mills' number-one dressing room by the side of the stage. Julia and most of the others had to leave the stage door and cross a shopping mall to reach their dressing rooms in another building. This meant they were continually going from a warm theatre into the cold throughout the show. It took its toll on Julia, who eventually became very ill.

Some theatre managements treated performers appallingly badly and the situation is no better today than it was then. A classic example is the local councillor who was showing the town's refurbished theatre to a local dignitary. When the visitor asked the proud councillor why there were no wash basins in the dressing rooms, he was told actors could wash before they left home.

Nat Mills was thrilled with the way our scenes worked. I got to know the little comedian very well during the run of the pantomime and watched his confidence grow as we worked together. Whenever he was pleased with my work he would always qualify the compliment by saying, 'Of course, Bobby was wonderful,' or 'But you should have seen how Bobby did it.' I did not mind. Nat was being loyal to his dead wife's memory and I appreciated his need to be so.

Sometimes, if he was invited out, he would ask my advice about a tie to wear or would want to know whether he was looking all right, and I would offer a suggestion or give a compliment. He was very conscious of his withered hand, which he went to great lengths to hide. Unless you knew about it you would not notice his disability. Like many comedians his nature was complex, but he trusted me and I learned a lot from working with him. He was also terribly proud of his brother, who owned Eastman carpets, and would sing his praises to me as if I were part of the family. Years later, he used to watch my career and took the same proprietorial interest in me as he did in his brother.

At the end of the run I was dying to get back to John and Brighton but Julia was seriously ill and could not manage to travel by train so I drove her back to her parents' house in Enfield before returning home. It was just as well I did. When I next saw her, she told me she had developed pneumonia and had been rushed straight into hospital. She said I had saved her life.

~

I BEGAN MARRIED life on the Brighton seafront, in our ground-floor furnished flat at 10 Marine Square. For a while it seemed very strange to be living with someone. Neither of us had lived with anyone before and slowly we both realized we needed our own space occasionally, something we had taken for granted before our marriage.

Mum had given me a Marguerite Patten cookery book. I studied it avidly trying to work out menus and budgeting not only for John and me, but also for Mike who was sharing the flat. John was earning fifteen pounds a week at the Brighton *Evening Argus*. Five pounds went on the rent and five pounds on housekeeping. I found all the cheapest shops down in Gardner Street, near the *Evening Argus* building, and managed to feed the three of us with a good mixed diet.

The landlord and his wife were a most peculiar couple. When John and I took the rent up to their first-floor flat on the first of February, we found them sitting on chairs with handkerchiefs on their heads. They told us to close the door quickly in case the 'budgie' flew out. As if on cue, a yellow budgerigar flew on to the landlord's head and began to twitter and chatter and walk about the handkerchief territory. John and I suppressed our hysteria. With great pride, the landlord told us he was a 'council rodent exterminator; in other words, he was a rat catcher. He told us in gory detail about killing rats and how, on one occasion, a cornered rat had leapt for his throat and he had heroically fought it off. He beamed as he described the rats' screams. We left him and his wife, not knowing whether to laugh or be sick.

My twenty-first birthday was coming up and at the next election I would be able to vote. John suggested that we go to London to celebrate. He had booked a table at a lovely restaurant in Piccadilly for dinner and arranged theatre tickets to see Tom Courtenay in *Billy Liar*. I was going to dress up for the evening and wear the red velvet coat I had worn for my wedding. Then Sonny rang to say that some Granada TV producers and directors wanted to meet me on the afternoon of my birthday. They were setting up an intriguing new series. So I went up by train early in my red velvet coat and arranged to meet John at the restaurant later.

Granada Television, under the leadership of Sydney Bernstein, was an exciting and innovative place to work. In 1960 it was decided to commission a series of one-hour plays by young writers, to be screened in 1961 under the title *The Younger Generation*.

Between 200 and 300 writers were interviewed and eventually eleven plays were selected for production. They were to be introduced by the poet Johnny McDonald.

Granada set up a repertory group of fourteen young actors and actresses called the Younger Generation Players. They would all play widely differing roles, often against type, and given an exclusive six-month contract to rehearse and record plays in Granada's Manchester studios. More experienced actors like Frank Finlay, Isa Miranda and Stratford Johns would be invited as guests to play the older parts. An unknown young actor also invited to appear in one play was Michael Caine.

The producer was Peter Wildeblood, and the three directors were Gordon Flemyng, Claude Whatham and Max Morgan-Witts. What I did not know as I travelled up to London was that Herbert Wise, one of Granada's top directors, had recommended me for the series. He had remembered me from my performance in *Murder at the Vicarage* in Llandudno in 1959.

So I turned up for the interview in my red velvet coat, apologized for being overdressed and explained that it was my birthday and I was going out to a posh restaurant later. A lovely woman called Margaret Morris asked me lots of questions about the work I had done. Peter Wildeblood was kind and put me at my ease. I thought I knew Peter Wildeblood's name from somewhere and cheerfully asked him whether I read about something he had done. The rest of the people in the interview room went quiet. With great charm, he said perhaps it was about a play he had just produced. 'It will come back to me,' I chirruped, with great confidence in my own memory. I was there for about half an hour and it was all over. Before I had even left the building my cheeks went hot as I suddenly remembered why Peter Wildeblood's name was so familiar to me. In 1954 he had been sent to prison with Lord Montagu of Beaulieu and another man for conspiracy to incite two young airmen to commit what were called 'acts of gross indecency'. Well, that's the end of my chances, I thought, but I did not let it spoil the wonderful supper and a brilliant performance by Tom Courtenay as Billy Liar. However, I underestimated the open-mindedness of Peter Wildeblood. The following day, Sonny phoned to say that

Granada had offered me a contract. John and I celebrated by shopping. A Daks sports jacket for him and a navy suit for me.

The contract was to start in March. We would be paid living expenses, rehearsal money, and sixty pounds for each transmission. To me it was a fortune. It could not have come at a better time because our friend Mike Taylor had been offered a job as a subeditor on the *Daily Mirror* and was leaving our flat. At the same time, our rat-catching landlord had given us notice because he could get more rent letting the flat for Easter and summer holidays. We quickly found another place further along the seafront in Burlington Street. It was a beautiful flat but more expensive at eight pounds a week. Now, we could afford to move there. With the Granada contract making me feel rich, I set off happily for Manchester.

A boy called Clive Colin Bowler and I were the youngest in the group of fourteen actors. We were all introduced to each other, photographed and given envelopes containing money – a lovely way to start a contract. One lively young actor was Johnny Briggs, who was to become a long-serving star of *Coronation Street*. That series had just started when we, the Younger Generation Players, began our rehearsals. Another, rather shy, young actor was John Thaw, who achieved fame through *The Sweeney*, *Morse* and many other television roles. Ronald Lacey was brilliant and rightly became an internationally known film actor specializing in nasty parts – though in reality was the most lovely man. He gave a memorable performance as Dylan Thomas.

We would get together in the evenings to discuss the plays and life in general, and it was during one of these evenings I discovered that most of us were from broken homes. Childhood memories were shared and I realized that the pain caused by the thoughtlessness, ignorance or selfishness of parents is never forgotten by their offspring.

To save living expenses, we decided to split into groups and share flats. Brian Hewlett, Bill Douglas – who had to call himself Forbes Douglas because someone in Equity was already known as Bill Douglas – and I decided to share a flat in Chorley. I insisted on one condition: just because I was the woman in the group I was not

about to become a skivvy and clean up after them. So began a wonderfully stimulating and creative six months. John would drive up
to Manchester at the weekends and liked Bill and Brian, especially
as they were teaching me how to iron shirts in a special way and
sharing the housework. Bill and I became great friends. He used to
write on a typewriter every night in our shared lounge. I too would
write and we would try out our ideas on Brian. Bill confided in me
about his deprived childhood in Scotland, being cared for by a
drunken mother. Later he went on to produce those ideas as films,
which won much acclaim.

The plays we worked on in the studios were mostly about our
generation's hostilities towards the previous generation, youth
holding contempt for a materialistic society. Although in real life
our generation was terrified that some lunatic would gain control
of nuclear weapons, the plays dealt with the more immediate problems of living in society and coping. But not all the plays were
heavy, 'social issues' plays. We had fun with some marvellous
comedies. I played the lead in Jeremy Kingston's *The Rabbit Set* on
a Thames houseboat. I kept rabbits, big white fluffy ones. When I
let Sybil Wise know she could hardly believe that rabbits were in
my life again. She went straight out and bought me two china rabbits for good luck. In the final moments in the play I was left alone
holding one of my fluffy pets. As the credits rolled over the picture,
my reluctant co-star rabbit, a filthy little beast, peed all over the
front of my frock. The director was thrilled and kept every frame.
The Rabbit Set was the first of the series to be transmitted and the
critics loved it.

By August our contracts were coming to an end but we had all
learned so much about working in television. Sonny called me and
said that I was to meet Laurie Wyman, the writer, and Alistair Scott
Johnson, who produced the *Navy Lark* radio series. The Younger
Generation plays continued going out until the beginning of
September, but by then I was Wren Cornwell aboard HMS
Troutbridge in the BBC's *Navy Lark*. It was a lucky move for me
because an ITV strike was to stop all independent television work
for a year.

~

BACK AT HOME in Brighton, the first-floor flat at number 8 Burlington Street was a well-designed bright and airy apartment, but we shared the bathroom and lavatory on the landing below us with the landlord, Michael Carmichael. He was a young, artistic man, sweet-natured and utterly different from the dreadful rat catcher.

Our street was full of characters. Max Miller's house was on the opposite side of the road. We would see the 'cheeky chappy' walking up to the shops and soon were on nodding terms with him. Lucy, an old wheelchair-bound lady who had run a pub in the East End of London, was directly opposite our flat. We found out that she would hide behind her lace curtains and watch us cavorting with abandon in the nude around our apartment. Next door lived two ladies whom we called 'Enamel and Emulsion' because no matter how early we got up in the morning they had their full, thick, theatrical make-up on.

There was great excitement when Laurence Olivier and Joan Plowright moved into the Royal Crescent Hotel at the sea end of our street. They were newly married and waiting for their house in Royal Crescent to be finished and ready for them to move in. Next to their future home lived John Clements and Katy Hammond. Two doors down on our side of the street, Sarah Churchill, Sir Winston's daughter, moved in with her new husband. There was a terrible noise one night when he 'folded her up' and put her bottom first into the dustbin outside the front door. She could not move but she could shout, and she did – loudly until the police arrived.

Behind our flat we looked down into Dora Bryan's house, a period cottage with a small walled garden. At the end of our street, overlooking the sea, lived actor Peter Copley and his wife Ninka with their daughter Fanny; above them, Pat Dunlop, a comedy writer who worked with Bob Monkhouse, with his wife Marion and their three children.

When Christopher Gridley, who had the best top-floor flat above us, left to return to London, we took over his flat. Poor Lucy from across the road was furious. We had deprived her of her daily dose of excitement, watching us prancing around.

I was nervous about starting the *Navy Lark* series. All of the cast were much older and very experienced radio actors and I was a novice. Early in September, just before the series started, there was a photo call on a ship moored by the Savoy embankment. The 'crew' of 'HMS *Troutbridge*', all dressed in naval uniform, posed together, and Heather Chasen and I – dressed as two wrens – held up a shield. I felt very much 'the new kid on the block', but everyone was very friendly and I knew Jon Pertwee, whom I had already worked with on the game show, *Can Do* in 1958. Leslie Phillips, another 'crew' member, had already started building his career as an ever hopeful Lothario with the film *Doctor in Love*.

When the series started, the drill was that we would receive the script in the post on Friday or Saturday morning. There was a read-through of the script at 2 p.m. Sunday at the Playhouse Theatre, down by Charing Cross, followed by notes and corrections from Alistair Scott Johnson and Laurie Wyman; then one more run-through, a break for a cup of tea and time for us girls to refresh our make-up. By then, the audience would have arrived and we would come on to the stage to be introduced and recording would begin.

I was pleased to be working with Jon Pertwee again and learned that the *Navy Lark* series was initially based on Jon's experiences in the Second World War and was created as a vehicle for him in 1959, a year after we had finished the *Can Do* game show.

On the first day's rehearsal I also got to know the wonderful actor Ronnie Barker, and the three fine character actors Michael Bates, Tenniel Evans and Richard Caldicott. Leslie Phillips and Stephen Murray were charming and I was terrified I might make mistakes. There are many pitfalls waiting for the novice radio actor, like rustling the paper of your script or accidentally banging the microphone while turning over a page.

During the read-through Heather Chasen took me under her wing. 'It's all very friendly now but come the show you've got to kick the men in the shins and elbow them in the ribs to get close to the mikes,' she said. She was right. I watched her pummel her way to the front and followed suit. I learned a lot about radio during my two seasons with the series.

Sometimes we recorded two scripts in succession. One of my favourite scripts was when we did a send-up of the film *Casablanca*. I played the nightclub cigarette seller called, appropriately enough in the film, 'cigarette'. In our radio version, I became 'fag-end'. To this day there is a *Navy Lark* Appreciation Society that keeps its members informed about news and the history of the series and 'the crew' through its newsletter.

The beauty of working on the series on Sundays was that I could do other work during the week. As the ITV strike was continuing I returned to Worthing repertory to work with Derek Fowlds who was playing Billy in *Billy Liar* – I played Liz. Derek was a wonderful Billy and he and I worked well together. Guy Vaesen was happy and on great form directing the play. Thankfully he didn't seem to need a whipping boy on this production.

There are moments during a play when, if you are lucky, you 'fly' – the audience, actors and words all come together and create 'magic'. You cannot re-create it, it just happens. Often, with technique, you create the moment, but 'flying' is a form of alchemy independent of one's own intentions. Working with Derek we often 'flew' in a scene, probably because we felt secure enough working together and the play and Guy's direction were so good.

In November, Sonny phoned with some exciting news. The *Daily Mirror*'s National TV Awards Poll had nominated me and Ronald Lacey from the Younger Generation plays, as Tomorrow's Star Actors. Shirley Bassey was nominated Best Singer. How strange life can be! The two sixteen-year-old kids who were both getting good reviews in the West End in 1956 were now, in 1961, nominated in the same awards poll. There was going to be a presentation dinner the following year.

Also in November, John was approached by the *Daily Express*. He had been scooping them in his column on the *Argus* and the *Express* editor, Bob Edwards, offered him a job on the William Hickey column. There was great excitement at number 8 Burlington Street. I decided not to do pantomime that year as I had already been away from John, in Manchester, and we wanted to be by ourselves for Christmas to spoil each other and wrap ourselves up in a cocoon of overindulgence. However, just before Christmas, a parcel arrived for us. It contained a Christmas card and a tape recording from my father.

Chapter Nine

1962

~

THE ONLY PERSON we knew with a tape recorder was Sybil Wise. She had a Grundig. After Christmas we arranged to go to her flat in Sussex Square to play Dad's tape. Apart from receiving permission to get married I had not heard from him for so long that I was feeling very nervous and emotional about hearing him again. John held my hand while Sybil set things up.

My father's voice sounded weak but his personality was the same as I remembered it. He welcomed John as a son-in-law and talked about books, music and journalism; he shared some of his favourite poetry with us, and gave me all the news about my old Gympie school friends. He also wanted to know about my brother and what he was doing and asked if both Brian and I would keep in touch and write to him. At the end of the tape, Sybil declared that he was a most wonderful man and John liked him. I felt relieved that Dad was all right and able to communicate again, but I still wondered why it had taken him so long to reply to my numerous letters.

Our friends Gordon Thomas and Annie Nightingale had married and found an unfurnished flat at number 5 Arundel Terrace, in Kemp Town. They had the top two floors of a beautiful Regency house owned by Count William de Bellroche. One weekend they got in touch with us and told us there was an unfurnished ground-floor flat to let in the house next door, owned by the actor Robert Flemying. With John working in Fleet Street and my work on the *Navy Lark* series, plus the occasional play at Worthing repertory, we decided we could afford to move into an unfurnished flat. The rent was reasonable but we had no furniture. G-plan was the fashionable but expensive furniture of that year but we decided to look around the old second-hand shops for alternatives. Some friends were selling their bedroom suite so we bought that from them.

During the week, while John was in London, I would go looking round the shops to see what was for sale, and at the weekend go in wearing a scarf and dressed in an old mackintosh to barter for the chair or whatever I had spotted earlier. When the deal was done, John would drive round in the car and pick it up. We moved into the ground floor of number 6 Arundel Terrace with chairs with their springs hanging out and slowly over the next few months got them renovated. Those chairs bought for a few shillings later turned out to be rather good antiques.

The most expensive purchases were the curtains. The ceilings were very high and the windows wide. We decided to splash out and order a pair of warm-orange velvet curtains for the sitting room and some light-mauve silk curtains for the bedroom.

Robert Flemying and his wife Carmen were the most wonderful landlords, often inviting us up to their top part of the house for dinner or a drinks party. Next door, at number 5, in the basement, lived Ziggi Phillips, an antiques dealer and the sister of Hermione Baddely. On the ground floor, Willy de Bellroche held court with endless parties; and on the first floor, Peter Spencer Churchill was busy writing his memoirs. Round the corner in Sussex Square, near Sybil, were several producers and Collie Knox, a famous journalist.

On the opposite side of Sussex Square Gardens, in a magnificent Regency house, lived Bill Owen and his wife Edie. Bill, who most people now remember as Compo in the BBC's *Last of the Summer Wine* TV series, was a well-known character actor with a string of theatre and film credits. Shortly after we had moved into our flat we were invited over to his house. Everywhere was marble, velvet and gilt. The chairs had gilt legs, even the matchboxes were covered in gilt. A huge marble fireplace dominated the sitting room. Arranged along it were extremely valuable ornaments and a huge clock. Bill was leaning against the fireplace when we arrived. As we took in the grand piano and beautiful antique furniture he said cheerfully, 'All this shit's Ede's.' Apparently, Edie was the only daughter of an extremely wealthy Scottish solicitor, who had left her everything.

Bill and Edie were an entertaining couple. She, so formal, immaculately dressed, not a hair out of place, yet with the deepest, most infectious laugh; and Bill, who looked forever crumpled, relaxed and happy, yet terribly energetic.

One day Bill asked me whether I would take part in a poetry reading with Leonard White, a producer who lived in Newhaven. They wanted to take Sussex poetry to the Newhaven Boys' Club to inspire the boys. I agreed to join them as I was writing a lot of poetry of my own at the time and looked forward to working on old Sussex poems. Leonard, Bill and I rehearsed at Bill's place and just before we were to travel to do the show realized we were one poem short. I offered one of my own. After all, it had been written in Brighton, which made it a Sussex poem, and they liked it, but I was too embarrassed to read my own work, so Bill said he would do it.

We got a wonderful response to the poetry reading from a packed house of young teenage boys. When it came to my poem I was so nervous. Bill read it brilliantly and when the boys cheered, I could feel my lungs filling up like a space balloon as I breathed in their appreciation.

～

IN THE EARLY summer I had a phone call from my old friend Wendy Mclure, who was now married. She and her husband were passing through Brighton and wanted to visit me. I remembered the romantic story I had written when working in Llandudno, modelling the girl's character on Wendy and having her fall for someone I had imagined to be like David Knight, the actor I had first seen filming in Seaford. When Wendy drove up outside our Arundel Terrace flat to introduce her new husband, I was astonished to see that she had actually married David Knight. Over tea I babbled on about the story I had written in Llandudno. Wendy decided I was 'fey' like some of the people from the Scottish islands. So laughingly we all agreed that it was probably my brief time as a child in the Hebrides that had triggered my 'feyness'. That incident was the first of many experiences whereby my creative writing became attuned to immediate or future events; with my later novels it became quite alarming.

The BBC TV producer Brian Bell sent me a six-part series written by Terence Dudley called *The River Flows East*. I was offered the leading part of Susan Melford, a journalist, who gets involved in a spy story. Gary Watson was playing the leading man while the villains were played by Harold Innocent, Burt Kwouk and Sheila Burrell. I was thrilled that the wardrobe department bought me a red Weatherall reversible suit to wear. It was the most expensive outfit I had ever worn and I managed to buy it from the BBC at a reduced price when the show was finished.

The series was a lot of fun to do and it was rewarding to be working with such experienced actors. During the final episode, however, I nearly ruined the filming by getting the giggles. Luckily I managed to control myself. The reason for my near lack of control was the dramatic sequence involving the hero, Gary Watson. He had to be overcome by the villains and tied to the end of a pier while the tide of the Thames was rising. When the tide finally came in it would probably drown him. My character was frantically rowing a boat across the river to rescue him. We shot the scene at Ealing Studios, where they had a large tank. Gary had to get into the tank and wait, bound in ropes, for me to be moved across the studio floor with men in the studio rocking me from side to side, as if I was rowing. It takes a lot of concentration to ignore the huffing and puffing of the chaps and pretend to be scanning a river while going through a rowing motion and shouting out dialogue. Unfortunately, during the dress rehearsal, Gary had complained that the water was too cold. So, the next time he climbed into the tank it was very hot. He was stripped to his nylon underpants and his skin was turning a definite shade of pink. It was a good thing it was shot in black and white, as most things were at that time. Along I came, rocking, rowing and shouting to him to hang on. By the time the stage crew got me lined up with him in the tank, Gary's nylon pants had become transparent. I looked down into what was supposed to be the river and saw his penis and testicles floating in the water. I nearly choked as I said my next lines. Luckily the director read my performance as being overcome with emotion, which just goes to prove that not all actors' emotions are what they seem to be.

While I was working on *The River Flows East*, the *Daily Mirror* held their National TV Awards Presentation Dinner on a Sunday at the Café Royal in Regent Street. I had finished my second series of the *Navy Lark* so was able to attend. John and I were seated next to Barry Took and Marty Feldman, two highly successful comedy scriptwriters. When Hugh Cudlipp, the chairman of the Mirror Group, proposed the loyal toast, 'Ladies and Gentleman, the Queen', Marty shouted, 'Whoever she may be.'

There was general hysteria. I slid under the table as I was laughing so much. This was a time when you still had to stand for the National Anthem at the end of films, plays or any public event. It was unthinkable to mock the monarch, but Marty was part of a new breed of comedians and actors, the new Sixties' irreverent rebels and satirists. The evening became quite raucous, especially when Charlie Drake got up, told the assembly he was going to retire, and everyone cheered. He was quite unpopular with many fellow performers.

∼

IN 1962, TRAVELLING abroad was quite expensive, nothing like as easy and reasonable as it is today. Annie Nightingale was pregnant so she, Gordon, John and I decided that, between us, we should buy a dinghy with an outboard motor, then we could bob about at sea which would feel like a holiday abroad. We found a boat for sixty pounds and armed with cushions and a picnic hamper, and making sure the pregnant Annie was carefully placed in a safe seat, we would shove off for the day in our boat. We spent most of the summer at sea, sometimes beaching in the most unsailor-like way on to the steep, shingle shorelines between Rottingdean and Hove. It was a beautiful summer and a warm autumn, and then in October came the Cuban missile crisis.

It was the moment our generation had most dreaded, the closest we have ever come to a nuclear war. On 22 October, when

America's President John Kennedy announced to the world the discovery of missiles in Cuba and demanded that Russia remove them, the Russians under the leadership of President Krushchev had already dispatched an arsenal of nuclear weapons on ships bound for Havana. Kennedy raised American military readiness to DEFCON2 and sent the US Navy to form a blockade round the island. Soon the Russian ships and the American ships were facing each other at sea. We all knew the dangers of radiation and the dangers to us and future generations.

Annie was heavily pregnant and the four of us were watching the television, listening to the radio, terrified one of the leaders would listen to the hawks of that time and fire the first missile. We all prayed for common sense to prevail. The whole world knew we could be facing extinction. Eventually Krushchev agreed to remove the weapons if the US would guarantee not to invade Cuba. They also demanded that the US remove their missiles from Turkey in exchange for the Russians dismantling theirs in Cuba.

An agreement was reached. The two leaders brushed aside the advice from their hawks and the terrifying moment was over. I hope no generation ever has to go through that fear and fright again.

Shortly after we had begun to recover from the dramatic event, I was approached by the Devonshire Park Theatre at Eastbourne. Their repertory company was producing a new play called *Love in Bloom* by Michael Brett and they wanted me to play the female lead opposite Edward Petherbridge. It was a lovely light comedy and I enjoyed playing the part enormously. While I was working on the play the company asked me whether I would play the princess in their pantomime *Puss in Boots*. Richard Murdoch, famous for his radio series *Much Binding in the Marsh*, was going to play the dame. As it was close to Brighton and I could travel home by train every night, I agreed. Two other people from Brighton, pianists Mary Hargreaves and Douglas Addey, in charge of the music, were also travelling on the train every day. I would be dancing and singing again in the pantomime and I would have my second Christmas at home with John.

One night, however, it began to snow heavily as the two pianists and I set off for the train after the show. We thought we would be all right travelling to Brighton, but one of the railway staff at Eastbourne got us on to the wrong train, and we eventually found ourselves in Bexhill. No more trains were running that night, taxis had finished, buses had stopped and snowdrifts lined every road. So we three thespians trudged along to the local police station and told them we were stranded. The duty sergeant offered us a couple of cells for the night and I phoned John but he could not get out of Brighton because of the treacherous road conditions. After a cup of tea in the morning we caught the first available train home. One night in a cell, even with the cell door open so I wouldn't get claustrophobic, was enough for me to vow to myself I would never do anything wrong in my life.

Chapter Ten

1963

~

IT WAS A short pantomime season and a very hard winter. The snow fell heavily in January. One night so many cars were stranded along the Brighton seafront near us that John and I invited people in for warm drinks and a rest while they waited for the strongest of the men to push and shove the stranded vehicles back on to the centre of the road.

John was encouraging me to write more short stories. I was also receiving tapes from Dad and felt I should return to Australia to see how he was managing. John agreed it was important for me to go back so I wrote to Dad to tell him I would try to get over to Australia that year. Shortly after I sent him the letter, a young nurse telephoned me. She was about to travel to Australia to join her husband, who was a British doctor working in Gympie and also my father's doctor. I was advised not to return to Gympie as Dad had very bad emphysema and the shock of seeing me could result in his death. I was devastated. For so long I had waited to return to Queensland to see my father, and just when I thought everything was possible he was being snatched away from me again.

Worthing repertory was going to be putting on a new play by Philip King, *How Are You, Johnnie?* It dealt with the subject of homosexuality, a very daring theme in 1963. Guy Vaesen was to direct it, and two male leads were to be played by Derek Fowlds and Ian McShane. They offered me the part of the girlfriend. The play was to tour for a couple of dates and then go to London.

We opened at Brighton to good notices, then travelled to Liverpool. I had some good personal notices in Liverpool but Guy was in a tetchy state from the moment we opened. I had seen him in this mood when he picked on a 'whipping boy' first in Llandudno and also at Worthing. It looked as though this time the 'whipping boy' was to be me. After we opened in Liverpool on the Monday he called a rehearsal early Tuesday morning. The atmosphere in the theatre was icy. Guy had the pursed lips I knew only too well and started with the sarcasm I had watched him dole out to others.

'And you, madam. What did you think you were doing?' Now it was my turn to have my performance taken apart while the rest of the cast looked uncomfortable but remained silent. As Guy bitched on I decided I was not going to put up with it and told him what he could do to himself in very explicit language. I was sacked on the spot. Someone was travelling up to replace me as I set off for home. While I did not regret what I had said to Guy, the shame of being sacked was terrible. John met me at Brighton station and soon cheered me up. Over the next few days I was spoilt and fussed over as he worked hard to restore my confidence.

But in fact, fate had been kind to me, although I did not know it at the time. The play did not run for long but if I had stayed in it I would have missed an even greater opportunity: the chance of working with Joan Littlewood. My guardian angel is a first-rate manager and the best agent any girl could have.

～

SONNY CALLED, AND after sympathizing about the sacking, told me that Theatre Workshop was doing a new production called *Oh, What a Lovely War*. I wanted to work at Stratford East and was thrilled to get the chance of an audition. But did they want a blonde or a brunette? He did not know. I went up to Regent Street where I had seen some black wigs in a hairdresser's window and bought one. I decided I would do the audition in the black wig and if they said they actually wanted a blonde I would pull the wig off, so getting a second chance.

I turned up at the Theatre Royal, Stratford East, in my black wig looking a bit like Harpo Marx. The audition was being taken by Gerry Raffles, Joan Littlewood's partner, and Kevin Palmer the stage director. When my name was called to go on stage, the voice in the auditorium had an Australian accent which made me feel cheerful. I sang, danced, improvised scenes on any subject they wanted and then I heard the words, 'Thank you.' As I was walking off the stage I shouted to them, 'Are you looking for a blonde or a brunette?'

'Why?' replied the Australian voice.

'I can be either,' I yelled, pulling off the wig and letting all my hair down.

There were howls of laughter from the front. 'Don't worry – you're in.'

'What as, a blonde or brunette?'

'Either – you're mad – you'll fit in perfectly.'

And so I started work with the great Joan Littlewood and the Theatre Workshop.

The first person I saw when I arrived at the theatre for rehearsals was my old friend Victor Spinetti, whom I had worked with at the Irving. He was warming up with some of the other actors who introduced themselves. Joan arrived in a cloud of Gauloise ciga- rette smoke. She was in her early forties, and had a large domed forehead partly covered by a beret pulled over her short, dark hair. Her grin, like that of a Cheshire cat, seemed to stretch across the whole of her face but could disappear in a moment. When she was concentrating or creating something her gaze was intense. She wore a crumpled cream mackintosh, the pockets of which held her supply of Gauloise, and comfortable trousers. She strode about the theatre in very soft, moccasin shoes.

A few years previously a book had been published called *The Donkeys*, a bitter story about the First World War. Charles Chiltern had then put a programme together for BBC radio with all the songs from the same period. Joan and Charles now had an idea for turning the whole concept of the war into a musical, *Oh, What a Lovely War*. With the actors' improvisations the show slowly came together. We actors became pierrots or clowns dressed in black and white, ostensibly appearing on the end of a seaside pier. We 'played' the 'War Game' by changing a hat or a prop, so becoming all the characters involved in the war.

While we danced, sang and played our roles, ticker tape over the proscenium gave the facts or numbers killed. I loved the rehearsals, the exploration, research and collective creativity. We were all paid the same money – ten pounds a week and shared communal teas, often of spam and bread and butter. The facts of the war horrified me. Our clowning while these facts were revealed had a profoundly emotional effect on the audience. Occasionally we could hear deep sobs from a member in the audience who had been overcome by the horror of it all. When John came to see the show and dropped into the dressing room later, his glasses were all steamed up from his tears.

Some people accused us of 'dancing on dead men's graves' but I think we were honouring them by making people aware of propaganda, the stupidity of some leaders and the profiteering that goes on during a war.

During the Stratford run, news came through that we were to appear at the Sarah Bernhardt Theatre in Paris, to be part of an International Theatre Festival. We would then return to England to open at Wyndham's Theatre in Charing Cross Road. Wonderfully, our ten pounds a week would be increased.

Just before we finished at Stratford I was sent a bouquet of flowers from Sonny wishing me luck for Paris. That night the tube train was late on the way to Victoria station so I knew I would have to run like the wind to catch the last Brighton train leaving at midnight. When I reached Victoria I took off my shoes so I could run faster. The train was still at the platform, but when I was about twenty-five yards from the gate, a pink-faced, surly-looking railway man, who had been watching me run for the train, closed the gates in my face. I begged, I pleaded, I tried to push the gate, shouting that it was the last train home. The train was still there but there is no greater obstruction to reason than a certain British bloody-mindedness. Helplessly, I watched the train pull out, and understood how spontaneous murder could come about. Instead I did a 'Hermione Baddely' – I whacked him over the head with my bouquet and called him quite a few names. Flower heads littered the platform. As I turned away to try to find a telephone to contact a friend who might put me up for the night, a watching station employee said, 'That's not very ladylike language is it?' He got the bouquet stalks thrown at him.

~

To GET TO France we were taken by bus to Kent, from where we were flown by charter plane across the channel. From there we travelled by coach to Paris. It was a long journey. A young journalist called Bernard Levin travelled with us and later wrote an article about our trip, 'The Clowns Will Inherit the Earth'.

The Sarah Bernhardt Theatre was opposite the equally beautiful Châtalet Theatre. After finding our respective hotels we all converged on the theatre to find the most enormous stage and vast auditorium. I was sharing a dressing room with Fanny Carby and Myfanwy Jenn. It overlooked the River Seine and was the most beautiful, large and airy room. Murray Melvin, Tony Holland, Kevin Palmer and I went to a friendly café next door to the theatre after rehearsing. Kevin suddenly grabbed my hand, 'Aw, Jude, isn't this great? How did a boy from Indooroopilly and a girl from Gympie manage to get to Paris, France? Aren't we lucky?'

We opened the following night at nine o'clock in the evening. The theatre was packed. Some French government ministers were in the audience with many famous French actors and writers. Film stars like Marlene Dietrich were also there. At the end of the show, when we sang 'Adieux La Vie', the French went mad. It was forbidden to sing the song during the First World War because it criticized the profiteering while the young conscripts were dying; anyone singing it could be arrested and possibly shot for being unpatriotic.

Flowers showered on to the stage. We had curtain call after curtain call and Dietrich was standing on her seat. Bottles of champagne were sent to all the actors, we were the toast of Paris and took all the prizes. We were also popular in Paris for another reason. For years the British had sneered at the sexual scandals involving members of the French government but now England too had just been exposed to a government scandal with the Profumo affair. The French had read all about the strange upper-crust English sexual habits and the English had gone up in their estimation.

During the time we were in Paris we hardly slept. The weather was warm, the nights balmy and we would wander together exploring Paris. We sat in cafés and watched the world go by, drinking our strong black coffees or *citron pressé*. On our last night all we had left of our expenses was enough to buy *œuf* and chips after the show. We were met at the stage door by a tearful waiter from the café we had often gone to, who thrust two big bottles of wine in our hands. We set off for the cheaper area of Paris, picking up some street entertainers on the way, and promised them some of the wine if they would play while we ate our egg and chips. So we had a party. Never did egg and chips taste that good. The man with the accordion played, the violinist became inspired and we danced around madly until early morning, when we rushed back to our hotels to pack for our journey back to England.

~

WE OPENED AT Wyndham's Theatre to rave reviews and played to packed audiences daily. Many Americans came to see the show and Keenan Wynn trudged all the way to my dressing room to say how much he had enjoyed the show and my performance. All my friends and family came. Mum saw the show and was moved to tears. She told me that her father had been gassed in the First World War and invalided out on some paltry pension.

We were also asked to appear at the Palladium in the show *Night of a Hundred Stars* where, as well as the famous stars of that time who were making an appearance, excerpts from the top shows in London were being performed. Excited and nervous, I stood in the wings with all the others waiting for my cue to go on, when I heard a wavering voice from the other side of the curtain, 'Oh God, Oh God.' It was a woman's voice, frantic with nerves. I peered round the curtain and found Dame Edith Evans wringing her hands with fright. 'Are you all right?' I asked her. 'Yes, dear, it's just the nerves seem to get worse as you get older,' she said. I assured her that I too felt sick with fright, but privately I felt a lot better knowing that a great actress like Dame Edith was as scared as I was.

Many of us were interviewed by the press during the West
End run, and a show business journalist called Barry Norman
arranged to take me for lunch. We met up but he seemed a bit preoccupied while we were talking and then told me that he was going
to be out of a job because his paper was folding. I remember looking at him and saying, 'You know, Barry, you're a respected
journalist, and not a bad-looking bloke; what about doing film
reviews or show business interviews for television? No one else
is doing it.' He very quickly established the genre for BBC TV and
rightly established himself as its best practitioner. When I bumped
into him at a film preview years later, we laughed as he remembered our lunch.

While playing in the West End I was able to catch the famous
eleven o'clock Brighton Belle. It was a beautiful train. Now of
course it is part of the Orient Express trains, as a result of the
following decade's cost-cutting, anti-elitism philosophy. But in
1963 actors, singers, journalists and many writers caught this train
and spent an hour of conviviality on the way home. There was
a saying around London during those days that if there was a
Brighton actor or singer in a London show, the third act would
go like the clappers so they could catch the Brighton Belle. For a
supplement payment of two shillings and sixpence we travelled in
carriages with individual armchairs and glass-topped tables with
lamps, and we could have supper of kippers, bacon and eggs or
Welsh rarebit. They served tea or coffee in china pots with proper
cups and saucers. We had spoons and standard British Rail cutlery,
now usually reserved for the grand long-distance trains.

Many passengers imbibed a bit too well on those comfortable
trains. I remember one man who in his inebriated state tried unsuc-
cessfully to be gallant. The lady sitting opposite him had got up
from her seat just before the stop at Haywards Heath. Seeing the
train was about to pull out of the station, he presumed that she
must have got off the train in the same state as himself because her
fur coat was still hanging from the coat hook. Thoughtfully he bundled up the mink coat and threw it out of the window on to the
platform as the train picked up speed. There was pandemonium
when the woman returned to her seat from the lavatory.

One matinee day I saw a man who I thought looked a bit suspicious walking up the stairs to the dressing rooms on the floor
above mine. I called Fanny Carby and asked her whether we
should alert anyone. The man might be a thief, I said. Fanny
clapped her hand over my mouth and pulled me into the dressing
room. 'Don't you know who that is?' she hissed.

'No.'

'It's one of the Krays.'

'Who are the Krays?'

Fanny then educated me about the London underworld. She
explained how when Joan was filming *Sparrows Can't Sing* in the
East End of London, the yobs who wanted to create trouble for
them disappeared like melting snow when they saw Joan had some
of the Krays' men protecting the filming. From then on I kept an
open mind about anyone I saw backstage.

By the end of September I was pregnant and experiencing morning sickness and was unable to drink tea or coffee without being
ill. The smells of cigarette smoke, petrol or any alcohol fumes
brought instant nausea. I told Joan, who said I could work for as
long as I felt comfortable. Apart from the morning sickness I felt
very well and could dance and keep up with the other members of
the cast. The stewards on the Brighton Belle spoilt me, making sure
I always had a seat and making me dry toast and Bovril for the journey to London.

At the start of *Oh, What a Lovely War*, the pierrots rush about
the stage enacting the panic caused by the assassination of the
Archduke Ferdinand and it is established that 'big fat Sophie was
with him in the car'. Speculation about the identity of the assassin
then follows with rumours of 'it's a Serb; no it's a Croat'.

By November the show was still playing to full houses and
many Americans were in the audience. On the twenty-second, just
as the curtain went up, John telephoned me from Fleet Street to tell
me President John F. Kennedy had been assassinated.

Life and art came together that night. John was getting news
from the *Express'* tapes and relaying the news to me in the theatre;
I would then tell the other actors. We heard that a kalashnikov had
been found. Was it the Russians? Who would shoot the President

of America, the most powerful man in the world? His wife Jackie was in the car. During the show the tension began to build in the audience as the word began to spread. By the time the curtain came down there was a seething mass of people around Charing Cross Road and Leicester Square. Americans were shouting, some were crying.

Fanny Carby and I fought our way through the crowds and made our way down to the *Express* office in Fleet Street, where John was able to give us more information. The three of us knew this was an important moment in history, and that everyone of our generation would always remember where they were the day President Kennedy was killed.

~

JOAN HAD AN idea for a pantomime, called *The Merry Rooster Show*, so we would all come in early to discuss and work on her idea; Lionel Bart would join us.

By December I was five months pregnant and beginning to get tired from all the travelling so I gave notice to Joan that I would leave in a fortnight. But I didn't work out my notice. The pains began on the Sunday and I was rushed into Brighton General Hospital. My old friend from Winston's nightclub, Barbara Windsor, took over my part and eventually went to New York with the show.

There is a great deal of nostalgia about the health service of the past, but I can assure you it is far better now than it was in 1963. I was put into an annexe away from the main women's ward. When the pains became terrible in the middle of the night, there was no bell to press, so I shouted for help but no one came. In the end I took my nightdress off and waved it across the door, hoping someone would see. They did and I was taken into a small, brightly lit room as it was obvious that I was about to miscarry. There was one really kind nurse, an Indian woman, who helped me by rubbing my back. The others bossily bustled about.

I was told it was a boy. The afterbirth had come away from the womb and suffocated him but I was assured that he had been perfectly formed and there was no reason I should not have other children. I cried for the rest of the night, then was moved to the women's ward and kept in for about ten days. I was amazed that so many people sent me get well cards, including one from all the stewards on the Brighton Belle.

Anyone who has ever spent time in a women's ward will know what a delightfully bawdy place it can be. There was a lot of humour and a lot of kindness during the day. But it was during the night that the haunting grief for a life lost and guilt for not trying hard enough to protect him returned.

When I went home I was very depressed. Every television programme I watched seemed to have someone losing a baby in it. It is strange how the mind works while in a depression. I felt a failure as a woman and also remember thinking that if the human race ever had to leave earth I would not be invited on to the space ship because I could not contribute to building up a new world.

My grandmother phoned and said, 'What's all this about you having a miscarriage? None of the women in our family have lost children. It must be from your mother's side.' Ah, the joys of family support. My mother was terribly upset but nagged on about the fact that I had worked for too long. I found out years later from a top gynaecologist that in actual fact the miscarriage was my body trying to save me by expelling the foetus. Being a mixture of my father's family, who were large-boned and tall, and my mother's family, who were small-boned and little, I would have difficulty giving birth. John came from a tall, large-boned family. If I had been living in the Middle Ages or even Victorian times, I would probably have died in childbirth.

Sybil was dreadfully sad for me but John was my strength, always seeking to divert my maudlin thoughts. He had quite a hard time. When we went for a walk half the world seemed to be pushing prams. I kept away from friends who had children and I did not want sympathy or encouragement for the future. Any reference to the miscarriage brought back the pain; it crept into my thoughts and my dreams.

Eventually, John encouraged me to start reading some American novels. Poor soul, he did his best, but the first one he picked for me was *For Whom the Bell Tolls*. I finished the novel in floods of tears and then saw the funny side of the situation. A sense of humour was coming back into our life; lingering despair was slowly replaced by optimism.

Chapter Eleven

1964–1965

~

THE NEW YEAR started well. Granada TV asked me to appear in an episode of *Coronation Street*, playing the girlfriend of one of the regular cast members. John was very pleased I was going back to work and thought it was the best thing I could do. I immediately started practising a Manchester accent.

Walking into the *Coronation Street* rehearsal room I was amazed at the transformation of the actors in the series. I had first seen them all when I was part of the Younger Generation company. Then they had looked exactly like the parts they were playing. Now they were rehearsing in luxury, with their own green room to rest in, their own telephone, glacé fruit on a centre table, and some very expensive fur coats were carefully arranged on hangers. Those who had rather drawn faces in 1961 now possessed a healthy, well-fed look. The women's hair was expensively styled and they all exuded that air of confidence that goes with having long-term, highly successful, well-paid employment. I enjoyed playing a floosie with most of my scenes in the pub.

While I was working on *Coronation Street*, one of Granada's top producers, Phillip Mackie, spoke to me about a series of Feydeau farces he was going to do. Silvio Narizzanno, a brilliant Canadian, was going to be the director. Phillip and Silvio wanted to keep the same company of actors for the whole series, and they wanted me for the juvenile parts. The rest of the cast were to be Adrienne Corri, Zena Walker, Alfred Marks, Henry McGee, Kenneth Griffiths and Paul Witson Jones, all very well known and experienced actors. I said I would love to be in it.

We rehearsed each play for two weeks at Granada's rehearsal rooms in London and went to Manchester for recordings. I was pleased to see Alfred Marks again. We had not worked together since Ben Lyon had cast me in the *Dickie Henderson Show*. He was always amusing during rehearsals, keeping us entertained with non-stop jokes. Whenever any other member of the cast told a funny story that Alfred liked he would disappear to the lavatory. We were all intrigued by the immediate urinary reaction to a joke, so it was arranged that one of the actors would follow him to see if he was all right. Kenneth Griffiths returned with a big grin on his face. He told us Alfred was writing down the story he had just heard into a little black book.

Most of us stayed at the New Theatre Inn while Adrienne and Zena stayed at the more expensive Midland Hotel. I would often join them for some smoked salmon sandwiches and a long gossip. The three of us became very close and had a lot of laughs together. It was the men who sometimes became tetchy with each other.

Once, I was woken in the middle of the night by the telephone on the landing outside my bedroom door. I got up to answer it and a woman's voice asked for Alfred. There was no one awake downstairs and thinking it must be urgent I knocked on every bedroom door shouting 'Alfred' until I found him. The next day at rehearsals he told us it was his wife, Paddy, who had shouted 'April Fool' down the line.

While we were making the Paris 1900 series of Feydeau plays, there was one play that had no part for me. Derek Grainger, who had been a producer of current affairs, decided I would be an interesting addition to *Scene at Six Thirty*, an evening news programme. By placing me with the news programme Granada would not have to pay me for kicking my heels and doing nothing. So on the Monday instead of going to the London rehearsal rooms, I presented myself to the newsroom in Manchester. I did not know what was expected of me and no one had told me anything about the difference in working with a camera on news rather than drama. At the morning discussion I was given a story about Harrods selling tins of chocolate ants, which I learned by heart while sitting in an office. The other reporter in the studio with me was a young

(*right*) My father Darcy Nigel Barry
  Cornwell, 1939.

(*below*) My mother Irene McCullen,
  1939.

(*above*) Me aged two, having
  dissected my doll to see how it
  worked, Benbecula, Hebrides,
  1942.

(*left*) Dressed for one of Miss
  Barcombe's concerts, 1945.

(*right*) Making sure Laddie does not throw my brother, Australia, 1952.

(*below*) A picnic in the bush near Gympie, Australia, 1950.

(*right*) Ballet student, Seaford, 1953.

(*below*) With my mother and Brian in 1952. I am in my new Lewes Grammar School uniform.

(*right*) Front of house picture, Panama Club, 1958.

(*below*) Playing Pippa in *The Spider's Web* in rep at the Palace Pier, with a young journalist I'd just met called John Parry, in 1960.

(*below*) Our wedding day, 18 December 1960. I married the critic!

The Younger Generation series for Granada, 1961.

(*above*) With John Thaw in *Flow Gently, Sweet Aston* by Patrick Garland.
(*left*) With Johnny Briggs in *Josie* by Maureen Duffy.

(*below left*) In *The Navy Lark*.
   Back row, left to right: Ronnie Barker, Jon Pertwee, Michael Bates and Tenniel Evans. *Middle row, left to right*: Stephen Murray, Richard Caldicot, Leslie Phillips. *Front row, left to right*: Heather Chasen and me.
   (Courtesy of the BBC)

(*above*) Playing Liz in Worthing rep's production of *Billy Liar* with Derek Fowlds, 1962.

(left) *Oh What a Lovely War*, 1963.

(below) Playing opposite Alfred Marks
in *Paris 1900*, one of an acclaimed
series of Feydeau farces produced
for Granada, in 1964.

(below) Playing Ruby in *Sweet
Fanny Adams* at Stratford East,
just after our son was born.

(below) Talking to the French
stuntman who had to look like me
when he crashed the coach in *Two
for the Road*, 1966.

(*right*) On location for *Rocket to the Moon* in Wicklow, Ireland, in 1966. Playing Lady Electra in a scene with Dennis Price and Burl Ives.

(*above left*) Playing Miss Smith with Donald Pleasance in *Call Me Daddy*, 1967. The play won an Emmy award. (Courtesy of ABC Television)

(*above*) Playing Filigree Fondle in Anthony Newley's *Can Hieronymus Merkin Ever Forget Mercy Humppe and Find True Happiness?*, 1968.

(*left*) Waiting to be called on set during the filming in Malta.

(*right*) My own chair, on location in Ireland, 1969.

(*left*) Playing Rosie opposite Susannah Yorke in *Country Dance* (renamed *Brotherly Love*), Ardmore Studios, Ireland, 1969.

(*above*) Playing Liz, Marty Feldman's wife, in *Every Home Should Have One* (now named *Think Dirty*) in 1969.

(*right*) We bought the house we always wanted in Brighton in 1970.

(*above*) Playing Nellie, opposite Harry Andrews, in *Wuthering Heights*, 1970.

(*above*) Meeting Princess Alexandra
  with Tim Dalton and Anna
  Calder-Marshall in the
  background, 1971.

(*right*) Playing Calpurnia in *Julius
  Caesar*, with Mark Dignam and
  Philip Mannikum also in the
  picture. (Courtesy of Reg Wilson
  Collection, RSC Archive)

journalist called Michael Parkinson. There was no autocue on the front of the camera as the presenters use now. I was perched on a stool and told to wait for my cue. But the studio floor manager used different hand signals behind the camera from the ones I was used to in drama. When he started gesticulating I was mesmerized but quickly realized he wanted me to start so I chatted on until the camera switched to Michael. An irate news producer stormed up to me afterwards to tell me I was dreadful. I agreed with him, which rather took away his anger, but I pointed out that if I did not know what I was doing, how could I be anything else?

The next day I was sent off to film an interview with a woman who had just lost her husband. Michael Parkinson came with me and really helped me. He showed me how to ask the relevant questions and how to react. He also was very patient, and needed to be because by now I felt a total idiot. When we finished filming the interview Michael said I deserved to be introduced to a Barnsley Chop, another thing I had never heard about. We all went for lunch and, once they knew I did not in any way take myself seriously as a presenter but was just filling in until I started on the next play, we got on well together. I was most relieved when rehearsal on the next Feydeau started.

In this play my character had a love interest. Silvio cast Nicky Henson as my young lover. I think it was Nicky's first television job. He arrived on a motorbike just in time for rehearsal. When we came to plotting our first embrace I found myself smothered by sweaty armpits. The weather was warm but not too hot, so it must have been his nerves. 'If we're going to work well together, Nicky,' I said, 'you're going to have to shower and get your act together.' He looked ashamed. 'Sorry, Jude, I got up late this morning.'

The next day at rehearsal a scrubbed-up, sweetly smelling Nicky arrived looking really handsome. He was also a fabulously funny young actor and I enjoyed working with him. Often when we have run into each other at various functions, we've had a joke about when we first worked together.

The series received many awards. It was beautifully and authentically dressed by John Bright, who had just started up his company, Cosprop. Silvio was a great director and we all worked well together as a team. Adrienne, Zena and I became good friends and I worked with Alfred and Henry again years later.

~

BUT IT WAS time to move on. I had a meeting with a director called Warren Jenkins, who eventually went on to begin the Welsh National Theatre. He wanted me to play a part in a new play called *Mr Whatnot* written by a new writer called Alan Ayckbourn. The play was to be produced by Peter Bridge and performed at the New Arts Theatre.

It was a play about a little piano tuner visiting a large country house where he discovers the eccentricities of the middle classes. He falls in love with the daughter of the house, takes part in a family tea party in the garden and plays tennis with them. I was offered the part of Agnes, the maid who kept asking him, 'Would you like a cup of tea?' The play required a lot of mime to fit in with a pre-recorded soundtrack which had the sounds of tennis, crockery and even the plops of sugar lumps dropping into tea. Julian Chagrin coached us in mime technique and I thoroughly enjoyed every session.

Among the members of the cast was my old friend from the *Navy Lark*, Ronnie Barker, and the famous old star, Marie Lohr, who was a lovely warm-heared woman with the most beautiful complexion.

While I was rehearsing in the play, I was asked to be on the panel of that Saturday's *Juke Box Jury*, a BBC TV pop music programme hosted by Pete Murray. On the same panel that day was Ringo Starr, the drummer with The Beatles. I liked Ringo. He was a cheery soul who kept calling me 'Judy love' and seemed as vague about the pop music we were supposed to have opinions about as I was. At that time newspaper reports were saying that panellists were being bribed to push certain records, but no one approached me with a bribe, or if they did I did not notice them.

Mr Whatnot opened to good notices. I had wonderful personal reviews, due in part to the brilliant ideas and comedy business Ronnie Barker suggested to me. I have often thought Ronnie should have directed. He had so much to teach young actors like me and was always generous with his ideas. Gloria Swanson came to see the play and sent me a very complimentary message. She said I was going to be a big star one day. I was thrilled.

Alan and I became friends. He had a quirky sense of humour and a feverishly creative mind. We had a lot of laughs and when the play ended he told me of an offer he had from BBC Leeds. He did not know whether to take it or stay on in Scarborough as an actor. I suggested that if he took the BBC job at least he would be able to give his wife some decent housekeeping money and he could write more plays. He took the BBC job and went on to write his first big commercial success, *Relatively Speaking*. On the last night of the show dear Marie Lohr came up to me and said, 'I want you to have my lucky brooch, dear. My career is coming to an end and yours is just beginning.' It was a half moon of rhinestones – I treasure it still.

~

As soon as the play finished, I started work on 'A Face in the Doorway', playing a university student in an hour-long episode of *The Sullivan Brothers* series which starred Anthony Bates. I was then asked to play the female lead in *Rookery Nook* with Richard Briers and Moray Watson. The play was to open in Oxford, play Manchester and then come to London. Jack Minster was directing.

At the read-through and first day's rehearsal I met the kind and gentle Hungarian actor Guy Deghy, who on the opening night in Oxford introduced me to someone who was to become one of my greatest friends, a Jesuit priest called Algy Shearman.

The rehearsals went well but when we opened in Oxford I began to feel tired. I went to dinner after the show with Guy and Algy and I suddenly noticed that I found the smells of cigarette smoke and alcohol fumes in the hotel unbearable; I also wanted only very plain food. I confided to Algy that I had all the early signs of being pregnant again and did not want to lose another baby but was worried about letting the company down. Algy discreetly advised me that if I was indeed pregnant I should make the baby my first priority.

We travelled from Oxford to Manchester, where we opened on

a foggy night. The fog was so thick that it had come into the theatre and we could just about see the front row in the audience but little else. That night I felt very ill. My friend Jenny Moss from *Coronation Street* shared a flat with a girl called Christine from Granada's make-up department. They called round to the New Theatre Inn to take me back to their place for lunch, but when they saw how dreadful I looked they called their doctor who immediately ordered me into bed and to stop work at once. Those two girls were wonderful. They took the medical certificate to the theatre company manager and telephoned John to come up and take me home to Brighton. They then collected my things from where I was staying and looked after me at their flat until John arrived.

At home my own doctor, Ian Hudson, came straight round and told me that I was to lie flat on my back, in bed, for the next few months. He felt that if we could get past seven months of pregnancy, the baby would have a chance of survival. I was not to get overexcited or worry about things but just rest. He also put me on folic acid and iron pills, which he said would help.

To survive those first few months I had to reduce my mind to focus on the minuscule events that happened within the confines of my bedroom. I could tell the time by the way the light moved across the room and I explored the texture of sheets and blankets. I remembered old black and white films where people were confined to iron lungs, or thought about how people had survived being incarcerated in a small prison cell. I began to play the same game I had played as a seven-year-old, only then I was watching the foaming trail in the ship's wake during quarantine at the back of the SS *Ormonde* travelling to Australia. Now I focused on a wall and travelled through my memories. I had to get rid of the occasional bouts of self-pity and concentrate on the small life trying to survive in my womb, so I meditated on the positive things in life and fed the little soul with lots of beautiful thoughts.

John joined in by playing records of classical music, which not only relaxed me but helped to fill my mind with wonderful images. He became my nurse, cook and a quite talented hairdresser, although it was very difficult having my hair washed over the side of the bed. When he went to work my mother arrived, chattering non-stop and thrilled to be needed.

After nausea abated and my appetite returned, I wanted the food of school dinner variety. My mother obliged, quoting, 'snaps and snails and puppy dog's tails'. She declared it was a boy. 'With you,' she said, 'all I wanted was melons and fruit; Very hard to find in wartime London.'

To try to get a measure of time I asked my mother to find me a knitting pattern for a shawl. The intricate pattern became my calendar. A Truefood booklet told me every stage of the baby's development. So I chose the right foods for each stage. By doing that I felt I was taking part in the creative process rather than just lying there like a blob.

~

BY DECEMBER I was able to get up occasionally and sit up in bed. Christmas was brought to us by one of our great friends, Kazzy, who was Polish and had a restaurant called The Four Aces. He and his wife Joy usually spent Christmas on their own as a welcome day off but he suggested preparing all the food in the restaurant and bringing it up to our flat. He also brought lots of folding tables and crockery for the gathering numbers who were joining us: John's mother and father, who came down from Birmingham to be with us; my mother, my brother and his girlfriend, Penny; and a friend called Richard Evans, a BBC TV producer – his wife was in a nursing home having her first baby. It was a great evening and I felt part of the world again.

I was also thrilled that I had managed to get my brother to start writing to Dad. Brian had listened too much to my mother's very bitter point of view before, feeling that it would be disloyal to her to write. Now he was enjoying the correspondence although we never discussed the subject in front of my mother.

Adrienne Corri telephoned to ask whether John and I would come to her New Year's Eve party. She said it would do me good to come up and see some of my friends and if John drove me up she would look after me until the party. John said he could not get there until later because of his work at the *Express*. I was not sure it was a good idea but I was tempted to go. The next day a composer-friend called Allon Bacon phoned us. He had been warned in a dream that I should not go to London and he offered instead to come and pick me up and take me to his place near by. He and his friend Umberto would give me supper and bring me home safely to wait for John's arrival after midnight. My guardian angel was at it again. We let Adrienne know that we were not coming and John drove up to the *Express* office in our sports car, a white Austin Healey Sprite we now had after trading in the Morris.

Allon and Umberto duly came to collect me on New Year's Eve and fed and entertained me until 1965 arrived. They then drove me home where I waited for John. By two o'clock in the morning when he had not arrived home I was seriously worried. At three o'clock he arrived in an ambulance.

He had been driving down the London to Brighton road, hoping to get home just after midnight, when the car hit black ice by Pease Pottage. The Sprite had rolled over and hit a tree. John was able to save himself from decapitation by throwing himself across the passenger seat. If I had been with him we would both have been killed. A passing lorry driver had got out and approached the wreck, fearful at what he might find, only to hear John yelling to come and help him out. He did not have a scratch on him.

The shawl grew longer as the pregnancy advanced. I began to have cravings for Indian curry. To satisfy this uncontrollable craving John hired a taxi and went down to the local Indian restaurant armed with saucepans. There were no such things as neat little takeaway packages then like they have now. He arrived home by taxi with an entire Indian meal. It was a trip he took many times during the following months.

As the weather was getting warmer, I was able to walk outside, sit on the front doorstep in the sunshine and watch the movement of the sea. Local elections were being held and I was dying to vote. I was supposed to wait until John came home but a very plush American convertible with the hood down pulled up in front of the building and the driver asked whether I would like a lift to the voting station. I told the man that I would have to be brought back again. He agreed and off I went on my adventure. Oh, the excitement of it all.

~

I WAS ONLY a few rows from finishing my shawl now. My brother got married and I attended the wedding looking like Humpty Dumpty. The baby seemed to be swimming with butterfly stroke across the womb and did not like sudden noise. He regularly kicked John in the bottom at night. We decided we were not tempting fate by looking for a bigger flat. However, no one wanted to lease a flat to a couple with a baby on the way. Some friends suggested buying a house with a mortgage, but as I was not able to get out, John had to choose one on his own. We were limited in choice because we wanted a ninety-five per cent mortgage, so it had to be a new house in the suburbs. I wanted to keep all my maternity allowance so I could pay to have the baby privately at Whitehaven nursing home, like my friends.

We managed to find a three-bedroom house with a garage at the back of Brighton, in Westdean, which cost £4,995. We borrowed our friend Kazzy's big soft-upholstered car for me to be driven to see it. The new car John had when the Sprite was written off was a red MGB and the ride was a bit bumpy for me. The house had everything we needed for the new arrival, an airing cupboard and a perfect room for a nursery. We decided that John would move in when I went into the nursing home.

Naïvely, I thought that when the time came for the birth all I would have to do was stand up and it would drop out. I practised breathing exercises with John, and as the time grew closer, Dr Hudson explained everything to me. I had now passed the seventh month stage and was nearing full term. I felt so proud and Mum, who had been knitting for England, rushed up to Harrods and bought a cot. She bought all the other paraphernalia needed for a first-born and we cooed and inspected the lot over and over again.

Then the pains came and I went into the nursing home, where I was a day and a half in labour. I told John to sod off when he started trying to keep me to the breathing rhythms. I kicked my doctor in the balls and my brother and his wife said they could hear my yells at the end of the street. 'It was like something out of a Hammer Horror film,' my brother told me. I think I also shouted that I had changed my mind, before I was introduced to gas and air, after which I opted out from the whole experience. When I came round, I was as mad as a skunk and my hair had gone grey, but I was given a beautiful eight-and-a-half-pound boy to hold. We had both survived the terrible ordeal. After counting all the baby's fingers and toes, John was beaming. He had seen the birth and was moved to tears whenever he spoke about it later. The matron told me that in her experience only one person had ever sworn more than me while giving birth and that was Joan Plowright.

Chapter Twelve

1965–1968

~

WE CALLED OUR son Dylan, Welsh for the ebb tide. But knowing how cruel children could be at school we gave him the name of Edward first, so he was named Edward Dylan. Edward was John's father's name. My father wanted us to call him Barry but I pointed out that Barry Parry was a bit much. It was just as well we had chosen two names. By the time he was at school the *Magic Roundabout* was a popular children's programme. In it was a rather goofy rabbit called Dylan, so the name 'Dylan' was dumped when my son reached the age of thirteen. His preferred name of 'Edward' has been used ever since.

After months of leading a sedentary life there was now hardly a minute in the day when there was not something to do. I became extremely placid and contented in my new routine. I suppose it was nature's way of making sure I protected and loved this new, innocent, vulnerable being. The whole of my day became a homage to this little human miracle and I would have been happy to stay at home for ever – but not so my agent. After three months Carole Golder, Sonny's assistant who had recently been put in charge of the drama section of the agency, came down from London with her husband saying she thought it was time I rejoined the real world. My mother promised to babysit, and after Carole had admired the baby and given him an expensive bib, we went to English's Fish Restaurant in the Lanes. It felt very strange being with grown-ups again, having discussions and opinions. Then I saw Carole putting some snail holders into her bag.

'What are you doing?' I asked, wondering whether she was a kleptomaniac.

'When Dylan goes on to a bottle these will be useful for pulling out the rubber teats when sterilizing them in boiling water,' she giggled.

We then planned how I could start work again very gradually. Carole agreed with me that a small baby was best with his mother but argued that she had turned down a lot of work for me while I was pregnant, including a film with The Beatles, and it was important for me to start again soon.

The first job she offered me was with ABC TV. Pamela Lonsdale was producing and directing *The Present Stage* from the book written by John Kershaw about some aspects of contemporary drama. It was to be presented by David Jones, who was with the Royal Shakespeare Company, and it meant working for four days a week in Teddington. We would rehearse excerpts from plays like *Look Back In Anger*, *Roots* or *The Fire Raisers* and then record them. I would be able to travel by train to the studios and get back in time to put Dylan to bed. A friend told me she had a Norwegian au pair whose friend wanted a family to live with for six months. Toril Grundvig arrived, a lovely, capable, friendly girl, who still keeps in contact with me after all these years. So when I started work I had no worries about the baby.

It was a huge shock to the system to be travelling on trains again. But Pamela was an inspiring director and the gossip and chat with other actors at rehearsals filled me with new energy. I also found out that Pamela was married to Reggie Collins, who had directed me when I was a raw student assistant stage manager at the Dolphin Theatre, Brighton, playing one of my first decent parts in *The Seven-Year Itch*.

I loved working on the part of Beatty in *Roots*. There were huge speeches to be learned and I studied them while travelling on the train. Pamela was very pleased with my performances and told me she looked forward to finding me something to do in the future. I could not have begun acting again with a friendlier or more talented company. I had been very lucky and the money was useful too.

~

VERY QUICKLY CAROLE booked me on to another show. 'Some money for Christmas, Judy. It's light entertainment for ATV. A sketch with Charlie Drake on his show. A week's rehearsal then a day in the studio.' When we started the read-through, I saw that my old friend from Paris 1900, Henry McGee, was in it, as was Pat Coombs. Charlie Drake introduced himself but behaved quite differently from anyone I had ever worked with before. He was more an observer than a participant. He was watching us all as we read. Someone else, his small stand-in, was reading his part. At the end of the read-through Charlie Drake went into a huddle with Shaun O'Riordan, the director, and one actor was called over. After a minute's discussion the actor left the rehearsal room never to return.

'What's all that about?' I asked Pat Coombs.

'Don't ask, don't look, you didn't see anything,' she replied with an overbright smile, as if we were discussing anything but the show.

Rehearsals were the same. We set the moves and the lines while Charlie Drake watched his stand-in perform. I was beginning to understand why everyone had cheered at the *Daily Mirror* awards when Charlie Drake threatened to retire. When the studio day came he would move a chair or some piece of furniture on the take so that the actor he was playing with was upstaged. He was a strange man; not the 'Hello my darlings' character at all. But I didn't mind. I had completed my part and they had to pay me.

Christmas was not far away now. Toril went home for a short break and it was lovely to have the house to ourselves again. Having a baby gave Christmas a whole new meaning. John's parents came down from Birmingham, Kazzy and his wife had another Christmas away from cooking, and my mother came too. I had made my own Christmas pudding, and with John's help the whole Christmas dinner was a great success.

As soon as Toril returned from Norway I began rehearsals for *Sweet Fanny Adams,* a musical written by Stephen Lewis for Theatre Workshop at Stratford East, with Kenneth Parrot directing. Ronnie

Barker was the barman who leaves his wife, played by Avis Bunnage, for Ruby, a barmaid, me – Grandma eat your heart out. The show ran for only a few weeks but it was just lovely working with Ronnie and Avis again.

Toril was going back to Norway and a new Norwegian girl was to take over from her but as Toril expressed reservations about her I was careful before taking on any work. She was dreadfully lazy and I did not quite trust her so she went and we found Jenny, a well-educated Sussex girl. I felt she was safe to leave in charge while I started work at ABC TV again on a science-fiction play called *Out of This World.*

Jenny was marvellous with Dylan, and I was able to get back from work in time to put him to bed every night. Then the producer Phillip Mackie offered me an episode in the Saki series for Granada TV. During rehearsals in London I could get home all right but it meant staying up in Manchester for two nights for transmission. Jenny said she could cope and John promised to get back early from Fleet Street for those two days, so off I went.

The young man playing my boyfriend in Saki was Cavan Kendall, whose parents I had teamed up with after my first pantomime. He had grown into a very tall and handsome young man. We had a lot of laughs together and went through all the numbers I used to do with his father, Terry. A year later, when I ran into Cavan in London, he had lost first his sister Kay Kendall to cancer and then his mother Doric to leukaemia; his father had given up the flat in Clapham Common and moved to America to live with his other daughter, Kim.

~

CAROLE WAS VERY excited when she told me that the famous American director Stanley Donan wanted to see me about a film to be made in France for Twentieth Century Fox, *Two for the Road*. Audrey Hepburn and Albert Finney to be were the stars. The first part of the film was about Audrey as a schoolgirl touring France, where she meets Albert. They wanted some actresses who looked youthful but would not make Audrey look too old. I was offered the part of Pat; the other 'schoolgirls' were Olga Piquot, Jacqueline Bisset and Joanna Jones.

The day came to leave Heathrow for Nice where the first part of the filming was to take place on location and in the studio. Joanna Jones had a little girl, Melissa, the same age as Dylan and she was as upset as I was about going to France – we both had a cry as we said our goodbyes to our respective husbands. We were travelling first class on a Caravelle which takes off almost vertically. I had taken my shoes off and they shot down the length of the plane, so I had to go crawling on my hands and knees looking for them in economy. By now, Joanna and I had the giggles, partly as a relief from our sadness, partly from the excitement of flying first class.

At Nice we were met by a chauffeur-driven car and taken to the Negresco, a magnificent hotel overlooking the sea and the promenade. We were given our schedules, call sheets and our envelopes of French francs for spending money. It was a totally different French experience from the time in Paris with Joan Littlewood, when we stayed in very cheap hotels and eked out our expenses.

Some people from the film company came by later and took us, 'the schoolgirls', out to dinner. Jacqueline Bisset spoke very good French; so did Joanna; Olga, of course, was French. I was able to converse in French quite well, thanks to all those extra private lessons Mum had paid for, though mime was needed occasionally. Going to sleep later in my luxurious room, I thanked my guardian angel for introducing me to privileged living.

Early the next morning we were collected and taken to the studio for our make-up and to be dressed by the wardrobe department. Audrey Hepburn had her own make-up man and hairdresser, an Italian husband-and-wife team who specialized in looking after big film stars like Sophia Loren and Gina Lollobrigida. Audrey's make-up would take about two hours and involved having coffees and cigarettes and general chat. The other make-up artists were two portly Frenchmen who worked very quickly on the other actors in the film.

On our first day at the studio, Olga and Jacqueline were the first to be made up. Olga's make-up man obviously adored her and lingered over every detail, making sure she looked perfect. Similarly, the one making up Jacqueline took great care and spent plenty of time on her. When they were finished, the make-up men looked at Joanna and me and waving their arms about implied we did not need any make-up. Very flattering but quite untrue; they were just being lazy. I called over the interpreter and told him to inform one of the make-up men that if he did not give me a proper make-up I was going to kick him hard in the balls. The change in attitude was immediate. At the very word '*testicules*' he leapt into action, was obsequiously polite and gave me an excellent make-up. Another English victory on French soil.

During the first shot the camera man asked me to get out of the hole in the road. I was not in a hole; the others were just taller than me. So for one scene I was put on a box to reach their height. When Audrey arrived to start shooting she looked beautiful, as always, but there was also a sadness about her and she was painfully thin. I asked one of the crew whether she was upset about anything and he told me she had just got over a miscarriage. My heart went out to her. Now I understood why there was such sadness in her eyes but I soon forgot all that when she began work. Her film technique was brilliant. She was so controlled in her craft that every moment I could I was trying to absorb and remember how she did it. She was also very friendly and showed great camaraderie of spirit towards us that reminded me of her dancer background. When Stanley Donan got carried away and started shouting directions to me in French, she was sympathetic. I was driving the van we were supposed to be travelling in, on the wrong side of the road, and he was urging me closer to an embankment down which the stunt people would eventually crash the vehicle for us. Only I was getting too close for comfort. I had Audrey sitting behind me and I did not want anything to happen to the 'schoolgirls'. I got out of the van and yelled at him to give his directions in English. Audrey was laughing. 'You give it to him, Judy. You tell him. It will do him good.'

One morning I began my make-up at the same time as Audrey, so I was able to watch her being made-up in the mirror. I was being made to look as if I had chicken pox. While red blobs were put all over my face I watched Audrey's Italian make-up man deftly and lightly applying the strokes to Audrey's face. Covered in spots, I left the room to go and rehearse and film the scene I had to do. After completing the scene, I returned to have the spots replaced with a straightforward make-up. By now Audrey's eyes were enormous but her make-up was still being applied. My man finished and I returned to the studio floor to rehearse the next scene while waiting for Audrey. When she eventually arrived she looked incredible, as always. 'I'm ready, so why are we waiting?' she said.

A good thing about working with a French crew is that the important things in life, like luncheon, are given plenty of time, and our lunch breaks were very civilized. Tables were laid out with brightly coloured tablecloths. Bottles of wine and mineral water were provided and the food was wonderful. Slowly we would return to work having eaten well and enjoyed everyone's company.

I was asked whether I wanted to see the rushes of the first day's filming – my first chance to see myself on a wide screen in colour. Albert Finney was already in the screening room. I was a bit in awe of him. I had first seen him starring in <i>Tom Jones</i> and thought he was a wonderful actor. Since then I had seen him giving the most brilliant performance as Martin Luther in a Manchester theatre when we were making Paris 1900. The screening started, and when I saw myself with my face spread across the screen, I hated how I looked. I thought I resembled a large Dutch cheese and I felt terribly depressed. There seemed no future in films for me. The lights went back on and Albert came up to me.

'It's awful, isn't it?'

'Yes, I was.'

'No you weren't. I meant the first time you see yourself on the large screen. I hated myself when I first saw myself. Thought I might as well give up.'

'That's how I feel.'

'Well, don't. We all feel like that. Come on, kid, I'll buy you a Coca-Cola.'

Albert was kind. He cheered me up and restored my confidence.

IT WAS TIME for Joanna and me to return to England. We weren't needed for a couple of weeks and then we would be returning to Paris to complete the rest of our scenes. I have never been able to travel in style. I do try to look like an elegant seasoned traveller but somehow I always end up with a plastic bag or two. I had bought some Belgian cotton cot sheets for Dylan and several little French baby sets. With the duty-free bags I looked like Mrs Bloggs with her Christmas shopping. When we reached Nice airport we saw David Niven and his glamorous wife waiting to board. From a distance she seemed very young. It was only when one got closer that you could see she was older than she had appeared. We were seated next to them and David wanted to know all about the film we were making and who was in it. He was a charming, friendly man. I kept wanting to pinch myself. This was an actor I had watched since I was a child. When we reached Heathrow we ran into Kirk Douglas, who was changing flights on his way to Los Angeles. He greeted David and we were introduced to him. Douglas too was charming and I felt slightly unreal, being with two film stars I had watched since childhood. Then Douglas said, 'Can I help anyone?' Not understanding the game of token politeness, and as I was struggling with my small cabin bag, my handbag and all my plastic bags, I took him up on his offer. 'Yes please,' I replied. 'Can you carry this?' I thrust my cabin bag into his hands. He looked slightly put out, but recovered and graciously carried my bag until he said his goodbyes and walked in the other direction for his connecting flight.

It was such a relief to be home with John and Dylan again. John wanted to know everything about Nice, and over a welcome cup of English tea I told him all about my adventures.

When I returned to Paris to film the rest of our scenes Carole Golder flew over to join me. She wanted to introduce me to a director who was in Paris for the weekend. We all went out for dinner on the Saturday evening and Don, the director, explained that he wanted to make a short film about two zany girls enjoying a weekend in London. Geraldine Chapman was to be the other girl. We would improvise according to the set-ups that he found. I thought it sounded fun so agreed to do it. It was only going to be for a few days after I finished *Two for the Road*.

The magic of Paris brings enormous energy and I took some of that energy back with me to shoot the film with Geraldine Chapman. It was a wild couple of days and we had a lot of fun but I never heard what happened to the film. I ran into Geraldine when we were both working in Budapest on a film in 1999. She had never heard anything about it either.

~

IN THE 1960s it was unusual for people of our age to own their own home. Even fewer of the previous generation owned theirs. England was more like Europe, where the majority of people lived in rented accommodation. Our friends watched with fascination as we braved the mysterious world of mortgages, home improvements and gardening. Soon they followed suit, realizing the benefits of owning rather than giving money to someone else. Annie Nightingale and Gordon Thomas bought an old house in the centre of Brighton. Annie was now well known as the first woman disc jockey on BBC Radio, and often pictures of her wearing her Courreges outfits with matching boots would appear in magazines; Gordon had left the *Argus* and now worked for BBC TV.

As my mother had only herself to look after now, she moved to an apartment close to the sea. My brother followed our example and bought a house. Thank goodness he and I did – a decade later, the whole property price lunacy began. In 1966 John and I lived in the suburbs but we had no intention of staying there. We often drove up one tree-lined street in the centre of Brighton because we loved the houses there. 'One day,' John said, 'I would love to live in one of these.' I made a mental note to try my best to make sure we did.

Another director named Don – Don Sharpe – wanted to meet me. Anglo Amalgamated Films were going to shoot Jules Verne's *Rocket to the Moon* in Ireland and he wanted me to play Lady Electra, the daughter of an eccentric scientist who was to be played by Dennis Price. The film was cast with big comedy stars. PT Barnum was played by Burl Ives; Tom Thumb, who was to be shot up to the moon from an extinct volcano, was played by Jimmy Clitheroe. Other big names were the German film star Gert Froebe, Terry Thomas, Lionel Jeffries, Hermione Gingold and the Israeli actress Daliah Lavi. I was booked for two months' filming and we were to be based in Dublin. I talked it over with John but two months was too long to be away from Dylan. So it was agreed that when I had settled into the film John would take his holidays and fly over with Dylan and Jenny, the au pair, and they would all stay with me in the hotel.

For the first week there were make-up tests, costumes to be fitted, photographs to be taken and wonderful, general rowdiness with the others in the evenings. Dennis Price immediately called me 'daughter'. 'Daughter, as we are not working today, I shall introduce you to one of the finer culinary experiences in Dublin. You are going to be taken, by me, to Jammet's.' Alas, the wonderful Jammet's no longer exists today, but I remember how right Dennis was about the wonderful food. Never before had I had wild strawberries with cream for pudding. Dennis loved the restaurant for its extended 'Holy Hour' which meant he could have more Guinness. He told me about his home on the island of Sark and how he had to behave or the Dame of Sark could ask him to leave. Sark was a tax haven. By then, lots of actors and writers had left England because of the high taxes. Some had gone to America, some to the Channel Islands or Ireland, and a few to Switzerland or Monaco. But of course, most of us just stayed in England and paid up.

One night in Jury's when Dennis was buying a round of Irish coffees a man came up to him and asked if he was Dennis Price, the actor. Thinking the man wanted his autograph, Dennis said yes. But he was from the British Inland Revenue and promptly served some papers on him. We were all shocked when it happened and commiserated with poor Dennis for the rest of the evening.

Don Sharpe was a brilliant director. He understood that with comedy actors you either got the take in the first two shots or the scene would take up to sixty attempts, so he set up everything to make sure that the actors were happy before the first take. When you are on a film location, it is like a small travelling community which sets up camp in different places. Once you know where the wardrobe is, the make-up van, the catering van and the lavatories, you can retire to your own caravan and work on your script. If you want to hear all the company gossip you head for wardrobe or make-up. They are the eyes and ears of the world and usually have the best coffee too.

I was fascinated by Burl Ives, who ate only a macrobiotic diet and had a lady to cook it for him. He explained to me that people who had the whites of their eyes showing below the iris are prone to die violent deaths so it is important to eat a calming diet. It was the latest theory coming from America. I looked into the mirror in my caravan and was happy to see I did not need to follow such a philosophy and could go on eating steaks.

Daliah discovered she was pregnant during the film and so had to keep having her costumes let out. There was a constant stream of journalists and photographers descending on the publicity caravan, and whenever I had a spare moment I seemed to be interviewed by someone, until I was sick of talking about myself. I wanted to be with all the naughty ones like Grahame Stark and Lionel Jeffries who had a constant fund of wonderful stories to tell. One day Lionel was filming a hunting scene and he asked some of the Irish extras for an Irish word for Tally Ho. 'Ah, that would be poke mahone,' one of the Irishmen told him. So with gay abandon Lionel yelled 'Poke mahone' as he galloped across the field. When the film was shown in Ireland and Lionel shouted it out on the screen, the whole cinema erupted with laughter. It meant 'Kiss my arse.'

After filming one day I asked for room service to bring me a pot of tea. The hotel porter arrived and placed the tray on a table but hovered about, shifting his weight from one foot to the other. He was staring intently at the carpet when he blurted out, 'You're with the fillums, aren't you?' I was cautious but replied that I was working as an actress on a film. He then nervously began to wring his hands, 'Do you have any contraceptives?' The penny dropped. The poor man. Contraceptives were banned in Catholic Ireland and he was hoping I could give him some. I replied that I did not personally have any but that I would ask the men on the unit whether they had any to spare. The porter's face lit up. Promising to call back the following evening, he fairly danced out of the room.

The next day I went round to all the crew and, after explaining the situation which resulted in a lot of ribaldry, asked whether any of them had some spare condoms. I collected about six packets. That evening, there was a tap on my bedroom door, and the hotel porter arrived with a tray of tea. I showed him my collection of packets. His face looked as bright as a child receiving his longed-for Christmas present and he was absent from work during the following week.

The family arrived for a fortnight and were fascinated to see the filming. Dylan was now nearly fifteen months old. Aware of how I could remember back to my childhood, I watched his curiosity and expressions very carefully. He loved the whole experience of pressing buttons for room service and watching all the actors running around in scenes on location. On the days I was not needed on the set we would go out to the countryside; we also took Dylan to the Dublin Zoo.

I was sad when they left for England but I knew I was going to be busy working for the remaining weeks. It was during this time I met an American called John Dolan who had been a photographer with Hearst newspapers. He was on the set one day shooting film and he was telling me that he and his wife, Joan, were moving to Ireland from New York. She wanted to visit London soon and would John and I meet up with them. I gave him my telephone number and told him to ring us when they arrived.

~

JOHN AND JOAN got in touch with us when they were in London and asked us to join them for tea at the Ritz. Joan was a wonderfully zany person, a character never to be forgotten. She was a Pisces, like me, and I found myself laughing like a teenager with a best friend. The tea was the most wonderful I had ever experienced – tiny sandwiches, small melt-in-your-mouth scones and seriously wicked cakes. The two Johns entertained us with journalist stories and we were sorry when the meal came to an end.

They asked us to come and stay with them for a week's holiday in Ireland, assuring us they had enough room for our son and the au pair and a garden where Dylan could play. We agreed to go over in October because I had a film to make for American International films in France in September, *The Wild Racers*, about life on the motor-racing circuit.

Fabian, a famous American pop star, was playing a racing-car driver and I was a groupie who followed the racers. I had lots of beautiful minis to wear in the film and lots of fast changes as we set up scene after scene, so I was often changing in the back of a moving van. One of my romantic scenes with Fabian took place in a boat. It was so small there was only enough spare room in the boat for the cameraman. Fabian was rowing so I had to use the clapper board, then go into the romantic love scene while occasionally stopping mid-sentence to warn Fabian that he was about to hit the river bank.

There were a lot of Canadian actors in the film, an Australian actor and some Americans. The French film crew were the team who had shot *Un Homme et une Femme*, which had won countless awards, and they worked really fast. I had a lot of fun working on the film but also noticed that some of the actors and American crew were using drugs like LSD and marijuana. I listened to the seductive voices' reasons for taking drugs and rejected them. To me, the philosophies were ersatz, substitutes for spending a bit of time and effort on meditation or thinking things through. Most of the people I spoke to wanted instant revelation or instant genius, when often they were not equipped to experience either.

When I returned home, John and I decided the MGB had to go because it was impractical. John was very sad because he loved the red sports car as much as I had loved my first Morris. We bought a white Mini, and when it was loaded up with toys and suitcases, we set off to catch the ferry to Ireland.

Everyone was excited about going on holiday. John had all the instructions to find Joan and John's house, in Black Rock, but we were quite unprepared for the huge house and gardens we found. It was a mini stately home. They had been right when they told us there was plenty of room. There were dogs everywhere and a cook, a cleaner and a secretary. John and Joan showed us to our rooms. They were giving a dinner to introduce us to some of their friends that night.

Later, when Dylan had eaten his supper and gone to bed, we all dressed for dinner and waited for the guests. The actor Ray McAnally and his actress wife Ronnie Masterson turned up with a few other people John and Joan knew. We sat at a long highly polished dinner table and there was a roaring fire at one end of the room. Just after the first course something ran down the centre of the table. Ronnie nearly fell off her chair. It was Joan's pet mongoose. She had bought it from Harrods, she informed us as we all recovered from the shock. While she was telling us all about the old house and we were wondering whether it was haunted, the large dining-room door slowly opened. Everyone froze. Then a little voice said 'Hello'. It was Dylan. Only we could not see him over the edge of the table, he was so tiny. He said, 'I think the man needs a bath he's so dirty.' The men got up from the table to see who he was talking about but there was no one there.

John told us the famous rebel leader Michael Collins had stumbled into the house after he had been shot. He was supposed to have died there. Whoever it was Dylan had seen I realized then that my little son had the same fey streak that I had. So it was not the influence of Benbecula for me but it was in the genes. I remembered my grandmother telling me about an Irish ancestor called Septimus Hennessy from Cork, who had been a seventh son of a seventh son. He had left Ireland for India, taken up tea planting and built a dam, then renounced his Catholic faith to become a Buddhist. Perhaps it was his genes we were carrying.

We had a wonderful week in Ireland visiting all the beauty spots with John and Joan. Joan and I decided that as we were both Pisceans we should pick a day between 22 February and 9 March each year and have a joint celebration of a birthday tea at the Ritz. The two Johns agreed it was a great idea and so a tradition began.

～

THERE WERE ALL the preparations for Christmas to be arranged. I was told that the local Scouts were raising money by one of the scout masters dressing up as Santa Claus and delivering presents on Christmas morning. All we had to do was wrap up our child's present and pay the Scouts a donation for it to be delivered. So I booked the Santa Claus for our house and began telling Dylan the traditional story about Santa. There was a lot of squeaking from the nursery one night. I ran up the stairs to find the toddler standing by the window, peeping through the curtains and shouting he could see Santa Claus. I thought maybe I had gone too far with the story telling until I looked out of the window. In the garden behind ours was a greenhouse, where a man was obviously trying on his Santa outfit for some function or other.

John loved the whole pre-Christmas planning. His family had never gone to the lengths that mine had over the celebrations, and he enjoyed every minute of it. Now my mother had grandchildren, she told us she would give a Christmas Eve lunch for the family and then she would come to our house for the Christmas Day dinner. Jenny went off for her Christmas holidays and we had the house to ourselves. It was wonderful to enjoy Dylan's first aware Christmas.

Unfortunately, my carefully laid plans for Santa Claus delivering a late present backfired. A thin Santa Claus with a black moustache from another organization came sauntering up the steps with the wrong present. It was meant for a child down the road. Dylan was watching from the window as I sent him away. As he left, another fat Santa Claus with a snowy-white beard was turning into the road. He was the one with our present and presented the parcel to Dylan with a lot of 'Ho Ho Hos' so one little boy enjoyed meeting Santa. However, after such a mix-up we kept to the mythical Santa for future years, that is until Dylan began to set booby traps to catch Father Christmas. We had cooked a goose for dinner that Christmas, and to hear his small piping voice sing 'Goosie Goosie Gander' as he associated the word with the words of the nursery rhyme was a moment I shall never forget.

For some time now, my brother and his wife had been writing and sending tapes to my father. I was really glad that at last they were getting on so well. On Christmas Eve Brian announced that Dad was hoping to come over to England for a holiday. I was surprised. If he was so ill that my arrival in Australia would kill him, how could he possibly manage a trip to England? Nevertheless, the idea that he was thinking about the journey gave us a lot of hope that we might soon see him.

∼

LEONARD WHITE, WITH whom I had performed poetry readings for the Newhaven Boys' Club with Bill Owen, was now the producer of ABC TV's Armchair Theatre series. In January 1967, he sent me a two-hander script written by Ernest Gebler, called *Call Me Daddy*. The story was about a rich businessman who blackmails one of his typists into spending a weekend at his apartment on the eve of her marriage to a despatch clerk. Instead of making love to her, he introduces her to the delights of good living to a point where she falls in love with him of her own free will. Donald Pleasance was to play the businessman, Mr Hoffman, and Leonard wanted me to play the typist, Miss Smith. Alvin Rakoff was to direct it. We had three weeks' rehearsal and then one day in the studio for a technical rehearsal before having three hours the following day to tape it.

I loved working with Alvin; we had the freedom to explore our characters and try all sorts of inventive business. Donald was a man with a great sense of humour and we got on really well together. Ernest Gebler would come to rehearsals and was so inspired watching our work that he eventually wrote a book about it. He used my photograph on the book cover and told me that I reminded him physically of his first wife, only I was more 'straightforward' – she was the writer Edna O'Brien. Just before we were to go into the studio we found we were a few minutes under time, so Donald and I improvised a scene until the play was the right length.

Straight after I had completed *Call Me Daddy* I went on to a play called *Go Tell It on Table Mountain*, by Evan Jones, Joanna Jones's husband. It was for BBC TV and the director was Toby Robinson. It was a play about racism and I was working with Paul Daneman and a fine black actor called Calvin Lockharte. We used masks for certain scenes to hide our characters' real feelings and then removed them to show the reality of relationships. It was while I was working on the BBC TV play that Carole called to say that I was wanted in Hollywood. I was to be flown over first class on TWA to Los Angeles where I would stay at the Beverly Hills Hotel. The William Morris Agency would be looking after me while I was in Hollywood and would go with me to the studios. There was much excitement at home and John reassured me not to worry about anything. So off I flew to Tinsel Town.

Arriving in Los Angeles was like taking part in a fairy tale surrounded by carbon monoxide. I was whisked away by car to the hotel which rose out of the ground like a large pink blancmange. I was given a beautiful suite overlooking a vast twinkling expanse of Los Angeles. There were flowers and fruit and lots of messages with a packet of dollars for spending money. When I sent for room service, the tray arrived with a single red rose carefully placed in a thin glass vase. Everything was beautiful and luxurious. I had been made to feel very welcome and had vivid Wizard of Oz dreams all night.

For the morning meeting with the agents I wore a white mini kaftan. They were obviously not used to minis but seemed to approve. I was looked at, sized up and told when and where I was to meet the studio heads that week, and one of the agents was chosen to look after me at all times and accompany me to meetings. This he did thoroughly and efficiently, wanting to know each day what I had been doing, who I had been seeing and advising where not to go and what not to do.

Among the suits I had to meet was Robert Wise, who was about to produce *Star!* with Julie Andrews. He was thrilled that I had a musical background and he was charming. My agent told me that in his opinion it was a most successful meeting but I was just glad when it was over. Many of the studio men had large smiles with beautifully white teeth, but their eyes were hard. For the first time in my career I felt more like a product rather than just me.

I was also invited out a lot. Once I went to the exclusive Daisy Club and danced until the early hours. I often went to Chasen's, the 'in' restaurant at that time, and I ran into a lot of British actors and writers. I saw my old friend Lionel Jeffries on the *Camelot* set. He was covered head to foot in metal armour and reclining on an armchair in his dressing room.

'Is that you, Cornwell?' he said.

'Yes.'

'This is what it all boils down to at a certain age – they dress you up like a tin man. I can't even pee without my dresser helping me. I mean, where's the dignity in that?'

The agents called to tell me that Twentieth Century Fox were offering me a long-term contract, starting with a part in *Star!* The agent in charge of me was thrilled and told me about the money offered; I said I would think about it. Everyone was excited about the Hollywood offer except me. I had been treated kindly by everyone I had met, had had a lot of fun and explored a lot of places, yet I felt homesick, both for my family and friends, and for a slower pace of life. Constantly smiling made my cheeks ache. 'Have a nice day' and the standard cheerful patter was thrown into confusion if an unusual question was asked. Life was on happy, happy automatic in LA; nothing of importance was discussed, merely the trivial, because everyone wanted to be liked by everyone. I realized that I did not have that 'divine self-obsession' needed to be a film star and became bored with the whole charade quickly. At the age of twenty-seven, I had to look hard at what was really important to me, not to agents. My husband and son were too precious for me to spend months away from Britain, and John was an English journalist whose career was as important as mine. I also weighed up work in England against working in LA. British TV was hugely varied at the time. Within ITV alone there were nine outlets producing drama and series. I enjoyed working on a variety of roles and had built up a reputation for being versatile so I didn't want to end up being typecast. I also knew I could earn more money in England, even with the high taxes, than the dollar income on offer. So I turned down the offer and flew back to England. That first cuddle from my Dylan when I arrived at Heathrow confirmed I had made the right decision.

~

As soon as I got home from America I was asked to attend the press launch for *Call Me Daddy*. I glammed up for the occasion and put on my white kaftan mini and wore some false eyelashes. To complete the ensemble I carried a newly fashionable bead bag. The first person I was introduced to when I arrived was a showbusiness journalist, David Nathan. As we shook hands my eyelashes came unstuck and dangled in front of my eyes like two big spiders; then my bead bag broke, spilling beads all over the floor. David found it highly amusing and had his story; I retired to the ladies' room to remove the eyelashes.

By now several scripts had arrived for me to read. One was another from Leonard White at ABC TV, *Wind in the Tall Paper Chimney* written by Robert Holles. The part I was offered was a spy posing as a model trying to seduce a rocket technician. I loved the script and began work immediately with Donald Sinden and Bernard Cribbins, who were wonderful actors and great fun. The second script was from BBC TV. A director called James Ferman, who years later became the British Film Censor, wanted me to play Maria in Vaclav Havel's *The Memorandum*. The play was about the destruction of communications by a bureaucracy inventing its own language, called ptydipe, and how, eventually, the freedom of speech and understanding is destroyed by control of language. Vaclav Havel was in trouble as a dissident at that time but after the Berlin Wall came down and he became president of Czechoslovakia, he visited London. During the visit, he was shown the play and was absolutely thrilled with it.

James Ferman was very clever with his casting of comedy actors in the roles of the bureaucrats, which added a wonderfully sinister quality to the play. Warren Mitchell, Alfred Marks and Hatty Jacques, all famous for their comedy performances, were just a few of the actors involved. So while the audience laughed at their antics, they realized they were being sucked into a totalitarian regime. My part was as the young girl, Maria, the one person who knows the code to the bureaucratic language, ptydipe, and manages to break away and escape from the collapsing regime.

I think it is time the play was resurrected by the BBC. Society needs to be warned about the destruction of language and meaning

and the control of free speech and information, especially nowadays as we head towards global gobbledegook and multi-national
totalitarianism.

We filmed the final scene of the play, which was Maria's
eventual escape from the regime, at St Pancras Station. And for the
first time I ran into the hatred and malice that is sometimes directed
at actors. A crowd of people had gathered behind the camera to
watch the filming. One young woman was enraged by me, or the
character I was playing. As I ran towards the camera she stepped
out from the crowd, screamed 'stupid bitch' and spat at me. She
was chased away by the crew. Luckily we had managed to get the
shot we needed before she stepped forward or I would have had
to do it all again. But I was shocked by the sounds of venom and
hatred. I suppose she saw me getting a lot of attention and working in what everyone always thinks is a glamorous occupation, and
it was too much for her. It is a strange and peculiar trait among
British halfwits, or should I be politically correct and call them the
emotionally challenged. Their usual targets are actors who play
tough coppers or villians on TV. The number of times these actors
are set upon in pubs by macho halfwits who want to challenge
them to a fight is legendary. Many young actresses, including
myself in the past, receive foul letters from dysfunctional idiots, or
should we say the sexually challenged. It is therefore rather com-
forting at this stage of my life to be associated worldwide with a
character (Daisy in *Keeping Up Appearances*) that has been accepted
as a real, underprivileged, sexually deprived, badly dressed,
placid, down-trodden person. There is no threat to anyone from
this character. She makes everyone feel that there is someone worse
off than they are. Although, if I step out of character as myself, I
can still offend people. As one very elegantly dressed woman on
the *QE2* said to me, 'That's a nice dress you're wearing.'

'I do have some nice dresses,' I replied.

'Well,' she huffed and puffed. 'Well, I shan't feel sorry for you
any more.' Then she stormed off; all because I was wearing a pretty
dress and looking reasonably presentable. I realized that I had
taken away her security blanket.

~

AFTER I HAD finished *The Memorandum*, Leonard White phoned and gave me some very good advice as he offered me another play. He suggested that at twenty-seven I should start playing the occasional older role so that people would be used to me moving in and out of age groups. That way I would not have a hard time as an actress when I got older. He wanted me to play Abbie, a sub-urban woman in her middle thirties, who was the 'other woman' in a story about a marriage breakdown. It was *Poor Cherry*, one of Fay Weldon's first TV plays, and had Dilys Laye, Peter Arne, John Wood and Jane Birkin in it. Fay came to watch the recording. The following day she sent me a great big bouquet of flowers from Harrods with a very complimentary note.

When I got home after recording *Poor Cherry* John was waiting for me with a very serious look on his face. I immediately knew something was wrong and wondered whether Dylan was ill. After assuring me that our son was all right, John then told me that my father had died. He was surprised at my reaction. I laughed. I think the reason I behaved so strangely was because I had already grieved so long for the loss of my father and the disappointment of being unable to go back to Australia to see him, that it was a relief for the continual emotional tug of war to be over. The final sense of loss and wasted opportunity did not arrive until a few months later, after it had been wriggling away underneath a heap of other layers of regrets. Only then could I finally let it go.

Some time later, John was offered a job with BBC TV as a reporter on *Tomorrow's World*, a new science programme presented by Raymond Baxter. James Burke was also employed at the same time. Excited by the new challenge, John handed in his notice to the *Express*.

My au pair Jenny decided it was time to leave as she was shortly going to get married, and a new girl called Beverley, from Yorkshire, joined us. We decided that it was time our son was christened and we asked my lovely mentor, Sybil Wise, to be his godmother. Kazzy, our Polish friend with a restaurant, was one godfather along with Mike Ritchie from the Navigational

Institute. He had sailed his yacht, *Jester*, single-handed across the Atlantic and back and was a wonderfully adventurous godfather to have. We asked Allon Bacon, the composer, to be the third godfather. Between the four godparents we thought we had covered all the different interests a child could pursue. Dylan loved Sybil's company. The two of them would sit happily talking to each other for hours. Kazzy too turned out to be a wonderful godfather.

My father's death had affected not only me, my mother and brother, but also my godmother, Musi. She had been writing to him ever since I had given her his address. Now, grieving for her lost friend, her letters to me were far more frequent. She insisted on repeating the tradition of supplying children's books, but to my son this time. As he was already having bedtime stories told to him, he and I now shared another bond, a cultural bond, and a cultural shorthand that we use to this day.

~

CHRISTMAS 1967 CAME AND went. Now both John and I were appearing on television. The Granada TV producer Peter Wildeblood, who had cast me in the Younger Generation Players, offered me the part of Lucy Hodges, a sort of female Tom Jones. Lucy was a sixteen-year-old girl from the country who tries her luck in London. After hectic affairs of the heart she ends up in Newgate Prison and is sentenced to death but at the last moment is transported to the new colonies of America. On the way there, she is shipwrecked and captured by Red Indians. The series of hourly plays went out under the title of *Rogues Gallery*.

There was thick snow on the ground when we started rehearsals in January, which meant leaving home earlier than usual in case the train to London was delayed. David Cunliffe, who had been a floor manager with us on the Younger Generation, was now a director, and a very good one.

After rehearsing in London we then had to go up to Manchester for the studio days. Aware that I was playing sixteen, I needed to be in bed early so booked into the Midland Hotel. Peter Wildeblood would walk me to the hotel after rehearsals to make sure I did not go off gadding with the other actors. At the read-through I found out that John Laurimore, with whom I had shared the cottage in Llandudno, was playing Pocahock, one of the Indian warriors. We caught up on all our news. He was no longer married to Zoe, with whom he had so romantically eloped to the strains of Sibelius' *Karelia* suite. A beautiful young man, playing one of Lucy's earlier seducers, was Kenneth Cranham. He was a wonderful actor and we made each other laugh a lot.

For Ralph Bates this was his first television job. Later he made many horror films, always playing the hero fighting against Dracula and other horrible entities. But in this television series he was cast as an Indian warrior who had just caught Lucy and was dragging her to the main wigwam to be confronted by the Indian chief. When we got to our scene in the play Ralph was very nervous. It was freezing and he only had his loin cloth on; there were goose pimples all over his skin and he was shivering with cold and nerves. The floor manager started the countdown . . . 10, 9, . . . and Ralph farted with fright in time to the countdown. I got the giggles. 'Don't laugh, Judy!' Ralph pleaded, still farting, and we were waved on into the scene. I could hardly breathe I was so convulsed with laughter. Somehow we did the scene. How I got any dialogue out I do not know, I hardly dared look at him.

When we had completed the recording I half expected to be made to do the scene again, but Peter was very pleased with it and said my breathless fear in the wigwam was very good. It was not quite breathless fear, but suppressed laughter, which all goes to prove what you see is not necessarily what is going on. One of the scenes had me talking to camera while ostensibly being seduced, while fully dressed, on a bed. My head was bouncing up and down while I spoke. Some of the extras complained that this was obscene and walked off the set. Oh, what would they make of the scenes they film now!

From playing a sixteen-year-old hoyden I went straight into a sophisticated BBC TV Wednesday play called *Infidelity Took Place*, written by John Mortimer. It was about a successful married couple whose combined salaries put them into the supertax bracket. They decide to divorce and live in sin and the wife consults a lawyer, giving him false grounds for divorce. But the lawyer sees her as a damsel in distress who would make a suitable mate when he has delivered her from the clutches of her dreadful husband. Ludicrous misunderstandings follow with the lawyer and his hired detective, a retired major, totally misinterpreting the married couple's actions. My husband was played by Paul Daneman and the lawyer by John Nettleton; Patrick Newell played the very round comic detective. On one day's filming, when the detective was following the wife to an island where she was secretly trying to meet her husband, Patrick had to grab a canoe and paddle in my direction. Unfortunately no one had anticipated the effect Patrick's weight would have on the canoe. He paddled gamely forward and then the canoe tilted up and sank. We were all roaring with laughter until we realized he was drowning. Someone leapt in to rescue him and he was put in the back of a car while the assistant floor manager took his clothes to the nearest launderette to dry them – The BBC is not known to waste filming time. Once dressed, Patrick did the scene again, only with weights in the front of the canoe. The play was very popular because everyone in Britain was sick of paying too much tax.

While working on *Infidelity Took Place* I was told Anthony Newley wanted to meet me. He was going to direct and star in a film he had written called, improbably, *Can Hieronymous Merkin Ever Forget Mercy Humppe and Find True Happiness?* It was going to be shot in Malta and I would be there for a couple of months. It was basically the story of his life, a film within a film.

I was to play Filigree Fondle, his first wife, who was modelled on Ann Lynn, Newley's real first wife. She was an actress whose work I had admired, so I was very flattered to be offered the role. His second wife, Joan Collins, would play his second wife in the film. I liked meeting Tony Newley and told him I would love to do the film but first I had to finish another play for BBC 2, *The Fall of Kelvin Walker* with Corin Redgrave and Harry H. Corbett. Corin knew I was going to Malta and gave me the telephone number of his wife Deirdre's family who lived there.

Malta is predominantly Roman Catholic and during my first night in a charming old hotel in Valletta, I was kept awake by church bells ringing, bands playing and the noise of fireworks as the Maltese celebrated a *festa* in honour of one of their patron saints.

The whole film was to be shot on a beach location. A car drove me to the unit base where I met up with all the other actors. Along the vast, white sandy shore I could see a big brass bed surrounded by lights and the camera all set up. That was where I would be shooting my scene.

There is nothing guaranteed to cause more neurosis than trying to time a speech for a lighting man who wants your speech to coincide with the sun just partly covered by a cloud. With a background of clear blue sky we would wait patiently until one small fluffy cloud meandered across the great blue dome towards our location on the beach. Make-up checks were done quickly, hair combed and the brain tried to keep calm and cool. We began the action as the first tendrils softened the sun and finished as the cloud finally passed. Cheers from the crew, while my back was drenched in perspiration.

Tony Newley was an actor's director. He knew the key words to give you so that you could give him the performance he wanted. I just loved working with him. My friend Victor Spinetti was playing the producer in the film and there were people like George Jessel, Milton Berle, Stubby Kaye, Bruce Forsyth, Patricia Hayes, Julian Orchard and Desmond Walter Ellis in the cast and lots of beautiful girls.

The respectable Maltese society was very put out by our miniskirts. We were not allowed to enter any churches and some of the older peasant women would spit at us. Often, while filming on the beach, we would see above the sand dunes, like stalking Red Indians, the tufts of hair belonging to young Maltese males trying to catch a glimpse of the girls.

Joan Collins spent most of her time with her secretary and children on the beach and posing for photographs not far from where any of the scenes were being played. I wondered whether she had read the script properly as she laughed and cavorted with some of her friends. I was shocked to see that what Tony Newley was telling her in the script was that after he had finished the film he was leaving her.

My new nanny, Beverley, arrived in Malta with Dylan, who inspected the hotel with great glee, and the hotel owners were prepared to arrange special supper times for him. Deirdre Redgrave's family, the Hamilton Hills, were very hospitable. I was able to take Beverley and Dylan on their boat, and when Dylan fell and banged his head their eldest son made sure he was examined by a good doctor. The greatest nightmare for working mothers is that accidents and illnesses with children always happen when you are up to your eyes in work. I was filming on the beach when Dylan turned up at the film set with his head in a bandage. I was beside myself with panic, guilt and all the other emotions that career mums go through. There was one stitch in his forehead but it soon healed. The warm weather and playing in the paddling pools near the hotel quickly turned him into a healthy little brown person.

Then the photographers arrived. Unknown to me, *Call Me Daddy* had won an Emmy. The fact that for the first time Britain had taken the TV drama Emmy away from the Americans had not been given much attention at home, and Leonard White had flown to Washington only to find the ceremony cancelled due to rioting in the streets after the assassination of Martin Luther King. He then flew to New York where he was unceremoniously handed the Emmy in the International Press Club. It was quite an anticlimax. However, I felt a quietly wonderful satisfaction that although I had turned my back on a Hollywood contract, I had gone on to beat the Americans at their own game in TV by taking the Emmy from under their noses.

ABC TV repeated the play and released a press statement about the Emmy. That coincided with about three other plays I had made going out at the same time. Fleet Street show-business writers accompanied by their photographers decided to take short breaks in Malta and I was photographed and interviewed.

When David Nathan turned up, the film company public relations woman arranged for us to have dinner after the day's filming. At dinner, David reminded me about how my eyelashes had fallen off at the press launch of *Call Me Daddy*. 'I hope nothing is going to happen to you over dinner,' he laughed. Just then I sneezed. The chain belt I was wearing around my waist broke and flew across the dining room, hitting a waiter who was carrying a tray of food which he immediately dropped. We laughed all the way through dinner.

~

ON ARRIVAL BACK in England after completing the film, Beverley gave in her notice saying that she was returning to Yorkshire, but agreed to stay while I worked on an hour-long episode of *Mickey Dunn*, starring Dinsdale Landen. It was a lovely zany comedy part to play and I liked working with Dinsdale. When Beverley left we advertised for another mother's help. John and I had the house to ourselves again and he was able to get some holiday leave from the BBC so we planned a holiday.

Our friend Allon Bacon offered us his studio flat in Saint Tropez to rent for three weeks. We were able to give him the rent money in England, as in 1968 no one was allowed to take more than fifty pounds out of the country. With Dylan counting as a person we could take one hundred and fifty pounds to spend, so would have to live quite frugally. We set off with tinned butter and packets of onion soup among other foods in the back of our Morris shooting brake and drove via Dieppe to the South of France. John had mocked up a tape of a request programme mentioning Dylan's name and playing all his favourite songs. With a talking Bugs Bunny in the back of the car with him he was happy during the long journey to Saint Tropez.

Late at night we arrived at the studio and had to clean the flat after a recent mistral had left dust everywhere. Our holiday started the next day. Armed with rubber rings, sunshades, an ice cooler and a plastic boat we would tramp across wonderfully hot beaches and spend the whole day in and out of the sea. In the evening we would occasionally go out for dinner at Gassin, where John proved how brilliant he was at inventing stories for small boys. Dylan enjoyed the French food and was picking up quite a few French words. He was now thoroughly used to restaurants with all the travelling he had done and was very well mannered for a three-year-old.

One morning, while we were walking along a new beach

carrying all our paraphernalia, Dylan shouted, 'That man hasn't got his costume on.' I looked up and sure enough we were on a nudist beach. We immediately turned round and walked all the way back with Dylan giving a running commentary on the various states of grown-up nudity while John and I kept our heads down. Somehow we managed to eat very well on our one hundred and fifty pounds, even having enough left over to buy some pottery to take back to England.

~

WHEN WE RETURNED home Bridget came to work for us. She had been the under-nanny at the Christies, who own Glyndebourne Opera House. She was a lovely girl and we were very lucky to have her. We also bought Dylan a puppy, which he chose himself: an oatmeal-coloured Cairn terrier we called Harry Parry, after the jazz clarinettist.

There were two television scripts and two film scripts waiting for me at home. The first TV script was an hour-long, two-hander love story called *Have We Done It Again?*, written by Robert Muller, about a photographer and a model. It was a story based on his own romance and eventual marriage to Billie Whitelaw. Barry Justice played the photographer. As it was for ATV and their studios were in Pinewood, I decided to stay in London, at the Connaught Hotel, the night before the studio day. John arrived back from a trip to America for the BBC the night I was there. After finding out where I was from Bridget he turned up at the hotel, where I was booked in under the name Cornwell. When he insisted on seeing me late at night the concierge came up to my room with him. Even though we assured him that we were married, he insisted in escorting John off the premises – they were very proper in London in 1968. I telephoned Barry Justice and John went round to his place and slept in the spare room there for the night.

After the love story I worked on a play for the BBC called *One Two Sky's Blue*, written by Charlotte Bingham and Terence Brady. It was a trivial play but had James Bolam and Brian Pringle in it who were great to work with. It was also the first time I worked for the director Bill Hays, someone for whom I had enormous respect. He was to become a great friend in the future. The story was about a zany ex-ballet dancer, which suited me well. I discovered that Bill Hays, like me, was also ex-ballet and the cameraman too was an ex-dancer.

As soon as I finished the BBC play I was on the night flight to Dublin, learning my script on the plane, to play Nuala, an Anglo-Irish nymphomaniac, in the film *Paddy*, from the book *Goodbye to the Hill* written by Lee Dunne. It was produced by American International Pictures and I worked with the lovely actor Milo O'Shea. Back from Ireland I worked straightaway on a film for the Children's Film Foundation, playing a villain in *Cry Wolf*. By now I was getting very tired, and it was a relief to be back home.

~

I WAS OFFERED another film but I had also received a stage play called *They Don't Grow on Trees*. The play read well and seemed very funny. The producer Michael Codron asked me to lunch so I could meet Val May, the director. I enjoyed the lunch but was a bit wary of the director. I should have listened to my instincts but, instead, went against them and I turned down the film – which I should have taken – and agreed to do the play. My agent Carole too thought it would be good for me to do the play. She had just broken up with her husband and was sorting out her own relationship problems. We both made a bad decision.

As soon as rehearsals started I knew I had made a mistake. Most of the directors I had worked with let me find my own natural way of working and discovering the humour in a situation. This director wanted to tell me every inflection, every movement, right from the first moment I spoke. I was working with Ronald Lewis, who was playing my husband. He was a lovely Welsh actor and seemed able to cope pretty well. The other members of the cast were Dora Bryan and Hugh Paddick. What had looked good on the page slowly became a rather second-rate comedy. I knew it was not going to work. When we opened in Manchester I felt ashamed to be part of it and told Carole she had to get me out. There was no way I wanted to go to London in this play. Eventually the producer agreed to release me providing I stayed until a replacement could take over. The press started sniffing around and I just said I had a previous film commitment, but I have never been so glad to leave a show. I was right, it did not do well in London and it was good to be home. A telegram from Bill Hays said, 'I wondered how long you would last on that play. Well done for leaving.'

Then a film public relations officer phoned me to tell me that a friend of hers, a producer called Ben Arbied, was interested in acquiring the filming rights of *Call Me Daddy*, and could I give them Ernie Gebler's telephone number. When I contacted Ernie, he immediately asked whether I knew an agent who could handle the deal, so I put him in touch with Carole. They got together and Carole let me know that the producer wanted Peter Sellers to play the main character, Hoffman. I was appalled that they were not going to offer the part to Donald Pleasance, who had given such a brilliant performance in the play. Sellers was quite the wrong sort of actor to play Hoffman. Also, I was told, Sellers did not want a well-known actress like me to play the part of Miss Smith but thought it would be better to have an unknown. The producer was worried that he would not be able to find a young unknown who could match my performance and asked whether I would be prepared to stand by in case they could not find anyone else. I was amazed that Carole could even think I would consider this sort of arrangement and I lost interest in the whole project.

It was at this time that I was introduced to John Mather. John was in charge of the London office of William Morris Agency, which was linked up to the Hollywood agency that had looked after me when I was there. He asked John and me to a Christmas party at his home just off Eaton Square, where we were introduced to Richard Eastham and his wife. John Mather told us that if I joined the agency Richard would be the agent to manage my career. I liked Richard, a dapper little man with a great sense of humour and extremely shrewd. Mather told me how he thought my career should be handled and asked me to consider the offer.

For a week I fretted about whether I should leave Carole and Kavanagh's. I had been with them for ten years and felt a great loyalty to them. I also knew that since Carole's break-up with her husband she was restless and I sensed she wanted to change her life, so I agreed to join William Morris.

Daniel Massey once told me, 'You know, Judy, I really believe one should change one's agent and one's wife every seven years.' It is not quite as light-hearted as that; to break with an agent is often a heart-wrenching experience. Luckily, Carole and I remained good friends for much longer than she was my agent.

Chapter Thirteen

1969–1971

~

IT WAS THE last year of the Sixties. Already midi-skirts were trying to enter the fashion world. I had worn one when I worked with Corin Redgrave on the BBC TV production of *The Rise and Fall of Kelvin Walker* the previous year. The BBC wardrobe department who had designed the skirt for me had wondered how long it would be before the fashion would catch on. Most of the men moaned about it. Naturally, they wanted the mini-skirts kept. I was perfectly happy to change to the midi. Minis were fine in the summer but when it was cold a midi was much kinder to your legs. Sometimes in the Sixties, especially in the winter, we would all look quite absurd wrapped up well in mini fun furs, with boots, gloves and warm hats but still exposing our knees and thighs to the cold. Towards the end of 1969 the maxi appeared; this was ankle-length, so hemlines became variable.

At the beginning of the year, Richard Eastham phoned to say that Herbert Wise wanted me to play Ginny in Alan Ayckbourn's *Relatively Speaking* for BBC TV. Celia Johnson, Donald Sinden and John Stride were to be in the play. This was the first of the commercial plays Alan had written while working for Leeds BBC Radio, just after we had worked together in *Mr Whatnot*. *Relatively Speaking* had received glowing reviews when it opened in the West End. I was thrilled to be working on my old friend's play, and also excited about finally working with Herbert Wise, the man who had recommended me to the Younger Generation producers nearly a decade earlier. I was a bit overwhelmed about working with Celia Johnson. Once, while taking part in a reading for a play written by

Hugh Williams, Hugh had told me that mine was the best comedy sight-reading since Celia Johnson had read for him. He had wanted me for the part in his play *The Flip Side* at the time but his producer wanted someone else. Just being praised and compared with Celia had given me an enormous boost in confidence. Now I was to be working with her. I had already worked with Donald Sinden and liked him, and I knew John Stride, but at the read-through I was almost tongue-tied – I was so in awe of Celia. However, she was friendly and charming with a wicked sense of humour and she soon put me at ease.

We began the three weeks of rehearsals in a church hall in St John's Wood. As I had admired Audrey Hepburn with her incredible film technique, so I was able to watch and learn from Celia. She had played the part in the West End and every gesture, every inflection was brilliantly timed.

In the middle of rehearsals my grandmother, Dearie, died. Dearie was a Buddhist. She had anticipated her own death and had travelled around the world checking upon all her grandchildren, including my brother's and my offspring. Having given each one a clock, she returned home, went to sleep and died. Sadly, because of the rehearsals, I was unable to join the large family gathering at her funeral, so my brother represented us both.

At the final technical run at the BBC TV studios in White City, Alan Ayckbourn arrived. I was thrilled to see him again and he was pleased I was playing Ginny. The recording went well and Celia invited us all back to her London apartment for a party. She was as gracious a hostess as she was the most brilliant actress.

～

AFTER I HAD finished *Relatively Speaking*, Richard Eastham took me to meet the film director J. Lee Thompson, who was casting *Country Dance* for MGM. The story was from a book by James Kennaway called *Household Ghosts* and set in Scotland. We were shooting it at Ardmore Studios near Dublin and using the Irish landscape for Scotland. Later the film was renamed *The Same Skin* before eventually ending up being called *Brotherly Love*. I was to play Rosie, a young Scottish girl with an illegitimate baby working for an eccentric baronet, Peter O'Toole, who had an incestuous love for his sister, played by Susannah York. I would have to be in Dublin again for about three months. Before I left for Ireland I agreed to model a Carl Schroeder evening dress for *Vogue* magazine. Patrick Lichfield was taking the photographs. I loved the dress and all of Carl Schroeder's designs, so he agreed to let me buy the dress at a reduced rate.

In Dublin I was told the early read-through and rehearsals were to be at the Shelbourne Hotel. The Shelbourne is one of those extraordinary places where you meet all sorts of people you know just sitting in the lounge having tea. When I turned up midmorning for the read-through, I was introduced to Ewan Roberts, who was the dialect coach employed to make sure we all had the right accent. He also had a small part in the film. Ewan was most conscientious about his work. When we were filming he would lurk behind the scenery and when he heard one false pronunciation his head would pop out from wherever he was hiding and we would be given the right inflection or sound. As I was going to be in Ireland so long, I rented a cottage so that when the family arrived we would all have plenty of room. Being in a hotel for three months could be very claustrophobic.

J. Lee Thompson, the director, decided that Susannah and I were too alike with both of us being blonde so my hair was coloured auburn. I enjoyed having long auburn hair; it certainly helped me to look more Scottish. The other actors – Michael Craig, Harry Andrews, Cyril Cusack and Brian Blessed – had all heard about the making of *Call Me Daddy* and wanted to know whether I was going to play the girl opposite Peter Sellers. They were stunned to hear I had been asked to stand by while the producer sought an unknown girl who could measure up to my original performance. Incidentally, our original director, Alvin Rakoff, had been booked to direct the film and I sympathized with the dilemma he must have been facing.

My first scene on *Country Dance* was with Peter O'Toole. I admired his work and his intense preparation for the scene. When I walked on to the set he was drinking a tumbler full of coffee, so I thought, until I drew nearer to him; the alcoholic fumes were quite overpowering. J. Lee Thompson was standing behind the camera while we rehearsed the scene. As we went through the moves and the camera followed us, he began tearing strips of paper which he would then screw up into a ball and throw on to the floor. I wondered what was the matter with him and asked the continuity girl whether he was feeling all right. She grinned at me and told me that he did that with every scene when he was shooting film. What with Ewan popping out from behind the scenery, the director tearing bits of paper and Peter exhaling alcoholic fumes, I began to feel like Alice in Wonderland at the Mad Hatter's Tea Party.

During any free time I had from photo calls, press interviews and dialect rehearsals, I was able to see my friends Joan and John Dolan and Ray McAnally. By now, Joan and I had celebrated three birthdays at the Ritz Hotel in London. We had a cake in the shape of a goldfish at the first birthday tea, the next year we had a wonderful chocolate dolphin, and this year we had a blue shark. By now, John and I and the Dolans had become very close friends and the staff at the Ritz entered into all the fun of the joint birthday teas by planning for the next fish to be chosen for the joint Pisces cake. Often too, on one of my free days in Dublin I would attend some art classes given by Michael Farrell, a famous artist in Dublin who was also working in the film art department.

Richard Eastham telephoned and asked me to fly back to London on the following Sunday for lunch with Ned Sherrin, Jim Clark and Marty Feldman. He had sent me the script of a new film, *Every Home Should Have One*, to read the part starring opposite Marty in this truly zany British comedy written by Marty, Barry Took and Dennis Norden.

I flew to London on the Sunday, enjoyed a hilarious lunch with Marty, Ned and Jim, and knew I would be happy working with them all. I also asked Ned whether I could be dressed by Carl Schroeder. He agreed, and I set off back to Dublin happy in the knowledge that even though it meant overlapping productions I was going to be working with people I liked – and wearing beautiful dresses!

The following week, I had an invitation from the producer Robert Ginna to attend a Saturday night soirée for a few of the cast at his rented house in Wicklow. I went with J. Lee Thompson in his car. The house was a beautiful, rambling place with large gardens. Robert had hired some Irish musicians to play for us, while we ate the most generous selection of food laid out on a large polished table. The musicians had an Irish drum, fiddle and pipes. As soon as we had eaten the first course, Susannah and I danced with abandonment across the gardens, with the musicians following us. Exhausted, we returned to the large sitting room to help ourselves to the selection of fruit and exotic puddings. A large dresser, along the length of one of the walls, had the most exquisite, antique, delicate china figurines on its shelves. We were all laughing and having fun when Peter O'Toole's face suddenly hardened. He had clearly consumed that one drink too many and took off one of his shoes and threw it at Susannah, missing her nose by a fraction of an inch. He then picked up some apples and oranges from a bowl and hurled them at the delicate china figurines. While the sounds of crashing china echoed around the room, J. Lee Thompson and I got jammed in the sitting-room doorway as we both tried to leave at the same time.

'Time to go, do you think?' he suggested.

'Definitely,' I replied.

What happened after we left I have no idea. It was such an ugly end to a perfect evening. I felt so sorry for Robert Ginna.

The cottage became a sanctuary of normal life once John arrived with Bridget – the nanny – Dylan and Harry Parry the Cairn. I could leave early in the morning for filming but return home in the evening to sanity and my family. The first drama we had was when Harry ran off. It is impossible to train Cairns. They do what they want, when they want, but they are valiant little dogs and we loved ours. We reported our missing dog to the Gardai and within an hour we were phoned with the news that he had been found sitting on the steps of the American Embassy. An embassy car was bringing him back to us even as we were speaking on the phone. Within half an hour a gleaming limousine delivered Harry. He was peering out of the back window. When he saw us, his ears drooped, as much as a Cairn's can. The wicked little dog knew he was in disgrace.

This was just one of Harry's escapades. On a walk out in the country, he was running around wildly, ecstatic with the freedom of miles and miles of rolling hills, when he disappeared. Suddenly, sheep we had not seen before were leaping out of clumps of bushes all round us. Harry was hanging on to the tail of the biggest sheep of them all. Worrying sheep can get a dog shot. The farmer would be quite within his rights to do so. We yelled and yelled for the dog to 'come to heel' and all the other useless commands for a Cairn. We whistled and ran after him but he hung on to the sheep's tail until eventually he was shaken off. Exhausted, he was put back on the lead.

As I would be finishing the film in Ireland soon, then flying back to London to start work with Marty the very next day, John arranged for me to stay in London with Chris Rainbow, a journalist friend, and his family during filming. There was no way I could cope with being picked up in Brighton by the studio car at five o'clock every morning, and arrive home at eight every night. That arranged I felt happy about working straight through.

Our nanny, Bridget, had met and fallen in love with a young doctor while she had been with us in Dublin. We were thrilled for her but I needed assurance that she would not leave us in the lurch, especially as I had to start filming in London. She agreed to stay on but would have to leave by early spring the following year as she was planning to get married.

Then I was asked to appear on the Gay Byrne chat show. I had no television in the cottage so had not seen the show's format but it was quickly explained to me. The other guest that night was a Roman Catholic priest. During a break between our interviews, a Dublin group entertained the studio audience by singing old IRA songs and I felt most alarmed. I had listened to the radio in the cottage, and heard all the ranting from the Reverend Ian Paisley. I sympathized with the Catholics in Belfast. It was a ludicrous situation when voting rights were restricted to householders only. No English county would have put up with such unfairness. To hear the words of the IRA songs sung with such feeling made me worried that there would be a civil war in Northern Ireland unless politicians moved quickly to rectify the situation about voting rights. I started talking on television about my fears, hoping to warn about the dangers of whipping up feelings which could escalate into action. The priest agreed with me. He also advised young men to control their anger about the situation. I talked as a mother, emphasizing that we mothers tried our best to protect our children; we certainly did not want them hurt by violence in society.

When I went home after the show, John and I discussed the incongruity of Neil Armstrong landing on the moon, while such sectarianism existed in Northern Ireland. We tuned into the radio to see what Paisley was saying that day. There was something about the sound he made. I had noticed the same tones on old film footage of Hitler's speeches. Arthur Scargill also used the same sounds when addressing a rally of union supporters. Each man started on a low note and worked his way up the scale, finishing his speech with the most noise and emphasis on the higher note – a trick employed by singers all over the world to get applause at the end of their song. Since then I have watched extremists everywhere using the same method. Was this a natural instinct, I wondered, or had they all worked it out musically?

When I finished on *Country Dance*, J. Lee Thompson gave me a beautiful little antique clock and thanked me for all my hard work. Then I was off to London.

~

THE FOLLOWING DAY, the first scene I had to shoot with Marty Feldman was a long one in the bedroom set. We were both dressed in orange, short nightshirts depicting the hippy nature of our characters. When we rehearsed the scene, Marty looked worried.

'I've never done an acting scene in bed before, Jude.'

'Don't worry,' I replied, 'it's just a scene where we talk and row, not a love-making scene.'

'Yeh, but what if I get . . . you know, . . . well . . . all unnecessary?'

'You won't. Marty, just think of me as a plate of meat.'

'Can't do that, Jude.'

'Why not?'

'Coz I'm a vegetarian.'

And so we started the scene. We improvised on the take and the scene got wilder and wilder. When Jim Clark shouted cut, the whole studio crew applauded. Marty and I were thrilled. Film crews do not applaud easily; to have earned their approval on the first take was quite an achievement.

I loved working with Jim Clark. It was his first film as director. His previous work had been that of an excellent film editor, often saving well-known film directors' tangled reels by turning them into beautifully polished films. Jim would still think as an editor when he was directing. By explaining how the ending of one scene was linking up to the next scene, he made it possible for me to adjust my performance. Jim made you feel part of the team and an important contributor to how any scene was to be played. He was far more generous than some directors who want to move you about like a pawn in a game of chess.

As well as the American Shelley Berman, there was a host of wonderful British character actors in the film including Dinsdale Landen, whom I had worked with the year before in *Mickey Dunn*, Francis de la Tour, Patrick Cargill – who had played my father in *Dixon of Dock Green* – and Patience Collier, a remarkable old character actress, whose libido was legendary. Her ability to attract younger men was formidable, especially as she was no beauty with a nose that could rival 'Schnozzle' Durante's.

Alan Bennett turned up in a court scene, and Penelope Keith was a leather-clad, German au pair who arrived at Marty's and my home on a motorbike. Another au pair in our home was a Swedish model called Julie Ege, who was quite beautiful but did not have a great deal of experience as an actress. She did not have to act; she was just perfectly beautiful. But in one scene, it really was important to be able to follow Jim's directions. We were doing a send-up of an old silent Mary Pickford–Theda Bara film, as seen in Marty's imagination. Jim was shooting the film by moving the camera from side to side and shouting out directions for us to follow. We were supposed to improvise according to his directions. Then he wanted me to chase Julie out of the set. She was to register fear and run for it. But each time we came to do it, she would glide gracefully instead of running. As a model she was more inclined to smile than register fear and Jim was getting more and more frustrated. So, I decided to use the 'Sister of Mercy' approach. The next time they shouted 'action' I threw a couple of apples at her just missing her head by inches. Julie registered a startled look. I then grabbed a broom and swung it wildly in her direction and she really looked fearful. So far so good. Letting out a blood-curdling yell I brandished the broom until she ran like hell off the set. It was a successful take and Jim was more than relieved.

I have always had great admiration for Ned Sherrin's numerous talents, but he has a wicked sense of humour. In one of the scenes I had to be pursued by a group of female dwarfs and midgets who rugger-tackled me so that I disappeared under a scrum of squirming bodies. We shot the master take and then I disentangled myself while waiting for the lighting and camera to be adjusted for the next close-up. I saw Ned, behind the camera, grinning wickedly. 'Enjoying yourself, Judy?' he said.

'I'm black and blue from all the grabbing and pinching,' I replied.

He giggled. 'Oh, I forgot to warn you. All the midgets are lesbians.'

When we came to the end of the film Ned gave me a beautiful present of a little figurine. It was a woman with a very fierce face and letters at the base of the figurine said, 'A match for any man'.

～

BY THE TIME I finished the film I was exhausted. I was due to start a TV play for Anglia, a two-hander with Michael Bryant called *Anniversary*, by Judy Gardiner. John suggested that I go to a health farm for a week. All the early mornings and car journeys to Shepperton Studios, plus sitting up late learning my lines, had taken their toll, and all I wanted to do was sleep. The studio car took me down to the Buxted Park Health Farm as soon as I finished my last scene. As we drove there, my thoughts drifted over events that had happened during the months spent filming *Every Home Should Have One*, now retitled *Think Dirty*. British troops were now in Londonderry, and my part in the film *Hoffman* had been cast with a young, unknown Sinéad Cusack, playing opposite Peter Sellers.

The owners of Buxted Park had named all the different bedrooms after famous writers or musicians, and decorated each room in the colours with which they thought such famous people would have surrounded themselves. I was put in the Goethe room where there was an awful lot of blue and grey. On the lawns, in the fading daylight, I could see two people playing croquet, so I went outside to watch. It was a couple of film people I knew. I joined in the game and it was the most vicious game of croquet. All three of us were feeling stressed-out and neurotic, as we had only just finished working. After a couple of days of saunas and cold plunges, followed by a session of Kneipe foot baths, vegetarian food and endless water with lemon, we were all like mad children. Whether it was the effect of Goethe's colours or just the peacefulness of the place I do not know but I started writing again. By the sixth day the three of us employed guerrilla tactics to raid the kitchen in the evening. We made ourselves some tea and toast with lashings of butter and collapsed in the lounge, drunk with the effects of so many carbohydrates and fats.

With all the money I had made that year, even taking tax payments into consideration, John and I decided that we could afford to try and buy one of the houses we had admired so much. We let an estate agent know that we were in the market and put our own house up for sale, but were told that the houses we liked rarely came on the market.

As someone had expressed an interest in buying our house it could possibly be the last Christmas there and I wanted it to be a super one. We still had not heard anything from the estate agent about any of the houses we were interested in. While preparations for Christmas were going on I worried about whether we could delay moving if someone wanted our house. The usual family gatherings took place. My mother's Christmas Eve lunch followed by midnight Mass. The next day the family and Kazzy and Joy gathered for our Christmas Day dinner.

Just before New Year's Eve I thought about the end of the Sixties. The whole cultural revolution of the early Sixties was in danger of being hijacked by the promotion of drugs and alcohol. There were writers I knew, good writers, who now sat in a haze of marijuana talking about plays they were writing – but they never finished them. There was an increase in drunk driving and lots more car crashes as a result. Famous actors, known for their capacity for drunken yobbish behaviour, were described as hellraisers by journalists and written about with admiration. After the discipline of the early Sixties there were now often bleary-eyed rehearsals, where actors sometimes lost all sense of timing after a previous night's pot smoking. Psychedelic living was a perpetual chase for the treasure at the end of the rainbow, only to find the rainbow had moved, and the seeker was up to his eyes in sinking sands. Librium and Valium were being prescribed to troubled housewives by doctors. I was worried that the drug culture would grow by the time my son was a teenager. Where were the government warnings? Why were pop stars behaving so irresponsibly by eulogizing about the effects of drugs?

On New Year's day 1970, the estate agent rang us. One of the houses we had lusted after was on the market, but the lady would sell it only to people she liked, people who she thought would cherish the property. He suggested that, if we were interested, we should meet her that morning. We scrambled into the car straightaway and drove there. We approached the steps of the house with some trepidation. Perhaps the owner would not think us suitable people to live in her house. An old lady in her mid-eighties opened the door and ushered us through to a bright sunny sitting room. Concentrating on me she asked whether we played bridge. I replied that we did not. She then wanted to know whether I was one of these women who threw Tupperware parties. I said I was not; I had no time for such things as I worked. Her eyes lit up and she wanted to know what I did for a living, so I told her I was an actress and I was also trying to be a writer. This seemed to please her. She asked John what he did for a living. When he told her he was a journalist, she beamed in approval and took us through to another room, a library. On one wall there were all the sorts of books that John loved; another wall had all the kind of books I read. We both knew that this was the right house for us with each room exuding a wonderful atmosphere and a feeling of warmth and peace.

Mrs Thomas, the owner, told us stories of when she was a suffragette. Her husband had been the editor of the *Listener* magazine. She said she would love us to have the house, and did I play squash. I said I did, so she said she would leave us her squash set as she was moving to America to join her son now that her husband had died. She had been happy in the house but it was too big for her now. When she wanted to know how soon we could reach a decision, John and I looked at each other, and John told her that we definitely wanted to buy the house. We left Mrs Thomas, unable to remember how many rooms there were, or any of the details. All we knew was that we wanted to live there and we would be happy in that house. Within a few weeks we moved in.

Harry Parry went mad with excitement, rushing around the new house and yapping at everything. Dylan was thrilled to have so much space in which to play hide and seek. Our collection of furniture seemed quite small when we first arrived but nowadays, after thirty-five years of family living, every room is filled.

~

JUST AFTER WE moved in I had to go to Norwich to work on the *Cork Moustache*. When I returned, I had to start looking straightaway for a replacement for Bridget. We were lucky to find the most wonderful girl called Margaret, who stayed with us until she married five years later.

Then Richard sent me a script for the American International Pictures production of *Wuthering Heights*, to be directed by Robert Fuest. They wanted me to play the part of Nellie (Ellen Dean). It was a lovely part but I had to age from seventeen to mid-forties during the filming and the director wanted us to wear hardly any make-up. So I made a graph, planning to have early nights when playing the younger scenes and late nights for when I was older. Of course the best-laid plans go wrong and a couple of times I got caught out when they changed the scenes round. Then if I was playing a young Nellie and I had enjoyed a late night, I had to rely on the lighting man. Tim Dalton was playing Heathcliffe, Anna

Calder-Marshall was cast as Cathie and the wonderful Julian Glover was playing Hindley. It was a friendly cast and we were based in Leeds. All the exterior filming was done out on the Moors. The interior scenes were done at Shepperton Studios. The original *Wuthering Heights* – with Merle Oberon, Laurence Olivier and Flora Robson playing my part of Nellie – was shot in Hollywood, where the occasional palm tree could be seen in the distance.

April on the Moors can be cold one minute, with rain the next, and on the same day one can be warmed by quite hot sunshine – a bit like Ireland really. But in Ireland you can expect to see some snow, hail or sleet thrown in as well. I had one very long scene with Anna out on the Moors. It was warm when we started the rehearsal but by the time we came to shoot, a wind was blowing, cloud covered the sun and the temperature had dropped to almost freezing. We worked for about two hours on the scene with breaks between camera adjustments when we would be given hot coffee and wrapped up in coats. When we finished we were both numb with cold and a studio car drove us back to the hotel. On the way, the heater in the car began to warm the muscles in our limbs. The thawing effect was so painful that we were almost crying.

Often when filming near members of the public, the occasional person will come up to me and say, 'I could do your job. It's easy.' They do not understand that if I am doing my job well it will look easy. But it is not; often it is repetitive, demanding intense concentration and self-discipline, and we also often have to work in terrible conditions, like cold weather, wearing the flimsiest of clothes. No sane person would work under these conditions.

From Leeds we all moved down to Shepperton Studios to complete *Wuthering Heights*. I stayed with John's friend Chris and his family again in London so that the filming days were not too long. At least I could have the weekends off to go home. After we finished filming I was recalled to fill in with some more narration to cover missing scenes. I saw Flora Robson on the train to London. We knew each other from many Brighton charity events we had both attended and she expressed sympathy for me, having to add some narration; she had been asked to do the same on the original film in Hollywood.

By now Dylan was nearly five years old and would start school in the autumn. He and John had come up to the Yorkshire Moors for a few days and we realized that this was the last time he would be able to come out on location with me. He had been attending a playgroup for a couple of mornings a week and was looking forward to starting school. The state school in our area was a five-minute walk from our house and the headmistress was charming. I was worried because friends of mine had told me about the new teaching methods for reading which had seemed like nonsense to me and I was rather hoping this school was going to teach the traditional methods. There were to be forty-eight children in the beginners' class. When I expressed concern about teaching that number of children in one class and the new reading methods, the headmistress was very understanding. She agreed there were too many children in the class and said, 'Do yourself a favour Mrs Parry. If you can possibly afford it, get Dylan into the private school system. He'll be a lot better off. I would if he were my son.' So I set off to find a school that was teaching the traditional way of reading and found a prep school that would take him until he was seven years old and enrolled him there.

Every Home Should Have One was released in the cinemas with a fanfare of publicity and received good reviews. A steady round of interviews and photo sessions followed. At the same time, *Country Dance* came out. Shortly afterwards *Hoffman* was released and compared unfavourably with the Emmy-winning *Call Me Daddy* TV version starring Donald Pleasance and myself. It was described as 'shallow, claustrophobic and jam-packed with third-rate epigrams'. Sellers was said to 'have failed to register in his first straight role'; his performance 'did not ring true. His attempts at playing suave instead of comic failed.' Thankfully, young Sinéad Cusack survived the critics with their appreciation of her youth, charm and freshness. I was so glad that I had chosen to work with Marty.

~

PETER WILLES, THE head of drama at Yorkshire Television, then offered me the part of Joan Last in *The Bonus*, a play written by Ray

Jenkins. It was the story of an ambitious company man, played by
Keith Baxter, and the conflict between his wife's aspirations and his
wish to rise up the company ladder. The play coincided with the
women's lib movement gaining strength and was a wonderful part
for me. The director, David Reynolds, was someone I had worked
with when he had been a studio floor manager. This was his first
time as a director and I did everything I could to help him. He later
rose to be head of entertainment at Yorkshire Television.

Just after I finished *The Bonus*, Marina Warner interviewed me.
While we were talking I told her I was also writing. I was working
on 'The Streamer', a short story I had written years before, which
I was trying to turn into a novel. A couple of days later Marina
phoned me to say that she had been talking to André Deutsch and
he wanted to meet me and see what I was writing. Shaking with
fright I arrived at the publisher's office clutching my five chapters
of badly typed manuscript. I was ushered in and invited to sit on
a large leather chair facing Mr Deutsch at his desk. He beamed and
encouraged me to talk about my writing. I liked him; he was a
friendly man and I felt at ease in his company. After a while, he
leant back in his chair and said, 'I have a feeling about you, and my
feelings are never wrong. You are a writer.' I got out my five chapters and asked him whether he wanted to read what I had written.
He declined, saying that he had an editor who read for him. I did
not see him press a button but a woman came into the office
straightaway and he asked me to give her my chapters. She was
very stern-looking and I really did not want to give them to her.
Like an experienced matron she extracted the chapters from my
tight grip and made off with them.

A week later she phoned me and offered me an advance.
However, during the week, waiting for her reaction, I had to face
the reality of whether I could finish the book quickly. I decided I
could not because I wanted to be in Brighton when my son started
school, there were lots of things to be done in the house, and
Richard had sent me a film script to begin in January the next year.
It was a leading part with Shelley Winters and Mark Lester. I also
felt that I needed to write another book before I attempted to complete the novel, five chapters of which I had shown them. So, I

declined the offer of an advance and told them I was not yet ready to proceed with my writing career.

At this point my guardian angel fixed it so I could stay at home and work. Sean Kenny had designed a theatre for Sussex University, called the Gardner Centre. A Belgian director, Walter Eysselinck, was producing several plays and he wanted me for two of them. The first was Sternheim's *Bloomers*, where I was to play the part of Frau Maske, who causes terrible trouble when her knicker elastic gives way at the beginning of the play, during a town parade, and her bloomers fall around her ankles. I was to be working with James Grout, Jack Shepherd, Ferdy Mayne and Gillian Raine, a smashing cast.

At the dress rehearsal Dylan came to see the play with Margaret, our new nanny. He let out a shriek of laughter when he saw my bloomers fall down. About a month or so before then, he had watched John on *Tomorrow's World* driving a huge steam train up in the North of England. He was so proud that his father had driven such a great big engine. The week he started school, the children in his class were asked what their parents did for a living. My son said, 'Daddy drives a train and Mummy drops her knickers every night.'

After *Bloomers* I worked on a play by Terence Feely, called *Don't Let Summer Come*, with Joe Melia and Carmen Munro. It was a wonderfully bizarre play with Carmen and me dressed in body stockings on which we stuck all our different changes of costume. We were the black and white parts of Joe's brain and enacted out all sorts of roles, from strippers to drum majorettes. Every bit of my past career was used for this role. I remembered how the strippers used to work when I worked at the Irving and the Panama clubs. I had to dance with a dummy and yet make it seem lifelike enough to be able to fight it. My knockabout comedy experience with Terry Kendall and Nat Mills was invaluable for creating this scene. The play was a great success. One night, Robert Helpmann, the famous Australian dancer, choreographer and actor, came backstage to meet me after the show. He was very complimentary about my performance and demanded to know why I was not with the Royal Shakespeare Company. I said I had never been asked to join them.

With our son well and truly settled in his school routine, I was able to accept a script Yorkshire Television had sent me. I would be working with James Grout again in *Husband and Friend*, an hour-long play in a series called Ten Commandments, with Judy Parfitt and Michael Culver. The play was written by Jeremy Paul and directed by James Ormerod. Peter Willes, the head of drama I had already worked for, had an incredible eye for detail. Nothing escaped his eagle-sharp observations. With him in charge the thespian troops in any production knew they were in safe hands. Judy Parfitt and I became good friends, and as she was thinking of moving to Brighton, I was able to offer her any help I could in finding her a suitable place to live.

~

IN OCTOBER 1970, a new producer took over on the *Tomorrow's World* programme. He brought in his own reporters and John's contract came to an end. I told him not to worry because my film, *The Gingerbread House*, was scheduled for January, so there would be enough money for the mortgage and any household bills. However, just before the Christmas celebrations began, Richard phoned to say that the film production had been put back until April. Panic ensued. I asked Richard whether there had been any other enquiries for me. He replied that there had been one from a company who wanted to make a commercial film about air conditioning and it was to be shown to their company only. He had turned it down as he did not think I would be interested. I told him to go back to the company and tell them I would have lunch with them to discuss the work.

When I met Bert Weedon, who was producing the film, I asked him who else would be in it. 'We're looking for an actor to work with you if you're interested in doing it,' he said.

'I am, and I know just the man for the part,' I said.

'Who?' he asked.

'My husband,' I replied.

Who was writing the script, I wondered. He said he had not found anyone yet and could I recommend anyone. 'Yes,' I said, 'my husband.'

By the time I had finished lunch with dear Bert, our family panic about the mortgage was over. John was employed, although what it would be like working together on a film we had no idea.

So in January 1971, John and I started work together. We had a lot of fun filming as a young couple thinking about air conditioning. John worked as scriptwriter on other productions with the company after I had finished and then joined Thames TV as a reporter on a motoring programme, called *Drive-In*.

Richard told me that *Wuthering Heights* had now opened in America and I had wonderful, rave reviews for my performance. Unfortunately for me Shelley Winters too had seen the reviews, and she had overall script approval in her contract for the next film. Before the shooting in Shepperton began, my part was almost deleted from the script. The best scenes were changed to become hers, and any of my scenes that were not essential to the story line were cut. When I was sent the final draft of the script I was horrified and I talked over the situation with Richard. The film company would still have to pay me the money that had been agreed but the billing was now ridiculous. I suggested that Ralph Richardson, whose name was in a box like Lionel Jeffries', should be given my billing and I should be put in a box instead. Richard arranged it all. He wanted to know whether I would rather pull out of the film, but I decided not to do so. I liked the producers of the film and this would be my fourth for American International Pictures. The heads of the company sent me Christmas cards. They were not to know that a certain actress would invoke her script approval clause.

I knew that Michael Bryant had worked with Shelley Winters on a film for television, so I phoned him to see what it was like to work with her. 'Tricky,' he replied. 'She makes mistakes when you are giving your best performance, so you have to do it again. This goes on until you drop your performance then she comes up and that is the take they use.' My heart sank. I hate selfish games during a performance. My experience of such behaviour had always come from older leading ladies jealous of younger actresses. The very presence of a younger girl reminded them that their beauty was fading and they were past their prime. I vowed I would never be mean to a young actress as some of the older women had been to a lot of my generation. The big stars were not like this, only those uncertain of their own futures.

In March there was a Royal Command performance of *Wuthering Heights* with the cast and the executives of American International being presented to Princess Alexandra. When I shook hands with her I noticed her flawless complexion and the most intelligent green eyes. She wore an incredible necklace of diamonds and emeralds. The emeralds were the exact colour of her eyes. I have met many royals since then but for me she was the most regal and beautiful. Later, after the film had been shown and she was walking through the foyer of the cinema with Bernard Delfont and other powerful and rich people, she caught sight of John and me standing together and walked over to us. She remembered John from meeting him in Marbella and Sardinia when he was a writer on royal affairs for the *Daily Express*. After reminiscing with him for a while, she then discussed my character in the film, having observed all the subtle things I had put into my performance. I was extremely flattered that she had noticed them. I also had some fabulous notices from the London critics and was pleased to see when I watched the film that all the graphs and games of having early nights for the young scenes and late nights for the older scenes had worked really well.

~

THE FIRST DAY of filming for *The Gingerbread House* arrived and I met Curtis Harrington, an experienced and charming Hollywood director. We talked through the scene and then Miss Winters arrived. I was introduced to her as the girl who gave the great performance in *Wuthering Heights*. She gazed at me with small beady eyes and said, 'I know. She's a scene stealer.' Curtis laughed as if she had made a joke; I knew she had not.

When we began preparations for the scene, as Michael had warned me, she fluffed and made mistakes. I kept steady, remembering how Audrey Hepburn had been so disciplined about each take. I followed her example, not panicking, just keeping up my performance and not dropping it for one second. Suddenly there was a wail from Shelley who said she had a headache and she stormed off the set, so we broke for an early lunch.

I knew some of the crew from other films. I had worked with Colin Brewer, who had been the first assistant when I had stood on a raft in the sea at New Brighton trying to get the job as a Can Do girl. We had a lot of laughs then and he was grinning at me now. 'Don't eat too much at lunch, Judy, or you could end up like her.' The Shelley Winters I remembered from films when I was much younger was a lithe, attractive, brilliant actress. Now she had put on weight and I felt she was coarse in her language. In a way I almost felt sorry for her. I was thirty-one and weighed about a hundred and twelve pounds; she was forty-eight and overweight. I wondered if my relative youth frightened her.

After lunch we returned to the scene again and this time she wanted me in a different position from before. Curtis tried to accommodate her. Every position that would work for the camera was unacceptable to her. I heard a couple of yawns from the crew. They did not like one of their own British actresses being put through the wringer by this Yank. Curtis began to lose his cool. 'Would you like me to put her under the table?' he said. I took several deep breaths and stayed calm. We began the scene again and suddenly she came up with a performance. So did I, and there was a shout of 'Take and Print'. I think she thought I was going to be thrown by the sudden change but I was not. I was tired at the end of the day, but the first scene was in the can and my next scheduled scene did not involve her.

The next time we had to work together she started again. I had had enough by now, so I let her have it with both barrels and told her that I had worked with some pretty big names, people with huge talent, and that none of them had behaved as badly as she had. I said life was too short for such games and could she please stop pissing about. Instead of wailing and storming off the set, which by now was frigid with silence and tension, she smiled, her face relaxed, and she said, 'My God, you remind me of me when I was young.' That was an alarming thought. But from then on she was nauseatingly nice to me, and I had no more trouble from her. It all proves, I suppose, that directors or actors who put up with nonsense on set deserve everything they get. *The Gingerbread House* often pops up on some late-night cable station, but is now renamed *Whoever Slew Auntie Roo?*

I shared all my experiences with my lovely mentor, Sybil, telling her about the fun and games with Shelley Winters. She loved all the gossip I brought her, especially as her health was deteriorating and she was not getting about so much as she had in the past. I made sure she was not alone and was holding her hand when she died in a nursing home on the seafront in May that year. The loss of Sybil brought me an enormous amount of grief that enveloped me like a shroud.

Shortly after her death the accountant I had been with since my days with Kavanagh's – in fact he was Carole Golder's cousin – had a nervous breakdown over the impending introduction of VAT, and many of us found that our tax affairs were in a terrible state. He had allowed the assessments to go through without any expenses being deducted and we all owed the tax man money for which we should never have been charged. There was no appeal. We all had to pay the rate the tax office had decided. Luckily, I found a wonderful new accountant, Barry Kernon, whom I have stayed with ever since. He got the tax man to agree that it was an unfair tax and negotiated for me to have time to pay it off a bit at a time. This was going to make our finances extremely tight as I would have to pay the current taxes at the same time. While all this was going on, a new boss took over the William Morris Agency, and my personal manager, Richard Eastham, left. I too wanted to leave the agency. The new head, Bob Shapiro, wanted me to stay on but it was time for a change and I moved to Larry Dalzell, one of the best agents I have ever been lucky enough to know.

~

THE FIRST JOB Larry got me was the part of Guste Daimchen in the *Man of Straw* serial, an adaptation by Robert Muller from Heinrich Mann's novel. The book had originally been banned in Germany as a subversive influence on society. I would be working for the director Herbert Wise again at the BBC. The leading man's part of Diederich was to be played by Derek Jacobi. It was his first big television role and he was quite nervous. On the first read-through day Derek said to me, 'I told Sir Laurence Olivier I was going to be working with you, and he said I'd be in safe hands. He thinks very highly of your work.' I thought that was a very kind thing for Olivier to say.

The play was about the rise of a devious man who manipulates people into giving him enormous power – a warning of the German propensity for being attracted to the future Hitler personality. There was a fine cast including John Cater, who had played the demon king in the pantomime *Puss in Boots* in which I played principal girl in Aberdeen in 1956. The girl playing my sister was Dora Reissar. During rehearsals Dora told me that her first memory was of looking through barbed wire from a ghetto. She was part of a Jewish family on the run from the Nazis. We became friends and she told me she was an ex-dancer turned actress but really wanted to be a dress designer. Her designs were wonderful and I was later able to get her a commission to design the clothes for my character in the television series *Moody and Pegg*.

Straight after *Man of Straw* Peter Willes asked me to begin work on *The Chinese Prime Minister* by Enid Bagnold, for Yorkshire TV. Christopher Morahan was directing; Francesca Annis and I were the younger women in it. I had met Francesca before, in 1958, when we were both practising singing in the Australian composer Ron Grainer's apartment. The older parts were played by Judy Campbell, Roland Culver and Alan Webb. Chris Morahan asked me how I liked to be directed. I told him I would do my own research and would ask for help when I needed it. As Judy Campbell always liked a lot of attention from the director it was probably a load off his mind.

At the technical run, Enid Bagnold turned up to watch. She came up to me afterwards and told me that I was the first actress to understand the part I was playing; no one else had ever been near the right interpretation. She wanted to know how I had worked it out. 'I bought your autobiography,' I replied, 'and looked up what you were doing and thinking in your early thirties.' She clapped her hands with glee. In fact, much of her family history was very similar to mine. She asked me over to her house in

Rottingdean and asked me to bring the book and she would sign it for me.

Duly I turned up with John one Saturday and we were greeted at the door by a huge man, who was her son. He shuffled along a corridor, the walls lined with pictures, theatre posters, and even a glass case containing Victorian Christmas crackers. Every inch of wall space was covered with memorabilia. Enid greeted us with the offer of some date bread she had made, some orange juice for me and a whisky for John. Then she signed her autobiography for me, and began talking about actresses and intuition, declaring the reason for her friend Dame Edith Evans's brilliance as an actress was that she did not have the capacity of intellectual thought. 'She is really quite stupid,' she said, 'but a brilliant actress.' She chatted on. Her big son was sitting in a chair in the corner of the room reading a newspaper. Every time she was stuck for a word he would prompt her without moving his position or even peering round his paper. Barefooted, she ran in and out of the kitchen to fetch some more date bread, which she wanted us to finish off. I became suspicious and wondered how long it had been there, so declined any more and insisted that we did not wish to overstay our welcome, and that it was time for us to leave. As soon as I said this there was a great sigh of relief from behind the newspaper. Her big son wanted us to leave too.

~

LARRY TELEPHONED ME and said that the Royal Shakespeare Company had enquired about me for the season at Stratford in 1972. Was I interested? If so, would I go along to meet Trevor Nunn and John Barton, taking a favourite sonnet to read. I wondered whether Robert Helpmann had recommended me to them. Larry thought it would be good experience for me. I was slightly nervous about working on Shakespearean productions but felt the need to test myself and, of course, a continuous contract for a year would help me pay off the tax bill. Margaret would bring Dylan and Harry Parry up to me in the Easter and summer holidays so Dylan would not miss me too much, and John would get up to Stratford as often as he could, so I told Larry I was interested.

I chose 'When out of Fortune with Men's Eyes' to read. The meeting went well and John Barton told me I had a natural instinct for the iambic pentameter. They offered me the parts of Adriana in *Comedy of Errors*, Calpurnia in *Julius Caesar* and Octavia in *Anthony and Cleopatra*. We would rehearse for a few weeks in January at Floral Street rehearsal rooms in London and then depart for Stratford. I arranged to rent a cottage in Ebrington, about twelve miles out of Stratford.

There was one more television play to work on before Christmas 1971. It was *Night of the Tanks*, part of the Love Story series of plays for ATV and written by Wilfred Greatorex. It was about a broken, refugee Czech journalist's meeting with a teacher living downstairs in a seedy house of bedsitters in the Cromwell Road in which they both lived. Alfred Burke played the Czech journalist and I played the teacher; the Frenchman Henri Safran was directing.

I asked Wilfred why he had chosen the Cromwell Road in which to set his play. He told me that one of his greatest fears was running out of ideas to write plays and ending up in the Cromwell Road, which is where he first started writing.

Also in the play was George Pravda and a young Czech actor called Milos Kirik. I was fascinated by Milos's own experience of being a refugee. He had escaped from Prague just as the Russian tanks arrived in 1968. He had no time to plan his escape and fled with only one tiny suitcase packed with the things that were most important to him: a couple of pairs of socks, some underwear, a jumper, a few family photos and a book with pictures of the beautiful city of Prague that he was leaving behind. It was a humbling experience to hear about this. Ever since, whenever I have been downhearted or fed up with the way things are going, I mentally pack a small suitcase of things important to me. It works wonders in getting a proper perspective of what really matters in life.

Chapter Fourteen

1972–1975

~

I READ EVERY book about Shakespeare I could find. I began learning Calpurnia's speeches in act two scene two; delved into all the superstitions of Shakespeare's time; learned about Francis Bacon's interest in Rosicrucianism and Freemasonry. I read *The Golden Dawn* from cover to cover and researched everything about Calpurnia and her family, whose connections in society I discovered had first helped Julius Caesar rise to his position of power.

On the first day of rehearsals the company was introduced to an American woman who took us through some psychological games – the aim being, I supposed, for us all to trust each other. The games varied from allowing ourselves to fall and be caught by comparative strangers to being lifted by a crowd of actors with the minimum of effort. Then we were told to sit on the floor and gaze at colours hanging on the four walls: yellow, red, blue and green. One actor was deeply affected by the colour red and leapt about a bit. The woman then asked us in turn what effect the colours had on us. I said what I instinctively knew she wanted to hear and fretted about getting on with breaking down the text. One bright cockney actor called John Bardon, who is now a regular in *East-Enders*, replied to the woman when she asked him how a colour was affecting him, 'The trouble is I can only feel it up to my knee.' I chuckled, and saw suppressed grins all round the room. Anyone who had read even basic psychology could have cobbled together this programme. After another day of dividing us up so that sometimes we were Romans feeling superior to the general rabble, and other times we were the rabble feeling inferior to the Roman elite, we began rehearsals. Three weeks later we went to Stratford.

It was a beautiful drive out to the cottage I had rented in Ebrington and I was more than happy to place some distance between the theatre and my temporary home. Knowing I was going to be with the company for a year, I would need to draw away from them once a day just to feel a sense of balance. The landlord was charming and everyone in the small village made me feel very welcome, offering their help for anything I needed.

The cosy thatched cottage itself was originally a tithe barn and had a small walled garden. At night, walking to the cottage in the dark from where I had parked the car, I could hear the occasional squeal of a hedgehog and the sudden, dry coughs from sheep in the fields near by. It was a bit alarming at first but I soon became used to it. The cottage beams too would creak during the night and I could hear the scuffling of birds in the roof. I noticed that everyone in the village placed flower pots over their milk bottles on their doorsteps and soon found out why when I caught a blue tit with its beak dipping into the cream at the top of my delivered milk. From then on I put out a daily saucer of milk for the birds and they left my milk bottles alone. Only one day did I forget and straightaway the beaks went through the top. I loved the village and much of the time spent there was inspiration for my first book, *Cow and Cow Parsley*.

Once I arrived at Stratford I met the wonderful Cicely Berry who was in charge of our voice production and breathing classes. She would rehearse the text with us individually and as a group. She also had a vast collection of poetry which we would read with her. John Barton was the director who helped me the most with the meaning of the text. He was wonderfully eccentric but his knowledge of the Shakespearean text was phenomenal. I loved the few sessions I had with him and admired his infectious enthusiasm. Often, because he concentrated so much on his work, he was unaware of things around him – a typical absent-minded professor. One day, when we were all on stage, he was moving up and down the auditorium and running up the steps to the stage to emphasize something or other. By chance one of the stage hands then moved the steps. Totally unaware of what had happened, Barton ran up as usual and somehow arrived on stage as if he had run up the steps. Mind over matter? Strange things can happen in the theatre.

Another day we were all called into the rehearsal room at the back of the theatre and shown a pristine white floor. We were told by the stage director not to bring in cigarettes or coffee in case we marked it. Then John Barton came into the room smoking a cigarette. We all held our breath. He talked away about a scene and we watched him flicking ash everywhere while he talked. One of the actors said, 'John!' and indicated the virgin white flooring. 'Ah yes,' Barton replied, and promptly stubbed his cigarette out on the new floor. We all gasped with shock. Oblivious to our sense of horror, he continued talking.

The Roman plays were directed by Trevor Nunn, who had two assistants working with him: Buzz Goodbody and Ewan Smith. After plotting the scene with Trevor we would then work with one of them. There were also some very good actors in the company. I admired Patrick Stewart's work. Patrick, of course, is now known for his role of Captain Jean Luc Picard in *Star Trek: the Next Generation*. Richard Johnson was another fine actor, as was Ian Hogg, who played Coriolanus. As I was not in *Coriolanus* I could sit in the theatre and enjoy the magic of Ian's performance during the first dress rehearsal. During the rest of the week, Trevor and his assistants were giving continuous notes on the production but, by the time they opened, Ian's performance, although extremely good, had lost some of the original magic seen in that first dress rehearsal.

I telephoned my agent and told him that I was not very impressed by the team's direction. 'Oh well done, Judy,' he replied. 'It usually takes my actors about six months to find that out, you've done it in six weeks.'

Other fine actors in the company included Maggie Tyzack, Janet Suzman, Don Henderson, Tim Piggot-Smith, John Woods and Corin Redgrave. I was thrilled to be working with Corin again. During rehearsals we arranged to go out for an Indian meal. He had changed a lot since 1968 and was far more interested in politics than I remembered. Over the curry we had a blazing row over our union, Equity. I called him a political extremist and he called me a middle-class mystic. Later in the season we would often argue, but I respected him both as an actor and as a sincere, highly intelligent man concerned about justice and the rights of others.

At the final rehearsal of *Julius Caesar*, before dress rehearsals began on stage, I was in a state of terror. I did not want to let the company down during the run by making a mistake. While I ranted as Calpurnia to Mark Dignam, who was playing Caesar, I could hear a knocking sound which I realized with horror was my knees. I was appalled to be so nervous. At lunch time, feeling very ashamed of myself, I came out of the stage door to find Ray McAnally sitting on the wall and grinning like a wicked leprechaun. 'I thought by now you'd need to be taken for lunch,' he said.

I was so happy to see him and told him about hearing my own knees knocking and how ashamed I was. He just roared with laughter. By the time we had eaten lunch, and Ray had told me some of his own embarrassing theatre stories, I had regained my sense of perspective and returned to the theatre with far more confidence.

At Stratford there was a remarkable make-up department with very talented people who arranged wigs and designed the make-up for each character in the play. Brenda was the girl in charge of it all. She was not only a brilliant make-up artist but also a member of a local coven. I found her intriguing. She gave me a wonderfully patrician nose for Calpurnia, and a long grey wig. I was dressed in a white flowing robe like all the other characters except for the soldiers. When we went on to the stage it was all white. The stage floor was a series of white squares controlled by a computer. These squares became steps, or a seat to sit upon or just a flat white area. Once the computer started, that was it. Nothing could be stopped, as we soon found out. One black actor who was giving a wonderful impression of being a big butch soldier, suddenly found the square he was standing on rising. He maintained his masculine stance until the square had risen high above our heads and then his knees turned in and his arms drooped in a queenie panic. I watched John Wood, as Brutus, run up the stairs in the most dramatic way only to let out a yell of surprise when he stepped into space where steps should have been. I became very wary of this set, and wrote some graffiti in the green room saying, 'In the beginning was the word – then came scenic design.' When the lights were full on, it was as hard on the eyes as if we were playing in the middle of a desert at noon.

In the scene I played with Mark Dignam, the stage was dominated by a colossal white statue of Caesar. Mark and I were waiting in the wings for our cue to go on and wondering whether anyone would notice us as all attention would be drawn to the statue.

'Let's put a spell on the statue,' I said to Mark, 'and make it disappear.' I then made up some pseudo magical words and pointed my finger at it. To our horror the statue's arm dropped off and crashed on to the stage. 'You must never play games like that in the theatre,' Mark said to me, 'Strange things can happen during a Shakespearean play.' He did not need to tell me again. I had frightened the wits out of myself.

Sometimes the dress rehearsals went on so long that we found ourselves starting a run of the play at midnight. By then we were tired, having been in the theatre all day. We also found out that unlike the backstage staff we were being paid only 25p an hour overtime. We stopped work, refusing to continue working into the early hours. The press covered the story, calling the stoppage 'Militants at Stratford'. Militants, rubbish! We were just exhausted and wanted to sleep. However, we did get a raise which brought our overtime more on an equal level with the dressers and make-up girls.

On the opening night of *Julius Caesar* the theatre was packed to capacity and the atmosphere was highly charged. When we Romans marched in time to a drumbeat on to the stage, dressed in our white togas, I could feel the electricity flow between the actors and the audience. It was a spectacular production and we received tremendous applause at the end.

My lovely Australian friend Kevin Palmer, whom I had worked with in *Oh, What a Lovely War*, left a message asking me to join him at the Dirty Duck for dinner after the show. It was a popular pub near the theatre that had an excellent restaurant and many people went there after a first night. Kevin was now working with Eddie Kulukundis at Knightsbridge Productions, and they regularly entertained actors from the theatre. It was a lovely, noisy occasion and I was relieved that I had not forgotten any lines or let the high standard down in any way. 'Gympie would be proud of you, Jude,' Kevin said. At one matinee, Les Killick, the Brighton policeman who first saw me take over the role of Cinderella at the Brighton Hippodrome when I was fifteen, turned up at the stage door with his wife, Mabel. They were the first people ever to have written me a fan letter in 1955, and they told me they wanted to make sure I was coping at Stratford. They were very pleased with my work and I was touched by their genuine concern for my well-being.

We had only three weeks to rehearse *Comedy of Errors*. I was playing Adriana. Clifford Williams directed and he knew what he wanted and worked very fast. The wooden stage floor of the *Comedy of Errors* set, placed on top of the computerized white blocks, had the most incredible rake. To make an entrance centre stage one walked up a ladder-like set of steps at the back of the stage. This was fine for the men, but for me, with my petticoats, wool dress and overdress, plus fan in my right hand, it was a nightmare of negotiation. One performance, before I realized what was happening, I had walked up the inside of my dress and made my first entrance by falling head first centre stage. Because of the tightness of my corsets, the sudden folding over of my body produced a large fart as I fell. I scrambled to my feet in the most ungainly way and began my dialogue, 'Neither my husband . . .' flapping the fan wildly to cool my bright red cheeks. Rosemary McHale, who was playing Luciana, was almost incoherent with the giggles. Because of the huge amount of breath control needed in the theatre, and because of the tightness of corsets, there are often discreet sounds of released trapped air backstage, but rarely on stage. When it does happen on stage, it is usually accompanied by collective hysteria. I was walking round the back of the stage during *Comedy of Errors*, when Don Henderson's head popped round one of the drapes. 'Bloody hell, Cornwell, you're like a motor bike,' he grinned. 'There's only one person who can fart louder than you and that's Peggy Ashcroft.'

The weight of the costume and the exertion needed to balance on the rake of the stage meant that during every interval I had to change my corset as it was soaked with perspiration. Costume designers often draw wonderful clothes for actors but these can be hell to wear and cause backache, tiredness and numerous other difficulties.

The part of Octavia in *Antony and Cleopatra* was a difficult but fascinating one to play. Corin was playing my brother, Octavius Caesar, and Richard Johnson was playing Mark Antony. Brenda designed a wonderful light-brown wig for me to wear. I fell in love with the darker-haired look and decided that to extend my range of parts in the near future I would change the colour of my hair to the colour I had as Octavia. When John saw me he wailed, 'But I married a blonde.' I reassured him that it would not be for ever, and that I was just trying to extend my range of parts.

Maggie Tyzack and I became great friends. We both missed our sons and husbands and would comfort each other whenever either of us felt homesick or confused by company politics. During the odd free day I would often go riding or write to my godmother, Musi. I told her how much I missed my mentor, Sybil, and how I wished she could have seen my performances at Stratford. She replied that she missed my father's letters to her and all the ideas they had shared over the years. Often during our correspondence a parcel would arrive with books of poetry she thought I would appreciate. After I sent her one letter discussing philosophy, there was a book sent back with a note saying, 'I think you are now ready for Epictetus.' I was. I spent much time contemplating his sayings. 'No man is free who is not master of himself.'

Then my mother came to stay with me for a while. She loved the cottage and saw all the plays. After *Comedy of Errors* she was full of compliments but my red wig had reminded her of her mother, Sarah. She could not stop talking about the fact that it had been like seeing her own mother alive again. When the Easter holidays came the family arrived with Harry the dog and bicycles. Harry teamed up with some layabout dogs who hung round the small local pub so we always knew where to find him; Dylan played with some other children in the area and had a copy of *Charlie and the Chocolate Factory* to read. I decided to let him sit through the plays so he could enjoy them instinctively before school possibly ruined them for him.

He was six years old and entranced by the production of *Coriolanus* and wanted to know how everything worked backstage. I let him see the swords, the costumes and how the trap door worked, and he could not wait to come to the next play. He loved *Julius Caesar* and laughed a lot at the *Comedy of Errors*. One night, when it was Margaret's night off, he came with me and sat in my dressing room while I was on stage. When I returned, he was covered in green make-up and looked like a mad imp. We drove home together through the dark lanes, the green imp shouting with glee as we spotted rabbits, foxes and other creatures caught in the headlights.

One Sunday evening, Harry did not return from his meeting with the layabout dogs and Margaret, Dylan and I went looking all over the village for him. When night fell, there was a whining at the front door and a creature soaked in pig muck was shivering on the step; sticking out of his mouth were the remains of chicken feathers. The demonic dog had obviously been caught chasing chickens by an angry farmer who had thrown a pail of muck over him. We had all been shamed by the wicked Cairn and his freedom was severely restricted after the pigswill incident. We gave him a really good bath, which he always hated, and dried him with my hairdryer until he was all fluffy again.

When the family returned to Brighton I missed them dreadfully but at least I knew that I was paying off the tax man. Phillip Mackie, the wonderful producer who had produced the Feydeau and Saki series among many other productions for Granada, lived in a large old rectory house in Cirencester. He came to see *Comedy of Errors* and asked Richard Johnson and me to a summer party at his house the following Sunday. I had a wonderful time. Andre Morell and Joan Greenwood were there with their small son and a host of well-known actors and actresses. After supper outside at tables covered with check tablecloths, we retired to his large drawing room and everyone did 'a turn'. Richard Johnson drove me back to Ebrington after the party. He was good company. Not only was he a fine actor but also a very decent man and a gentleman, not at all egotistical – a rare combination in the theatre.

Working in repertoire, the season soon passed and the family was back for the summer holidays. During my free days we would go strawberry picking or would explore the Cotswold countryside. I even found a village called Cornwell.

When the family left for Brighton I was counting the days to the end of the contract. Trevor Nunn called the company together and asked us whether we would all like to do a television production of *Antony and Cleopatra*. Those who wanted to take part would then open at the Aldwych Theatre in the Roman Season. I declined the offer. One year in the company was enough for me. The thought of working on the same plays again appalled me; I wanted to do some different work.

~

I WAS GLAD when my agent sent me a new play written by Rosemary Ann Sisson, *Finders Keepers*, a love story for ATV. It was a wartime romance between an RAF pilot and a WAAF which had ended in 1944 because the pilot had been married. When the pilot's situation changes fifteen years later, he contacts the ex-WAAF again. It was to be directed by Ken Hannam and produced by Henri Safran, who I had worked with as a director; John Standing was playing the pilot.

We began work on, *Finders Keepers* in December, as soon as I had left Stratford. The weather was freezing cold. John Standing and I played our most romantic moment in a churchyard. I had to stand on a box so that our heads were level and whatever breath escaped our lips during the conversation condensed into little wispy clouds that hovered around our faces. 'I've never kissed such cold lips,' John said as we shivered through the scene. Make-up had to keep wiping the dewdrops from our noses. When the play was shown on television there was not a sign of freezing noses and lips thanks to the lighting man.

Dylan was now seven years old and highly suspicious of the

whole Santa Claus story. This Christmas when we tried to creep quietly into his bedroom to deliver all his presents we ran into a trap. A tin tray balanced on the door came crashing down. John and I hit the ground like skilled commandos and slid along the floor just out of sight of the sleepy child staring into space. We were there for ages waiting for him to snuggle back down under the sheets. Later, having quietly arranged his toys, and almost helpless with suppressed laughter, we decided that perhaps the time had come to let him know the truth about Santa. On Christmas Day he told us that he had been tipped off about Santa by our bank manager's son. Of course those were the days when you knew who your bank manager was and even talked to him. Sometimes, as in our case, he became a family friend.

January the first 1973 began with learning from the prime minister, Edward Heath, that we British were now all members of the European Economic Community. Stories were told of butter, grain and meat mountains that would protect us from price changes during famine, pestilence and disease. His government's education minister, Margaret Thatcher, had abolished all free school milk, which had sustained so many children over the years. Thankfully, because my son was in the private system, he could still have fruit juice or milk for elevenses, but I felt angry for those children in the state system who had lost out.

Our friend Johnny Porterfield, who had run the successful restaurant The Harpsicord with his friend George Nicholson for so many years, had become a Benedictine monk at Worth Abbey upon his friend's death. Worried that he might become too holy I had told him that any time he felt in need of some healthy irreverent humour he could bring some of his monk friends to our house for a jolly lunch. Duly, two cars of monks pulled up in our street and parked in the two-hour bays. In the middle of a noisy, merry lunch discussing all kinds of subjects two monks went rushing out to change the parked cars round. It reminded me of some of Jonathan Routh's wonderfully funny nun paintings. The house was blessed by the monks so often that people have commented our dining room has an almost sacred atmosphere about it. If they had heard all the yelling and shouting from the exuberant monks over lunch they would hardly have considered the atmosphere sacred – innocently joyous perhaps.

I was then asked by the Abbot of Worth to give an after dinner speech to the boys at the school. Johnny, now Brother Anthony, told me that I was the first woman asked to speak in the dining hall and that it was a great honour. I thought very carefully about what I should talk about and decided that I would warn the boys of the rising problems of alcohol and drug abuse and debunk the whole advertising campaign claiming greater machismo to beer drinkers. So I began by quoting Shakespeare: 'It provoketh the desire but taketh away the performance.'

The talk went down well and the next thing I knew I was asked by the London School of Economics Catholic Society to give a talk at their annual dinner. Lord Longford was to be the male speaker and I was to follow him. I was a little nervous about it, especially as I was going to be sitting next to the Apostolic delegate. At that time there were many strikes going on – rail strikes, strikes by civil servants, fuel shortages and power cuts. Lord Longford got up to speak to a candle-lit room as all the power had gone. I got up after him hoping the power would stay off but as soon as I started, the lights all returned. 'Let there be light,' I said to a lot of laughter, and then discussed the various paths we choose seeking truth in our lives.

~

PAMELA LONSDALE, THE director who gave me my first job – in *The Present Stage*, at ABC TV – after my son was born, was now in charge of *Rainbow*, a children's programme that had a guest story teller each week. By now ABC TV had become Thames TV and Pamela wanted me to tell the story of Smith, the lonely hedgehog. So off we went on location to film a couple of hedgehogs, supposedly Smith meeting another hedgehog called Matilda. I had learned the script thoroughly and was sitting close by on a tree stump telling the story when over the shoulders of the camera crew I could see some curious horses making their way over to us to see what was going on. I kept going, chatting away, until the horses stuck their heads between the camera and the producer and blew through their lips, making the most dreadful noise. Realizing that the viewers would think it was me making the frightful noise, the crew chased the horses away and we started again. In the distance I could see the horses begin to walk back but this time I was able to speed up and finish the story just before they stuck their heads round the camera again. Ah, nature during filming! We filmed a second story about two baby hedgehogs, Smith and Matilda's progeny, a fortnight later. This time, however, it was in the calm atmosphere of the studio.

Meanwhile my agent sent me a play written by Keith Waterhouse and Willis Hall called *Who's Who*. The play's theme was infidelity, mistaken identity and a confusion of names: Black, White and Brown. Those who are called White in Act I become Black in Act II. I was to play Miss Brown. It was a very fast-delivery farce which would mean impeccable timing and, I thought, a real challenge. It was going to be put on at the Fortune Theatre at the beginning of the summer. I admired the work of the director Robert Chetwyn, and had enjoyed all his productions I had seen in the West End. He liked my work but wanted to know whether I could lose some weight before rehearsals started. My clothes were a size twelve and by no means could I have been called plump, but Bob wanted me to lose weight to have a certain look. I agreed to lose some weight and accepted the part. It was a four-hander and Francis Matthews, Joe Melia and Josephine Tewson were to play the other parts.

It was a strong cast and I was happy to be taking part but first I had to play Joyce, a tea-drinking, slatternly ex-prostitute in one of Joe Orton's earliest black comedy plays, *Ruffian on the Stair*, for Peter Willes at Yorkshire TV. The production was for the company's Sunday Night Theatre slot. My old friend David Cunliffe was directing the play but wanted me to be blonde for the part. So I had a blonde wig with dreadful black roots for my character. Michael Bryant played Mike, a petty criminal married to Joyce, and Billy Hamon played the sinister Wilson out to avenge a murder. It was lovely to play opposite Michael Bryant again. He was such a fine actor and great fun during rehearsals. Working on the Orton play with its black humour, I was reminded of the story my husband

John had told me of Orton's funeral in 1967. All the press were gathered outside Orton's place waiting for the coffin to be carried out, when from round the street corner came an ice-cream van playing the usual tinkling tune. It was a hot day and many of the journalists rushed to buy a whippy ice cream. They were all stand-ing licking their ice creams as the coffin was brought out and placed in the hearse. Pure Orton black comedy.

Straight after playing Joyce I was booked to play Serafina, a young lady from Petersburg, in a radio play set in Russia, Constantinople and Paris during the Bolshevik revolution. It was called *Flight*, a play in eight dreams by Mikhail Bulgakov. My old friend from Worthing repertory days, Gary Bond, played my lover, Golubkov. Gary had always made me laugh and to try and do a love scene with him to a radio mike in the centre of the studio was difficult. With Gary kissing the back of his own hand passionately while I kissed the back of my own hand with equal passion, it was guaranteed to reduce our overdeveloped senses of humour to a state of helpless mirth. In the end we had to look away from each other while slobbering over our respective hands. The brilliant John Tydeman adapted and produced *Flight* for World Drama. He and Enyd Williams were two of my favourite radio producers.

Then Peter Willes sent me a telegram asking whether I would return to Yorkshire TV to play the second wife, Lady Sims, in *The Twelve Pound Look* by J.M. Barrie. Gwen Watford and Michael Denison were playing the first wife and Sir Harry Sims. Mike Newell was the director. Gwen was a lovely down-to-earth woman and an actress I had admired for years; Michael Denison was a charming man who spoke with pride about his wife, Dulcie Gray's literary achievements. They lived in part of a stately home in the country but had a small apartment in London. After we had finished rehearsals in London he offered me a lift to Leeds in his very old Rolls-Royce. During the journey it began to rain and I was a bit alarmed that he had to work the windscreen wipers manually. But his whole approach to the journey was a bit like stepping back into the forties: he supplied a rug for my knees, a small bag of sweets and endlessly interesting conversation. He was from the old school of gentlemen actors and I was lucky enough to work with many of them.

~

BY THE TIME we started rehearsing for *Who's Who* I had lost weight for Bob Chetwyn and was now a size ten. It was a good thing too as I was dressed in a Mary Sarrin dress that clung to every part of my body.

It was a hot summer in 1973. Women were gamely trying to walk in platform shoes that nearly pulled their knees out of their sockets. Car bombs, planted by the IRA, had exploded in London earlier in the year as the troubles from Northern Ireland spread to England, so everyone was wary of strange packages. Naturally, there was a drop in the number of American tourists visiting London when they knew there might be danger of bombing. Most of them were so politically ignorant they did not even realize some of their own countrymen were supplying the IRA with funds to continue the fight. Just before we opened the play, I walked through Trafalgar Square on the way to Victoria to catch my train, and I could sense the wind of change. Gone were the wonderful freedom and optimism of the Sixties. Instead there was the start of collective fear and a sense of aggression.

We opened the play on 27 June and the production and players had rave reviews. But the play was exhausting to perform. It was so fast and the dialogue so complex that by Thursday, after a matinee, we were all on our reserves of energy, bewildered, and not quite sure which part we were playing or which act we were doing. The stress of the intense concentration took its toll and by Saturday night all four of us were wiped out and fit for nothing but sleep. After a couple of weeks of this fast pace I began to lose more weight and was now getting too thin. When I was down to a size eight, I began to eat all the things I had given up just to keep my energy levels up for the play.

During this time a neat, smartly dressed, red-haired lady in her late twenties called Gladys M. Hart turned up at the theatre and announced that she was secretary of my American fan club. I often had fan letters, to which I always replied, but I had no idea there was actually a fan club. She showed me all the write-ups and reviews in America of *Wuthering Heights* and other features. We had lunch together and she saw *Who's Who*, which she was going to write about for the fan magazine. I promised to keep her informed about any film or TV show I was doing and we corresponded for years until she moved from New York and gave up being the secretary. These days I am dreadfully behind with my fan mail but I hope a lot of the questions usually asked will be answered by this book.

While the play was on at the Fortune my agent told me that Gene Kelly wanted to see me about working with him on a film. I was thrilled as I was a great fan. When we met I was surprised to see how much smaller he was than I had imagined. We talked about the film script and then he said he thought I would have to lose some weight. By now I was less than a size eight and my clothes were hanging on me. If I lost any more weight I would look like someone out of Belsen. It would be dangerous and could make me ill. So I told him firmly that losing any more weight would not be a good idea for me. Mentally I said goodbye to the chance of working with him and went on to the theatre to do the show. By the time *Who's Who* closed, I was quite skinny.

~

PAMELA LONSDALE WANTED me back to do another *Rainbow* story, this time about an ostrich and a rabbit. I wore a wonderful Ginna Fratini dress with a smock to make me look a little more wholesome; I did not want my bony look to scare the children. There were two pages of story to learn, with one very dangerous line when the rabbit, in his nice warm burrow, addresses the ostrich, who did not want to face something and had stuck his head inside: 'And the rabbit said, "What are you doing with your head in my hole?"'. I knew that if I caught one grin on anyone's face when the line came up I would be utterly destroyed and unable to continue. Somehow I managed to get through the story in one take and could breath a great sigh of relief. Then the jokes on the set started and I was very grateful no one had uttered a word earlier.

John was now working as a freelance broadcaster for *World at*

One on Radio 4, so even though I had paid off the tax bill, money was still tight. Some friends of ours had moved from Brighton to a large old manor house in Somerset. They asked us to come and spend some holiday time with them; we were thrilled. With the dog in the back of the car we drove to Williton in Somerset and enjoyed the most wonderful time. Dylan knew their daughter and spent the days examining beehives, collecting eggs from the chickens and exploring the local countryside, while I helped my friend dig up the new potatoes and other vegetables, or pull lettuces as well as picking raspberries for dinner. Harry was in his element chasing everything that moved but we had to watch him carefully in case he went after the chickens again.

While we were in Somerset we explored a rough track which led to Culborne, a tiny village consisting of about three houses and a small church. It was a magical place and the memory of that day, as well as my time in Ebrington, contributed to ideas for my first book.

Back in Brighton, I was wandering round the Lanes one day when I found an art shop with a solitary piece of sculpture displayed in the window. It was called *Man on a Bench*. The sculptor was Peter Perri, a German Jew who had destroyed all his works in Germany rather than let the Nazis take them. He escaped to England, became a Quaker and began to create a whole body of work reflecting his new beliefs. I fell in love with the piece straightaway and went inside where the owner of the shop, John Lloyd, told me the price. During the following week the man on the bench haunted me, so I went back only to find that it had been removed from the window. I rushed into the shop where John Lloyd reassured me he still had the piece. He then took me into the back of the shop and showed me a whole collection of Perri's work. I bought *Man on a Bench* and carefully carried it home feeling shocked at my own extravagance but thrilled that I could now look at this wonderful piece of work whenever I wanted. Today, it sits in our sitting room in place of honour and is a continual source of inspiration to me.

BY THE END of 1973 Britain was in a terrible state. OPEC had put up the price of oil and disputes involving miners, railways and power stations were crippling the country. Many people were working a three-day week. As a self-employed person I now had to pay VAT, which was turning all self-employed people into tax collectors; and we had the added expense of employing accountants to make sure we did not make any mistakes.

By the beginning of 1974 there was talk of a possible early election. We, however, were rejoicing about John being offered an annual contract by Andrew Boyle, the editor and creator of BBC Radio's *World at One*. At the same time, Robert Love, a producer at Thames Television, sent me a script from a series to be called *Moody and Pegg*, written by Julia Jones and Donald Churchill. It was about a civil servant from Bolton (Bankruptcy Division) whose unconsummated, long-term relationship with her boss is over, as he has found someone else. Her boss has her upgraded and transferred to London. Daphne Pegg arrives in London with her hamster, Jarvis, to find that there is a mix-up with the lease of her new flat and she has to share the place with Roland Moody, an antique dealer, who is enjoying bachelorhood after a happy release from a seventeen-year marriage. There were to be six one-hour productions and Derek Waring was cast as Moody. We had some excellent directors: Richard Martin started off the series; Jonathan Alwyn and Mike Vardy directed the other four. June Roberts was the story editor. She and I became great friends, and later she was influential in my progression as a writer.

I had never been to Bolton but found out that a woman I knew called Lucille, who worked in a fish and chip shop in Hove, was from there. I used to go into the shop and sit and take notes of the lilt of her accent and her vowel sounds. The research worked well and there were many people from Bolton who thought I was from their town – I have still never been there.

I loved developing my character of Miss Pegg and the studio crew also enjoyed working on the series. I remember one scene when Jarvis, the hamster, had run into Moody's bedroom and disappeared under his bed. Daphne, knowing he was about to bring a girlfriend into his room, tries frantically to catch the animal before he comes in but finds herself trapped under the bed when Roland returns. Having grabbed the offending animal she tries to extricate herself but is squashed as the bed springs come down on her head. She gives a discreet cough, which stops the lovers' antics, and after coming out from underneath goes into a long speech of apology by the side of the bed. I remember looking at the cameraman at the end of the scene. He had tears running down his face and a hand-kerchief stuck in his mouth to stop him laughing out loud.

The series was a great success and rocketed to number four in the ratings. The turnaround between studio recordings was ten days, which included the rehearsal and any filming to be done. As Derek and I carried the show, it was a lot to learn in the time so I locked myself away in our friend Chris's house in Fulham, away from the family, so I could concentrate on the work. By the end of the series Thames was already starting to talk about a follow-up series for the next year.

~

THEN MY FRIEND Bill Hays telephoned and asked me to read the scripts of *Cakes and Ale*, adapted from the Somerset Maugham novel by Harry Green. The BBC was producing it as a three-part drama. He was offering me the part of Rosie Gann, the blonde bar-maid with the heart of gold, and heroine of the story. I loved the script and the idea of filming in Kent during the wonderful Indian summer we were experiencing. It was back to wearing a blonde wig again – this time, honey blonde. I also had to listen to lots of tapes to learn the Kent dialect. One problem I could see in the third part was when Rosie is eventually found as an old lady in New York. Somerset Maugham had described her as having a set of extremely white dentures with very red gums. I talked to my den-tist, Arthur Sturridge, who had designed Laurence Olivier's gap in his teeth when he played Archie Rice in *The Entertainer*. I showed Mr Sturridge the appropriate section in the book and he designed the most wonderful slide-on teeth with red gums. It had the right ageing effect without the make-up department having to resort to using loads of latex. The only problem with the teeth was when Michael Hordern, who was playing Willie Ashendon, sat down to have tea with me. He was supposed to be the young man I had influenced so many years ago now visiting me, an old lady and much older than himself – in reality, Michael was almost twice my age. I had warned props to make sure the cake was moist when I came to eat it, but they had forgotten and given me dry cake. The result was that I sprayed Michael Hordern with crumbs and the cake went up into the gap between my teeth and the slide-on teeth. Hordern, who was a notorious giggler, began to shake with laughter. His teacup was rattling, and even though I tried hard not to give in to laughter, we both had to start the scene again. After washing out the teeth and props moistening the cake we got through the scene without the hysteria.

There were some wonderful actors in *Cakes and Ale*. James Grout, whom I had worked with both in the theatre and on television, played Lord George Kemp; Peter Jeffrey played Alroy Kear; and Mike Pratt was an inspired Edward Driffield, the author who runs off with Rosie and marries her. I adored Mike. He was funny, wise and the most talented human being. He had composed the song made famous by Tommy Steele, 'I've Got a Handful of Songs to Sing You', and was a great musician. Lynn Farleigh played the second Mrs Driffield who, while helping to prepare the biography of her late husband, tries to cover up the fact that Rosie had inspired her famous writer husband's great works of literature. The story was based on Thomas Hardy and Willie Ashendon was really Somerset Maugham having a go at the literary establishment at the time.

In order to film one scene set in an oast house full of hops, the cameraman had to straddle across some beams in the roof. It was a noisy, lusty scene between Jimmy Grout and myself, rolling around in the hops. Bill Hays was out of sight in the corner. The smell of the hops made us soporific and giggly and the hops themselves seemed to get into every orifice; despite my tight corsets they even ended up in my bellybutton. We had finished the scene in the late afternoon and Bill, Jimmy and I were discussing how the scene had gone when a mournful voice from the rafters said, 'Oi feel like the village peeping Tom.' The effect of the hops and the cameraman's tone reduced us all to gibbering laughter and we all lay in the hops, except the cameraman who was still in the roof, howling with laughter.

When the programme was shown and received good reviews I was nominated for the Society of Film and Television Arts Award for Best Actress, 1974. Derek Waring's wife Dorothy Tutin was also up for the award for Shaw's *Major Barbara*; as was Janet Suzman for an Ibsen play, *Hedda Gabler*; and American actress Lee Remick for her performance in a Thames production called *Jennie*.

Dorothy Tutin then telephoned me to see whether I had won it. I told her that even though the BBC men in suits had a table and *Cakes and Ale* was their production they had told me I could come to the dinner if I paid twenty-five pounds. I guessed correctly that I had not won! In any case, I was a little apprehensive about winning. All the actresses I knew who had won in the past had been out of television work for at least two years after receiving the award. Dorothy did not want it either for the same reason, although Yorkshire Television paid for her ticket. We both hoped the American would win because the Americans liked winners, and the same wilderness for two years would not apply to her. Lee Remick did win and I watched the whole thing on television in the comfort of my own sitting room. The meanness of the BBC TV suit brigade did not surprise me.

～

SHORTLY BEFORE CHRISTMAS that year, John Lloyd, who had sold me the *Man on a Bench* sculpture, got in touch with me. He told me that Brighton Council were planning to make the decision to pull down the West Pier. He was trying to organize a protest march to stop them, and he asked whether I could help. Within days we had all organized a march, which was covered by the press and national television, and had thousands of signatures on a petition which I was going to present to the mayor. We did stop them pulling down the pier and over the years formed ourselves into The West Pier Society. We organized dances and all kinds of events to try and raise money. We also managed to get enough to improve the foundations and I served on the committee of artists, engineers, businessmen and all other lovers of the pier for fifteen years before resigning and letting some more high-powered people take over. Alas, in 2005, after storms, arson, in-fighting and sheer incompetence, the pier is now resembling a burnt old fishbone sticking out of the sea. I believe they will shortly demolish what remains.

Thames Television then offered me another series of seven hour-long episodes of *Moody and Pegg* to start in the late spring of 1975. They were also going to pay me a lot of money. However, I was worried that the general public were beginning to think of me as Miss Pegg. Anonymity is a most precious commodity only appreciated when it is lost. In the past people had recognized me, especially when I wore make-up. I had also received plenty of fan mail, but I could still merge into the background and listen or observe without anyone paying me any attention. I remember going to a party and joining a group of friends when one man, whom I did not know, blurted out that he hoped I would not be insulted, but, he asked, had anyone ever told me that I looked a bit like Judy Cornwell. Intrigued, I asked why I should be insulted. 'Ah well,' he replied, 'she's a lot older than you.' The group I was with pulled his leg mercilessly after that.

Similarly, I was once on a train, sitting opposite two women, one of whom was telling the other how well she knew Judy Cornwell. I was reading a book and looked up at this woman. I had never met her in my life. She prattled on about all sorts of things in my life which I realized she must have read in magazine articles, but she did not recognize the person sitting opposite her. That was the sort of anonymity that I loved. As an actress it is important to observe people's mannerisms and their characters. Also as a writer, it is important to listen to conversations and observe situations without people noticing. When the first series of *Moody and Pegg* went out I began to lose that precious anonymity, so I would mentally cover myself in an invisible cloak and try to disappear from the curious gazes I met in the street. When the offer came for the second series I was also concerned that I could become typecast whereas I had enjoyed a versatile career up to then. So I made up my mind that I would do the second series but no more.

Before starting on *Moody and Pegg* I was offered another television play by the BBC, playing Frieda von Richthofen, in a play called *Frieda*. It was a beautiful, bitter-sweet play about the over-powering love Frieda felt for D.H. Lawrence so that she left her husband, Professor Weekly, and her two children and ran off with him. Professor Weekly was to be played by Michael Bryant; and D.H. Lawrence by Michael Kitchen. The script had been written by Fay Weldon, and Don Taylor was directing. Frieda was a fabulous part for an actress. I was thrilled it would be shown giving me a totally different character from Miss Pegg. Unfortunately, even though the play was shown as a trailer for the following week, it was cancelled when the BBC found out that the copyright of everything to do with Frieda von Richthofen was owned by an American. The production, which cost a fortune to make, is still sitting in some vault at the BBC. The producers told me it was very good, but I have never seen it.

Meanwhile my old friend Verity Lambert had been made the executive producer of *Moody and Pegg*. It was good to see her again and we caught up on all our news and gossip. And two other directors had joined the team by now: Baz Taylor and Roger Tucker – both brilliant directors.

My instincts for not doing more than two series were reaffirmed when the writers put a shower scene in one of the later episodes. At the reading I told the producer that they would only be able to shoot my shoulders because I would be wearing a swimsuit. Donald Churchill said that his wife had shown her breasts on television and everyone was now used to nudity. 'That may be,' I replied, 'but I think it would take something away from Miss Pegg to be seen nude. And I'm most definitely not prepared to do a nude scene.' What I had loved about the writing, and what the viewers had enjoyed, was the delicate balance between the comedy and reality of the storyline. The last episode was beautifully and sensitively directed by Roger Tucker and I felt glad to finish the story there, with the audiences saying they wished there could have been more of the series. Verity also felt the same about it.

At the end of the series I drove down to Somerset to join the family at our friends' manor house again. There I could relax, slop about and commune with nature, and sit with my morning coffee dressed only in my dressing gown if I wanted. Bill and Isobel were such good friends. When we returned home there was a calamity! Our wonderful nanny, Margaret, was in love and going to get married. John, Dylan and Harry the dog became the male guardians of her honour. We invited the young man round for lunch and it was not just Harry growling; I have never seen such male possessiveness. When she left to get married the whole house mourned for her. She had been our anchor, a member of the family and confidante to all of us.

The Belgian au pair arrived soon after. She liked motorbikes but was inexperienced in the home, so I started to teach her about our way of living. She was going to stay with us for six months then we would have to look for someone else.

My agent them sent me a play called *Old Flames,* written by A.E. (Ted) Whitehead. It was to be performed at the Bristol Old Vic studio theatre and was to be directed by Jonathan Hale. Four women in a man's life get together and share their experiences and disillusionment with each other. They then kill him and eat him. My old friend Gary Bond was playing the man. I played Diane, the strong but bitter ex-wife; Anne Dyson played his mother; and Jane Asher and Susan Tracy played the other women in his life. My agent said I should do it even though the money was lousy. He thought it would be good for me and, anyway, I had made lots of money that year. Such economic reasoning only seems to apply to artists, I think. The play had extremely explicit language in it and when we came to rehearse, all of us felt a little embarrassed. We even had special swearing and rude sessions so we could feel more familiar with the words. Jonathan Hale was a very patient director who let us all work at our own pace. He guided us through the exploration of our characters until he had a very powerful production.

When the play opened it received critical acclaim and as it would be transferring to the New Arts Theatre in London in the new year I was asked to go with it. Gary agreed to go, so did Anne Dyson, but Jane and Susan had other commitments and were replaced by Barbara Ewing and Katherine Fahy.

Ted came down to Bristol and was very pleased with the production. He confided in me that he had wanted me for his original production of *Alpha Beta*, a play I loved and wanted to do, but the producers had wanted someone older.

Just before the end of the run at Bristol, my mother let me know she was coming with a friend to see the show. I was horrified and tried to put her off but she was determined to come and told me they were taking me out for dinner afterwards. During the meal in Harvey's restaurant after the show my mother's pursed lips let me know exactly what she thought of the play. Over pudding she blurted out, 'Why do you come all the way here to be in such a dirty play? Why don't you take nicer plays?' I told her it was a challenge and explained what the play meant. She simply changed the subject to what she considered to be more pleasant matters, such as our Christmas arrangements.

Chapter Fifteen

1976–1980

~

WE BEGAN OUR rehearsals for *Old Flames* at the New Arts Theatre in London amid further bomb scares. At the end of rehearsals late one afternoon after I had walked along Shaftesbury Avenue and reached Piccadilly Circus, I noticed that the usual bunch of scally-wags hanging around Eros were nowhere to be seen. I was going to go into Swan and Edgar's but my instincts told me to grab the first bus out of the area. Just as well I did, as the bomb planted close to Swan and Edgar's went off shortly afterwards. Harold Wilson's labour government was back in power with a slender majority, and there was still industrial unrest and national economic problems. In our house we were just thrilled that John's annual contract with the BBC had been renewed and that I was working as well. Our son was now at Great Walstead Preparatory School, which meant us taking part in a school run with other parents. He was so happy there that the inconvenience of the long daily trips to school were inconsequential.

Katherine Fahy and Barbara Ewing, an extremely talented New Zealand actress, needed the same amount of rehearsal time to explore their characters that we had been given in Bristol. For those of us who had already performed the play it was useful to have a second examination of the text.

The play opened to excellent notices. Although laughing nervously in the first act, the audience was frozen into silence in the second act, which is what Jonathan Hale had intended the reaction to be. Over twenty years later, in the 1990s, I worked with two directors who had been young students when we were performing

Old Flames. They both confided in me that they had been inspired by the production and my performance to become directors.

At that time Sue Lawley had a late-night chat show on BBC television. After the first night of the play I was invited on to it to talk about the show and my own career. Waiting in the hospitality room to appear after me was a young politician called John Prescott. My husband John and I talked to him after the programme was finished. The poor fellow was terribly worried about our fishermen possibly getting hurt in the row between Britain and Iceland over cod fishing and had been trying to get a meeting with Harold Wilsons who seemed to be avoiding him. I asked him whether he and his wife would like to come to see the play. Unfortunately, because of the crisis, he was unable to make it. Struck by the man's sincerity and concern for the fishermen I told John that if there was any justice in the world of politics John Prescott would end up at least as a cabinet minister! – Well spotted, even if I say so myself.

When my friend Joan came over from Dublin for our annual birthday tea at the Ritz, I was given the remainder of the birthday cake in a box to take home with me. It was a measure of the general paranoia in London when, after he dropped me at the New Theatre, the taxi driver wanted me to take the box out of the cab before I paid him. On the late train travelling home to Brighton I received numerous suspicious glances at my box containing the birthday sponge fish.

Shortly after the show finished the run I was walking up Harley Street to see my dentist when I spotted what I thought was someone who looked like an older version of my chum Mike Pratt walking towards me. As he drew closer I realized with horror that it *was* Mike; I was shocked at his appearance. 'I've got the big C, Jude,' he said with a wry smile, 'haven't got long now. See you over the other side, kid.' As I sat in the dentist's waiting room I had a good cry. Mike died a few months later.

~

IN APRIL 1976, my agent sent me a script, adapted by Gerald Savory, of Dion Boucicault's *London Assurance*. The BBC had me in mind for the part of Lady Gay Spanker and Cedric Messina, the producer, wanted to discuss the play over lunch at the BBC's tele-vision centre at White City. I had just returned from Dublin where I had been staying for a few days with some friends who kept horses. Each day we had gone riding around the Wicklow Hills. One morning I had galloped up the drive of my old friend Gordon Thomas, who was living in tax exile in Wicklow. He had married Edith, a lovely German woman, after his divorce from Annie Nightingale – I had gone to his wedding in London and wept dis-gracefully all the way through the ceremony. When I rode up his drive I yelled out various rude things and he came out of his front door outraged at this unexpected invasion of his property. When he saw it was me, his face broke into a large smile. 'What the hell are you doing here, Cornpoke?' he shouted. My friends and I then had coffee with him and we had a wonderful time catching up on all our news. Over lunch at the BBC Cedric Messina, knowing I had just returned from a riding holiday in Ireland, asked me whether I could ride side saddle for the filming of Lady Gay Spanker's scenes as the play was set in 1841 and the ladies all rode side saddle then. I said I could take a few lessons and, providing I was riding a mare, could see no problems in doing the scenes.

We started rehearsals at the BBC's Acton rehearsal rooms. Charles Gray was playing Sir Harcourt Courtly. He had just finished playing Blofeld in *Diamonds Are Forever*. Nigel Stock, whom I had worked with in the theatre, was playing the squire; James Bree, whom I had also worked with before, played my hus-band. The young lovers were played by Anthony Andrews and Jan Francis. Dinsdale Landen was playing Dazzle; and Clifford Rose, another actor I had worked with over the years on different pro-ductions, was playing Cool.

We rehearsed during the hottest British summer I could remem-ber, and the ground became extremely hard. In Sussex, the farm-land was bleached almost white with the heat. Aware of the dangers of riding on hard ground I asked the producer's assistant whether I was covered in case of an accident. He assured me this was so. Unfortunately, I did not read the small print on the BBC contract stipulating that the only people covered by insurance were members of staff. I have never made that mistake again. Now I read every word of any contract I sign.

We began the filming near Tetbury in Gloucestershire. I had to get the horse to leap over a hedge with the cameraman hidden on the other side. All these scenes went well despite the fact that I had been given a steeplechasing stallion to ride instead of a mare.

On the last day of filming, it was extremely hot. Nigel Stock was bitten by two of the dogs and the horses were very edgy. We were lining up for the wild gallop across the fields when my stallion began getting tetchy. He obviously did not like the white stallion that Anthony Andrews had just ridden out to where we were to begin. One of the assistants started shouting at us through a loud-hailer and my horse panicked. He started bucking, trying to throw me. With a side saddle there is only one stirrup for the left foot, the right leg is hooked over the leaphead. Because the play was set in 1841 I was unable to wear a safety riding hat; just a period hat of the time was pinned into my red wig. The stirrup slipped off with all the bucking and then the horse threw me into the air. I landed flat on my back on the hard ground and I heard the sounds of cracking in my spine. Looking up at the hard blue sky I wondered whether I would be playing wheelchair parts for the rest of my life. The camera crew had filmed the whole thing and found it hilarious. A perfect comedy throw. I slowly tried to move and found I could get up. I was rushed off to the local hospital for an X-ray, where the doctor just gabbled on about television programmes he liked.

When he gave me the all clear, I returned to the filming where they had dressed up a local rider to wear my wig and costume to complete the galloping scene. The rider came up to me having completed the gallop scene and said he had found the horse really strong, and the effort of holding the reins had nearly pulled his arms out of their sockets. He was amazed that I had been able to handle him at all.

Although I was in pain, I got back on the horse and completed the rest of the riding scenes. Then I drove home to Brighton. The next day I woke up unable to move my head, my arms or legs. John knew of a naturopath in London who had helped many of his BBC friends so he made an appointment for me and drove me there.

The man was brilliant and it was confirmed much later by an orthopaedic surgeon that he had in fact saved my spine from being permanently damaged. I had five vertebrae out between the neck and the middle of my back, and the base of my spine was slightly out of place. He manipulated them back into position and showed me how to help myself if the base of my back played up. It did continually. I would find myself suddenly seizing up and unable to move in shops, on a walk, or just climbing the stairs at home. Once the naturopath had to instruct me over the phone how to click myself back in place so I could move again. I went to see my GP who referred me to an orthopaedic consultant. He X-rayed the whole of my spine and found that I had a fracture just above the top of my hips. He suggested heat treatment, ultrasonic massage and exercises to strengthen the muscles supporting the spine. If I was lucky enough to have good bones, he told me, it could possibly heal. However, he warned me that in order to protect the sciatic nerve the body would probably put on weight.

I told Equity, my trade union, about the accident. They referred me to the industrial injuries board so they could take the matter forward. The industrial injuries board sent a report to Equity and they began a lawsuit against the BBC for negligence. My friend James Grout was also injured by a horse that year, but he was working for ITV who treated him with great care and settled generously. The BBC insurers came back to Equity with the reply that it was not a BBC horse. Well, it certainly was not mine. They dragged out the case for a couple of years, as only insurance companies can, until we were about to appear in court. Just before my case was to come up, my friend Dorothy Tutin was in court claiming compensation for having been thrown by a camel she was riding at a charity event in Chipperfield's Circus. She had a considerable number of injuries and the court found in her favour. After Dorothy's case, the BBC settled with us out of court.

There were numbers of actors who told me I should not sue as I would never work for the BBC again. This was absolute nonsense. The insurance suit brigade was nothing to do with the makers of programmes. I was even employed by the BBC making *Mill on the Floss* – with the same director, Ronald Wilson, who had directed me in *London Assurance* – when the settlement came through. Any actors reading this book should learn from my experience. I have always advised young actors to be more like the Americans: never ever volunteer to do anything that could be remotely dangerous, especially when working with animals. Make the company employ a stunt person.

It took ten years for my back to heal and, strangely enough, you can get used to working in pain. It is only when you have a day free of it, and the memory of how life used to be returns, that you dread the next restriction of movement through pain.

~

MY FRIEND PAMELA Lonsdale was going to produce and direct a musical version of Mrs Gaskell's *Cranford* for Thames Television. She sent me the script, which was written by John Wells, asking me to play Miss Matty. I would have to play both the young and the old Miss Matty – different wigs of course. It was a well-written script and the composer for the musical score was Carl Davis. The musical was set in 1830 and playing the old Miss Matty was helped by the pain in my back restricting my movements so that I walked and moved like an arthritic old lady. Playing the younger Miss Matty was painful, especially when I had to dance as well. Colin Douglas and I had a beautiful duet called 'Days Gone By' and the whole cast were mostly people I had worked with before, including Clifford Rose who had been with me on *London Assurance* and who was most concerned about my back injury. It was a happy time spent on the production of *Cranford* with a cast of most talented people. The musical was shown over the Christmas period and was well received by the critics.

A month before Christmas 1976 my agent called me to tell me that Lindsay Anderson wanted me to take over the leading-lady part in *Bed Before Yesterday*, a new play written by Ben Travers, which was on at the Lyric. John and I went to see it and I found out it was the most demanding role as, apart from about five minutes, I would be on stage for the whole two hours. Sheila Hancock was playing the part and her contract had come to an end; Joan Plowright had played the part before her. I met Lindsay and asked him why he wanted me. The other women who had played Alma were at least ten years older and I was worried that I was too young for the part. Lindsay explained that the other women had found the part demanding and exhausting which is why he wanted someone younger. Also he wanted my authoritative presence on stage as well as my comedic ability. A wig and the right clothes, he assured me, would soon help me to age. I told him I was not interested in reproducing anyone else's performance but wanted enough rehearsal time to discover my own character. He agreed to let the theatre go dark for a week in order to let me have enough rehearsal time; and my agent agreed a very good salary plus a percentage of the box office receipts.

So in January 1977, I went to London for the read-through of the play. I liked the cast. Playing opposite me was Michael Aldridge, a wonderful actor with a great sense of humour. Royce Mills and Jonathan Cecil were remarkable farceurs; and Susie Blake, later to star in *Coronation Street*, was the young ingenue. June Ellis, Leonard Fenton, Gabrielle Day and Paul Foulds made up the rest of the wonderfully talented and supportive cast. After the read-through I went with Michael Aldridge, Lindsay Anderson and the ninety-year-old Ben Travers to a pub near the theatre for a spot of lunch before starting to plot the play. I sat next to Ben at the table, but while waiting for my food to be served I felt his hand groping my bottom. I could not believe he was capable of anything so naughty. I eased over to Lindsay and whispered in his ear, 'He's groping. What shall I do? Will you change places with me?'

'Don't be such a spoilsport, Judy,' Lindsay replied. 'He's ninety and having a wonderful time. Leave him alone.' I looked at Ben. There was a great beaming smile on his face. Okay, I thought, this time grope away because you are not going to get another chance, you old devil.

After the first day's rehearsal, and while making my way home, I queued for a bus to Victoria opposite the theatre. My name was up in lights and yet I was standing in a slight drizzle feeling quite anonymous – an observer again pondering over the incongruities of life.

When we opened the show to really good notices, Ben became quite cunning. He would visit backstage during the interval when I had to change. He would let himself into my small reception room and pretend he could not hear my shout from the dressing room that I was changing. Armed with a box of chocolates from Harrods, he would squeeze my arm and say, 'We don't want you to lose weight with all this running about, do we?'

I had to wear 1930s high-heeled shoes in the play and at the end of the show each night my back would be killing me. When my weight fell below a certain figure, the orthopaedic surgeon was proved right when the sciatic nerve almost made me scream with pain.

Because of the early school runs, I trained myself to catnap. I would always arrive two and a half hours before the show and then with a promise from the stage door man that he would wake me in an hour, I would go into a deep sleep on my couch in the dressing room. The local Soho priest used to drop in to my dressing room for a few minutes about half an hour before curtain up. He was a lovely man who went out every night round the Piccadilly area looking out for young people in trouble. Before he set out on a rather depressing time outside, he would come for a laugh and a chat, knowing I kept Ben's Harrods chocolates in my dressing table drawer. He would never accept more than two chocolates, but would then, with a sweet tooth satisfied, set forth into the night to save souls.

A car picked me up at the stage door each night and delivered me to Victoria station in time to catch the eleven o'clock train home. The wonderful Brighton Belle, alas, was no longer in existence because of some cock-eyed philosophy about it being elitist. Instead, all the West End thespians would crowd around the plastic-topped tables in the buffet car and gossip and share all recent news. My old friend Jack Tinker, by now the *Daily Mail* critic, was usually returning home from a first night so we could hear from him about the new shows. If there was no one serving on the buffet car, whoever got to the station first would grab some refreshments so we had something to drink and eat on the way home. All of us were in different shows. When we shared the same matinee we would take it in turns to entertain the others to tea between shows. The routine was fun and I enjoyed my work and the travel during the run of the show.

~

BY NOW TED Whitehead had written another play, called *Mecca*, which was going to be put on at the Open Space fringe theatre. Jonathan Hale was going to direct again and they wanted me to play the part of Jill. Lindsay had been offered the play *The Kingfisher*, which started rehearsals before *Bed Before Yesterday* completed its run. I asked Lindsay whether I should take Ted's play. Working at the Open Space Theatre would mean taking a huge drop in salary.

'I think you should,' Lindsay replied.

'But what about you?' I said. 'You're taking a real establishment play. What is your message for the rest of the seventies?'

'Survival,' Lindsay replied.

After talking to Jonathan Hale about the play, we agreed that Ted was going to rewrite some of the scenes in the second act, which needed to be shorter. I then went off with the family to Tunisia on holiday. During the weeks in the seaside resort of Hammamet, I was relieved to see that warnings to my son about paedophiles had been well and truly digested. I had used *Star Trek* as an example of how people, no matter who they were, could think in an alien way. I had told him that if any teacher, stranger or even a family friend ever said, did, or mimed certain things, he was to run like hell and tell someone. While John and I were lazing round the hotel pool one afternoon, Dylan came running to us shouting that there was an alien in the men's lavatory. John and a group of British and German men pursued the guilty-looking man along the beach but they lost him. The whole event had a strange syn-chronicity with the play *Mecca*, which has British tourists in Morocco killing a young Arab boy who is believed to have raped a young British girl.

When I returned from holiday the script still had not been amended. I talked to Jonathan on the phone and suggested that

(*left*) The cottage I rented for the Stratford season, in Ebrington Village. It inspired a lot of my first novel *Cow and Cow Parsley*.

(*below*) In ATV's *Love Story* with John Standing, 1972.

(*below*) With Francis Matthews in *Who's Who* by Willis Hall and Keith Waterhouse 1973.

(*below*) With Gladys M. Hart, the head of my American fanclub, in 1973.

(*above*) Playing Daphne Pegg in *Moody and Pegg*. Roland Moody was played
   by Derek Waring. (Courtesy of Thames Television)

(*below*) Playing Rosie Gann in *Cakes and Ale*. On the right, Mike Pratt on the
   piano and James Grout behind him. I was nominated for Best Actress by
   the Society of Film and Television Awards (the early BAFTA) for this role.

(*above*) We Brightonians formed a society to preserve the West Pier from being pulled down. (Tom Blau/Camera Press)

(*above*) John preparing to feed a hungry family, 1976.

(*left*) Playing Lady Gay Spanker in *London Assurance* for the BBC – before I was thrown from the horse. In this photo, with my red hair, I look like my grandmother Dearie.

(*above*) All made-up
with a blonde wig as
Miss Trant in *Good
Companions* with Nigel
Hawthorne. (Courtesy
Yorkshire Television)

(*top right*) Presented to the
Queen Mother at Windsor
after a private show of
Most Gracious Lady.
Later in the 1990s, the
Queen Mother was to
become one of *Keeping Up
Appearances* greatest fans.

(*bottom right*) Playing Anya,
with Dudley Moore as
Patch the Elf and David
Huddleston as Santa
Claus, in *Santa Claus: The
Movie*.

(*above*) Playing Mrs MacDipper in
    December Rose for the BBC, 1985.

(*right*) Playing Aunt Belle in
    Bergerac – smuggling cigarettes
    and whisky, 1986.

(*below*) I played Anja and Sir
    Anthony Quayle played my
    husband, the mayor, in *The
    Government Inspector*, 1988.

(*above*) Rehearsing for *Keeping Up Appearances*.

(*below*) And in character. I played Daisy, Geoffrey Hughes was Onslow and
Mary Millar was Rose, 1991.

(*above*) With my Aussie friend Kevin Palmer and Joan Littlewood at a party in
 London, 1993.

(*below*) The fairy godmother in *Cinderella* – opposite Rolf Harris and Gary
 Wilmot in Birmingham.

(*left*) Playing Josie in Carlton's *The Wrong Side of the Rainbow* in 2000. (Courtesy of Carlton)

(*below*) With my old friends Brian Murphy, Victor Spinetti and Carmen Silvera while touring with *You're Only Young Twice*.

three pages could go with the summing-up of one line, 'a Marxist with a mortgage'. Ironically, much to Ted's amusement, when the critics talked about the writing they singled that line out. The play was set in a Moroccan holiday resort, which meant a stage covered with sand, and a white wall and blue sky in the background. The sexual Puritanism of a group of British tourists is explored through the characters of two married couples, a pretty young medical student, played by Brenda Cavandish, and a Liverpudlian soccer star, played by David Schofield. I played Jill, a woman married to a supercilious, homosexual army bore, played by David Bailie. Jill has somehow worked out a way of living with the situation. Jean Boht and Glyn Owen played the middle-aged couple whose relationship is uneasy now the children have grown up and left home. The first act was a witty if sometimes vicious build-up of sexual tension until the young medical student wanders outside the compound in her bikini and is raped by one of the locals. The group outrage that follows her degradation is thwarted by her refusing to cooperate in the cry for vengeance.

In *Mecca*, Ted had saved all his diatribe against women for my character to say. The racial bile and explosion of criticism for the young medical student was relentless. With the close proximity to the audience in the Open Space theatre in the round, I could feel the audience's hatred for my character. The hairs on my neck were nearly bristling with the waves of anger I was receiving for and creating with my inflammatory speeches. We received very good reviews but I was very careful on my way home. With the amount of anger I knew I had generated I did not want to run into a member of the audience who might have taken the speeches too personally.

~

NEXT I WAS offered *Viktoria*, a supernatural play set in Budapest in 1873, for the BBC. I was playing an English governess to a Hungarian child, Viktoria, whose father (played by an Australian actor, Lewis Fiander) has married again after the death of his first wife. The second wife was played by the beautiful Catherine Schell, who was going out with my old pal, director Bill Hays; the

Hungarian Peter Sasdy was directing. In the play the child has a
malevolent doll which hates the second wife. The doll was played
by a midget actress. While we were rehearsing, Catherine and I
would take it in turns to lift her up to the food counter in the BBC
canteen so she could choose what she wanted to eat.

I got on well with Catherine and during one scene where I had
to stalk her round a darkened room, I was supposed to look sinister. It did not work because Catherine was taller than me. So the
wardrobe department put me in elevated shoes to make me taller.
But these platform shoes made a clumping sound as I walked
towards her, reducing Catherine to helpless laughter. We both got
over the giggles only to find that the designer had placed an owl
chained to a steel perch in the drawing room. As I continued to
stalk Catherine, clumping away in my elevated shoes, the owl took
fright, tried to fly, and ended up dangling ignominiously from his
perch. We had to wait for the owl to be tied more firmly to the perch
and we had to calm down after all the hilarity before we could start
again.

Travelling up and down from Brighton to London during this
time was not easy. Jim Callaghan had taken over from Harold
Wilson as prime minister and Britain was having its policies
dictated by the International Monetary Fund. There was high
inflation and there were many strikes and shortages, as well as the
continual threat of IRA bombs. My husband John, having been sent
over to Iran by the *World at One* programme, was now in Paris,
where he became one of the few journalists able to meet the
Ayatollah Khomeini in exile. He talked to George Brown, the
Foreign Secretary, and told him that if the Ayatollah returned to
Iran there would be the most terrible upheavals. George Brown
replied that journalists always looked on the black side of things –
another politician who did not listen.

When *London Assurance* was transmitted, it received wonderful
reviews. I was sent a script by a director whom I had once watched
performing as an actor with the Caryl Jenner Players in the Seaford
drill hall, Harold Snoad. Years later he was to cast me as Daisy in
Keeping Up Appearances; for now, however, he was interested in me

playing the part of a lisping aristocrat in the Dick Emery Christmas Special.

I loved taking part in the show which was pure madness from beginning to end. June Whitfield and Roy Kinnear were two of the really talented comic actors also in the show. Years later, Roy was killed when he was thrown from a horse while filming. After the news of his death, I was appalled to hear what problems his wife experienced at the hands of the film company's insurers.

We had the usual family Christmas and bought Dylan a special chessboard as he had done well in the National Junior Chess championships. We now had the old 1940s Aga we inherited with the house working on solid fuel. With all the power cuts we had been experiencing it was invaluable, as we were still able to cook, heat water and keep warm when all the lights failed. We kept some paraffin lamps too, so we could continue living normally. Some friends of ours had bought small generators, but we managed all right with just the Aga. It was during these times that I had more ideas for the book I intended to write. Having been brought up during the war I was used to thinking in terms of survival. I also learned how to make my own bread and pasta. Often the kitchen was full of rising bread or strings of drying pasta.

The BBC sent me a script in January 1978 to be filmed first in Manchester and then North Wales. It was written and directed by David Wheatley and was about the Brothers Grimm. David Collings, a brilliant Brighton actor, and Ian Marter were to play Jacob and Wilhelm Grimm, who slowly over the years collected all the European stories, although some were reputed to have begun in India, and produced the Grimm's fairy tales. I was to play Dorothea Grimm, their mother, who had told them so many bedtime stories that when the stories were to be shown during the production I, as Dorothea, played all the dominant women in them. I loved working with David Wheatley. He reminded me of Jim Clark on *Every Home Should Have One* in the way he prepared for filming. David would have a series of drawings which he would show us so we could see what he was trying to achieve and in this way we could help him.

The two twelve-year-old boys playing the brothers when they

were children were looking droopy-eyed when we came to film them listening to the stories. They were self-conscious in their period nightshirts and David wanted more animation. I whispered to him that if he just rolled the camera, instead of telling them the story I was supposed to tell, I would sing them a rude song. Then he would get the right reaction. So I sang them a rude song, 'Ma's out, Pa's out, let's talk rude. Pee Po belly button drawers. Let's all dance in the garden in the nude. Pee Po Belly Button Drawers.' The two boys' faces lit up and they yelled with delight. One of the boys, Garth Bardsley, is now an actor and a writer. He got in touch with me when he was writing Anthony Newley's biography and reminded me of the rude song I had once sung him.

While I was in Manchester filming *Brothers Grimm*, I was walking along the street to the Midland Hotel when I saw Donald Pleasance walking from the station on the other side. He waved frantically and yelled, 'I've got to be interviewed about a children's book I've written. Do you know, they don't even pay for writers to travel first class any more.' I understood his chagrin. Equity had agreed with the television companies who had said that they were having a hard time, that actors would waive the right to automatic first-class travel. The result was that often actors would be travelling second class when make-up girls and other staff were travelling first class. The whole situation was potty.

When we left for North Wales to film, we were greeted by a landscape covered in snow. The castle was freezing but quite wonderful for the programme. On the ceiling of the main hall I saw the names of the thirteen Welsh tribes, and was able to tell John when I arrived home that the Parry tribe was one of them. When I saw the programme go out I was so proud to have been a part of it. It was shown again about fifteen years later and the quality and depth of the programme were still most impressive. I hope the BBC have kept it in their archives because each generation should see this wonderful production.

~

THERE WAS TO be an anniversary gala celebrating John Counsel's forty years of running Windsor Theatre and the Queen Mother, now in her eightieth year, was to attend. There would also be a private performance of *Most Gracious Lady*, a two-hour show which was a series of sketches of sixteen queens from Queen Elizabeth I to the present day, devised and directed by Peter Clapham. Peter wanted me to take part with Francis Matthews, Martin Jarvis, Mary Kerridge and Elizabeth Counsel. I was given speeches or letters written by Queen Charlotte and Queen Victoria to read. I also had the daunting task of being the Queen Mother during the darkest days of the Second World War; and finished with the Coronation speech by the present Queen, Elizabeth II.

There was an invited audience of stars who had appeared at the theatre over the past forty years. I have a good ear, as they say, and when I started on Queen Elizabeth II's Coronation speech I managed to hit the exact note that I had heard on news clips in 1953. There was an intake of breath from the audience. I knew that from that particular sound I had made, one could either satirize the speech, which is what they feared, or I could give my own interpretation of the words. I put in as much passion as I could and felt the audience sigh with relief. When I met the Queen Mother afterwards, she looked me straight in the eye and said, 'I blubbed. You made me blub.' She mimed wiping tears from her eyes, and said again, 'Yes, you made me blub.'

I was fascinated by this woman. She was nearly eighty and yet had only tiny, thread-like laughter lines around her eyes. Showbusiness writers had always written about my skin being as smooth and wholesome as fresh eggs, but the Queen Mother's skin was as flawless and smooth as the finest bone china. Like Princess Alexandra, she looked directly into your eyes, and for that moment of meeting seemed only interested in you and what you had to say.

Shortly after the show, I arranged a meeting with Verity Lambert at Thames to discuss an idea I had for a television comedy drama series. It had been inspired by a conversation with my brother. Verity loved the idea. When I asked her who should write it she told me that I should and promptly commissioned me to write an hour-long pilot and further breakdown for twelve more episodes. I wondered whether June Roberts, the story editor on *Moody and Pegg*, had spoken to her as June had always encouraged me to write. Knowing that June had nagged me into writing quickly, I asked John whether he would like to work with me so we could bounce ideas off each other. John agreed and we had more rows over working together than we had during the whole of our marriage. The rows were basically about our different senses of humour, and we were forever asking Verity to mediate. We finished the pilot and Verity was really keen to produce the series. We were paid a handsome cheque for our efforts and I have a photograph in our album of me holding the cheque and looking slightly insane with happiness. The fact that I had been paid for writing was a seal of approval for something I normally did in my own time and then filed away in a cupboard. It gave me an enormous boost of confidence.

Unfortunately, Verity was transferred to Euston Films and although our pilot was still under option to Thames, the new Head of Drama brought in his own writers with their own ideas. With the pilot still under option, however, we could do nothing else with it. I was then booked to be in another BBC television play written by *The Good Life* authors, John Esmonde and Bob Larbey, called *A Touch of the Tiny Hackets*. It was about a burglar dwarf, played by Rusty Goffe, who's caught and bashed on the head by the householder. The householder is then ostracized by his family and friends for his unsporting actions against a minority group; his wife even takes a lover in protest. It was a hilarious anti-politically correct comedy play and was directed by James Cellan Jones who was the BBC's Head of Plays. Ray Brooks, another Brighton actor, played the householder and I played his wife. My chum Tony Selby and Brenda Bruce were also in it. During the rehearsals at the Acton BBC TV rehearsal rooms the cast went up to the canteen. Seated at one table was a group of actors who had been working there when I was working on *Viktoria*. During those rehearsals they had seen me lift a midget up to the food counter. Now they saw me queuing up with a dwarf.

'What is it with you and little people, Judy?' they said, as I passed their table with my tray.

~

WHILE WORKING ON the play I was approached by another BBC producer, Barry Letts, who was preparing to put out eight twenty-six-minute episodes of *The Mill on the Floss*. He wanted me to play Bessie Tulliver. I took the manuscripts home with me to read and let my agent know that I wanted to do the part. Ronald Wilson, who had directed *London Assurance* and had worked with me as an actor on a radio show when we were both in our early twenties, was going to direct, so I knew it would be a good production. When we began rehearsals at the BBC rehearsal rooms at Acton I found I was working with a wonderful cast of experienced actors and extremely talented young people. Young Tom was played by a highly intelligent young boy called Jonathan Scott-Taylor, who played the role of Damien in the film *Damien: Omen Two*. The older Tom Tulliver was played by Christopher Blake; Pippa Guard played Maggie and Anton Lessing played Philip Wakem – three brilliantly talented young actors. Ray Smith played my husband, Mr Tulliver.

After weeks of rehearsal we set off for the filming. We were all staying near Stratford in an old hotel which was owned by Danny La Rue. During the first night there I was woken up in the early hours by someone in the next room snoring for Britain. I put on my dressing gown and went down to the receptionist and asked him to ring whoever was in the room next to me and tell him to turn over on his side. When I returned to my room the snoring had stopped. I never discovered who the person was but perhaps my complaining was a help to his wife when she next grumbled about his snoring.

I had to drive a pony and trap while filming. Now forever cautious, I walked the entire length of the rough path chosen for the drive to check for any sign of a pothole or anything that could make an accident possible. I also had the children as passengers and I did not want to worry about our safety.

One day, while filming, we heard that Robert Shaw had died. Ray Smith, another actor and I returned to the hotel and, shocked by Shaw's sudden death, we went into the bar, where we sat up on bar stools and reminisced about what a marvellous actor and writer he had been and the glorious uncertainties of life.

The hotel pianist then entered the room on the other side of the bar and was listening to our conversation while he drank his beer. While Ray was waxing lyrical about Shaw, the pianist suddenly let out a cry and disappeared behind the bar. We followed the barman into the other room to see what was happening. The pianist was lying on the floor and it seemed he had suffered a heart attack. Everyone rushed around trying to do something. Someone called an ambulance and we waited for it to come. Minutes went past and the man was beginning to turn blue. I remembered watching a nurse give first aid to someone who had collapsed in a similar way and asked the others whether I should try to help. They all decided I should try to do something. So I did what I had seen the nurse do, thumped his chest and rhythmically pressed up and down for a while. The blue colour disappeared and the pianist began to breathe again. Still the ambulance had not arrived and the man started to turn blue a second time. Encouraged by the others I repeated the exercise and again he began to breathe. Then a decrepit ambulance arrived at the hotel and a nurse got out carrying a bag. As the pianist began to go blue again, Ray Smith became terribly worried and excited. In his broad Welsh voice he said, 'Let Judy do what she did before.'

The nurse agreed and I repeated the whole thing again; the blue colour went and he began breathing. 'Well done,' said the nurse. When we saw that the doctor had arrived, we felt more confident about the situation but by the time he reached the pianist and examined him, the man had turned blue again and the doctor pronounced him dead. We were shocked and all went off in different directions with our own private thoughts.

Moments later Ray, the other actor and I returned to our original positions on the bar stools – a bit like the three wise monkeys. We sat in silence for a while and then Ray said, 'Well, if that's how quick it is, what is the point of worrying? I'm going to drink, smoke and fornicate every day.' All the black humour of the situation was too much for us. We rolled around with laughter, clutching each other for support, and left the quiet thoughts of the tragedy of the situation for contemplation on our own.

~

WHEN WE RETURNED to London and the studio work, Bill Hays, who was working on another production, asked me out to dinner. He told me that Alan Plater had written a musical television series of J.B. Priestley's *Good Companions* which Bill was going to direct for Yorkshire Television early the next year. There would be nine one-hour episodes and he wanted me to play Miss Trant. According to her description in the book, I would have to wear a blonde wig again; and as I had put on some weight for Bessie Tulliver, Bill wanted to know whether I could take it off for Miss Trant. It was not long before Christmas but I told him I could diet after the season's festivities in time to start the series. I was given a bundle of scripts to read and then told my agent I wanted to work with Bill. But one thing bothered me: in the script I was supposed to dance down Llandudno pier. I hoped my back would be able to cope with it.

After I finished on *Mill on the Floss* I was a size fourteen. A friend of mine, who was a member of Weight-Watchers, volunteered to help me shed some pounds for the series and we worked out a goal weight which I would attempt to achieve after Christmas without hurting my back.

Britain now entered the period that became known as the Winter of Discontent, with strikes, shortages and more strikes. Even the dead were left unburied. I got used to stockpiling food and when there was a bread shortage I made my own bread. The British people were looking depressed and downhearted wherever one went. I began to write my first novel, *Cow and Cow Parsley*, and discovered a world – both extraordinary if sometimes alarming – that Carl Jung called 'synchronicity'.

I was angry at what was happening to Britain. I hated seeing grown men looking shabby and defeated; loathed hearing the confusion of language by socio-babblers; and abhorred sensing the people's fear of a growing violent youth. I decided to use Celtic mythology and old folklore in a modern setting to bring back the feeling of community. I also had to learn how to type on an old typewriter John no longer needed. Slowly but surely, using two fingers, I typed up what I had written in longhand. By the new year of 1979 I had finished my first chapter and began working on the scripts of *Good Companions*. I achieved my goal weight with my friend's help and got down to a size ten. Bill was more than pleased when we started rehearsals in Kennington.

David Fanshawe was composing the music for the series. I had a singing session with him to find the sound for Miss Trant and he composed some wonderful numbers for me. While we worked together we discovered that both our great-grandfathers had been soldiers and had fought in the same battles. David's great opus, 'African Sanctus', inspired me when I was writing my third novel.

Travelling by train and tube to rehearsals in the morning I would study the script for *Good Companions*; and travelling back in the evening I would write more of my book. In my prologue, I referred to Dagda, a Celtic god and King of the Tuatha de Danaan. No one seemed to speak about Celtic gods any more and I wanted to reintroduce them to the reader. One day, on the way to rehearsals, standing on the tube station platform waiting for a connection to Kennington, I suddenly saw a poster advertising an Irish musical group, called Tuatha de Danaan. I was astounded; I had never heard of them before. Sixteen years later I met the group and told them about the strange coincidence. They told me they just thought up the name at the same time that I had.

John Stratton played the wonderful character of Jess Oakroyd, who teams up with Miss Trant on her intended motor journey through the cathedral cities of England. The vicar, who suggests that she goes on the tour after the death of her father, was played by Nigel Hawthorne. We filmed the scene, walking in the garden on a typically grey English day. When Nigel said, 'Why not do a tour of the cathedrals?' and I replied, 'What a good idea,' a beam of light like a spotlight came through the murky clouds and lit us beautifully. My guardian angel had obviously taken up electrics. Bill yelled with delight and decided that was the shot he wanted.

I was given a 1920s car with cork brakes to drive. You had to enter the car on the passenger side and slide across. John Stratton was a little nervous when he knew what the brakes were made of but I assured him that if I felt there was any danger I would yell for him to jump out of the car.

Inigo Jollifant was played by Jeremy Nicholas, who was also a brilliant musician. When the three travellers link up with the Dinky Doos and the story takes off we were filming in Bradford, Scarborough and all over Yorkshire. The interior scenes were mostly done at the Yorkshire TV studios in Leeds. As soon as the day's filming was over I would go back to the hotel and, after checking I knew the words for the following day, would settle down to write.

Then I heard that now Thames' option had run out for the pilot John and I had written, ATV had taken an option on it. Alas, then came the electricians' strike and we could not work; neither could the producer at ATV do anything with the idea. We were all sent home but were unable to do any other work because we were still under contract. Lots of other shows were all in the same boat. I took advantage of the subsidized time and got on with my book. The strike went on for months. As Yorkshire TV had already spent nearly a million pounds on the production, the contract for the series that should have finished in the autumn of 1979 had to be extended well into 1980 otherwise the money would have been wasted.

It was a warm summer in 1979. My son, who was now at Hurstpierpoint College and using the name Edward, was working for his O-levels and so I was happy to be home. Next door, Professor McKenzie and his wife Jean were working on a book on Dickens. I would hear their typewriters going during the day and that would get me into a highly agitated state if I was not writing; I wrote mainly at night, which in turn would often drive them mad. When we went back to rehearse at Kennington again, I had almost finished the book.

My second experience of synchronicity came during the rehearsals. I wanted the stars to be in a certain position in my book, as their position would foretell an event to come. I was sitting on the train returning to Brighton after work and wondering how I could find out whether the stars could actually be in that position – I know nothing about astronomy or astrology. I had my notebook out and wanted the position of the stars to warn the people in my book about the year 1986, which then seemed a long time away. The warning was about a nuclear incident.

Suddenly, Patrick Walker got into the carriage. Here was a man who was an expert astrologer. I could hardly believe my luck and asked him if what I was trying to write was possible. Could the stars be in this position? I did not tell him why or for what year. 'Not only is it possible,' he replied, 'but it will probably be in nineteen eighty-six that they are in this position.' We then talked about other things but I felt a bit overwhelmed by what he had said.

I finished the book just before leaving to go off filming again. It is a strange feeling, finishing a book. When the story is over, the book exists in its own right, to be read and understood by each according to their imagination. Someone once described writing as 'licking honey off a thorn' and I cannot think of a better description. I told Alan Plater I had completed my book and he said, 'You've come out of the cupboard,' and wanted to read the manuscript.

Then I was told I was in for a treat. During the filming J.B. Priestley was coming to watch and we were to have lunch with him. I was thrilled. When the day came I had some of his books I hoped he would autograph, including *Literature and Western Man*. I sat next to him at lunch. He was very old, about eighty-six, but his eyes, though rheumy and heavy-lidded, were observant. I wanted to know who had inspired him for his characters in *Good Companions*. Who had he modelled Miss Trant on? Susie Dean? Had he had an unfortunate love affair with an actress to write so bitterly about Susie Dean? When his wife Jacquetta Hawkes, who was younger than he was, joined us for lunch, I could see who had inspired him for his Miss Trant.

I asked him during the main course what he thought of actors.

'Dreadful people, actors,' he replied.

'And actresses?' I enquired.

'All women are actresses,' he said. I watched him carefully as he replied. With his eyes half closed he answered every question too quickly and easily. I realized he must have been asked the same questions time after time. Over pudding I told him that I had just

finished my first novel. His eyes opened and his expression softened. Now he was listening. He wanted to know what the book
was about. All the questions I had asked him were now coming
back to me! He signed all the books I had brought with me and
wanted to know specifically what I had thought about *Literature
and Western Man*. As I chatted on I noticed that his head was drooping and, although his pipe was still in his mouth, he had gone to
sleep. His wife laughed. Oh yes, she was definitely Miss Trant.

'Don't be offended,' she said. 'He always drops off after pudding. I can always tell if he's fallen asleep in the bath by the hissing
sound his pipe makes when it comes in contact with the water.'

~

BY FEBRUARY 1980, we were all up in Scarborough. First we had
a scene in the theatre where some scenery is supposed to fall on
Miss Trant's head so that she ends up in hospital. I told Bill to get
a stunt girl to do the scenery-falling shot because in no way was
I going to risk being hurt if anything went wrong. He could not
understand such wimpishness. 'Hadn't I been perfectly all right
cycling along a wall with a steep drop in *Cakes and Ale*?' 'That was
before I was thrown from a horse,' I reminded him. They set up for
the scene which I removed myself from just before the long shot of
the accident when the stunt girl stood in for me dressed in my
clothes. It all went horribly wrong and the girl was knocked uncon-
scious. Grudgingly, Bill admitted I had been right to be cautious.

I celebrated my fortieth birthday on 22 February 1980 travelling
on the train from Scarborough down to Brighton. My mother telephoned in the evening to say she was bringing my present round.
'Life begins at forty, so make the most of it,' she warbled. 'You start
dropping to bits at fifty, and from sixty it's downhill all the way.'
She was furious when she reached sixty, and threatened me with
all sorts of dire repercussions if I told anyone her age.

The day which I had been dreading finally arrived. It was time
for the big song and dance number down Llandudno pier. My song
was 'By the Sea' and we had already recorded it with an orchestra.
The pier was long and Bill had the idea we could do the whole
number in one take, but there were the extras and all the dancers

including the sailors with whom I had to do my high kicks and lifts. We started our rehearsals and then spotted a body floating by the side of the pier. The coastguard was called and we congregated like seagulls watching the gruesome scene of a bloated corpse being fished out of the water.

Rehearsals started again and this time Ann Stallybrass got her handbag containing all her credit cards kicked over the side. Luckily the coastguards were still around and fished the bag out for her. Body and bag all sorted out, we began to film the number. Finally, Bill agreed that it was a long way to travel during the song so we split the film takes. By the end of the day the dancers dressed as sailors were groaning with each lift and accusing me of eating too much at lunchtime. They were just tired and my back was killing me so I could not help them with the lifts. When we finally finished and I saw the scene later with all the singing in sync and smiling sailors, no one would have guessed the number of groans, blasphemies and expletives that had been part of the number.

Leonard Lewis, the producer who also directed some of the episodes, threw a great big party at the end of the day. I soaked in the bath before the party, filling and refilling the tub with hot water until my back felt normal again. I felt so relieved I had got through the scene. From now on all the filming would be easy in comparison.

~

AFTER READING THE manuscript of *Cow and Cow Parsley*, Alan Plater was very complimentary about my book and urged me to keep on writing. A young editor, Maureen Waller, was just about to move to Hodder & Stoughton and wanted to take the book with her. However, Fay Weldon had also written what is now called an 'Aga saga' and so there was no room for my book with the publishers. I put the novel back in the cupboard where it was to stay for the next four and a half years, resting on top of the television pilot.

A social worker I knew told me there was to be a meeting in Brighton chaired by the area health officer, Dr Robin Brims Young. Knowing how I believed in health education regarding the dangers of alcohol abuse she asked whether I would like to go with her. Peter Bunker, a solicitor, and Geoffrey Williams, the managing director of the insurance company Ansvar, were on a panel with Jim Hill, who was going to be the director of a newly formed council of alcoholism. After a talk the panel asked if there were any questions. I asked two questions about how they intended to tackle education in schools and industry. They had no answers. After the meeting Dr Brims Young came up to me and said, 'If you're going to ask questions like that we'd much rather you were on our board than at a public meeting. Will you join us?' I agreed because I felt very strongly about the subject. I joined the board and soon after joined the executive board of the National Council of Alcoholism in London as well – this was chaired by Sir Bernard Braine with Derek Rutherford as director. After a few years with them, I was invited to become a board member of the Institute of Alcohol Studies when Derek Rutherford took over running it. The National Council eventually disbanded to re-form as Alcohol Concern.

I enjoyed my time involved with these people and found I had a talent for ideas and communication that I had not realized before. I also discovered I had another talent for spotting really clever people who did not have enough nerve to push themselves forward, and giving them the confidence to do so. Once inspired and having discovered their own talents, these once shy and retiring people rose into veritable warriors for the cause.

~

YORKSHIRE TELEVISION GOT in touch with me again and offered me a lovely play called *A Little Rococo*. It was to be directed by my friend David Cunliffe and was produced by Pat Sandys. It was written by Anita Bronson, and was the story of a thirty-nine-year-old widow, April, who finds herself unwittingly in competition with her eighteen-year-old daughter for the attention of Sam, a very dishy antiques dealer who is too old for one and too young for the other. Although he had starred in many musicals, playing Sam was Paul Nicholas' first experience of TV drama. Geoffrey Palmer played the mother's neighbour who quietly fancies her and is her accepted friend until Sam turns up.

When Paul Nicholas first walked into the rehearsal room we all gasped with admiration. This young man was seriously attractive. He oozed with sex appeal and I knew every female viewer would envy my character for the brief love scene we had. Paul was a little nervous working on a drama but he gave a splendid performance and his acting career took off immediately.

After the play was shown on television, I was shopping in Waitrose with no make-up on and in my old jeans, when a woman, perhaps a few years older than me, popped her head over the tins of baked beans and said, 'Well, if you can pull someone as young and beautiful as Sam, there's hope for all of us.'

Part Three

Chapter Sixteen

1981–1985

~

JUST AFTER CHRISTMAS 1980, I was looking through a magazine when I came across a picture of the Waikanai Caves in New Zealand. From a sitting position in a boat moving along an underground stream, the photographer had taken a picture of the myriad glow worms lighting the roof of the cave. It was a magical spectacle and I longed to go there and see it for myself. My guardian angel obviously thought I had put in a request, because in the first week of 1981 my agent called me to say that a New Zealand theatre company wanted me for a tour playing the title role in the play *Rose*. There would be three weeks' rehearsal in Wellington starting early in October and the tour would end back in Wellington in the middle of December. I could not believe my luck. Not only would I be able to see the Waikanai Caves, but from New Zealand I could easily fly to Australia.

The director was going to be Eric Thompson, Emma Thompson's father. I had met him over lunch a couple of years earlier to discuss a play which in the end I decided not to do.

The part of Rose was extremely demanding and, except for the interval, it meant being on stage for two hours non-stop. I said I would take it; the money was good and the chance of getting back to Australia too seductive. I arranged for the family to join me in Sydney, where we would have Christmas with friends of ours from Sussex who had emigrated some years earlier.

But that was all months away. First, I had to film a play I had been sent by the BBC, *The Guest*. It was adapted from a story by Gerald Durrell about a married couple who are on a gourmet's tour of France only to find that the pleasant chef cooking one of their meals has designs on them being the meat for next year's pâté. A new young and award-winning director, Paul Bemborough, was going to direct the play, which was to be filmed in Dieppe first, and then just south of Rouen. Usually the BBC just offered me a role to play; this young man wanted to meet me first.

After talking for a while, Paul asked how I would play the part. 'I'm not going to tell you that,' I replied. 'Do you seriously think I'm going to give away my ideas when you might employ some-one else and pass them on?' He looked shocked at my response. 'I'll tell you when I see a contract and the money is agreed,' I added. By the end of the day my agent was able to tell me the deal and when the contract was to start. Later, of course, I discussed my ideas with Paul.

The make-up girl suggested that I might like to go back to being blonde again, or at least to have blonde streaks. She promised to take me to a first-class hairdresser where, if I felt like wearing my hair shorter, I could have a really good cut. So I went back to being blondish and my long waist-length hair was cut into a beautiful bob.

I was working with Anton Rodgers and Brewster Mason, who were excellent comedy actors with years of experience. After filming at Dieppe we were all based at Rouen where we would travel each day to a gourmet restaurant out in the countryside for the rest of the filming. French politicians were reputed to drive there from Paris for the exquisite food. During a time of so many union problems, I have never seen a film crew so happy. Nothing was too much trouble for anyone on the film. The director was talented, the actors knew what they were doing and all got on well with each other, and the food provided – from the French apple tart at coffee break to the luxurious lunch we all sat down to enjoy each day – kept smug smiles on our faces throughout the filming. Every day we would think of fellow actors and crew back at the BBC studios and marvel at our luck.

On the last day, while waiting for the bus to drive us to Dieppe and the ferry home, I sat on a bench with my suitcases and men-tally talked to my guardian angel. I was involved with a lot of different committees as well as my work and I wondered whether I should hand over some of the responsibility to others. Somehow I wanted to be shown a sign so that I would know what to do. I sat there waiting, aware that at any moment the bus would arrive. Suddenly, out of some bushes, scrambled a young French boy of about ten years of age. He had been sleeping rough and was dirty with matted hair. He stared at me with glazed eyes, clutching an almost empty bottle of spirits, and staggered off in the direction of the shops. I was shocked that anyone so young could have a drink problem. 'OK,' I said to my guardian angel, 'I'll stay on the committees.'

~

THE FLIGHT TO New Zealand was exhausting. We had to change planes at Los Angeles and wait five hours for a connecting flight to Auckland. After an hour of waiting there, we flew to Wellington and were met by the producer, Stewart Macdonald, who wanted to put me straight on to a TV chat show. 'Not a chance,' I told him. 'I'm going to have at least six hours' sleep before I speak to anyone. Even then I shall probably not make any sense at all. We've been travelling, and in and out of airports, for about thirty-six hours. It's too much.'

I have often wondered how politicians or business people can step on to planes, have an important meeting or make important decisions in another country and then turn round and fly home. When I eventually went on the show hours later, I was still off my head. The most banal question could reduce me to uncontrollable laughter, as if I were feeble-minded. Ray Lonnen was being interviewed with me. He had set off earlier than I had and stopped over in Hawaii, so his trip to Wellington had not been as arduous. Even so, our jet-lagged madness must have seemed rather less than our chat show host had expected of us.

When I woke up in the motel suite the following day, I flung open the balcony doors and took a deep breath of fresh air. I nearly died of shock. Despite all the beautiful morning sunshine, the breeze was directly from the Antarctic. I felt I had just breathed in a lump of ice; only an immediate cup of tea restored my breathing to normal. A car picked us all up and took us to rehearsals. Jack Gallagher and Jean Hayworth had also flown out from England; and we were joined by the New Zealand cast. Alice Fraser I knew from when she was in England and I worked with her at the Worthing repertory company.

The rehearsals for *Rose* were continually being interrupted by publicity photo calls until we really had to call a stop to them. Everyone worked hard and Eric managed to communicate with us, despite the restrictions to his speech after his stroke. Sometimes he would lose his temper with his disability but we would all wait for him to calm down, then we would make a joke about it and he would regain his natural sense of humour.

Jean had played her part of mother in the West End when Glenda Jackson had played the title role. She found it fascinating watching my discovery of the role compared to Glenda's way of working.

The play went well and some of the people in the audience had travelled huge distances to come to see the show. As we set off to play split weeks up one side of the North Island, the Queen and the Duke of Edinburgh were on their tour down the other side. We reached Auckland and were to open at the theatre on Auckland's Rose Day. When I went into my dressing room, it was covered from floor to ceiling with bunches of roses from well-wishers and fans. I felt really touched by so much of a welcome.

Among the bunches of roses was one posy with an invitation to the past. My memories of childhood and being a frustrated six-year-old swearing an oath of vengeance were reawakened. The letter attached to the posy reminded me that I had once attended preparatory school with her daughter, and the woman wondered whether it was possible that I remembered them. Oh yes, I remembered them. I remembered her snubbing my mother and the hurt look on my mother's face and my rage and anger at being unable to say anything rude because she was a grown-up. The oath sworn by the six-year-old child promising revenge was about to be fulfilled. I telephoned the vicar's wife, told her I did remember her and that I most definitely would not be coming for tea.

'But I've changed a lot,' she said.

'Good,' I said and put down the telephone. Mother's hurt had been avenged, but I, as an adult, felt ashamed that I could not have risen above 'an eye for an eye' thinking.

I did get to the Waikanai Caves, and drifted on board the canoe along the underground river looking at all the glow worms lighting the darkness. It reminded me of the legendary River Styx that leads to another existence. Now we were all secure with the running of the play, I could fully appreciate the mystical, ethereal, inspiring countryside. Everywhere I went I ran into people I had known from Sussex who were now living there.

I also visited many people involved in the field of addiction. The people in London whom I had told I was touring New Zealand had got in touch with their contacts and asked them to show me around while I was there. I found myself visiting the Beehive, which is the New Zealand parliament, and talking to health workers in every town I played. The system in their country was far better than in Britain. They had a tax on alcohol sales that went into a fund to pay for detoxification centres, preventative health education and wonderful hospitals. I nearly cried when I saw the facilities available to a population of three million and thought of the lack of investment in care in our own rich, heavily populated country. One earnest worker in the field asked me what they could learn from Britain. My reply was, 'Nothing – they should be learning from you.'

I was very impressed by their dedicated research and care. I was also getting more and more worried about the problems of the foetal alcohol syndrome, which was causing great concern in Sweden at the time. I once saw a child in an English children's home with this syndrome. It was an experience that haunted me for years. I can still see his tiny head and sharp rat-like teeth, his long skinny arms that reached past his knees. He was hyperactive and emitted shrill squeaks like an animal. He seemed angry at all times and was vicious towards the children's nurses. The poor little soul did not live much longer than his ninth birthday. Still, even now in the twenty-first century, I do not see enough government health warnings about drinking alcohol during pregnancy.

A Maori actor friend introduced me to a Maori *paar*, a place where – when a Maori baby is born – the afterbirth is buried in a special plot of ground. The Maori then always knows where a part of him belongs. I also ate *poo haa*, a sort of dandelion plant, to become a blood sister. Later during the night there was an earth tremor. I did not know whether it was the *poo haa* working havoc with my stomach or a genuine earthquake, but it turned out to be both.

During the last week in Wellington, a radio producer I had got to know asked me to lunch and promised me a great surprise. I turned up at the restaurant and shortly afterwards another woman, about ten years younger than me, joined us. She was about two inches taller but apart from that and the age difference she could have been my clone. We looked absolutely identical. My producer friend introduced us, 'Judy Cornwell meet Judy Cornwell.' We gazed at each other in amazement. She was working with the American Embassy, and started telling me the story of the Tasmanian aunts who had been sent to England for the season but because of bad behaviour were sent back to Tasmania in disgrace. This was a story my father had once told me. We realized with all the stories we shared that we were distant cousins. That we had both been given the same name was remarkable.

~

WHEN THE TOUR finished I caught the plane to Sydney, the city I had left so many years ago when leaving for England. My friends Bill and Margaret were waiting at the airport. They took me back to their home in Saint Ives where we would all be spending Christmas together. John and Edward were flying in a day later to join us. Everything my father had hoped for Australia had come true. Sydney now was a city of optimism, style and thoughtful planning. The Australians had taken the best ideas from Britain, Europe and America and discarded the worst.

My old friend Kevin Palmer had returned to Sydney and was now running an agency. He wanted to know if I was returning for good, as he had decided to do, and was disappointed when I told him that I was returning to England in January. But first I had to get to Gympie to see my father's grave. After Christmas in Sydney, John, Edward and I set off for Brisbane, where we stayed for a while. Brisbane was so clean; streets were washed several times a day in the city. The easy-going gentle lifestyle was reflected in a friendly attitude towards strangers.

So many creatures have a natural instinct for finding their way back home. From the moment I arrived in Australia all my senses became acutely sensitive, as if some part of me had been left behind there, like Peter Pan's shadow, and was now binding itself around me again. New Zealand had heightened my awareness, almost as if in preparation for my return to Australia. I felt whole again.

I was able to show my family the farm in Dagun, the school and the small railway station. John declared that he now understood why I was as I was, and he and Edward decided that my mother had been quite right to leave the farm. Even though roads and buildings had changed, I was able to find our old house in Gympie. We then looked up one of my mother's friends and my father's solicitor and found out where my father was buried. There was no headstone on his grave. Within a few hours and with my friends' help, I had everything organized. Remembering the evening walks with my father, I asked the stonemason to write on the stone, 'There is no religion greater than truth.'

It was hard leaving Australia again but deep down in my heart I knew I would return. Because my ticket was via New Zealand, I had a horrendously long journey back to England ahead of me. Anticipating this I had arranged with a travel company in Wellington to give me a stopover in San Francisco. After flying through the most awful storm over the Pacific, where it seemed half my stomach had dropped down to my knees, I arrived to find the hotel booked for me was mostly peopled with men in tight black leather trousers and transvestites. Standing at the reception desk in my tweeds I looked like Miss Marple who had wandered on to the wrong film set. The camp male receptionist gazed at me as if I were someone from outer space. I guessed this whole situation was some New Zealander's idea of a joke. Or perhaps he had not enjoyed the play. I was very comfortable though. The young men behind the front desk took great care of me, warning me to be careful where I explored and to hold on tightly to my handbag. I managed to take a ride on one of the trams I had seen in American movies and to visit Fisherman's Wharf and Alcatraz.

Then it was off to the airport, where baggage handlers tried to look cool like Lee Marvin and where I had a screaming row when I threatened them with the British consul for weighing bags in a different way from the rest of the world. In the end we compromised, in order to stop the rest of the queue behind me also getting angry and difficult with them. They tied two bags of mine together so that it became one item, and I boarded the plane for London.

~

IT WAS 1982 and I was nearly forty-two. Back in England I thought about Leonard White and his good advice about ageing up as an actress while I was still young, so that I would have no problem as I got older. The forties are sometimes the death rattle of actresses who have played glamorous roles most of their lives. Some of them, of course, resort to plastic surgery and other methods to look younger, but character actresses go on to play each age group. By taking Leonard's advice I had extended my working life.

I was asked to do a quick film with George Cole and Maureen Lipman giving information about people's legal rights. It was fun and we had a lot of laughs. I was also doing a lot of radio work, which I loved, and dubbing films from Eastern Europe and doing voice-overs for advertising. Margaret Thatcher was now prime minister. She had won the election in 1979 after the most terrible winter of strikes and shortages. At first I was thrilled that a woman could be prime minister until she quoted Saint Francis of Assisi. Then I became a little worried. National leaders who easily and publicly call on God always worry me a bit. In 1982 there were three million people unemployed and a new philosophy not practised before in my places of work before Thatcherism. It was a belief held dear by Michael Heseltine, a member of her cabinet: 'Keep everyone, especially freelancers, waiting at least ninety days before paying them any money owed.' It became commonplace to wait for ages before being paid. Agents reminded companies politely that 'payments were overdue' but to no avail. Fortunately agents never pass on the various threats and expletives uttered by actors over many deals or while waiting to be paid.

Radio Luxembourg owed me money from an advert and kept delaying payment. Then they booked me again while I was still waiting to be paid for the previous session. John Bennett and I turned up at the studios all ready to work – John had just returned from filming in Egypt. We were given our scripts and I asked John to bear with me while I sorted out something. He looked curious. The producer in the control box spoke over the feed-back: 'Are we ready?'

'No,' I replied.

'What's the matter, Judy?'

'I can't get inspired.'

'Why?'

'I can't get inspired until you pay me for the last session – and in advance for this session. If you write me two cheques then I won't waste any more studio time.'

Poor John Bennett looked horrified. 'I'm writing the cheques now,' came the reply. I went to the control box, collected my cheques and returned to work on the script with enormous enthusiasm and speed.

Afterwards John and I went for coffee. He expressed great surprise at my behaviour. I told him to wait to see how long they would take to pay him and then he would understand. Now, in the twenty-first century, with New Labour in power, the Heseltine 'ninety days' lives on – especially with freelancers, whether they be actors, journalists or indeed anyone who is self-employed. Farmers are kept waiting for up to six months before being paid by the supermarkets. This is one of the unacceptable faces of capitalism – there never was the 'trickle-down effect' that Thatcher promised.

By now I was also elected on to the executive committee of my trade union, Equity, representing the South-East. I served on it for three years. By 1982 I was seriously worried, especially for the future of trade unions. I met two friends of mine for lunch. One was a professor of history, the other a professor of Russian studies, both Tories. I asked them whether they were as worried as I about the economic philosophy of centralization. Not only did I consider it to be dangerous for a government to follow, but businesses were also centralizing. They were removing the autonomy of regional managers to make decisions for their areas, and making their savings and so-called 'efficiencies' by cutting jobs on the ground. But they contradicted the whole philosophy by increasing management and bureaucracy. My friends agreed and said they too were worried, especially for the future of education. The professor of Russian studies pointed out to us that no leader since Stalin had centralized like Thatcher.

John was offered the job of Southern African correspondent for the BBC, and I was all set to go with him to Johannesburg for the three years he was to be there. I told my agent that I would be unavailable during this time and would probably get on with my writing while in Africa. About three years earlier John had put forward the idea of adding an arts correspondent to the BBC hierarchy, arguing that stories about the arts should be included in regular news and current affairs programmes. At the same time that he was considering the African job the BBC offered him the first ever arts correspondent position. He found the arts job irresistible, especially as he had helped to create it; so every arts correspondent since then has John to thank for their job. There were huge celebrations at the BBC's *World at One* office because John was the first contract journalist to win a staff correspondent post – a huge leap in those days.

~

MY FRIEND BILL Hays asked me to read Molly Keane's book *Good Behaviour*. Hugh Leonard had dramatized it for a joint BBC–RTE television production to be shown in three sixty-minute episodes. Bill wanted me to play Mrs Brock, an eccentric nanny working for an Anglo-Irish family who dies tragically in the first episode. I would have to play the piano, sing, drive a pony and trap, cope with mice, two children and swim. The setting for the series was Ireland at the time of the First World War. Bill had cast some wonderful actors, including Joanna McCallum, Hannah Gordon, Dan Massey and Michael Denison.

We rehearsed in London before leaving for Cork at the begin-

ning of April. We were all booked into a very modern hotel close
to the town. Some of my ancestors had lived in Cork; Molly Keane
told me she knew of them. On the first day of rehearsals, Terry
Coles, the producer, who had also produced *The Guest* which I had
filmed in France, came up to me and said, 'I don't know what it is
about you, Judy, but when we put you in a play, no matter what it
is, we can increase our viewing figures by five million.' He paused
for a minute and then added, 'But perhaps I shouldn't have told
you that.' Of course, I was thrilled.

I found Mrs Brock a real challenge. It was a wild and outrageous
part to explore and there were two hurdles for me to leap. One was
swimming with the children; the other was to be dead on the shore.
We had a lifeguard who strutted about the beach in a wetsuit and
assured me that the water was perfectly safe. I had my doubts.
There had been a storm not long before we filmed and a lot of weed
was floating about. I set off in my striped, old-fashioned bathing
costume holding hands with the children. We were supposed to
swim out. As we entered the water I felt the weed wrapping around
our legs. I shouted out to Bill that I was not going to drown the
children and myself for the shot so he had better shoot up to our
plunge and make the most of it. A young New Zealand actor who
was playing the boy when he was older went in next. He was an
extremely strong swimmer and when he came out of the water he
told me that even he had felt a sense of panic when he hit the weed
– it had almost pulled him down. I had been quite right not to go
in any further. The stupid twit strutting about in his lifesaver outfit
had not even tested the water.

The day came for me to be found drowned, and washed up, on
wet sand. It was very cold and I was in my striped bathing costume
again. The camera was set up and Bill showed me where he wanted
me to lie. Some Irish extras were to find me and bring my lifeless
body ashore. I lay down on the sand and began to sink slightly. Bill
threw a bucket of water over me and the surrounding sand so it
was all smooth. I told him to hurry because the sand seemed to be
sinking. He told me it would not take long and there was a lovely
hot bath for me in a private house near to the location. I lay there
doing my dead acting and then came the Irish extras to pick me

up and carry me off. I went limp. One lot took my right leg and
the others took my left leg, a few of them lifted my shoulders
and nearly dropped me. I inwardly cursed but remained limp.
Unfortunately, the men carrying my right leg and the ones carrying my left leg turned in different directions, giving the camera a
great shot of my bottom. As neither side gave way, I was being
pulled in different directions. Eventually the left side conceded
defeat and I was carted off to dry land. The camera crew and Bill
were nearly wetting themselves. The screams of laughter broke out
when they knew the shot was complete.

It was a take. I was given a blanket to wrap around my muddy
body and driven to the house, where I anticipated a lovely warm
bath.

'Stay there,' a voice shouted as I walked up the garden path.
I stopped in my tracks. 'Take the blanket off, Miss Cornwell, will
you.' I took off the blanket wondering what was going on. 'Walk
forward, will you.' I walked forward and was hit by a jet of icy cold
water from a hose. It was horrendous, but the owner of the house
was having no sand on his carpets. I even had to walk on a plastic-
covered route to the bathroom where I sank into a hot bath and
wanted to stay there for ever.

It was during the filming, when I had a long walk with Dan
Massey, that he announced his belief that 'One should change one's
agent and one's wife every seven years.'

The hardest part for me was when, having been seduced and in
love with the master of the house, a deranged and bitter Mrs Brock
says some horrific things to the young girl, who was played by
Joanna McCallum's real daughter. When children rehearse over
and over again they often get quite blasé and sound like automa-
tons. I talked to Bill and suggested that to get the child's best
reaction I should not rehearse in the deranged manner I planned
for the final take. Before we did the scene in the studio I told the
little girl to be prepared for a different Mrs Brock. When I gave the
full, wild performance, the little girl had the most horrified look on
her face – it worked wonderfully. Afterwards, I joked with her,
showing her that everything was all right. When I met her a couple
of years ago, she had grown into a lovely young woman and

beamed when she realized she was looking at the Mrs Brock who had scared her out of her wits.

At home the house was in mourning after Harry the dog died in August. He had been with us for fifteen years since he was picked out from a litter by our son. I think I wept more over the loss of that little dog than over any of my relatives'. He had been a part of us, a delightful, shaggy creature, and we all felt the loss dreadfully.

~

I HAD RECENTLY been reading a book about Thomas Garrigue Masaryk, a man I admired enormously. He had been born a serf, was educated by the Jesuits until he was seven, then apprenticed to a blacksmith. He begged the Jesuits to be allowed to continue his studies, then went to Vienna to tutor in order to educate himself further. Eventually he became president of Czechoslovakia, having brought the Czechs and Slavs together forming one country. When I finished the book I thought about him a lot.

Synchronicity, or my guardian angel who felt like more travelling, then arranged it that I had an offer to go to Prague to make *The Devil's Lieutenant* for Bavaria Atelier, a German film company. It was also going to be shown on Channel 4. Jack Rosenthal had written the script, which was an adaptation of the novel by Maria Fagyas. The story was set in Vienna in 1909, when the Austro-Hungarian Empire was shattered by the Dorfrichter Affair – an ambitious first lieutenant is accused of poisoning nine of his comrades. The judge advocate, Kunze, was played by the German actor Helmut Griem; the first lieutenant was played by the late Ian Charleson; I played Rose, the judge advocate's mistress who becomes his wife. John Goldschmidt was directing. All the other actors were German, Czech, Italian or French, so Ian and I were flown over to Vienna for dress fittings and make-up and wig tests.

The European actors' unions were not at all as strong as our own union Equity at the time, and all the other actors were waiting to see what the Brits would insist on when they arrived in Prague. Ian got a lunch break introduced into the day's filming, and I made sure that a lavatory was available for the women on the unit.

When I first arrived at the old grand hotel, in a street just off Wenceslas Square, the secret police took my passport away. It would be returned when I left Prague, they told me. The hotel was incredibly warm with very powerful central heating. Two women sat at the end of the corridor knitting and watching every time I came out of my room. I was given coupons for my breakfast and evening meal, which allowed me no more and no less than the coupons dictated. I was woken at five thirty every filming morning and the first of the coupons gave me two rolls, two pieces of wrapped butter and a pot of coffee – the butter, I noticed, was from the European Common Market.

The half-hour lunch we were allowed during filming consisted of anything that could be bought that day, sometimes cheese and bread, occasionally some salami. By the time we were finished filming in the evening and I was back at the hotel I was ravenous. My evening coupon bought me some soup, a little meat, usually pork, potato and a small portion of vegetables, then a small pudding and coffee. I spent most of my time in Prague thinking about food. On my few days off I would join the back of any queue in the city to see what was at the front. In a special shop for foreigners I managed to find some chocolate. When I returned to England I had lost a stone and a half.

On my first free day I set off on the trail of Thomas Masaryk. When I asked anyone where I could find his picture or statue their eyes would look shifty and I was told by one person that it was a name not to be mentioned. I did find his statue just by chance; it was tucked away in the corner of the big museum in Wenceslas Square. I paid homage to his memory and when I came out of the museum and looked across the huge square, I had a strange experience. I had been wishing for freedom for the Czechs and thinking about Masaryk's selfless devotion to Czechoslovakia when I saw, instead of the normal day in the square, an image of crowds of people standing in the dark holding lighted candles in their hands. Around them was a soft glow of candle light. At that moment I knew they would soon be free. I suppose it was a sort of vision, but it was intensely real.

Most of the time I spoke German so I could communicate with

the film crew and the other actors. I also learned a few Czech words. The Czechs were watched all the time by informers, who slid about the different film sets eavesdropping on any conversation. We foreigners were also watched by cameras inside the hotel, and I learned how to spot the various cameras in the city. During one scene I began talking to a young Czech actor called Vladimir. I was reassuring him that his English was very good. Although we were not supposed to fraternize with the Czechs and the spies were forever lurking, Vladimir asked me whether I would like to visit him and his wife. I said I would love to meet a Czech family in their home and he told me to wait for a phone call at the hotel and then run like hell up to the underground station from where he would take me to his place – there were spies in the hotel and we could not speak on the film set because it was too dangerous for him.

I made sure I ate my supper quickly that evening to be ready to take the call. A couple of people looked at me with curiosity when it came but I ignored them, shot out into the street and ran up to the underground, where Vladimir was waiting. We had to dodge all the cameras that were placed around the city but we eventually made it to a delightful apartment on a hill. The Czech actors, like their Russian counterparts, were all given rather pleasant apartments. Vladimir's wife had made a cake in my honour. I knew how difficult that must have been for her as I had seen the queues for food all over the city. They were thrilled to be able to talk freely. Their children were out for the evening, otherwise they could not have risked my visit in case the children talked to anyone about it. They told me how, too, they had to be careful about the books their children saw them reading, for the same reason. When I told them about working with Milos Kirik, they became terribly excited. They told me that Vladimir and Milos had been students together. In 1968, when the Russian tanks came into Prague, they were supposed to escape at the same time, but because he could not find his girlfriend, who was now his wife, Vladimir missed the opportunity.

They were thrilled to know that Milos was safe in England and told me about the boosters on their radios so that they could listen to the BBC World Service and how careful they had to be not to get caught. They also wanted their children to learn English in case there was a chance of freedom but they had accepted the fact that they would never see freedom during their lifetime. Remembering my strange experience outside the museum, I blurted out that I could guarantee they would be free in a few years' time and they were not to give up hope. I promised that as their letters were censored I would send them cards with symbols they could understand. But I could promise they would be free. They wanted to know whether I had contacts with the underground. I said nothing about my strange experience, but told them I just knew they would be free.

Before I finished filming in Prague, a few Czechs, knowing they could trust me, gave me messages for the BBC Free Czech radio station. I tried to remember them all but made little symbols in my diary to make sure.

As I queued up at the airport to leave Prague, I watched a number of Czechs shaking with fright as they approached various officials and I felt my own mouth become quite dry. We were searched about six times in different booths. At one time they looked through my diary and shook it. They ignored all the clinking in my holdall. These were the different bottles of spirits with plants in them which I knew would go down well at Christmas with our Polish friends. As the Aeroflot plane rumbled out I felt enormous relief and was determined to get the right messages to the Czechs in London.

As soon as we landed in Heathrow I telephoned John at Broadcasting House and told him I had messages for the Free Czechs. He got in touch with them and when I reached his office I was able to remember all the things I had been told to pass on.

During the following weeks I found any experience of shopping in a supermarket disgusting. So much choice, so much food. I kept thinking of the people in Prague and the queues. Vladimir and I kept in touch, and when the velvet revolution happened in November 1989 I saw the same picture on television that I had seen in my vision the day I had stood looking down the square from the museum. That night I spoke to Vladimir and his family. They were shouting and laughing with joy. Some time later the whole family came to stay with us for a holiday in England and we have remained friends to this day.

Sometimes I look at all the CCTV cameras now monitoring our roads, our shopping malls and streets, and remember how horrified I was in 1982 to see such spying on people in Prague. How easily we have accepted so much prying into our lives because of 'crime', 'terrorism', 'anti-social behaviour', and so on.

Christmas was a wild affair, especially with the bottles with plants in them that I had brought back from Prague. After Christmas pudding we served the vodka in the Polish way, in iced silver liqueur glasses salted at the rim, much to the delight of our Polish friends, the apprehension of my mother and the glee of my father-in-law. My brother played wild flamenco on the guitar afterwards and a noisy night was had by all.

~

IN JANUARY 1983, I was sent a play by Southern Television. It was part of the Dramarama series and was called *Mighty Mum* – a spoof on the Superman comic. I was to play an ordinary mum who, when called to fight crime, would spin round until she was in a lycra Superwoman costume, then went into battle with her frying pan, wielding it ferociously against all kinds of incompetent villains. It was fun to do but more importantly it was a chance to work with Renny Rye, a brilliant director, who I was to work with again two years later.

After *Mighty Mum* I was contracted to play Mrs Reed in *Jane Eyre* for the BBC. Barry Letts was producing the series and the director was Julian Amyes. Timothy Dalton, whom I last worked with in the film *Wuthering Heights*, was playing Rochester. It was good to see him again and he was quite brilliant in the part. It was a wonderful production and received great notices.

From the sublime to the ecclesiastical . . . I was invited to join a conference sponsored by the British Council of Churches to contribute some ideas for the future of churches in Britain. Neither I nor any of the other lay guests – they seemed to be from every kind of background – knew why we had been chosen. During the discussions I managed to embarrass everyone in my group by bringing up the subject of paedophilia within the Church and the absolute need for getting rid of it. It was as though I had dropped my knickers. After some uncomfortable verbal shuffling the group moved swiftly to safer subjects, such as the use of pop music in church. Having been sidelined on that issue I came back later with another. It was time, I suggested, for the Church to disestablish itself from the monarchy. In a moment of astonishing prescience I warned that if the heir to the throne behaved in any way to embarrass the Church, it would make it difficult for him to assume the role of Supreme Governor of the Church of England. After the briefest of discussions we were interrupted by the call for afternoon tea.

By now the television scene was beginning to change. There were few productions and many actors were feeling apprehensive and moving to different agents, hopping around as if in a game of musical chairs. The agent I was with lost many of my contemporaries. Agencies were splitting up, moving premises or joining with other agencies to save costs. Reluctantly I too changed agents.

The first job I was offered after the change was a delightful play for the BBC called *Kisses On The Bottom*, by Stephan Lowe. It was directed by Jeremy Alcock who had been a first assistant on *Good Behaviour*. In the story the characters in Donald McGill's British seaside postcards come to life and, between funny poses for the postcards, lament the changes in society and the loss of good old vulgar English humour; the characters were changing with the times. Hetty Baynes and Max Hafler, who played the honeymoon couple, were now going to take part in syndicated strips, while my character as the fat, polka dot-dressed Mam wondered why her husband, Dad, the thin wiry man with the handkerchief on his head, had not been given greater chances in the comic postcards. The husband was played by the excellent actor Peter Benson, who is brilliant at droll humour. One of my most favourite moments in the play was when we had to paddle in a blue plastic sea.

～

LATER IN 1983 I was asked to become chair of the Brighton Alcohol Rehabilitation Service, BARS. This was a committee hoping to set up a detoxification centre in Brighton where those arrested for being drunk and incapable could safely sleep it off. It was to be similar to the ones I had seen in New Zealand; drunks waking up there the next day would be advised what to do and where to go if they had a drink problem. The committee was particularly concerned for young people who, getting drunk for the first time, might be in danger. There were magistrates, probation officers, police, business people and prison officers on the committee. The police wanted to have a place to deposit drunks because for every one in custody it took one policeman to check them every fifteen minutes and turn them on their side in case they died of vomit inhalation. Violent drunks had to stay in police cells. We also needed a doctor on hand in case someone was wrongly diagnosed as drunk when picked up; they could be having a stroke or some other life-threatening episode.

The aim of BARS was to find a building near the hospital and the police station that could be developed into the centre. When I took over the chair, I said I would do it but only for two years, because if we had achieved nothing in that time it could only become another talking shop.

We tried our best but every time we found a building the public response was 'not in my backyard'. Eventually we wound up the committee and gave what money we had collected to the Saint Thomas' Fund, which was run by a wonderful Catholic priest called Father Mark. His group was providing halfway houses for those coming out of treatment centres or prison for crimes associated with addiction. By having a different structure in their life and by attending regular meetings with Alcoholics Anonymous, these people were later able to rejoin society and discover their real worth.

While I worked for BARS, the Chairman of the Bench, who had known me since I was fifteen, asked me whether I had ever considered being a magistrate. He and his deputy said they wanted more women like me who knew the area, understood the social problems and worked for a living. They were also both strong union members. I agreed to let them put me up before the selection committee.

It was about this time that Peter Hall, then director of the National Theatre, asked me to take part in an excerpt of Shakespeare's *The Tempest* for the BBC. Sir John Gielgud was to play Prospero; Barbara Jefford, Juno; Sarah Kestleman was playing Iris; and I was to play Ceres. We were shooting at Ealing Studios and I do not think I have ever laughed so much in a show. Barbara, Sarah and I were performing our dialogue in recitative. During the rehearsals at the Acton rehearsal rooms we were already finding everything hugely amusing but it got worse when we got to Ealing. There, Sir John was cavorting with nymphs and shepherds; Barbara, looking majestic in blue, was stuck up in the air on a polystyrene cloud; Sarah, draped in flowing rainbow colours, was looking uncomfortable on a swing dangling from high up in the air; and I had to negotiate a way by stepping on two wooden boxes to pass through two wooden sunflowers that creaked open to allow me on to a steeply raked stage. I had corn dangling from my ears, my hair dressed like plaited wheat sheaves, and I was wearing a gold dress – I resembled a slightly underdone granary loaf. When we started the recitative and caught sight of each other we cracked up with laughter and had to start all over again.

All the time we rehearsed, Peter Hall sat with headphones on his ears smiling benignly. I thought how dedicated and calm he was listening to bursts of laughter from us as we staggered through our verses. Then I found out he was not listening to us at all; he was studying German for the next opera he was about to direct.

After the Falklands War, we had elections in 1983 and Margaret Thatcher was returned to power for a second term. My friend Joan Dolan asked me over to stay at her home in Dublin. Her husband had died a few years previously and I had gone over to help her with the funeral. We kept up our tradition of our shared birthdays at the Ritz, but the only man with us now was my husband, John. Joan felt very lost without her husband and often came over to England to stay with us. In the winter she would travel to Hong Kong, where she had other friends. When I arrived in Dublin for a few days I found that Joan had arranged a dinner in my honour at the beautiful Hibernian Hotel. It was a wonderful evening with lots of interesting people. I was especially thrilled to be sitting next to the famous Irish actor Micheál MacLiammoir and his friend Hilton Edwards. Micheál entertained us with poetry in many languages. He was a natural linguist as well as possessing so many other talents. I was enormously grateful to Joan for arranging it so that I had the opportunity of meeting him. Alas, the beautiful Hibernian Hotel no longer exists; a bank stands where it used to be.

~

AT THE BEGINNING of 1984, my friend Joy, who was married to our Polish friend Kazzy, asked me whether she could read my novel *Cow and Cow Parsley*. I had to pass her house driving to London to rehearse for a new comedy series for Yorkshire Television, so I grabbed my carefully typed manuscript from the cupboard and thrust it into her hands at her gate as I passed on the way. I was working on a series called *There Comes a Time*, with Andrew Sachs; and Ronnie Baxter was the producer/director.

Andrew played a man who finds out he is dying from a rare disease and tries to seek answers about what life is all about. In one episode he tries to tell his gin-soaked, Librium-taking wife, played by me, he is dying, which makes her fall about laughing. Unfortunately the world was just beginning to hear about a deadly disease called AIDS, and although the script by Wally K. Daly was hilariously funny, we could all see a looming problem for the show as we worked during rehearsals.

Joy rang, telling me how she had been unable to put the manuscript down. She wanted to know if she could give it to a friend of hers, a publisher, who wanted to read it. I was thrilled and agreed but had to concentrate on learning my lines for the comedy series.

My agent meanwhile asked me to meet some Americans, producers Ilya Salkind, Pierre Spengler and director Jeannot Szwarc, about a film called *Santa Claus the Movie*. It was to star Dudley Moore as an elf, and they wanted me to play Mrs Claus, Santa's wife. The screenplay had been written by David Newman, and the film was to be released by Tri-Star. Anne Henderson, the casting director, kindly advised me what to wear when they wanted to see me again. I heard that Dolly Parton, among several other well-known actresses, wanted to play Mrs Claus and wondered whether

I should bother turning up at all. But Anne insisted that I should and, indeed, the part was mine. It would be twelve weeks' filming at Pinewood Studios starting in the summer so we had a family celebration.

Then Joy telephoned and asked us all over to dinner. She wanted me to meet her publisher friend, Carol Biss, who was in some way related to Kazzy. Carol and I got on really well. She told me she wanted to publish my book; that there was a little editing needed but not much. When she heard that I was starring in an American film with Dudley Moore, she decided it would be a good idea to wait until the film came out and then pick up on the publicity. Although the film was not due out until November 1985, Carol suggested that as a writer I should be thinking about my next book. I had already decided what I wanted to write next and the theme was running around in my head. I wanted to call it *Fishcakes at the Ritz*.

The first day of filming arrived. We were shooting in the large studio which had huge industrial fans and bags of plastic snow standing by for me and my husband Santa, played by David Huddleston, caught in a snowstorm. We were dressed in furs and thick woollen clothes, but it was August and we were sweltering in the heat. When the fans were switched on, the plastic snow hit us full force. Trying to speak our lines was a near lethal effort. I was trying hard not to breathe in the plastic snow or to swallow it. For two days we battled with heat, plastic snow and coping with driving the reindeer through our man-made blizzard. For the worst of the snowstorm, the reindeer were taken out, and the puppeteers, inside reindeer puppets, were brought in. There was to be no discomfort for the animals – but bugger the actors.

When we had completed the most difficult scenes, David Huddleston and I returned to our dressing-room suites to find Fortnum and Mason hampers from Ilya and Pierre. Little cards told us how thrilled they were with the scenes and how much they appreciated our hard work. I thought how generous they were to give us such lovely presents. Although I had enjoyed tea and sometimes a milkshake at Fortnum and Mason's, I had never had a

1981–1985   *291*

hamper from them. I carted it home in the back of the car that weekend so John too could have the pleasure of unpacking it.

Dudley's suite was opposite mine but his lifestyle was quite different. I would arrive at the studios already having eaten my
breakfast. Dudley would start the day with the most enormous
dinner. From the make-up room I could smell all the cooking: trout
with garlic, or some other exotic dish, all mixed up with the delicious aroma of freshly brewed coffee. By lunchtime, when I was
ready to eat a meal, Dud was having a light snack and playing the
piano he had in his sitting room. He believed one should work off
the food eaten at breakfast all through the day, and in that way stay
slim.

Jeannot, the director, was great fun to work with and I enjoyed
making the film enormously. The company of elves had many
small actors I had worked with throughout the years – comedians
from my days in Variety and revues and young men who had been
my sons in different plays. The company had advertised exten-
sively for small men to make up the numbers. One man, an eminent
nuclear scientist, said he had never enjoyed so much respect from
his grandchildren as he had while working on the film.

While I was enjoying myself making *Santa Claus*, my great
friend Joan Dolan died. For me it was like losing a sister. She had
been my best friend, someone who had shared so much of herself
with me. We used to telephone each other regularly for a gossip,
wherever we were. Suddenly she was gone and I missed her.

The seventeenth of September was David Huddleston's birthday. I could sense something was going on in the studio from all
the elves smirking and Dudley's strange behaviour. I asked Dudley
what was going on and he told me that I had to promise not to let
my face give away the secret. I promised, crossed my heart and
everything else. Dudley had dressed up a stripper in an elf's
costume. After lunch, we were supposed to enter through huge
wooden doors to the great hall of toys. Behind the doors would be
the stripper. When we started the rehearsal for the take, Jeannot
and all the crew were hovering like naughty kids. I stared at the
ground terrified of giving away the secret. The doors opened and
out came the stripper. My goodness she was fast at taking off her

clothes. Then everyone sang 'Happy Birthday' round a birthday cake, while David was beaming.

John and I celebrated Thanksgiving Day with David. He was staying in a rented house in Fulham and a group of us from the film joined him so he would not feel homesick for America. He took great delight in telling us all about the history of the tradition and had cooked everything that went with this very American celebration. When the last day of my contract was finished, Ilya, Pierre and Jeannot took Dudley, David, John Lithgow, who was playing the baddy in the film, and me to the Russian restaurant in Fulham for a farewell dinner. Apart from any dubbing, I would not be seeing them again until the film opened in New York. After New York there was to be a Royal Command Performance and a short publicity tour around England, Scotland and Ireland. I said I would participate for no other fee providing I was allowed to plug my book. They agreed I could. There were huge mounds of caviar on the table, black and red; and Dudley told me how much he had enjoyed working with me because, 'You don't get offended by fart jokes, Jude.'

It would have been impossible if I had been the type to be offended by crude jokes. I was the lone woman among lots of naughty elves and David, all of them determined to top the others' jokes. If the audiences could have heard half of the naughty comments, like 'Let's all rush Anya,' or 'Come on, Mrs Claus, show us your boobs', they would never have thought the film so innocently entertaining.

Towards the end of the shoot Dudley presented me with a tape of the most ferocious fart noises. Always honouring the agreement with my agent to pay him ten per cent, I gave him a copy. Unfortunately he was driving an open-top car when he played it. The rude noises coming from his vehicle attracted quite a lot of attention from other drivers, especially when he was waiting at a set of traffic lights. He never forgave me.

～

AT THE BEGINNING of 1985, I was sworn in at the Brighton Court as a magistrate. I did all my training and sat for as many sessions as I could before work took me away. I was expected to sit for forty sessions a year to carry my load, but as I was working on my new novel at home I was easily able to do so.

Later I was offered a lovely part in a two-part dramatization of E.F. Benson's novel *Paying Guests*. I was playing Mrs Bliss, an eccentric lady who believed in mind over matter when it came to trying to beat her arthritis. She joins many other characters at Wentworth, a respectable guest house, close by the health-giving waters of a fashionable spa. The period was 1923. I loved Benson's books, particularly the Mapp and Lucia stories which had me in stitches. The director was the talented Michael Simpson and it was produced by Rosemary Hill, who had also worked on the production of *Frieda* which still sits in the archives of the BBC.

After rehearsing at the BBC Acton rehearsal rooms we were sent to Malvern for the filming. The cast was a most impressive group of actors. Barbara Leigh-Hunt was one of the ladies running the guest house with Avril Elgar playing her sister. Other arthritics were played by Annette Crosbie, Benjamin Whitrow and Richard O'Callaghan. The more fit health enthusiasts were played by Robert Hardy, Angela Thorne and Joanna David. I had never been to Malvern before; the air was quite wonderful. I do not think I have ever been in a place where the air gave me so much energy and I have been back there often playing in the theatre. Each time I return it is like being given pure oxygen.

By now I had also been sent scripts written by Leon Garfield called *December Rose*. Renny Rye was directing the series for the BBC Children's Drama Department. The story was set in London in the 1870s and involved a group of politically powerful people brought to justice by the courage of a young Victorian chimney sweep, who stumbles into one of their secret meetings. On the run for his life he is befriended by Tom Gosling, a Thames bargee. The young chimney sweep slowly adapts to his new river life and meets Mrs McDipper, owner of a rival barge, and her daughter who is the same age as him. It was a beautifully written script and I was looking forward to starting rehearsals and working with Renny Rye again; Paul Stone was the producer. We began the read-through the day after I finished filming *Paying Guests*. Two extremely talented children had been cast. Cathy Murphy was playing my daughter and Courtney Roper-Knight was playing the young chimney sweep. Actors I had worked with in the past, like Michael Aldridge, Ian Hogg and Patrick Malahide, were there too. It looked like it was going to be a really good company.

Then the man who was going to play the bargee, Tom Gosling, turned up. I knew him mainly as a comedian, Dave King. His attitude towards everyone was condescending and rude. Something about him made the hairs on the back of my neck prickle. After the read-through, all the other actors were sent off and we began the early scenes with the children. The comedian started directing us, telling us what he thought we ought to be doing. The children looked to me; they were confused by his behaviour.

'Excuse me,' I said, 'but you see that man over there?' I pointed to Renny Rye. 'He's the director. Why don't we wait to see what he wants us to do.'

The comedian glared at me. 'We're not going to get on are we?' he said, challenging me.

'We won't if you try directing,' I replied.

'Let's face it,' he went on, glaring at me, 'I don't like you and you don't like me.'

'You're absolutely right,' I said. 'And I'm not leaving.'

'I can't work with her,' he shouted at anyone who was listening, 'I'm leaving, You'd better recast.' Then he stormed out of the rehearsal room.

I was shocked. The children were wide-eyed. The producer and the director were beaming. The producer straightaway telephoned another actor, Tony Haygarth, who arrived a couple of hours later. Tony was lovely, a great actor.

I was confused and asked Renny how they managed to get an actor like Tony so quickly. He told me that he and the producer had never wanted the comedian, but other voices had prevailed. Renny was not sure how long it would take, but he knew I would not put up with such rudeness from the comedian and would probably 'see him off'. So, on the quiet, they had asked Tony to stand by. The fact that the man had walked out meant they did not have to pay him, so everyone was very happy.

I loved working on *December Rose*. The whole cast and crew were the most friendly and happy people. We also had a wonderfully talented camera man, Remi, who gave the film the most incredible atmosphere. I was very proud to be on the production. One day Leon Garfield turned up on the set and we talked for hours. I told him I had my first book coming out the day after I finished filming on *December Rose*, 11 November, and I was now working on my next one. He volunteered to introduce me to his literary agent, Andrew Hewson, of John Johnson, who was happy to represent me. At the end of the filming, Renny gave me a china cow with a milkmaid for good luck with my *Cow and Cow Parsley*.

A few weeks before publication Carol had solemnly presented me with a bound copy. How can I possibly describe the emotional moment of holding your first book in your hand? It is your mind's child. The pages represent months of thought and inspiration, aching shoulders from sitting hunched over a typewriter, despair when being stuck not knowing where to go next, and anguish when the story has come to a natural end, the created characters, almost part of yourself, now locked away from further exploration.

My book received very good reviews, sold out and went into reprint. It was also put on the long list for the Booker Prize. I was thrilled and proud, even though it was not selected for the short list.

~

SHORTLY AFTER PUBLICATION and when I had done the round of book signings, I flew to New York for the premiere of *Santa Claus the Movie*. I had decided to stay at the Algonquin Hotel. As so many writers had stayed there in the past I thought some of the inspiration might rub off on me. At Kennedy Airport I was met by a chauffeur and a long stretch limousine. I had never been in such a vehicle. The roof was glass so I could see the lights of New York stretching up to the heavens. At the hotel were bowls of flowers waiting in my room and a message from David Huddleston's agent, Michael Thomas, saying he would pick me up at six thirty to take me to Sardi's where all the others were having dinner. When I got there they all wanted to see my book. David Newman was full of admiration for the cover and wished me luck for good sales. I felt I wanted to pinch myself. Here I was in Sardi's and enjoying every moment of the fun.

The following morning I had a breakfast meeting with the publicist. I am useless first thing in the morning and to make any sense at all over a breakfast meeting meant getting up terribly early to pull my head together. While she and I talked over scrambled eggs and coffee, I was aware of various other writers discussing deals in the dining room.

I dressed up in the evening and a limousine took me to the cinema. It was the first time I had seen the film right through on a big screen and I felt sure children and grown-ups would love it. Afterwards we were all taken to a big party at the Inn on the Park. While I was there I desperately wanted to write; so many ideas were bursting to get out and on to paper. As soon as I returned to the Algonquin, Andrew Ansbach, the hotel manager, asked me how the premiere had gone and I told him everything had gone well but all I wanted now was a large pot of cocoa, some paper and a pencil so I could write in the corner of the sitting room. He rushed off and came back with a pad of paper and a ballpoint pen. I curled up in the corner, sipping my cocoa, and wrote a whole chapter.

When we returned to London, we were met by complaints from newspapers that the reindeer in the film had been killed and eaten. Whoever started this rumour and for whatever reason, it was all bosh. The deer had been taken up to Scotland to live out their days on a private estate. Also, by being in the film they had avoided the annual cull that takes place in Canada. Animal rights activists were all round the cinema and I spotted one with a notebook taking down our names, halfway behind a potted palm in the Dorchester where we were all to have dinner afterwards.

The Prince of Wales and Princess Diana walked along our line of dutifully well-dressed elves and Mrs Claus. Poor David Huddleston was asked to dress up as Santa Claus for the occasion. As the film was called *Santa Claus the Movie*, he was rather more than surprised when Prince Charles asked him what he had to do with the film. 'At that moment, Judy, I was proud that I was American and a Republican,' he told me afterwards. Prince Charles asked me what I had to do in the film and I replied, 'I am the symbol of motherhood.'

'Hooh, intriguing, intriguing,' replied the prince. Well, what else could one say?

Before we set off for the publicity tour, I received a telephone call from Susie, Musi's daughter, telling me that my godmother had died. I felt very sad. She had known I was having a book published and had been so excited about it. She and I had written to each other for so many years and her words of wisdom had been a beacon of light for me. Later I was to meet Susie, my father's first love before my mother whisked him away. We have become great friends since.

The publicity tour began with David and I sent all over the place for radio, television and newspaper interviews. During each interview I mentioned my book. Sales went up. From cities in England we flew to Scotland and then on to Ireland. The film company provided wonderful suites in each hotel and the young publicity man in charge of us turned out to be the son of my friend Lee Dunne, the Irish writer whose film *Paddy* I had been in.

When we arrived back at Heathrow, customs officers pounced on us. I suppose they were not to know that a large suitcase for a few days' travel was necessary for the number of outfits needed on a publicity tour. A very bossy officer demanded that I open my suitcase. Out of my case fell a selection of hotel plastic shower hats, soaps and shampoos. The customs officer looked very disappointed.

Every Christmas the film is shown on one television channel or other. I often get strange looks from young children I meet who are being told about Santa Claus. One parent told me that her daughter thought I was Mrs Claus in disguise keeping an eye on children to see how they were behaving. In such a way is a new generation of conspiracy theorists begun.

Chapter Seventeen

1986–1989

~

JUST BEFORE CHRISTMAS 1985, John and I celebrated our silver wedding anniversary. Our closest friends and family came to the party. My mother was in her element. She had read my book and seen the film of Santa twice; and John's mother had moved to Brighton after his father died. The two mothers plotted together about the silver soup ladle they were giving us. Our Polish friends brought a Georgian silver condiment set and our son bought us some silver coffee spoons. When I looked at all the presents later I could see years of silver polishing ahead.

I moved out of the study I shared with John in the new year of 1986, and commandeered a spare bedroom on the lower ground floor for my study. This meant I could type away into the early hours without disturbing the men in my life, who both had to get up early.

During one night's work I forgot to draw the curtains. I was sitting at my desk in my therma-wear nightdress, oblivious of everything except my typing, and did not see the flasher who was exposing himself at my window. In desperation for a response, but cunning enough to hide his face, he pulled himself up on our balcony above but left his legs dangling by the window. He then kicked at the window to attract my attention. I looked up to see a pair of legs with trousers down at the ankles and a pair of blue Marks and Spencer's Y-fronts. I picked up the telephone and dialled the police. With great physical dexterity the chap managed to drop down with his head far from my gaze and he legged it off down the road. I described the blue underwear and the direction the man had taken to the police and was asked whether I was upset. I replied that I was not, but as someone had been flashing with a bin liner over his head at the girls school round the corner, perhaps it was the same man and they might like to catch him. The police turned up the next day for a statement, and I remembered to draw the curtains at night when working.

Some time later I was asked to present prizes at the girls' school near me. When I met the headmistress she turned out to be the lovely, caring young girl who had escorted me to the Seaford convent in the 1940s, Jane Simmons. As we laughed and reminisced together, I thought how little we change from childhood. It was natural for her to be a teacher and to be concerned for the welfare of children. That side of her character was already apparent when she took me by the hand to make sure I walked safely on the pavement to school. 'Give me a child until he is seven, and I will show you the man,' as the Jesuits say. Or, in this case, the woman.

I was asked to say a few words to the girls and began, 'Anyone who says that schooldays are the best years of your life must be seriously retarded.' Great cheers from the girls greeted this opening statement. I then went on to tell them that what you learn at school, however, will always stand you in good stead and gave examples. My afternoon at the school was very enjoyable, and as I walked home, I thought how strange my life was, with people from my past constantly returning.

~

THEN THE BBC sent me a lovely episode of the series *Bergerac*, 'Memory Man', with an offer to play an eccentric smuggler called Belle Young, who is also Susan's aunt. Susan was played by Louise Jameson and Bergerac, of course, was played by John Nettles. As I was now in my mid-forties, I had obviously been put into the category of eccentric roles. It was a lovely part and it meant flying to Jersey where it was to be filmed. The producer was Jonathan Alwyn, whom I had worked with when he directed some of the *Moody and Pegg* series. Graeme Harper, who was directing, had worked with me on *Mill on the Floss* when he was an assistant. When I got into my hotel, the thoughtful John Nettles had left a message welcoming me to Jersey and asking me if I would like to join some of the cast who were going to the theatre that evening. I turned up, found all the cast to be friendly souls and immediately knew I was going to have fun on the show. At the theatre that night, I also found out that a friend of mine from the old non-stop revue days, Peggy Ray, was now living in Jersey. Her husband ran the theatre. Peggy and I met up when I had a free day and sat drinking coffee and reminiscing over our youth and the five shows a day at the Panama Club.

We were filming at sea when the nuclear accident at Chernobyl happened. I was suddenly reminded of my book and the year 1986 that I had imagined to be so far away when I was writing it. I also remembered the conversation I had with Patrick Walker on the train.

During the filming it began to rain. I made sure I was under cover as I suddenly realized what dangers there were for fallout over the Northern Hemisphere. I also decided that when I returned home the only meat I would be buying for the next few years was New Zealand lamb.

In one scene, when Belle knows the customs are on to her and about to raid her for smuggled cigarettes, she empties the cartons and throws them into the sea. All the film crew were on another boat filming me throwing the cigarettes into the water. Those who smoked had little fishing nets to try and catch any precious contraband before they hit the water. I found it hilarious to watch and it became a game to see how many cigarettes were rescued during a take.

My husband John was going to Edinburgh for the Festival. I, meanwhile, had been sent another script from the BBC for an episode in the *Dorothy L. Sayers Mysteries*, called 'Strong Poison'. I was to play a Miss Booth, a nurse who was interested in spiritualism. The leading part of Lord Peter Wimsey was played by Edward Petherbridge, whom I had once worked with in the Devonshire Park Theatre in Eastbourne. Christopher Hodson was directing. We began rehearsals at the Acton rehearsal rooms and then filmed in the Lake District before finishing in the studio at the BBC TV centre at White City. When I had finished my filming at the Lake District

I had a few days free before the studio work, so I drove to Edinburgh to see John. The summer of 1986 was dire, with endless grey clouds and murky weather. As I set off to drive back down to Brighton I yearned to see some sunshine.

~

WHEN I REACHED home there was a message on my answer phone from my agent. Richard Attenborough had asked if I would come over to Zimbabwe to film a small part on *Cry Freedom*, the story about a South African journalist called Donald Woods, his friendship with Steve Biko, and the terrifying ordeal Woods goes through after he tries to let the outside world know about Biko's death by escaping house arrest and getting out of South Africa dressed as a priest.

I had read a book once about Steve Biko and his black consciousness philosophy, and found it fascinating. I had thought at the time how he was echoing Carl Jung's theory about the collective consciousness.

Richard Attenborough was asking people to come to Zimbabwe because he could not cast there, and if someone wanted some warmer weather it would be a nice break. I was told he would really appreciate it if I came out. If I was interested they would send me a script. As I was not likely to visit Zimbabwe by choice but would like to see the country, and I needed some sunshine, I said I would do it.

Biko was being played by Denzel Washington, and Kevin Kline was Donald Woods. My scene was with Kevin Kline at the British High Commissioner's office in Lesotho. As I suspected it would be all very chaotic in Zimbabwe, I took a couple of suits and blouses which I thought suitable for a receptionist at the British High Commission.

It was a long flight and the actor travelling with me, who had agreed to carry some film reels over for the company, was taken apart by the customs. The Third World Non-Aligned Conference was taking place in Harare. I was told by the girl who met me that everyone on the film had had to vacate their hotel rooms in Harare to make way for the overseas politicians. After I was picked up in a car I was to wait in a house for a while and then I would be flown to Mutara, near the Mozambique border where the film crew were now working. I sat in the house for a while watching some ants winding their way over the window sill and waited for the girl to come back. When she returned, I asked when I was to fly to the rest of the film unit and settle into my hotel. I emphasized how tired I felt and how much I would like to sleep. She said I could sleep in the house for a while until the flight for Mutara could be arranged. 'TAB, TAB', I remembered, John's shorthand from his regular trips to Africa when he worked there for the BBC. It meant, 'That's Africa Baby'. It was the stock response for everything that ever went wrong there. I did not want to sleep in the house, I wanted to get to wherever I was supposed to be going and unpack and find out when I was wanted. I felt very nervous and unsettled.

Eventually I was taken to an airport where a small aircraft was waiting. I got in next to the pilot and off we went. The pilot knew of my uncle who had lived in the country when it was called Rhodesia. He had an estate which he sold when Mugabe came to power. He had since moved down to South Africa. It was a long but fascinating flight. I tried not to fall asleep but to take in the full breadth of the extraordinarily beautiful countryside. We landed at a small runway where I was met by Terence Clegg, the executive producer, who wanted me to go for a wardrobe fitting. I assured him that I had brought my own wardrobe and that I was tired, and all I wanted to do was to sleep in a clean hotel bed.

When I climbed between the sheets at the Owl Hotel, I fell into an exhausted sleep, only to be woken a few hours later by an army helicopter flying low over the hotel. I fell out of bed with fright. The hotel was near the Mozambique border and there were rebels in the hills. I was beginning to think it might have been better to have taken a quick package tour to the Canary Islands if I had been so desperate for a bit of sunshine. Through the window I heard the voice of an Australian. Feeling safer already, I dressed quickly and went in search of the voice. It was the lovely John Hargreaves, who had just arrived. I introduced myself and he was as relieved to see me as I was to see him. We sat by the pool gossiping until the unit returned and we got our schedules. I was to shoot my scene the following day.

I got up early, dressed in the suit I thought appropriate for the scene, and got into the car allotted to me. When we drew near to the place where they were working I saw heavily armed Zimbabweans surrounding the area. They were to protect us, I was told. 'From whom?' I asked. From BOSS agents, was the reply. BOSS was the South African Secret Service. As we wound our way towards the unit I spotted the honey wagon, the portable lavatory carried by all film units. It stood in a cloud of flies. I decided I was going to be the fastest actress ever employed because there was no way I was going to use that honey wagon.

I met Donald Woods, whom I really liked, and we chatted for a while. Then Richard Attenborough and I discussed the scene. He wanted the receptionist to be hung over from the New Year celebrations the night before while trying to type and smoking a cigarette. Kevin Kline would then arrive in the office breathless from running, dressed like a priest, and try to see the commissioner. The following dialogue was a series of misunderstandings. Someone told me that when they saw the film at the BAFTA preview theatre, the scene got a huge laugh. We completed the scene and Richard Attenborough emphasized how thrilled he was that I had taken part. He was so thrilled in fact that he spelt my name incorrectly in the credits and put it almost at the bottom of a very long list. I never forgave him for that. Ah well, I never was much of a luvvy.

After the scene I was asked if I would like to stay on for a bit of lunch but I declined, saying I felt I ought to get back to the motel. I could not wait to leave a place with armed men and a fly-covered honey wagon; and I wanted to use my own bathroom. John Hargreaves was by the pool when I returned from location. It was beautifully warm in the sunshine and after changing into my bathing costume I joined him. We talked about Zimbabwe and I warned him about the dangers of swallowing any river water while he was there. He could ingest something which caused bilharzia.

'What's that, Jude?'

'Well, they're small snail-like things that can get into your system and, like malaria, they can cause cyclical illness where you pee blood.'

John squirmed at the thought. I then got into the pool for a swim, and as I was halfway across the pool he shouted, 'Watch out, Jude, a snail might swim up your fanny.' I nearly drowned with laughter. I liked John. He came to visit us in Brighton when he had finished filming and before he went on to Paris.

As the hotel rooms were needed for other actors arriving, I was sent back to Harare and on a trip to the Victoria Falls, with an excursion down the Zambezi River and a visit to a crocodile farm. This was a wonderful day and worth the whole trip for me. The Falls were massive and awe-inspiring, and as I travelled along the river past submerged hippos and elephants washing themselves, I counted my lucky stars. When I held a baby crocodile in my hand, even though it peed all over me, I felt very happy I had come to Zimbabwe.

I arrived back at the house in Harare in time to see Gwen Watford, who had just arrived from another trip so that her hotel room could be used by another actor. Since I was waiting for my flight out to England, the following morning Gwen and I went shopping in Harare. Every shop wanted English pounds. There was an air of desperation about the place. The only things Gwen and I could find worth buying were some very cheap plimsolls. I had listened to the radio while I was in Harare, listened to Mugabe and Gandhi denouncing the British and the Western world. I had also talked to a black driver who had been employed as a detective under Ian Smith's white government. The driver told me all the key positions were now held by people from Mugabe's tribe who had little experience. Anyone in the police from the driver's tribe was immediately replaced when Mugabe came to power. He told me that nothing was being maintained properly, fire engines did not work, and 'Quite honestly, we were better off under Smith.' From the rantings I had heard on the radio, I could tell this was a racist society. How ironical, I thought, that while everyone criticized white racists, no one ever called black Africans racist. India is even worse. Its caste system makes it one of the most prejudiced countries in the world.

The flight back to England took forever because some birds were caught in the engines near Nairobi. We waited for about eight hours for the next plane. By the time I finally got home I was shattered.

~

MY MOTHER WAS about to have a knee operation and was very nervous about it. I had started work on an episode of John Mortimer's *Rumpole of the Bailey*, in which I was playing a civil servant, Miss Rosemary Tuttle, who wears a lot of woollies, and is accused of leaking classified information. It was lovely working with Leo McKern again, who played Rumpole defending an innocent civil servant. It was good to work with Paul Daneman again too, who was playing the Lord Chief Justice. I thought I could make it back to Brighton after I finished taping the show at the Thames studio in Teddington. With any luck I would be able to be there when my mother woke up from the operation. It had been a long day rehearsing and recording and when I set off in the car for Brighton it was cold and dark. I put the heater on and just before I reached Brighton I fell asleep at the wheel for a brief second. It was a terrible shock to wake up on the wrong side of the road with traffic approaching in the distance. I wound down the window and breathed in some fresh cold air. Reluctantly, I realized that I could no longer do a whole day at the studio and then drive straight home as I had in the past. I did manage to get to the hospital in time so I could reassure my mother when she woke that no one had cut off her leg.

Straight after working as a guest star on two episodes of the situation comedy *Farrington F.O.* I had a wonderful treat. I was asked to be in four episodes of *Dr Who*, with Sylvester McCoy playing the Doctor. The four-part adventure was called *Paradise Towers*. Elizabeth Spriggs, Brenda Bruce and I were playing 'Rezzies', dreadful old women who lived underground and hunted young people to eat. Liz Spriggs and Brenda Bruce came to a terrible end by being eaten by a waste disposal unit, but I, as a younger Rezzie, reformed, stopped trapping young people, and helped Bonnie Langford and Sylvester trap some Daleks. I used a huge crocheted shawl to entangle them. Richard Briers ended up dressed like a tin man as the chief caretaker, and I looked like an egg cosy.

As I walked past Richard's dressing room at the BBC Centre, the door was open and he was perched on a chair looking extremely uncomfortable. He shouted out to me, 'This is how it all ends up as we get older, Jude. Look at me all dressed up like the tin man in the *Wizard of Oz*.' The last person who had said that to me was Lionel Jeffries on the Hollywood set of *Camelot*.

'Don't worry, I look like a lemon-coloured tea cosy, Richard,' I said.

He grinned, 'Yes you do a bit,' and burst into laughter.

Being in *Dr Who* was fun and I have been amazed at the huge following for the series. Sometimes, *Dr Who* fans admonish me for not including *Dr Who* in my credits in a theatre programme. As I always point out, space is restricted in the programmes and I usually only put my theatre credits and recent TV or films. I would not dare offend them by not writing about the four episodes in this book.

~

On 15 October 1987, I drove to Portsmouth to visit a youth detention centre as part of my magistrate's continuing training. It was a well-run place and the men in charge were mostly ex-servicemen. The young boys were often unused to any form of structure or discipline in their lives. Many had never possessed a toothbrush and some did not even know that it was usual to sleep between the sheets on a bed. When I left the centre I felt enraged and saddened that so many young people had such an awful start in life and often had to learn from places like a detention centre such basic standards of living. How could a civilized country not notice the needs of these children until they committed a crime?

On the way home I noticed the sky was a strange greenish colour, like nothing I had ever seen before. Starlings too were behaving strangely and were wheeling in different formations from the ones they usually made.

After I had returned home and we had all had supper, I went down into my study to finish my book. I was on the last chapter and trying to get the pages free of typing errors so I could deliver the manuscript to Andrew Hewson. At half past two on the morning of the sixteenth, I finished my book and carried the pristine chapters up to the dining room and laid them out on the table. There was not one smudge or blob of Tipp-Ex. I was very tired as I made my way up the stairs and decided that, instead of disturbing John who would be up in four hours, I would go up to the spare room at the top of the house and sleep there.

The room was directly above my son's room. I quietly got into the spare bed and snuggled down. I was just drifting off to sleep when the bed moved about six feet to the side from where it had been. I sat up on the pillow, hugging my knees, wondering whether I had imagined the movement, but no, I was in a totally different place from where the bed had been earlier. I sat for a while wondering what had happened when there was an almighty crash and the fourteen-foot chimney on our roof crashed through the ceiling. I screamed. Edward heard the crash and my shout, and rushed up the stairs to where he thought I was, only to find the roof open to the sky, a screaming wind, and wooden beams and debris across the bed where I was sitting. He reached through the beams and got hold of my hair and pulled me out, just as the whole floor and chimney stack crashed through to the room below and on to his bed. By now John had got up and saw us both covered in soot coming down the stairs. The wind speed of the hurricane was over one hundred and ten miles an hour. Curtains, furniture, clothes, papers and almost everything in one part of the house were being wildly blown around. Then the power went and we were in darkness.

We groped our way down the stairs and lit some candles. I went straight to the dining room, grabbed my pristine chapters, found a chair and sat on them. There was no way I was going to type all of the book again. The wind was screaming at the front door. We all huddled together in the sitting room wondering what had happened. John's and my first fears were that it was a nuclear blast. Our son guessed it was a hurricane. We found a battery radio and tried to listen to the BBC. Eventually we heard that the hurricane had struck along the south coast and London, and power lines were down everywhere. It was a long, terrible, frightening black night, with the wind sounding like a million banshees. Edward decided to go down to the lower ground floor where he felt safer. I told John about my bed moving just before the chimney came down. The fact that hearing my shout woke Edward and got him out of his room just before the chimney fell on to his bed was extraordinary; the fact that I was sitting on the pillow with my knees drawn up meant the falling beams had not broken my legs or trapped me. John was very quiet, realizing that he had nearly lost his wife and his son but for my bed being moved. Who or what moved the bed six feet from where the chimney fell? I decided it was definitely all our guardian angels working hard together.

As soon as it was light I telephoned a friend who had a scaffolding business. The builders who had been working next door covered the roof with plastic to keep the rain out, and we had scaffolding throughout the house, in the kitchen, in the upstairs bedrooms, the hallway, outside and inside. So much damage. We called the insurance company; the estimate by the architect and builders to restore our home to its original state was eighty thousand pounds and it was going to take months to repair the old house. It was a strange Christmas that year of 1987, with tea towels on the scaffolding in the kitchen so we would not bang our heads. I began to swing around the kitchen like a monkey. We kept very quiet about the damage, avoiding all publicity. As half the wall was out at the back, the last thing we needed was burglars. When I delivered the manuscript to Andrew, the first page of each chapter had a sooty fingerprint on the corner.

It was impossible to keep the house clean with all the work being done. Every time I did the washing fine dust would work itself through to the washroom and settle on the clean clothes. We had salvaged as much as we could as soon as we were able to get into the damaged rooms. Luckily, a curtain had wrapped itself across Edward's bookshelves, so protecting all the children's books Musi had sent him. We were able to clean them and store them until his room was redecorated again. When my mother first came to see the damage she behaved very strangely. She just looked at it, announced that we were all unhurt, and then started telling me about my brother's garage being damaged.

While the men went off each day I was left with the dismal time of endless noise, dust and making lots of cups of tea for the builders. So, when I was offered a tour with Anthony Quayle's company, Compass, in Gogol's *The Government Inspector*, playing Anna, the mayor's wife, I immediately said yes. My old friend Brian Murphy, whom I had worked with at Theatre Workshop in *Oh, What a Lovely War*, was playing Ossip. Phillip Manikum, a brilliant character actor whom I had worked with in *Comedy of Errors* at the RSC, was playing Bobchinsky; and it was being directed by Don Taylor, who had directed me when I had played the title role of *Frieda* for BBC TV. When we started rehearsals in London I was over the moon.

~

ANTHONY QUAYLE WAS one of that rare breed of men, a successful, talented idealist with a strong sense of duty to his fellow countrymen. He had been influenced by touring theatre companies as a child growing up in the Isle of Man and now, in his twilight years, wanted to take good-quality plays back into the regions so young people could have the chance of experiencing the theatre in their home towns. He spent a good deal of his own money setting up the Compass Theatre Company and, like the loved and respected person he was, set the standard and tone of the company's collective attitude to each other. Everyone worked hard and looked out for their fellow actors. As rehearsals progressed we became a disciplined but zany family.

A young Paul Rhys was playing Khlyestakov, the trickster. It was a wonderful chance for him to play the role with such an experienced company of actors. Everyone sensed then he was going to go on to do great things and we have not been disappointed.

Tony wanted us to go to Belfast. He thought that with all the terrible things happening to the people there it was our duty to take the play over to their theatre. I was not so sure. I really did not feel like risking bombs or any random shooting. We arrived in Belfast, where I was staying at the Europa hotel. It was surrounded by barbed wire and guarded by armed police. I had to pass through three checkpoints before actually entering the foyer. When I looked out from my fourth-floor room and saw small tanks moving along the street I really did not feel like walking across the road to the theatre. How could people live like this, I wondered.

I remembered the Gay Byrne chat show in Dublin, in 1969, when the priest and I had both warned about the dangers to Northern Ireland. Now, almost twenty years later, there were armoured vehicles on the streets. Why could it not have been sorted out before now? I felt so sorry for the people of Belfast. Perhaps Tony was right, we should be here to cheer them up with a play.

Full of trepidation, I passed through all the barbed-wire checkpoints and walked over to the stage door of the theatre only to be confronted by an armed policeman in a flak jacket who asked my name. I looked up into a security camera then I was let inside.

We were all summoned to the stage where Tony was waiting for us. He told us that the ship with all the scenery had been delayed in England so we would have to open the play without it; luckily the costumes had been brought over on the plane. Brian Murphy and I looked at each other with glee. This was going to be like working with Joan Littlewood again. Colin Small, our company and stage manager, put together a wooden door frame and also found some furniture. Apart from that, it was just a black stage. We began our rehearsal and whooping with excitement managed to make it work. The following night, when we opened, unknown to us the theatre critic from the *Observer* was in the audience. That week we received a glowing review, saying that it was one of the most exciting nights in the theatre he had seen for a long time. We were very pleased with ourselves. Tony was right. Lots of young people were waiting for autographs and to talk about the play. They saw the parallels between the corruption in the play and events in their own city.

However, this same play was seen as too middle class by the stupid Arts Council, when Tony applied for a £30,000 grant towards his next production. They kept him waiting for hours in the corridor – this wonderful old man who had done so much in his life for the theatre. In the end, they turned down his request for a grant and yet were doling out thousands of pounds to productions that no one wanted to see or could understand. Astonishingly, the Arts Council still survives and, in my opinion, continues making not always the brightest funding decisions.

When we arrived in Nottingham, Tony suggested that he and I could help promote the show by dressing in our costumes and driving through the city in a pony and trap. We met the mayor of Nottingham and off we went. It was very cold and Tony's nose was almost blue. We looked absurd, waving like lunatics at passers-by as we trotted past. Then we became helpless with the giggles. I had once heard a pompous music impresario describe all artists as 'performing animals'. At the time I had wanted to punch him hard. Sitting with Tony in that pony and trap, I did indeed feel like a performing animal.

When the tour reached Newcastle, several old men called at the stage door to see Tony. Later, as they said their farewells, they would half salute him. Tony explained that during the Second World War he was in the Office of the Strategic Services (OSS). When it looked as if it was possible that the Germans might invade, Tony had to set up a network for guerrilla warfare. Miners with a knowledge of the passages of disused mines were recruited to find and set up hidden bases where small groups of soldiers could mount guerrilla campaigns. The men calling at the stage door were these old miners. The more I talked to Tony the more I found his stories fascinating. I also realized that even though he had been treated for cancer, he was fighting a losing battle. I talked him into writing his autobiography, urging him to take it easier and let someone younger take on the mantle of Compass. His treatment by the Arts Council was disgraceful and I did not see why he should subject himself to that sort of stress.

He had also picked up a Czech refugee from Gibraltar during the war, who was later to become Robert Maxwell. After many years, when Maxwell was a rich and powerful publisher, he and Tony met up. 'If you ever need any help, come to me,' Maxwell had told him. When the Arts Council turned him down Tony had gone to Maxwell, who had said how grateful he was for being picked up in Gibraltar. Tony explained how he needed some financial backing. 'Leave it to me, I'll be in touch,' Maxwell had said. But Tony never heard another word from him.

When he began his book he told me he had not realized how much those days in the army had meant to him. I wanted him to tell the story about meeting two actors from the original Russian Stanislavsky company and I wanted to know what Stanislavsky thought to be the most important aspect of an actor's work. Tony laughed. 'That is exactly what I asked them, and do you know what they said?'

'No.'

'They said "learn the lines thoroughly" was Stanislavsky's advice.'

My friend Father Algy turned up to see me in Newcastle. He was now the chaplain for Durham's top-security prison for women. He loved the play and invited me to lunch the following day. He told me I could visit the prison; as a magistrate I had security clearance. I had already telephoned Algy and told him about the bed moving before the hurricane hit Brighton. He had agreed that it was definitely a miracle. 'The Boss does not want to take you back yet,' he said.

He did not want me to know what each prisoner had done but wanted me to talk to them without any prejudice. I spent a couple of hours talking to the women. As Algy drove me back to the theatre he told me that most of them had been imprisoned for murder.

When the cast flew to Aberdeen we were met by a coach and dropped off at the theatre. Brian and I were staying at the same hotel, which was further from the theatre than we had imagined. As we set off to find it, wheeling our suitcases along the pavement, we started to laugh. 'How long do you think we can go on carting our bags to the digs like this, Jude?' Brian asked. 'God knows,' I replied, pulling my case out of yet another crack in the pavement. We asked ourselves the same question thirteen years later when we were on tour together again.

Just before the end of the tour we played Brighton's Theatre Royal and I threw a party for the company at my house. John cooked all the food and the party was the noisiest we have ever had before or since. When the tour ended we all felt sad about parting as we had been so happy together. Tony and I remained in touch and often met for lunch. Tim Piggot-Smith took over running Compass and when Tony died he left money for a large party for his friends to be thrown at the Garrick Club.

~

As soon as I finished the tour I met Joanna Goldsworthy at Gollancz, who was going to publish my second book, *Fishcakes at the Ritz*, and liked her immediately. She wished to know what I wanted to write next and I told her about *The Seventh Sunrise*, which I had started to write in the sixties but realized was too ambitious for me at the time. Now that I had completed two novels, I knew I was ready to write it but I was not quite sure how to structure the book. As I told her about my love for Australia and how I was torn by belonging to two countries, I found out that Joanna had been brought up in Kenya and felt exactly the same. We went on to discuss how I could go about trying to bring all the strands of the book together.

Joanna had inspired me. Suddenly the structure of the book began to take shape, so I went home and started to write. As all the main characters in the book had to travel to Egypt I knew I too had to go there. Although I could research a lot of it from historical books, I knew I had to experience Egypt for myself and decided to put aside some money and plan a trip carefully so that I could visit all the places I wanted to see without cutting corners on my research.

When he knew I was serious about going, Father Algy phoned me with a great deal of advice. He had been a missionary in the region and was determined I should not get sick at all. I knew I could rough it for research as long as I could return to a five-star hotel at night and sleep in a fresh bed and use a spotlessly clean bathroom. Algy advised me to travel to Egypt in the spring of the following year, so I called my agent and told him I needed plenty of voice-overs and radio work to make some quick money. The launch of *Fishcakes at the Ritz* was also happening in the middle of April 1989 so I had to be back by then. I decided to go at the beginning of March.

By now the scaffolding had been removed from inside the house but was still up outside. The painting and redecorating was going on and slowly but surely the house was being restored. I decided that no one would ever again sleep in the room at the top of the house where I had gone to bed in the night of the hurricane. Instead, it would be my study. I bought a barometer and placed it on the wall close to the window, so that if it ever began to behave strangely I would know a hurricane was coming. The room also had the most wonderful views of the sky, the sea and the sloping rooftops – a perfect place for contemplation and creative thoughts.

The people running the Marriage Guidance offices in Brighton then asked me whether I would take over the position as their president. As I believed in the work they were doing, I agreed. When I made my first speech as president the name had been changed to Relate, and now included counselling for relationships that were not always sanctified as a marriage. I remained their president for six years.

To help pay for my trip to Egypt I had agreed to write a travel piece for a magazine. With all the other money I had saved I knew I could travel comfortably. I had every inoculation there was to be had, took boxes of antiseptic wipes and water-sterilizing tablets. At Algy's insistence I also carried a mosquito plug that deterred the insects. I had tablets for everything. John was very dubious about my travelling alone, but I was adamant that I could not worry about anyone else. I was not going there for the food or a holiday but to explore and research my book. I had to be free to move as I wanted and to be alone to think.

John saw me off at the airport. I had my binoculars, camera, tape recorder and several writing pads. I wore a cream linen trouser suit and a straw hat; and carried a capacious shoulder bag into which everything went that I would need on any excursion, and a sheaf of Biros. I was the original eccentric Englishwoman travelling abroad!

A car was waiting for me at Cairo airport. The Thomas Cook representative whisked me through the customs, leaving the rest of the British tourists standing in a long queue. Unknown to me, the travel agent in England had written that I was a VIP on the form sent to Thomas Cook, and the Egyptians were rising to the occasion. I was driven at speed through Cairo and checked in at a wonderful hotel right in the centre of the city. From my balcony I could see everything with my binoculars.

After unpacking, I wandered over to the Thomas Cook office and discussed the trips I wanted to make. I needed to go to Ismalia and find the old British air force bases and explore round Lake Timseh, right through to the Suez Canal and Port Said. I also needed to explore Cairo, Giza, the mosques, the oldest synagogue, the museums, then go to the Fayoume Basin, the Coptic monastery at Wadi Natrun and then drive on to Alexandria. After travelling back to Cairo I would board an overnight train down to Aswan to take the trip to Philae. From there I would take the flight to Abu Simbel for the day before returning to Aswan, where I would wait to board a ship going up the Nile to Luxor. We mapped out the whole schedule, which was going to cover many weeks, and agreed that a Muslim would take me to everything except the Coptic monastery, where I would be accompanied by a Coptic Christian. I would also have a female Coptic guide in Alexandria.

I ran into other women travelling on their own through Egypt; they were all Australians. Each time we ran into each other we would share information and experiences.

If I had been a spy I could not have gathered more information. On my travels I managed to spot every launch rocket hidden among the sand dunes. Once, when I had stopped and was admiring one, a jeep drew up and soldiers with guns jumped out and yelled at my guide. I reckoned the best way out was to attack or I might be in serious danger of ending up in an Egyptian jail. I yelled at the soldiers, 'I am old enough to be your mother.' The guide translated. 'I'm writing a book and I'm doing some research. God knows you must be used to British women writers by now.' Again the guide translated. The young soldier grinned from ear to ear and told the guide that perhaps we should go and look at some other sights, then left. I decided it was lunch break and wanted to find the nearest lavatory. After wiping everything with my antiseptic wipes I counted the flies and my lucky stars that I had avoided trouble with the army.

My guides were wonderful. When we reached a place where I wanted to be on my own, they would let me wander, make notes, talk into my tape recorder or write. I knew I was safe as they would hover discreetly, making sure I did not run into any trouble. It was one of the most important journeys of my life. Not only could I gather all the information I needed for the book but my inner self too was rewarded with answers to questions I had pondered for years. When I reached Aswan, another guide, called Aboudi, met me from the train and took me to my hotel, which was situated on an island in the middle of the Nile. My room had a balcony where I could watch the river and all the life upon it. I drifted on the river in a felucca, marvelling that I was at that moment living among people whose lives were as they had been hundreds of years ago. The magnificence of the statues in Abu Simbel was awe-inspiring; one walked with reverence for their creators. As a dramatic change in the evening, I took myself to a nightclub and watched the belly dancers while having dinner. The interesting thing for me was that I never ever felt alone. The characters in my book were dominating my need to explore places and the questions I needed to know were being answered daily.

When I joined the ship cruising up the Nile to Luxor, the British contingent looked upon me as an oddity, I suspect, as I was not part of a couple. I watched them often taking ice in their drinks while I would send a bottle of water back if the seal was broken. I did not get gippy tummy but they did. I also added sterilizing tablets to washing water, bath water and any water for rinsing my teeth, despite assurances that the cabin tap water was safe. When we set off on a tour of the Valley of Kings, I had my straw hat, my torch, my tin of sweets, an industrial mask for when we went into the tombs and a bottle of water; and I wore my linen trouser suit, socks and shoes and carried an umbrella. Some young couples, dressed in just singlets and shorts, nearly wet themselves with laughter when I joined the group. But by midday they were all suffering from dehydration and were grateful to be allowed under my umbrella.

There was one tomb I particularly wanted to visit. In old maps I had studied, it was situated in Luxor, but it was never mentioned in any of the modern tourist books. On the morning of the day when we were all to be taken around the temples in Luxor, I instinctively knew I was going to find it, and that I would be taken there. The group set off to tour the temples with the ship's guide. He said I could go off on my own for half an hour before moving on to the next place. I watched all the tourists move away but stayed where I was, thinking about the tomb.

An Arab approached me, looking at me carefully, and named the tomb I wanted to see. I nodded. He beckoned and I followed. He led me over rough ground until I came to the tomb, which was locked and guarded by a soldier. I gave them both some money and the soldier unlocked the door and let me in to the dark tomb and closed the door behind me. It turned midday as the door closed and the sun was directly overhead. A light streamed through a small hole in the roof and lit up the incredible statue of an ancient Egyptian deity. The effect was both terrifying and wonderful. As the light moved, the great shadow brought a movement to the deity's face. I was full of wonderment. I had managed to see what I had been trying to find, but I cannot say the name; it would be a blasphemy to the old Egyptian priesthood.

I left the rest of the tourists on the Nile tour and took a plane from Aswan back to Cairo. While visiting Giza I passed the Nile Hilton Hotel and saw that Ralph Bates was opening in a play on a Derek Nimmo tour. I left a message for him saying, 'This is not from a belly dancer from your past, just Cornwell wishing you luck for the play and hoping you enjoy Egypt.'

By the time I left Cairo I had just enough money left to give my Coptic guide a good tip. I could not even buy any duty-free goods and I did not have enough for a train ticket to get home from Heathrow. I hoped John would remember to collect me from the airport. He was there, waiting, with a look of relief that I had returned safely. He confessed later that he had been very worried about how I would cope on my own and feared I might disappear somewhere. All I could think about was getting on with the book. John gave me his old Amstrad word processor, and taught me how to use it. This was much better than all the fun and games with the typewriter, but I still wrote everything in longhand first.

In early April I was busy with all the pre-publicity before the launch of *Fishcakes at the Ritz*; endless chat shows, interviews and photocalls. At the launch, at Hatchard's book shop in Brighton, the Gollancz people came down and provided drinks and snacks for a huge crowd of people. Just before it all started, when the shop had closed and locked the doors, there was a banging on the door. One of the book sellers answered, then came to me. Pointing to a man in a duffel coat outside, he said, 'He says he knows you.'

'Never seen him before,' I replied.

The man in the duffel coat kept knocking on the door. The book seller returned to the door and came back to me again. 'He says he's your agent.'

I was appalled at myself. Poor Andrew had been locked out because I had not recognized him. That is the trouble when you build up a relationship on the telephone, only meeting a couple of times. I apologized profusely to dear Andrew, who found it all a great joke. At the end of the launch, Andrew and the Gollancz team came back to my house where we had dinner and lots of laughs.

Another week of signings, talks, radio interviews, TV chat shows and my promotion time for the book was over; now I was able to get on with *The Seventh Sunrise*.

My writing, however, was interrupted with an offer of a lovely part in an episode of *Boon* for Central TV, playing a matron of an old people's home who steals from the wealthier residents in order to give special treats to an old woman who does not know her son has died.

As soon as I finished the television work I returned to my writing. I was planning on spending less time acting and continuing with my career as an author. After all, I had done all the things that I had originally set out to do as an actress and I was having difficulty remembering my acting agent's telephone number. Now, I thought, is the time for writing. 'The best laid plans of mice and men . . .' It was not to be. While I was happily writing, trouble was looming.

Chapter Eighteen

1990–1993

~

MY SON, EDWARD, had built up a business over the years but was now about to sue a large company over a wrong valuation. The company handed the problem over to their insurance company who thought, by dragging out the time before the court case, the legal costs would force him to go away. But my son is a fighter, and decided to take them on. John and I realized that we would have to back him in this fight and that it would cost a lot of money. So by the end of 1989, I knew I would have to go back to work as an actress and write again in my spare time.

In January 1990, I changed my agent. The first thing Ken McReddie wanted to know as my new agent was why I wanted to leave my old one. I said, half joking, that I could not remember his telephone number. Ken thought that was the most terrible thing he had ever heard, and ever since regularly asks whether I can remember his number.

The first day I joined him he got me a part in the *Van Der Valk* series, playing Harriet De Kuyper, a Dutch madam in a brothel in Amsterdam. On the same day, Harold Snoad tracked me down to my new agent. He had been given a pilot for a new situation comedy series called *Keeping Up Appearances*, written by Roy Clarke. He had very little time to cast it and wanted people he had worked with before and knew would work quickly. I was asked to play a character called Daisy. After reading the script I knew it would be a successful formula, depending on the casting, so Harold and I met at his office at the BBC and I told him that while on paper poor old Daisy did not seem to have a lot going for her, I

thought I could make something of the character. I was also thinking that as the person playing Hyacinth was carrying the show, I
would be able to learn my part quickly and get on with my book.

My agent did the deal with Harold for the pilot and for any sub-
sequent series and I flew off to Amsterdam to film the hour-long
Van Der Valk episode with the lovely actor Barry Foster playing the
title role. I had never been to Amsterdam before; I thought it was a
beautiful place. While I was there the first of the season's herrings
arrived at the hotel and I was talked into trying raw marinated her-
ring. Yuk! I prefer my herrings cooked.

The Dutch wardrobe department bought me a wonderful,
leopard-skin patterned dress from a tart's shop. The dress opened
quickly, secured only by Velcro at the waist. Apparently when a
prostitute is trying to fit in a lot of clients, the quicker she can get
her dress off and on the better. I was also given some really high-
heeled red shoes, which meant I towered over Barry Foster during
our scene. So the director decided that the scene, apart from a few
moves, would be better played seated. And I had to work with a
big white Persian cat, who as the scene dragged on was making
those rumbling sounds of anger which I knew could result in a
nasty swipe with claws.

On a free morning, when I went to find the famous red-light district, I missed it but found a wonderful Christmas shop instead. As
I had been steadily building a Christmas collection for years, I went
in . . . and was immediately recognized as Mrs Claus. The people
in the shop were very friendly and after signing some autographs
I bought a Christmas butter knife and carried it triumphantly back
to the hotel.

Nobody in the unit could understand how I had missed the red-
light district so gave me new directions. This time I found it. Seeing
all the strange wares out on display reminded me of when my
mother, who had been reading about a sex shop opening in
Brighton, had wanted to go and see it. But she would not go on
her own and wanted me to go with her. The most embarrassing
moment for me was when my mother thought she had found a
fur-lined tissue box. I had whispered that it was not for tissues.
I really am quite bright about workings things out.

'What's it for then?' she had asked loudly.

I had hustled her out of the shop and explained as we walked away. The young man serving had looked at us as if we had come out of the Ark. I felt sure he could hear the 'No, surely not, you're making it up, Judy', followed by a lot of giggles.

The date arrived for the filming sequence for the *Keeping Up Appearances* pilot. As Daisy was very poor and the wardrobe budget was very tight, I happily sifted through the vast BBC wardrobe for some old clothes. I fell in love with an old grey cardigan, some tatty jeans and a truly dreadful dressing gown; I also had some old shoes at home which I felt were suitable for the character. After my drive up to Leamington Spa where the unit hotel was based, I found Shirley Stelfox, who played the first Rose, wandering round the hotel. Shirley and I had tea together and talked about the script; I knew we would work well together, so I went to sleep very happily.

The following evening we were driven down to the location and straight to the make-up caravan. Shirley, as Rose, was going to be made up to look glamorous; I was getting hardly any make-up. Harold Snoad introduced me to Pat Routledge, who was playing Hyacinth. She and I had once shared the same agent and I thought she was perfect casting. As Hyacinth was the brightest sister, Rose the quick-thinking if always romantically inclined, and Daisy a little slow, passive and good-natured, I decided to use some of the personality I had once used for Gretchen when I was working as stooge with Nat Mills.

After the filming we all turned up for the read-through and rehearsals of the studio segments at the Acton rehearsal rooms. I met Geoffrey Hughes, who was playing Onslow, Daisy's husband. Like Pat, he too was from Liverpool and I thought perfect casting. Clive Swift, whom I had worked with at Granada, was playing Hyacinth's husband Richard; and Jo Tewson, whom I had worked with in *Who's Who* at the Fortune Theatre, and had a great sense of comedy, was playing Hyacinth's neighbour, Elizabeth. It looked like it was going to be fun working together.

When Geoff and I came to rehearse our scenes I could see he worked quickly. I was very relieved; it meant we could finish early. The rehearsal period was until Sunday when we went into the studios and, after a couple of technical rehearsals, taped the show in front of a live audience. In the studio we were introduced individually to the audience. This did not worry Jo, Geoff, Clive, Shirley or me; we were used to it and known to TV viewers. Pat, however, was better known in theatre circles and was a little nervous, but she soon got into her stride and Hyacinth, aided by Harold's brilliant direction, quickly became a great success with the audience.

When it came to our scene in bed, Geoff and I climbed in and sat up ready for the floor manager to cue us to begin, when the top of the bed collapsed and we ended up with our legs in the air. The audience went wild with laughter, and it took ages for them to calm down and listen to the scene. We got all our laughs and the whole pilot went really well. Harold was very pleased with us; so was the BBC and they promptly booked us for another six shows. The series would be shown in the autumn.

There was high unemployment in Britain in 1990. In the street in Coventry where we filmed the scenes of Onslow and Daisy's house, many men were unemployed. The best of British community spirit was on show when the BBC paid the people in the street a fee for any inconvenience caused, and the residents gave the lion's share of the cash to those who were unemployed. During all the years of making *Keeping Up Appearances* we returned annually and watched the children grow up and noticed various improvements to people's homes. Often the residents would join us during a tea break to discuss the different scenes. The children too, when returning from school, would come and have a sandwich or biscuit and treat us as their friends and tell us their news.

Close to the base we used in Leamington Spa when filming Hyacinth's house, a man had bought a plot of land. When we first arrived in 1990, he told us it was for his son and new daughter-in-law, and he and his son were going to build a house there. They were just laying the foundations when we first arrived. Each year we saw the house growing and by the time we finished the series, in 1995, a beautiful house stood on the ground, surrounded by a mature garden.

While working on the first series I was also writing *The Seventh Sunrise* and found the same synchronicity was occurring that I had experienced while writing *Cow and Cow Parsley*. In my first chapter I created a character called Machtum. Why I called him that name I do not know but I think it was probably the most perfect chapter I had ever written. I loved Machtum, who had become so real and led the story into all kinds of situations, placing himself ideally for when I wanted to introduce the next characters, three women, into the story. At the end of the first part of the book, Machtum dies by the bank of the Nile. As I finished writing I felt incredibly sad that it was the end of this beautiful character. The next morning I was reading the paper at breakfast when I saw in the obituary column that Sheikh Rashid bin Saeed Al-Maktoum had died. I was utterly shocked. I had no idea there was someone so important with that name. The sheikh was from one of the ruling families in the Gulf States and an eminent, highly respected spiritual leader. He had died about the same time that my character had died by the bank of the Nile.

I have often found that a strange alchemy happens when writing a book. After intellectually perceiving a character, and working on that character's personality, a form of alchemy takes place, when the character created takes on a life and a will of its own and then leads me into areas and situations where I follow. It is a magical time. I suppose these moments are the equivalent to what actors or other entertainers would call 'flying' during a performance.

Joanna, my editor at Gollancz, often arranged 'get togethers' where I met other writers in her stable. On one occasion I saw Michael Denison and his wife, Dulcie Gray. Michael had just completed an autobiography for Gollancz. I soon learned that ninety per cent of writers have a day job; in my case it was often a day and night job – few can devote their entire time to writing.

~

BEFORE I BEGAN the second series of *Keeping Up Appearances*, the director Pedr James – who was one of the directors influenced by *Old Flames* and my performance in it – offered me a wonderful part in *Nice Town*, an extraordinary production to be made on film for the BBC. I was to play Aunt Peggy, who had been incarcerated in a mental hospital since a teenager. She had been sectioned there by her family for being promiscuous and after giving birth to an illegitimate child.

For my research, I asked a friend who was with the Brighton Health Authority to arrange for me to meet someone, like the Aunt Peggy character, who under the new mental health laws was being allowed to return to ordinary life outside the asylum. My friend, a fellow magistrate, arranged for me to meet someone who was attending a mental health day centre. I talked to lots of patients and watched those on medication, so that by the time it came to filming I knew how I wanted to play Aunt Peggy. What I did not know at the time was that I would be returning to the same mental hospital in entirely different circumstances within a few years.

I loved working with Pedr, and luckily the filming finished just in time for the start of the second series of *Keeping Up Appearances*.

After the first series, Harold Snoad had to replace Shirley Stelfox as her other commitments cut across his schedule. Mary Millar took over the part of Rose and David Griffin came in to play the part of Emmet, Elizabeth's newly divorced brother.

On the first day's filming Mary was highly nervous; having mostly worked in musicals she felt inexperienced when it came to drama. She asked whether Geoff and I would tell her if anything she did was wrong. We told her to go for it and we would help her in any way we could. So she did, and was great, creating a wonderfully bizarre Rose whom everyone loved.

Mary was a lovely person, deeply sensitive and very religious, with a wonderfully naughty sense of humour. One day Jo Tewson, Mary and I went to the pictures while we were on location. As none of us was wanted first thing in the morning, we felt we could have a late night. When we were seated in the cinema some children were making a terrible row so I went to the manager and told him to come in and control them. Dutifully, the children calmed down. The real noise came later from Mary, when there was cruelty to an animal in the film. She let out a great wail. Jo and I tried to pacify her. 'It's only a film, Mary,' I whispered in her ear. 'They are not really being cruel to the animal. It's just effects. Shut your eyes.' The manager rushed in again, thinking it was the bunch of children yowling. By now, Jo and I were trying to stifle the wailing Mary. Thankfully, the scene soon finished, and Mary's muffled snorts and sobs died down.

~

As FAST AS I was making money it was going out into the fighting fund for the lawyers preparing our son's case. The insurance company kept dragging out the time, were unable to find papers and took an age to answer our lawyers. It was obviously going to be a dirty war.

I kept writing at every opportunity and my book was growing. One night while working, and tired, I pressed the wrong button on the Amstrad. I had not put in a backup floppy disk and lost three months' work. John and Edward rushed up the stairs when they heard my screams of rage. Thankfully, I had written it in longhand first so could start typing it up again.

I had been asking both John's mother and my own what they could remember about the 1920s and 1930s hoping I could find things of interest to add to my book. What I did find was that whereas my mother had always been reluctant to talk about her childhood, she began to reveal a lot more to me because I was writing a book. She told me about the lifestyle and traditions in her home before her mother died; and how she had loathed her father's drunkenness, which was why she had joined the Temperance movement. She had wanted to be a teacher but after her mother died her father wanted her to leave school and work. So she had run away to join her sister Gladys in London, leaving her younger brother Ronald behind. He joined her a few years later. Now I understood her and her attitudes to life much better than I had before. Her father died a few years later when, while drunk, he had stepped out in front of a tram.

In the autumn of 1991 she had to go into hospital for a hysterectomy. After the operation she was never the same again. I suspect she must have had a small stroke during the operation and nobody noticed, or if they did, they failed to tell me.

At Christmas, some friends joined us for dinner and I noticed my mother would bring up the same subject that we had just finished talking about. I knew that sometimes she switched off when she was bored and would make the occasional gaffe but this was unusual for her.

One afternoon I phoned her and she said, 'What time do you call this to be phoning me, Judy?'

'It's four thirty, tea time,' I replied, presuming she had just taken a nap. 'Are you all right?' I asked.

'Why shouldn't I be?' she replied angrily. I thought she was in a mood and left her alone.

~

WHEN THE NEW year of 1992 arrived, so did a contract for the third series of *Keeping Up Appearances*. After the success of the first two series we were now booked for Christmas specials as well.

By now, the marketplace philosophy promoted by Mrs Thatcher had permeated everyone's life. Our union, like all the other unions, was no longer a closed shop and much weaker. I heard various actors in the rehearsal rooms talking about their financial advisers, who had referred to creative accountancy. Creative accountancy? I thought surely accounts had to be based on true facts; creativity belonged to the world of make-believe and invention. I stuck with my good solid accountant whom I knew would keep me out of trouble.

John Birt was now changing the nature and shape of the BBC. He was a man who had come from commercial broadcasting and in my view had no feeling for or understanding about the ethos of public service broadcasting. While everyone within the corporation accepted that the BBC had to be made more efficient, to some of us, Birt's introduction of internal marketing seemed disastrous. Wasn't something wrong when radio producers in Broadcasting House found it cheaper to walk down Oxford Street to the HMV store to buy a record for their programme rather than pay the new marketing fee from the BBC's own comprehensive library? Or when drama producers in Broadcasting House chose to rent a luxury suite in the hotel next door for rehearsals rather than pay the exorbitant fee for a BBC rehearsal studio? BBC Television rehearsal rooms stayed empty while local church halls around London thrived on the business from BBC productions using their premises for rehearsals; and the unused BBC rehearsal rooms were slowly turned into offices. The whole philosophy seemed flawed. My John was under a lot of stress with the changes and I watched many of the producers I knew leaving, or taking early retirement. My old friend Bill Hays took off for France with his new wife, Catherine Schell.

I told my literary agent Andrew Hewson I had nearly finished my book. Then Gollancz was taken over by another company and my lovely editor, Joanna, who had been with the publishing house for almost twenty-five years, left. It was arranged that I should have lunch with Maureen Waller, who had first tried to take *Cow and Cow Parsley* to Hodder & Stoughton in 1980. Now she was the commissioning editor for Simon & Schuster. She had read the manuscript of *The Seventh Sunrise* and wanted to know what I planned to write next. I told her my ideas for a murder mystery, *Fear and Favour*, which I hoped to start soon. She wanted time to think about the editing needed on *The Seventh Sunrise* and definitely wanted *Fear and Favour*, so Andrew arranged a two-book deal with her while I went off to the West Country to film an episode of *Miss Marple* starring Joan Hickson. She was absolutely the best Miss Marple of them all.

In the Miss Marple story called *The Mirror Crack'd from Side to Side* I was playing Heather Babcock. The first person I ran into when I turned up to start filming was Gwen Watford; I was able to find out how she had got on after I left Zimbabwe. Claire Bloom and Barry Newman – the American actor – were also in the film. All of us had a laugh with Barry when we were told about his American agent dealing with the BBC producers. Agents fight for good terms when negotiating a contract for their clients. But American agents, on the whole, are much tougher than their English counterparts. Barry's agent, knowing Joan Hickson was the star of the show, had insisted that his client should have everything that Joan had, such as standard of hotel, billing and all the other details that go with a guest starring role, and was astonished when the BBC producers happily agreed to all his demands. For the truth was that dear old Joan Hickson had none of the things that Americans associated with stardom. On location, she did not have a great big caravan fitted out with all the luxuries that American and these days our stars expect. Joan, when not wanted, would just quietly sit on a chair under the shade of a tree. So Barry Newman had one hundred per cent of nothing.

~

BACK AT *KEEPING Up Appearances*, Mary, Geoff and I were now happily confident playing our characters on the 'wrong side of the tracks'. By the time we began the third series, our senses of humour and close working friendship had bound us together like a real family. When hanging around in the old banger of a car we would sit sharing sweets and jokes until we had to drive into shot and start the scene. We all worked very quickly on our scripts and were never called in on a Saturday to rehearse, which used to infuriate Clive. Pat, who had so much more to do, enjoyed working on a Saturday, and as all Clive's scenes were with Pat, he used to be called in to rehearse with her and would groan, 'Why can't I go and live with them in the series? I wouldn't have to rehearse on a Saturday then.'

Once during the filming, Onslow, Daisy, Hyacinth and Richard are travelling in Onslow's car when smoke starts pouring out of it. We were pushed for time and the man in charge of the pyrotechnics was rushing to finish setting up when Harold shouted 'action'. A stuntman was driving dressed as Onslow. I was strapped into the front seat and the tube from which all the smoke was going to appear was tied over my safety belt. We were driving along when the back of the car caught fire. Pat and Clive leapt out of the car and ran away. I was trapped by the tube across the safety belt and could smell burning hair and knew it was my own. The stuntman got me out and the make-up girl quickly smoothed my hair, saying, 'No Judy, hardly anything. You won't notice it.' I insisted on seeing a mirror, and saw lots of little singed ends.

'Right,' shouted Harold, 'let's try again. It's all fixed now.'

'Not me,' I yelled. 'If you think it's safe you put on my grey cardigan and risk your hair being singed.'

He did and it all worked perfectly well.

A lot of the things that went wrong on location ended up in the out-takes programmes. It was always the unexpected silly things that made me laugh. Like when Geoff got his cigarette stuck to his bottom lip in a scene in the car, or when Mary and I got caught on door knobs, or had not seen our cue light and thought we were still waiting to begin. Things do go wrong, and especially when working with animals. The beautiful dog which used to frighten Hyacinth into the hedge time after time was called Alice. I had worked with her trainer on other productions where animals or birds had been involved. She was a brilliant trainer and we all grew very fond of Alice. However, she was replaced by a younger dog of the same breed but a slightly lighter colour. So she had to have a water rinse to tone her fur down. When we patted or cuddled her during a scene the colour would come off on to our hands.

At the end of the third series, Maureen came to Brighton and we went through my manuscript. She decided that it was more marketable if the book began with the second chapter and we lost the first chapter. I nearly went mad. This was my perfect chapter. She was a tough editor and the fight over the chapter lasted for a few hours. Finally we agreed that I could thread all the information in the first chapter into the rest of the book and I would have a prologue to set the story up. After the session I was deeply depressed, but there was a deadline for delivery and a lot of work to do, so I got on with it. I had to deliver the finished manuscript by the beginning of December. While I was working on the rewrites, I had an offer from the producer Michael Rose to play Ida in a national tour of *The Cemetery Club*. It was about three Jewish widows and was to start early in 1993. I would have to have a perfect New York Bronx accent.

～

BY NOW I was tired. Working on the book was taking up all my time and I felt unable to cope with the usual family Christmas. I arranged that my mother would spend time with my brother and that John's mother would go to her sister's; Edward had his own plans. John, stressed out of his skull with the BBC changes and the impending court case, agreed to come with me to a health farm, Grayshott, for Christmas and the New Year. I delivered all the rewrites on time to Andrew, who merely said 'Bravo', then 'Happy Christmas'.

John and I entered a sanctuary of peace, switched off our brains, and let Grayshott smooth away our worries. It was one of the best Christmas/New Years ever. We started 1993 reinvigorated and ready for battle with the world. Not so my poor brother. Christmas with my mother had been terrible. She had complained about the children, the food and everything else, and then demanded to be taken home earlier than was arranged.

In January a fourth series of *Keeping Up Appearances* was being talked about but the dates were not fixed. My agent went ahead and booked me with Michael Rose. We were to start rehearsals fairly soon and I wanted to work with a good coach for accents before I started on the play. Millicent Martin and Ann Charlton were also going to be in it. I went to the brilliant coach Joan Washington, whose work I knew about from friends who worked at the National Theatre, and she gave me confidence and a really good accent.

While I toured with the play during March, April and May I promoted my book, which was due out in October. After ten weeks of the near sell-out, twelve-week tour, the filming for *Keeping Up Appearances* was starting. Luckily I was playing at the Wolverhampton Theatre so I could get to the first scenes I had to film, although it meant getting up at five o'clock in the morning and having a car drive me to location and bring me back in time for the evening performance in the theatre.

The big problem was that in the theatre I was using the lower register in my voice for Ida and I had to remember that Daisy's voice was in a much lighter, higher range. When we started filming I tried to hit Daisy's timbre and it sounded like a choir boy's voice on the break. Pat got the giggles, so did Mary and Clive; Harold looked worried. I tried again. This time it sounded as if I was being strangled. After Geoff and I did a bit of improvisation of our own, I got Daisy's voice back. My attempts to find my Daisy voice ended up in some of the out-takes. By the time I got back from the filming and put on my make-up for the theatre, I was shattered.

After the show on the Saturday, I was heading home, driving south to Brighton. Our last date on the tour after Wolverhampton was Swindon. Luckily, my next filming day was going to be near Arundel, so I could get there in time for the shooting on the Sunday, and then travel on to Swindon. After the week in Swindon I could join the rest of the cast filming *Keeping Up Appearances*. Already Michael Rose was talking about another tour in the autumn. He had made a lot of money with *The Cemetery Club* and wanted it to go on. I said that nothing was going to get in the way of my book launch at Hatchard's in Piccadilly in October, so it would have to be after that. Everyone agreed to wait until the launch and the following week of promotion were over.

While I was in Swindon a woman who booked the writers to lecture on *QE2* cruises came to see me. She had read in the programme that I was a published novelist and wanted to know whether I would be interested in taking a cruise as writer on board. I told her that one of the episodes we were filming during the making of the fourth series of *Keeping Up Appearances* was going to be on board the *QE2*. So, if I enjoyed the experience, I would certainly come on a cruise – especially as she had promised that I could take John with me.

Harold was watching me closely when I rejoined the gang. He was worried I might have forgotten Daisy's character, but I soon settled back in to the role and he was happy again.

Only Pat, Clive, Geoff and I were in the episode on the *QE2*. We were sorry for the others left behind, and promised to tell them all about it. There were great grins on the film crew's faces as we travelled in luxury to Copenhagen. Most of the time, we actors were sitting in our cabins waiting for the assistants to come and fetch us for a scene, but the evenings were free, and we would all meet up to listen to jazz, see a show, or go to the ship's cinema. I made friends with the librarian and told her I might be coming on board again to give a lecture.

Harold had the best-dressed extras that any director could wish for as many of the passengers volunteered to take part in the crowd scenes. The final scene involved the four of us dancing in the ballroom. Pat panicked when she realized that neither Clive nor Geoff were really good at dancing, and there was only one or possibly two takes with the use of volunteer extras and the band. 'What shall I do? What shall I do?' she shouted. I showed her quickly how she could fake it by moving her arms and shoulders extravagantly, which would look like dancing. Nobody would be able to see their feet on the dance floor, I assured her. She did it brilliantly.

After filming, the trip back to Southampton was wonderfully wild and indulgent. I got in touch with the lady organizing the lectures on board and told her I would be interested in lecturing on any future cruises providing I was available.

~

WHEN MAUREEN WALLER left Simon & Schuster, I was handed over to Lucy Ferguson, another editor. She decided to buy the paperback rights of *Cow and Cow Parsley*, which was now out of print, and wanted to bring it out while they were waiting for me to finish *Fear and Favour*. I was shown the jacket that marketing had chosen for *The Seventh Sunrise* and hated it. To me it looked like a penny dreadful. I had wanted something much plainer – a darkened pyramid, perhaps, with the sun rising behind it. I was told marketing thought it was the best kind of cover. As marketplace and accountants seemed to be ruling the world, I stopped complaining and let them get on with it.

By the end of the fourth series of *Keeping Up Appearances* Harold was uncertain whether there would be another the following year. Pat wanted to play a new role as a private detective, and said she would be too tied up to do any more. Harold explained that there was still a Christmas special to be made the following year. I went off to promote *The Seventh Sunrise* on endless chat shows, newspaper interviews and soroptimists' dinners. Just before the launch at Hatchard's, I agreed to do two days' filming with a director I had worked with before, in the 1950s and 60s, Robert Tronson. It was part of a series written by John Mortimer, called *Under the Hammer*. I was playing an old girlfriend of Richard Wilson, nicknamed Batty. Batty was a teacher taking some schoolgirls on a trip to Paris where she meets up with Richard in a bar. It was a lovely scene to do, and I already knew John Mortimer from other productions.

The day of the launch arrived and I got to Hatchard's early. It was pouring with rain but lots of people came, including the gang from *Keeping Up Appearances*. They closed the door at a certain time and my poor husband found himself locked out in the rain. After he was let in, there was more banging on the door and it was Joanna Goldsworthy saying, 'She is one of MY authors.' It was wonderful to see Joanna. I hugged her tightly and gave her a copy of my book. Afterwards she wrote me a wonderful letter about how well the strands of the plot had come together and how much she loved it. I was very touched by her words. After another week of promotion I was off again, with an increase in my salary, to do another six-week tour of *The Cemetery Club*. I was also going to be doing book signings in every town we visited.

Again we packed the audiences in to the theatres and I was really beginning to appreciate the enormous popularity of *Keeping Up Appearances* as everywhere I went people were coming up to me and telling me how much they loved our characters. At every book signing, *Keeping Up Appearances* fans would take the opportunity to get my autograph as well as my books and I was unable to keep up with the huge amount of fan mail.

By the end of the tour I was very tired. It had been a hectic year and I could not wait to go home. Michael Rose wanted me to agree to another tour the following year, with an increase in salary again. I said I would think about it, but eventually turned the offer down and Carmen Silvera took over my part.

The final tour date was Birmingham. On the last night of the show, I knew I should really wait until the morning to travel, but I yearned to go home. I set off with that wonderful feeling of freedom knowing I did not have to do anything, smile at anyone or make any sort of effort – I just wanted to hug my family. As I approached the Sussex Downs in the early hours of the morning, I wound down the car window and breathed in the fresh, cold Sussex air. I was home again.

Chapter Nineteen

1994–1996

~

ON A SUNDAY night, just after Christmas 1993, John and I were watching a film on television when we heard letters coming through the letter box. I went into the hall and found about twenty cards in envelopes by the front door. They were all addressed to me in my mother's handwriting. I looked out of the front door but she had gone. We opened the cards and found they were all Christmas cards. Now I was seriously worried. What was she doing out at this time of night dropping cards through our letter box? We went looking for her in the car and drove through every street in the area but to no avail. We went to her apartment and waited for her to return. After a while she came tripping down the pavement with her keys in her hand. She was wearing an old raincoat I had not seen her wearing for years. The buttons had come off and she had safety pins keeping it together.

'Oh,' she said, when she saw us, 'what are you doing here?'

'You've just posted twenty Christmas cards through our letter box,' I said.

'The man said you had to have them. They're important letters.'

'What man?'

'The man said they were important and you had to have them straightaway. Isn't it a lovely moon?'

'Are you going inside now?' I asked.

'Yes. But I've got to watch out for that yellow van.'

'What yellow van?'

'It's often parked near here. I think they're watching the house. See you soon.'

We watched her let herself into her apartment and she waved to us from the window. It is a terrible moment when you realize that your mother has gone quite mad.

The next morning I called my mother's doctor. He told me he had asked her to get me to ring him months earlier. Her condition was due to a series of small strokes which had resulted in a form of dementia. Her condition was worsening and she would need to be in a home within six months. He advised me to get power of attorney straightaway so that I would be able to take decisions on her behalf. I got the forms from a solicitor friend and telephoned my brother. He and I went round to see a highly suspicious mother, who signed the forms but insisted she was perfectly capable of staying in her own place and looking after herself. Strangely enough, she did seem to be almost normal that day.

I also got in touch with a social worker for advice and found out that there was a group she could attend; and to make sure she was eating properly she could have meals on wheels. However, she would not go to the group and she would not take meals on wheels. I called in to see her and found her looking like a small grey-skinned pixie. She was pleased to see me but then moaned that my brother never came to see her. As I knew he had visited her a few days before, I took no notice. When I asked her whether she had eaten, she described the elaborate meal she had just finished, but I did not believe her. There was no smell of cooking, and when I looked in her refrigerator, there was hardly anything there. I drove to Sainsbury's and went straight to the delicatessen counter. As I started ordering amounts of cold meats for her, an old man was staring at me. I ignored him and then he shouted to his wife, 'It's her, it's Daisy. You know the one with the dirty kitchen. She's buying some ham on the bone and some tongue.' I wanted to hit him hard. Faces all over the store were turning in my direction. I kept my head down and flushing with embarrassment tried to give my order quietly without it being relayed down to the old man's wife. By now the odd shopper was following me to see what else I was going to buy. The whole experience was a nightmare and I wanted to get back to my mother as fast as I could.

When I put some cold meat and salad on to a plate for my

mother, she wolfed it down. I made her promise to eat more; her fridge now had food in it. But she did not want me to go into her bedroom. Her bathroom was neat and tidy. She had always been a fastidious housewife. I realized that she had fooled us for ages about her condition by keeping her lounge in perfect order. We were so used to her guarding her own privacy that my brother and I would never have dared to intrude.

Her seventy-seventh birthday was near; it was also my fifty-fourth. I called my brother and we arranged a surprise party for her with all her grandchildren because we knew at this rate of decline it would probably be the last birthday when she would be able to understand what was happening. We had a beautiful cake made with 'Happy Seventy-Seventh birthday, Irene' written on it. I telephoned her beforehand to make sure she knew what time I was collecting her, and then had three angry calls back asking me when I was coming. When I picked her up in the car she had one eyebrow pencilled on and the other eye had blue shadow. I did not dare say anything. She was grumbling and anything I might have said would have been interpreted as criticism. However, she rose to the occasion when she saw all the family. No one mentioned the odd eyebrow. Even the grandchildren knew that no one ever rebuked my mother about anything. My son charmed her and so did my brother's children, who paid her a lot of attention. The party was a success.

My brother and my son promised to keep an eye on her when I had to go to Manchester to record a radio play. It was a beautiful script written by Lavinia Murray, an adaptation of *My Beautiful Career*, an Australian book. The Christmas special for *Keeping Up Appearances* also took me away from home for a while but by Easter I was back and the date had been set for Edward's court case. It was expected to take a week in the High Court.

A ridiculous system exists in the courts when you are suing someone. If the defendant thinks the case against them is strong enough they can lodge some money in court. The judge is not allowed to know about this. The person bringing the case can either take the money and drop the case or proceed. If the case goes to court and the money awarded to the plaintiff is not as much as the money lodged in court, the plaintiff can then be made to pay all the costs. It is catch twenty-two with a vengeance. The whole system is absurd and makes a mockery of justice. The insurance company had placed some money in court. My son and his solicitor now had to work out whether it was worth taking.

At the same time we heard about the date of the court case, my mother went into hospital. There was an infection in her knee replacement. I was running up and down to the hospital with clean nighties and making sure she was all right, while trying to look after my husband and son who were working with the barrister on the court case. I was also trying to write my book.

When I let myself into my mother's bedroom I found chaos. I hardly knew where to begin to sort things out and realized there was no way she could look after herself and would have to go into a nursing home. I found somewhere that was absolutely beautiful and the matron agreed to come to the hospital to meet my mother, who was in a very good mood and agreed she would come to the place to recuperate. As I cleaned up her hospital locker I noticed she had old tissues and a crust in her handbag. When I opened it up to remove the old tissues, I found a condom in the bottom of her bag.

'What is the definition of an optimist?' I asked my husband and son when I got home.

'All right,' said John, 'What is the definition of an optimist?'

'A seventy-seven-year-old woman with dementia who keeps a condom in the bottom of her handbag.'

'She's obviously been influenced by the ads on TV,' Edward said loyally. 'You know, the safe sex ads.'

'Either that or she fancies the consultant,' I replied.

As the court case progressed I read all John's notes each night and I did not like the way it was going. In spite of a defence witness admitting lying to court, I could smell what I can only describe as an establishment carve-up.

On the day of the judge's summing-up my mother came out of hospital. I had cleaned and marked all her clothes and hung them up in the wardrobe in her room at the nursing home. I waited at the home for her to be dropped off by the ambulance; my nerves were as frayed as they could be. I was anxious she should like the place and I was worried for my son. When the ambulance pulled up in the drive, she descended the steps of the vehicle like the angry witch in the *Wizard of Oz*. 'What's the meaning of this, Judy?' she almost hissed at me. The matron greeted her and distracted her from attacking me further. I was beginning to feel like a deflated balloon and I wanted to cry. I was so tired from all the clothes marking and the effort of getting everything ready for her. The matron took her in to meet all the other residents. Lunch was about to be served and I said I would be back later to see that she was settled in. Then I rushed home to wait for news from my son.

I could hardly eat anything, I was so worried about him. I remember talking to my guardian angel and saying, 'I don't think I can take any more of all this,' while I sat by the telephone waiting for news of the court case. When it did ring it was the matron of the nursing home. My mother was creating havoc, saying she knew her rights and wanted to leave. I drove up to the nursing home again and was told that they really could not keep her there. Her personality had changed as soon as I left, the matron told me. It was almost like schizophrenia. She had been threatening them with all kinds of legal action if they held her against her will. I threw all her clothes and possessions into the car and took her back to her apartment. I told her how silly she had been; how the nursing home was one of the best in Brighton and she had blown it forever. I also told her that the judge was summing up in court so I had to rush back home.

'I hope you lose the case,' she snarled, sounding like the worst kind of fiend in a horror movie. I could have strangled her if I had not been so intent on getting her back to her apartment. When I took all her things back into her place she changed again and as I left she cheerfully said, 'See you soon, Judy.'

My son lost the case. He and John arrived home utterly dejected. We had been advised an appeal would not be wise. The three of us sat together trying to come to terms with the situation. When someone hurts those I love I normally fight. This time I turned the whole problem over to my guardian angel. That day, and the period of time before it, was my experience of 'the dark night of the soul'.

Never before or since have I felt so inadequate, so unable to cope with the events surrounding me, and so dependent on a power greater than myself.

The nightmare with my mother continued as she 'rage, raged against the dying of the light'. She was in and out of hospital and finally she was sectioned when one of the residents in the apartment above her reported her to the social services for leaving the gas on. She was taken to a part of the mental hospital where I had gone to research the role of Aunt Peggy. They got in touch with me to meet a committee made up of a psychiatrist and social workers.

It was lucky I knew so many people who worked or had worked in the health service. I also had friends who had gone through the experience of having parents with Alzheimer's or dementia. They told me what would happen when I attended the meeting. Pressure would be put on me to take my mother into my house. My brother and I decided to play 'good cop, bad cop'. I would be the callous daughter from hell and he would be the soft son who could not possibly take the time off from teaching. We both knew our lives would become nightmares if she lived with us. I could not give up my work and neither could he.

Duly, we turned up for the meeting and the most sanctimonious psychiatrist said to me, 'If it was my mother, I would want to take her into my home to look after her.' I did the best impersonation of Bette Davis that I could and played a hard, detached woman. 'Well, she's not your mother,' I said, looking her straight in the eye. 'I don't like her that much.' I watched the look of distaste appear on her face. 'And you might be able to afford to give up your job but I can't and won't. I'm not having my life ruined by her.'

She looked at me as if I had crawled out from under a stone. Then she turned on my brother. He gave the best impersonation of a slowed-down version of Woody Allen I had ever seen. He almost had tears in his eyes when he said how he would love to look after her but he had to work to keep his family. They agreed to keep her there for a while. I knew it was one of the best places she could be and where she would be well looked after.

When we left their office we saw the tail end of a conga winding through the building. Shuffling people with Alzheimer's and dementia were hanging on to each other as they hissed the conga tune. We knew who was leading them. Sure enough, there she was, right at the head of the long line. I think she thought she was on holiday in Bournemouth.

~

IN OCTOBER 1994 I was booked to play Mrs Musgrove in the BBC TV's production of Jane Austen's *Persuasion*. It was a lovely role and I looked forward to playing it. Just before I started on the contract, Edward entered a *Times* travel competition and won it. The prize was a two-week holiday for two in Grenada, in the Caribbean. As he did not want to go there, he offered it to us as a thank you for standing by him. I said I would swap with him for a trip where he wanted to go. He chose to go to California. The flight to Grenada was on the day after my contract ended with *Persuasion*.

My brother promised to deal with all my mother's affairs so I started work knowing she was safe and well looked after; and he would take care of everything to do with her welfare while I was away. John by now had resigned and taken early retirement from the BBC, which removed a great deal of his stress. He returned to written journalism with a column in the *Spectator* and writing travel and arts features for *The Times*.

Working on *Keeping Up Appearances* had cushioned me from many of the changes in the BBC. We still had our rehearsals at Acton and all the benefits of that excellent rehearsal studio. The introduction of internal marketing at the BBC had changed everything. Productions now had to rent rehearsal rooms and deduct it from their budgets. The read-through for *Persuasion* was in the production office of Threshold House in Shepherd's Bush, with all of us squeezed up together as we read our parts. One actor I knew came up to me and said, 'I can't believe it, Judy, I'm working on this for less than I earned in the early Seventies.' I was very relieved that my agent had done a good deal.

Our week of rehearsal was in a church hall, which was cheaper than using the BBC's own rehearsal rooms in Acton. I thought the whole concept of the internal marketing system absolutely insane management. What accountant dreamed up this scheme to make himself look good, I wondered. I had not rehearsed in a church hall for the BBC since the 1950s and early 1960s.

My old friend Corin Redgrave was giving a wonderful performance in his role as a fop; it was good to see him again. The whole cast from Amanda Root to Ciarran Hinds was made up of the most talented actors and I felt sure it would be an excellent production. I joined the filming at Bath. The way the scenes were lit gave a wonderful feeling of the period.

I was sitting with some of the cast in a caravan one day, waiting for the next scene to be called, when Fiona Shaw began saying how much she admired Princess Diana. The others joined in the discussion and I remember saying, 'One day I'm afraid she'll go too far and really upset the establishment.' Someone asked what could possibly happen to her.

'She could be killed in a car crash,' I replied.

'What a terrible thing to say,' Fiona said. 'They wouldn't dare.'

In 1997 I wondered whether any of them remembered that conversation we had in the caravan three years earlier.

~

As soon as I finished shooting the film I drove back to Brighton and packed for our trip to the Caribbean. Edward had already taken off for California.

John and I had the most wonderful holiday in Grenada. We needed it. The stress of the last four years had taken its toll on both of us. Whenever I am under stress, I eat. So I had gained a lot of weight. John, too, needed to lose weight. We swam, basked in the sun and went exploring the beautiful island. The people were friendly and many of them recognized me from the television. Then a newspaper reporter arrived. It was not a dreadful intrusion and as soon as he had his interview we were left on our own again.

Before Christmas I learned that there was to be another series of *Keeping Up Appearances* the following year, so 1994 ended in a great spirit of optimism.

I had nearly finished *Fear and Favour* when my editor Lucy moved to another publishing house. Clare Ledingham became my new editor and she was brilliant. When she went through my manuscript she gave me some wonderful suggestions with which I agreed absolutely, and I rushed off to finish the rewrites on the book. It was going to be published in 1996, just after Easter.

In the spring of 1995 the mental hospital got in touch with my brother and suggested that as my mother was greatly improved, we would be able to move her into a home. I had been recommended a lovely place where a friend of mine had placed her mother. The matron of the home, having been assured by the social worker attached to the mental hospital that my mother would be fine, immediately accepted her and I moved her in.

As she settled into her room she looked at me and said, 'I'm loopy, aren't I?' I did not know what to say. 'Tell me the truth, Judy,' she said.

'Yes,' I replied, 'but don't worry, Brian and I will make sure you're all right.'

She did not last long in the home, and the matron was furious with the social worker who had told her my mother would fit in. So I found another home and moved her in there. Within weeks I was asked to move her again because they said her language was disgraceful. Her language? The man running the place was most apologetic. He described her as disruptive and violent. If I had not seen the sudden changes in her myself I would probably never have believed him.

Back she went to the mental hospital, where she seemed much happier. I would slip in to see her at odd times to check that she was all right. Sometimes she was like a little child, treating me as if I were her mother. Another time I found her sitting alone in the dining room, having taken a seat which she knew one of the other patients thought of as theirs. 'Are you an illusion or are you real?' she asked me. I assured her I was real. 'How did you find me?' she continued. Just then another woman shuffled in complaining she was thirsty. 'Don't worry, the bar will be open soon,' my mother said. Where did she think she was, I wondered. Another woman said to her, 'That's my chair. I sit there.' My mother's eyes became malevolent slits as she said, 'Well, I've got it now.'

~

After I finished the book, I went back to working on *Keeping Up Appearances*. As we filmed the scenes with Hyacinth, Rose and Daisy's father getting into all sorts of humorous scrapes, I thought how many people facing similar problems with their parents as I had with my mother must appreciate a chance of laughing at situations in *Keeping Up Appearances* they understood only too well. Humour is one of the most important things in life. You can overcome anything with humour. Governments can be brought down if enough people can laugh at their lies or corruption. Tragedy and Comedy, two halves of the same mask.

I had so many letters from fans who told me that when the husband was unemployed, and the whole family was feeling utterly dejected and poor, Onslow and Daisy's situation made them laugh and feel better. At least here were some characters, trying to make something of their lives, who had less than they had.

While we worked on the fifth series I sensed that it would be the last one. Harold and the BBC wanted to make another series but Pat felt it had run its course. She wanted to move on to other things. I could understand her position as I had once made the same decision myself over *Moody and Pegg*. I shall forever be grateful to Pat for introducing me to magnifying mirrors. 'All women over fifty should have one,' she told me. And she was right. I carry mine everywhere with me. It is a shocking reality, gazing into one first thing in the morning on location, but as one's eyesight changes it is an absolute necessity.

In one of the episodes of the fifth series Pat had to be driven in a Rolls-Royce to a very posh hotel. Outside were parked some very expensive cars, including a Jaguar sports car. I talked to the lady who had brought the Jag down to the location and told her I would love to take it for a drive. She gave me the keys and I took off, whizzing around country lanes. It was exhilarating.

At the end of the series we all gave each other presents at a party. Many of us have kept in touch since. Mary, Jo and I arranged to have lunch the following year on Mary's sixtieth birthday. Harold showed us all the out-takes he had collected and they were made into programmes later.

~

PAUL ELLIOT, WHO ran the pantomime company E&B, offered me the part of Fairy Godmother in his number one pantomime date at the Birmingham Hippodrome. It had been years since I had been in a pantomime and I realized quickly that the way they were put on was quite different from how I remembered. It was normal to have only one week's rehearsal now; I had been used to at least three weeks' rehearsal when I had last taken part in a pantomime. E&B made me an offer I could not possibly refuse, so I agreed to do it. I would be working with Rolf Harris and Gary Wilmot. They would need me to go up to Birmingham as soon as my costume was ready, for publicity photographs and press interviews. I was shown the most wonderful designs for my costume and met up for dinner with Carole Todd, who was directing. We got on well and are still good friends today; I knew I would be safe with her directing.

On my one free day during the making of *Keeping Up Appearances* I travelled up to Birmingham for the publicity call. There I met the two men playing the ugly sisters, Nigel Ellacott and Peter Robbins. Their costumes, which they had designed themselves, were amazing. I also found out that the champion ice-skater Robin Cousins was going to be Dandini, and Bob Carolgees and his dog Spit were also in it. It was strange returning to the Hippodrome. The last time I had appeared at the theatre was when I was a sixteen-year-old dancer performing in *Slaughter on Tenth Avenue*. Memories came rushing back.

Rolf, Gary and I were all in the same hotel in Birmingham for the pantomime. Gary was the first person we met when John dropped me off at the hotel. We had tea together and Gary confessed he used to watch *Moody and Pegg* when he was a young lad. He was an open, friendly person and we got on at once. Rolf was like a big sweet-natured cuddly bear while Robin Cousins, whom I had watched skating for Britain and cheered from the comfort of my armchair, was a warm, kind, gentle soul full of fun. He wanted to move to Brighton, he told me, and I promised to help him in any way I could. The whole cast was utterly professional and friendly, and we were looked after by the best ever company manager, Ian Sandy, whom we all loved.

It was hard work, two shows a day for over eight weeks. When the pre-publicity was given to the press, E&B took a million pounds in advance bookings. The shows were packed at every performance. Between shows, Ian Sandy would order us pizzas or other goodies and we would have a nap before the next show. There was a standing joke in the company that if you walked down the corridor you could hear Rolf, Gary and me, in our respective dressing rooms, snoring our heads off; the younger ones like Robin and Jodie Jackson, who was playing Cinderella, would be just resting. Nigel and Peter's dressing room became the green room where we would call in and help ourselves to any biscuits or chocolates left on display for visitors. As we all became familiar and confident with the show, so the jokes began.

The most hazardous time for any fairy godmother is when the ponies arrive on stage pulling the coach to take Cinders to the ball. Inevitably there was one naughty pony. I think he must have had the soul of a dreadful comedian. He would wait until I was in full voice and about to wave my wand for Cinders to go to the ball, then he would drop about a hundredweight of poo on the stage. This would immediately reduce the children in the audience to hysterics; and the cast. It was really hard to get them back to the magic of the moment again. I soon dealt with the pony. The moment he lifted his tail I turned and looked at him. 'Any nonsense from you,' I said glaring upstage at the pony, 'and I shall turn you back into a mouse.' His ears went back. It stopped him from ruining the scene, but he would drop the poo backstage, in the wings, so all the dancers had to step over it.

As we all got to know each other well there was an outbreak of fart jokes. We would pick our moments when we could make a fart-like noise guaranteed to make the other person laugh. It was always done discreetly. The audience was never aware of what was going on.

John and Edward joined me at the hotel for Christmas and we had a wonderful time. The management of the Swallow Hotel had put up decorations and a tree in my suite, and the lunch in the dining room downstairs was accompanied by singers and entertainers. We had no clearing up to do and just relaxed in each other's company.

Because of the heaviness of my costume, it needed strength to fasten all the clasps, so I was given a male dresser, Brian. I think my guardian angel had a hand in choosing him, because he was also a trained Samaritan. Early in January 1996, I began to have strange dreams, as if my mother was trying to send me messages. After this, my brother telephoned to say that Mother was dying and was now being given diamorphine. I had two shows that day and Brian helped me through them. If ever I wilted, he would gently talk to me until the bad moment passed.

My brother was with her when she died. He made all the funeral arrangements so that I could go back to Brighton for the service on the Sunday. The day she died, Rolf's favourite uncle also died. In the hotel car park, as we got into his car to go to the theatre, we both broke down and cried together. But we still made the matinee audience laugh.

At the funeral, while my brother publicly gave way to grief, I remained controlled with the stiffest of upper lips. My audible grieving came later, at night, in the privacy of my hotel suite. It was at night the haunting occurred, in dreams and the half twilight of sleep, with dreadful images of my mother's madness. It took four years before the dreams became more positive, giving her a new life. Now, I can remember her as she once was, beautiful and cheerful again.

The E&B management could not believe there had been no fights or arguments during the season. They were amazed that we had all got on so well together, and all loved working as a company, so they booked us all for the following Christmas at Woking. I was over the moon. It meant I could stay at home and drive to work every day. I was so proud of being in that Birmingham production of *Cinderella*. People still talk about the show today as being one of the best pantomimes ever. My agent, who came up from London to see it on one of his 'duty to clients' visits, was enthralled and returned again another day with his whole family.

After the pantomime finished, BBC Radio wanted me to make a

travel programme, travelling to Miami, from where I would take a short cruise to the Bahamas. They knew I liked travel and had written travel articles for magazines. I asked if John could be my producer. They agreed and off we went to Miami, and the warmth. John and I had a whale of a time. When we docked at Nassau we recorded all the calypso music that greeted the tourists; and the howling wind aboard the ship during some rough weather. He and I often argued about the script, but if I say so myself, we put together a really good programme, and had a short but wonderful holiday at the same time.

As soon as we returned home, the *QE2* publicity man, Eric Flounders, offered us a part of the world cruise from Cape Town to New York via Rio and the Caribbean – a wonderful trip. We could just manage it before returning for the week of promotion and the launch at Hatchard's of *Fear and Favour*. I agreed to give two lectures and John gave two lectures and was writing a travel article for *The Times*. They flew us out to Cape Town, where we stayed for four days before joining the ship. John was able to show me all the places he knew from when he was on the BBC's *World at One* and covering South African affairs.

It was the most fascinating trip and we enjoyed every moment of it. I also signed lots of books. It was in the early hours of the morning, and raining, when we came up the Hudson River. We could hear the sounds of church bells drifting across the water. Then the Statue of Liberty loomed into sight. It is really the most impressive way of arriving in New York.

We were staying for a few days before returning to England and we were going to meet up with our friend Stella for lunch. She was in New York visiting her daughter. Stella and I had been good friends for a long time. When I first began writing *Fear and Favour* I told her I was going to use her name for my heroine in the book and she had been pleased. When we met up for lunch at the Inn on the Park, she told us about returning from a holiday in Grenada to Gatwick and finding her car covered in snow. My hair nearly stood on end. I had no idea she was going to Grenada.

'Stella,' I said, 'this is weird. The second chapter in my book, where I introduce my heroine Stella, begins at Gatwick, when she has just returned from Grenada. I have written about her car being all snowed up.'

We discussed the strange coincidence for a while, then I asked her if she had met a new man in her life.

She beamed, and said, 'As a matter of fact, I have. He's a policeman.'

Now my scalp tingled. 'Oh Stella, this is too much. My heroine in the book meets a policeman.'

We became silent. Eventually, I asked her his name. When she told me, I got up from the table. 'That's the name I've used in my book,' I said. I went outside the restaurant and had a cigarette. How was this possible? Synchronicity? When I returned to the table, Stella, practical to the end, said, 'Why don't you write another book and let Stella win the lottery?'

The cover for *Fear and Favour* was excellent. Simon & Schuster brought out the hardback and the paperback versions at the same time in April with another super launch at Hatchard's. We had some good reviews and the hardbacks sold out very quickly.

~

IN THE SUMMER of 1996 I was offered the part of Mrs Baker in an episode of the *Famous Five* series. The story was 'Five on a Hike Together' and filming was in the West Country. I was called at a civilized time in the morning for my scenes with the children. As I waited in the hotel to be picked up, an actor who had just finished his work greeted me with the words, 'Judy, all I can say is, these children are the children from hell.'

'I'm usually quite good working with children,' I said. 'They don't worry me.'

'You are in for a surprise,' he laughed. I kept an open mind. Sometimes actors like to wind each other up.

When I started my scenes with the children, everything went well and they behaved, knew their lines and worked reasonably quickly. But too many scenes had been scheduled for one day. It should have been a two-day call. The children were getting tired and began to get naughty. We had covered the final scene from all angles and now the camera was on me for a long speech and they were bored. They got into my eye line and started pulling faces and behaving as only naughty children can. I waited for the director to tell them to stop, but he said nothing. So I launched into them like a headmistress and told them if they wanted to be actors they had to learn some self-discipline. I said they were behaving like selfish brats and they looked shocked. After that they sat quite still until I had completed my speech. As I left the location, the make-up girl was hugging herself with glee.

'I warned them,' she said. 'I warned them not to play you up or they'd cop it. Someone needed to tell them off.'

The real problem was they had been working far too many hours. There are supposed to be rules governing this but they are obviously not effective.

For the rest of the year I worked in radio and on TV shows like *Call My Bluff*, and I started research on my next book.

We all hugged each other when we began rehearsals for Woking. My friend Robin Cousins was now living in Brighton and we saw him often. He was going to drive up and down from Brighton too. Rolf had been overdoing the work that year. It happens to us all at some time or other. He became ill and had to have time away from the show. Gary Wilmot was great and so was everyone in the cast covering for Rolf's absence. After we were all settled into the run, the naughtiness began again and we had a great time.

Rolf decided to retire from pantomime. He found it too much strain. Two shows a day, when you put in as much energy as he did, does take its toll – as I was to find out a year later. After the pantomime, he headed off to rest on the island of Mustique in the Caribbean, with a copy of *The Seventh Sunrise*, while John and I flew off to Grenada for a working holiday on a voyage with the *Black Prince* which was part of the Fred Olsen Line. We were picked up at St George's harbour and cruised through the Caribbean, across to the Azores and on to Dover. It was a wonderful way to begin the year.

Chapter Twenty

1997–1998

~

I STARTED 1997 with three jobs lined up. BBC TV offered me the part of Mrs Quigley in a play called *Student Prince* with Robson Green. Again, the director had been influenced by *Old Flames* and my role in it when he was a young student. The vibrations from that production have rippled through my whole career. Immediately afterwards, I was to play wildly eccentric May Cuttle in an episode of *Midsomer Murders*, with John Nettles. The director was Baz Taylor, whom I had worked with on *Moody and Pegg*. I had also been offered the part of the nurse in *Romeo and Juliet*, for the Stafford Shakespeare Festival. I really wanted to play the nurse so I told my agent to accept. It looked like it was going to be a busy year.

Until I began the play for the BBC, however, I wanted to get started on my new novel. While I was writing, Gail Wiltshire, who runs the Twelfth Night Theatre in Brisbane, arrived in England and drove to Brighton with her assistant, Lisa Broadby. Gail wanted me to appear in a play at her theatre, and then for a short tour, in 1998, and had brought me three plays from which I could choose. The thought of returning to Australia again was too tempting to resist. I told her it would have to be after I finished the pantomime in Nottingham and had had a chance to rest. I chose to do *Bedroom Farce* by Alan Ayckbourn; I wanted to play Delia, which had originally been played by Joan Hickson in London.

Edward, by now, had taken off to America to work in California. John had agreed to create and then edit a new magazine for the Royal Society of British Sculpture to be called – in its first year –

Sculpture '97. He was looking forward to creating a very special periodical using all his contacts in the arts world to write for him. He and I were asked to dinner by the sculptor Michael Rizzello, at his home in London. He wanted to show us his new work which would have a prominent site on a building in Oxford Street. As soon as we entered his front door and had glasses thrust in our hands he was urging all his guests to walk down the path at the back of his house to his studio to see his new work. I followed everyone, misjudged the steps, and fell over. I felt intense pain and knew I had broken my right arm or shoulder. We had no dinner. As there was no way I was going to go to a hospital in London, we drove very gently back to Brighton to the casualty department of the Royal Sussex Hospital.

The nurse began to ask me some most extraordinary questions before sending me to the X-ray department. She would not let John sit near me while I told her how I had fallen over on the way to see a sculpture at the bottom of someone's garden. I suppose it did sound a bit weird. I suddenly realized that she thought my loving husband had given me a thumping. I got the giggles, assuring her that if any man ever raised a hand to me I would thump him first. I was certainly not a victim of marital violence. The radiographer was obviously tired. Either that or she was having a bad hair day. Because I could not use my broken arm, when my jacket slipped off I asked her if she could replace it round my shoulders. She draped it over me as if it was a soiled nappy. I began to feel gritty.

A registrar came to see me, having looked at my X-rays. He told me that I would never have full use of my arm again, because the arm had broken so near the joint with the shoulder. He said I would be very restricted in my movement and suggested I attend the hospital physiotherapy group, where I would be looked after by the very consultant who had operated on my mother's knee. 'No way,' I raised my voice. 'I'm placing myself under Mr Barry Fearn, who is a friend of mine. I want you to keep all the X-rays for him.' There was an immediate reaction. Barry was the senior consultant orthopaedic surgeon. More X-rays were called for and they promised to give them to Mr Fearn in the morning. Barry was the wonderful orthopaedic surgeon who had saved my spine after I had been thrown from a horse. He and his wife had become great friends of ours and I trusted him completely. John was appalled at my name dropping, but I told him I did not accept that I would never have full use of my arm again. 'Besides,' I said, 'if I can't raise my arm, how am I going to wave my wand as fairy godmother in the pantomime at the end of this year?'

Barry came round to our house the following morning and told me that intense therapy, providing the bones were healing properly, should get my arm working well again. The filming for the BBC play was drawing close so I explained to the producer that I had broken my arm and suggested that he might like to recast the part. 'Just use your left hand and we'll shoot round you,' was the reply. Within two weeks my bone was growing like coral and the physiotherapy had begun.

The first scene I had to do was when my character lets herself into a room and is startled by a stark-naked Robson Green pointing a gun at her and shouting 'freeze'. He was playing a bodyguard to a prince. I used my left hand to open the door and entered the darkly lit set. My right hand was involuntarily twitching, wanting to do things normally. I felt like Quasimodo, leading with a right shoulder and rolling to the left. At the shout of 'freeze', I turned, trying hard to look with fright at the gun, and not down at Robson Green's testicles – a difficult thing to accomplish if you are as curious as I am. Self-discipline prevailed, however, and I never did see his private parts. I think if I had, I would have reacted like Frankie Howerd in a *Carry On* film – 'Ooh! Ooh I say.'

Although nervous and wary of any condition that would lead to another fall and breaking the left arm, I managed to complete the scenes. John had to chauffeur me to the studio because I could not drive. I could not even dress myself and taking a shower was a nightmare. But I completed the contract and went back to the physiotherapist. I could not write or use my computer. The only way I could make notes was by pulling a pad of paper across with my left hand while keeping my right hand in the same position to write. The result was a spidery scrawl. But my arm was getting stronger.

During the first two days of May the whole country was in a

state of euphoria. The sun was shining and people were walking around with smiles on their faces. The general election results showed that the British people had voted against Thatcherism. They wanted a change from a philosophy which had released the worst of greed and ruthless opportunism into society. In the past, this unpleasant aspect of the British psyche had been cloaked under the mantle of standards of public behaviour and concern for the welfare of others. While John Major was a likeable enough person, he was surrounded by the most awful, disloyal, sleazy people in government. New Labour, under the leadership of Tony Blair, promised a new, sleaze-free Britain. Ah well! At the time of writing this book, I cannot forgive him for creating such political cynicism in the British people.

By the time I started work on *Midsomer Murders*, I could use my right arm a lot more. However, I had a lot of difficult things to do as the character May Cuttle. For a start, I was supposed to play the cello; I was also supposed to be dressed as a Roman soldier in a dream scene and drop dead from being poisoned; I had to be able to dance and take part in rituals in the garden, avoid a large piece of falling masonry in rain and drive a car. Hey diddley dee, an actor's life for me! I got to grips with the cello, moving my right arm from side to side, with the help of a brilliant cellist who showed me the movements I should be making for the pre-taped cello music. Striding around as a Roman soldier, however, proved a little more difficult and was not helped by the hysteria among the film crew at my attempts to be masculine. As I had no wish to hurt myself in any way, I had a huge mattress on the ground so that when I was poisoned I could fall backwards on to it safely. I could hear the prop men sliding the mattress as I slowly tasted the poisoned mushroom soup. When I fell down, of course, I could not use my arm to get up so the guys had to heave me up by lifting me from the waist. We all had a lot of laughs during that scene, and Baz was patient and amusing as our director.

I enjoyed working on *Midsomer Murders* and all the cast were great fun. When we had to dance round the garden during our rituals, the stifled giggles and snorts of laughter were infectious, at times nearly reducing me to tears of uncontrollable laughter.

I was just as lucky with my director when I travelled to Stafford for four weeks of rehearsal for *Romeo and Juliet*. She was Julia Stafford Northcote, and the young cast of actors were extremely lucky to have the inspiring experience of working with her. Juliet was played by Kelly Bright. I have not seen a performance of Juliet that has ever measured up to hers. For a young girl, she had the most mature appreciation of the words and meaning. Working with her was exhilarating. I was the oldest in the cast and because they knew I had an arm slowly mending, these young people were very supportive. We would work outside on a raised stage in the shadow of the castle; the audience would sit inside an arena of covered seating. When it rained, the stage could become slippery, and the young actors would wait at every one of my exit areas to help me down.

There is no greater test of concentration than working in the rain. To see a seat where a puddle is forming, and know that at any moment you are going to have to sit in it, and play the rest of the scene in wet knickers, can be daunting.

I loved that production of *Romeo and Juliet* and learned a lot from the sensitive, well-educated, thoughtful and kind young people in that company. It was also a bonus to work with Julia, who set the tone of the whole production.

My friend Mary Millar, who had played Rose in *Keeping Up Appearances*, was dying of cancer. I had known for some time that she was fighting the illness. We used to talk on the telephone regularly when she would tell me about what it was like to go bald after chemotherapy. With her usual indomitable spirit, she would describe her trip to the supermarket when she wore a jockey cap to cover her head. Catching anyone staring at her she would raise her cap and curtsy. They would then leave her alone. When she felt really depressed we would talk about spirituality and the Christian religion.

I was next offered the part of Mrs Palmer senior in *The Life and Crimes of William Palmer* for Yorkshire Television. My old friend David Reynolds was producing and Alan Dossor was the director. By now, my arm was much more flexible. The muscles were damaged but with a lot more work and exercise I knew I could rebuild them. The leading man, Keith Allen, playing my son the murderer William Palmer, gave a brilliant performance, and I loved working with him. He knew my work and was considerate and generous in every scene we played together, despite the enormous pressure and stress he had while playing such a complex character.

As we were filming in the autumn, it was much colder. My first long scene with Keith was a discussion while we walked past a gaggle of geese. The scene then continued as I descended some steps leading to a boat moored to a jetty by the river. It was a long scene and the director wanted to film it in one take. Here we go, I thought. Working with geese is going to be fun. The animal trainer shooed them into position. First they went the wrong way. All stop and start again. We had so much dialogue to say and yet everything depended on these geese going the right way and the cameraman getting them in shot. After endlessly repeating our scene, the necessary miracle happened. The feathery fiends turned the right way and we had a take. Yorkshire Television had found some wonderful locations and the designers, wardrobe and property departments created a great sense of the period.

I was now beginning to feel quite cheeky again as my arm felt pretty normal. I practised swinging it up and down so I would eventually be able to wave my wand in the best fairy godmother tradition.

Gary had to work on another production so Bradley Walsh, an extremely funny comic and later a regular in *Coronation Street*, was playing Buttons in the Nottingham production of *Cinderella*. Bradley was great fun and full of naughtiness and I knew I would be happy working with him. Nigel and Peter were still playing the ugly sisters and Bob Carolgees with Spit was also one of the original cast. All the other cast had changed. Instead of Rolf, Peter Baldwin, who had been a regular in *Coronation Street*, was playing the baron.

We began our rehearsals in London for a week before moving to Nottingham. I booked into the hotel nearest to the theatre so I could easily walk there every day. The flooring on stage was a serious problem. Dancers began complaining about aching limbs and strained muscles. Carrying my heavy costume was hurting my legs and ankles. I was not worried about my arm any more but my knees. I was finding the two shows a day very tiring. However, I was still having fun, especially with Nigel and Peter. We discovered that from my dressing-room window we could see the young men in the restaurant across the road changing into their waiters' uniforms. I told the girl dancers, who crowded into my room, and waved and made cat calls at them. They responded by mooning at us. Nigel and Peter soon joined in and it became a regular game.

One night there was a bomb scare right near my hotel and the street was sealed off by the police. I stayed in a bar with Nigel and Peter for a while, and then after I thought the police had had long enough to sort out whether there was a bomb or not, decided to return to my hotel. I was stopped by a young policewoman. I told her where I was going and she talked into her walkie-talkie, 'There's an old lady here, who's trying to get back to the hotel.' What old lady is she talking about, I wondered, looking round. With horror, I realized she was describing me. I suppose I was hobbling about a bit as I walked.

When John came to collect me at the end of the pantomime season in February 1998, and saw how much the hard flooring had affected my legs, he said that was the end of my pantomime days. I agreed. Like Rolf, I had to accept my limitations. Since then I have been offered many pantomimes and have turned them all down.

～

BEFORE SETTING OFF for Australia I had a good rest. By now I had resigned from all of my committees, and as a magistrate. The only position I still held was as president of the Brighton and Hove Entertainment Managers Association, which met once a month. As soon as I stopped working on the hard stage my legs improved and I could walk more easily.

I worked on a couple of radio plays but that was easy compared to the pantomime. I also began working again on my novel. Fan letters continued arriving and the pile needing a reply grew to a mountain. Many fans greet actors or other entertainers at the stage door of the theatre or often outside a studio if they know they are appearing on a programme. They are usually polite, thoughtful and happy to wait patiently for an autograph and a chat. I had gone to the National Theatre with my friend Stella. I can assure you there is nothing more inhibiting than being followed into the lavatory by a party of schoolgirls and their teacher who are waiting outside your cubicle for you to sign autographs. I did not come out of the cubicle. In the end they gave up and left. Stella, rightly, was aghast. Teacher and pupils had behaved abominably.

I arrived at Brisbane airport in the early hours of the morning. Even so, Gail and Lisa were waiting, bright-eyed and bushy-tailed, and drove me to the apartment they had found for me overlooking the Brisbane River. I had two days to acclimatize before starting rehearsals. After they left, I went out on to the balcony and breathed in the fresh Queensland air. I was back in Australia; I was home. The emotions I felt overwhelmed me.

After unpacking and sleeping for a few hours, I awoke to a perfect blue sky with the river already full of life. The fishermen were out with their nets, young school children were rowing their canoes in time to the accompanying shouts from their instructors. The sleek City Cats, a public transport speedboat service, were picking up people heading up the river for work in the city. There were joggers pacing themselves along the river walk, and there were people swimming in the apartment block pool below my balcony. So much life, so much positive energy.

Since I had last been in the city, Brisbane had grown architecturally into a model of optimistic design. Whoever was in charge of the planning and the running of the city possessed a sense of vision and inspired taste. The Brisbane people appreciated the public services and were proud of their city, and proud of being Australian. They did not throw rubbish in the streets or scrawl graffiti. Wherever I travelled in Queensland I was aware of how much care the people took of their towns and cities.

The Australian cast were friendly and welcoming. When we began the read-through the director, Peter Williams, knew it inside out and the ideas just flowed; we got on immediately. He was wonderfully extrovert and demonstrative and made me laugh a lot.

The publicity calls were non-stop. Australia loved *Keeping Up Appearances*. The fact that a Gympie girl was appearing in it was a source of great amusement and pride. Charmaine Dobson, who was with Channel Seven, approached me. She was from Gympie herself and wanted me to fly back to the town in a helicopter, then take the train that I used to travel on to my bush school. It had just been renovated and was now a historical tourist attraction that was going to be operating in the region. Because I had described the old train in my book *The Seventh Sunrise*, Channel Seven wanted me to read that section of my book while travelling on the train. I agreed to take part, although I was a bit nervous of flying by helicopter. We took off from the studio grounds and my stomach disappeared to somewhere near my ankles.

The whole vast countryside between Brisbane and Gympie opened up before me: the extraordinary Glass Mountains; the winding Mary River that flowed past our house when I was a child twisted and turned through the exotic landscape. I lost my fear of the flight as the beauty of it all overwhelmed me. As we circled around the landing site in Gympie, I could see my old home, and a circle of women with greying hair.

'Who are those ladies?' I asked Charmaine.

'They are your old school friends,' she replied.

They were all waving and had books in their hands, copies of *The Seventh Sunrise*.

I was amazed. As they greeted me, the faces were all familiar. Their names came back to me in a moment. Girls I had known from schools in Gympie and Dagun – like Margaret Sharman, now Margaret Stallard, whom I had fought in the convent playground. Some of the older ladies were my father's friends. They told me wonderful things about him. What a friend he had been to them, how much he had contributed to the town. Then I was whisked off by car to the station where I boarded the train and sat with the Channel Seven interviewer. The train shunted off on its journey.

Despite being overcome by so many emotions, I managed to read the piece from my book to camera. We passed the small bush stations and I felt as excited as a child, the child I used to be. I forgot the camera as I yelled out the names of the stations and the farms there. The herds of cows looked so healthy, the fields so lush, I was falling in love with the land as my father once had. It was beautiful. I was shattered when I returned by helicopter to Brisbane, both physically and emotionally. When the programme went on air, it knocked out every other channel. They had never had such high viewing figures. The programme's popularity was reflected in the theatre's bookings. We were sold out. When the play opened, charabancs of farmers and people from the Gympie area arrived in Brisbane for the show. In Toowoomba, again some of my father's friends turned up to tell me how much they had loved and respected him. The vast theatre there was sold out. It was an excellent production, beautifully directed by Peter. His ideas for comedy were formidable and brilliant. It is lovely to hear an audience howling with laughter, and to see them grinning when you come out to meet them afterwards.

After a week on the Gold Coast, we returned for a few more weeks at Brisbane. John had flown out to see the show and found it very funny. He returned to England via Los Angeles so he could see our son. I arranged to travel back the same way so I could meet up with him too.

The audiences continued to pack into the theatre. One night, I came on to the stage in my smart cocktail dress – I had the first lines in the play. I looked down into the stalls to see three rows of people all dressed as Onslow and Daisy. The women had Daisy hairpieces, patterns on their T-shirts and down their tights. I nearly fell off the stage. I had seen people dressed like Rolf Harris in the pantomimes we did together but never Daisy look-alikes in any play I had performed in England.

One Sunday, Charmaine drove me back to Gympie. Margaret Stallard had organized a girls' lunch for me and I wanted to put some flowers on my father's grave. I had a great time. All the women were so interesting and very strong people. We joked about the past schooldays and caught up on all the gossip of the town. I found out quickly where one of my mother's friends was staying in an old people's home, and visited her on the way to my father's grave. The stone was there, as I had arranged it to be in 1981.

While Charmaine went off to talk to her granny who was buried in the same graveyard, I told my father how I understood why he had stayed in Australia. He had done what was right for him.

Gail asked me whether I was interested in returning to the Twelfth Night Theatre again some time and I said I would love to return. We arranged to meet when she was next in England and I flew down to Sydney to see my old friend Kevin Palmer; then on to Los Angeles to see my son. It is a very long and tiring journey from Australia to Los Angeles and I was physically and emotionally exhausted from my work and from reviving all my childhood memories of Gympie.

~

EDWARD, WHO WAS now heading two film distribution companies, greeted me at Los Angeles airport with American speed and energy. He had arranged for me to stay at a lovely hotel in Rodeo Drive in Beverly Hills for a few days before taking me for a trip to Las Vegas. His apartment nearby was a little small for both of us. He left me to sleep for a while before taking me out for dinner. We gossiped for hours and caught up on all our news. California agreed with him. He was bouncy and full of beans, and far more positive than when he had last been in England. The trip to Las Vegas was amazing. Ed had arranged a very good deal and I was astounded at the size of my hotel room. We hired a car and went exploring everywhere. We went to extravagant shows, ate in wildly different restaurants, and saw the wonderful, musical water display at the Bellagio Hotel. For three days we had a ball before returning to Los Angeles.

Everywhere we went people would come up to me, looking curiously at my son, and tell me how much they loved *Keeping Up Appearances*. The series was enormously popular in America. I would introduce my son to them and they would always look relieved. They could not cope with the idea of Daisy with a handsome toy boy.

It was difficult for both of us when I left him at the airport. I missed him dreadfully when he first left for America, but he had begun a new life in a country where he was happy, and I, as a mother, had to let him go.

~

BACK IN LONDON, my agent wanted me to go and meet a Hungarian director called Peter Medak who was over from Hollywood for a few days. He would be making a film, *David Copperfield*, for Hallmark Films and wanted to see me for the part of Clara Peggotty, a beautiful substantial role. We met up in London and seemed to get on well. I went home and thought no more about it but my agent was determined I should be in the film. When an offer came up to play a wonderful old tramp lady in an episode of *The Bill*, he was worried the timing might clash with it.

The film company was playing games, saying they might offer the part to Joan Plowright. I told my agent to book me with *The Bill* regardless. So I started work with the director Chris Hodson, whom I had worked with before. I was playing Brenda, a tramp, in the episode 'S.A.D.' As soon as the film company knew that I had started work on *The Bill*, they offered me Peggotty and wanted me to fly to Dublin to start rehearsals with the dialect coach so that we all had the same Norfolk accent. Now they would have to wait until I had finished my work playing the tramp.

The week before I was due to start work on *The Bill*, my dear friend Mary Millar died. I missed her, missed our long talks on the telephone and her zany sense of humour.

When I turned up at the place where the production office and changing rooms are on *The Bill* I saw a group of other actors waiting in the lobby. I asked them where the read-through was taking place and they all fell about laughing. One of the actors told me I just had to put my costume on, show it to the producer, then just turn up for the filming.

The regular cast work incredibly hard, often filming three productions at the same time – I saw my friend Herbert Wise was directing one. He seemed as confused as I was about the new way people were working. One of the regular actors in the series told me that my chum Dorothy Tutin was horrified about there being no rehearsal when she had been booked for an episode. I knew I could cope with the new way of working, but I realized how fortunate I had been during the past few years with the work I had been doing.

I was covered in muck for my part of the tramp. The best

compliment I received was when a bystander watching the filming told the director how lucky he was to find an old tramp who was co-operating with them. I had to play the mouth organ while sitting in a shop doorway, have a punch-up with a passing shopper and end up in jail. This was the tramp's moment of triumph as her intention was to be in a warm place, clean and deloused, with food for Christmas.

~

WHEN I FLEW to Dublin for *David Copperfield*, I was taken to a very grand hotel where the cast were staying. The two Americans in the cast were in a different hotel and also had a much bigger caravan than the ones we had on location. I began work straightaway with the dialect coach, a wonderful Irishman and a great teacher, who filled me with confidence. It was a ridiculous time of year to be filming. It was cold, some of the locations were muddy, and they wanted us to work long hours until after three in the afternoon before having lunch. That was when the light faded. We would then work into the night, often not finishing until ten thirty. As the car had picked me up at six in the morning, this was a long day.

A wagon, nearly the size of a double-decker bus, was brought on to the location with one carthorse pulling it. It looked wonderful as far as period authenticity was concerned. Freddy Jones, playing Barker, was in the driving seat, having gone round the lanes a couple of times. The riggers hauled me up to sit on the seat, where I found there were no sides to hold, and no barrier between the actors' feet and a sheer drop to the horse's hooves. The child playing the young David Copperfield was dressed in white satin which was slippery to hold. Warning bells went off in my head. This was an accident waiting to happen. The wagon was top heavy. The lane, along which we were supposed to travel was bumpy, and led over a small bridge. There was only a narrow wall separating the lane from a drop into the stream below. One slip and we would all be over the edge. The young boy could fall down to the horse's huge hooves, especially if I could not hold on to the slippery satin suit he was wearing.

I told the director the whole set-up was too full of risks. I also reminded him that no American would ever set foot on such a potentially dangerous carriage. The line producer was called, and the first assistant, who told me they would never risk our lives. I pointed out that no insurance company would ever pay damages for an accident as there were no safety guards and no barrier between the seat and the horse's hooves. I also told them that while I had the utmost respect for Freddy Jones as an actor, a skilled horseman should be in control of the reins. We argued, and I offered my part to be recast. They agreed to rebuild a smaller wagon, and to put sides in so we could hold on, and to have a horse handler to control the reins. The line producer also told me he would show me the insurance cover to reassure me. Afterwards the young boy's parents thanked me. They too had been worried about the carriage and the safety of their son. I could have hit them. Why had they not complained? Why did I always have to fight the battles? Freddy was a bit miffed as well. He felt confident that, as he had gone round the lanes a couple of times, he could handle the horse. I assured him I was concerned about the unexpected happening when only a trained horseman would be able to cope.

Later on in the filming my fears were confirmed. We were about to get on to the smaller carriage when a sudden gust of wind blew a makeshift sail over the horse and carriage frightening the animal, which tried to bolt. It had to be quite forcibly restrained.

We were given a short Christmas break from the filming. I was picked up at Gatwick by the studio car and driven home. I began telling the driver something, the next moment I was home and he was waking me up. He was laughing. He told me I had zonked out mid-sentence, and snored all the way home. My brief holiday break was much needed. I was feeling dreadfully tired and dreaded the thought of returning to Dublin with the tough schedule of filming.

John and I spent our New Year's Eve at a splendid dinner party with our friends Barry and Gay Fearn. I sat next to the witty Earl of Limerick, an appropriate person to be with, as I was flying back to Dublin on New Year's Day.

At the Dublin hotel I found Murray Melvin. We were both working on the same scene the following afternoon. Murray and I had had enormous fun in Paris with *Oh, What a Lovely War*. I was able to pass on all Kevin Palmer's news, and we gossiped for hours about all our old friends from Theatre Workshop. I told him about turning up for Joan Littlewood's book-signing in March 1994. She had written a huge autobiography called *Joan's Book*. All of her ex-theatre workshop actors had loyally turned up, and were standing in a queue to pay homage, and receive her signature. We had met up quite often while she was writing the book and she knew I had gone through the baptism of book signings with my novels. Various people were sitting at her knees as we slowly filed past. She was loving every moment. As I reached her, she waved her arm at the long queue. 'Did you have as many people queuing at your book signing?' she challenged me.

'No,' I replied, 'but I know two women who did.'

'Who?' she demanded.

'Margaret Thatcher and Joan Collins,' I replied.

'Cow,' she said, and wrote 'To Judy, the sexy actress, with my love, Joan.'

I felt anything but sexy as Murray and I began our scene in the rain. With wind machines blowing at you and water pouring down your neck, you feel like experimental animals being tested for water endurance. You have to shout your head off so the sound operators can get your words recorded, which always means swallowing a lot of hose water. It is an uncomfortable experience, strictly for people like Gene Kelly.

I began the beach scenes in mid-January. Ostensibly, Nigel Davenport – who was playing my brother – and I were sitting mending fishing nets in the sun. I could hardly move my fingers, I was so cold.

There were many well-known British actors who worked on the film. The caravans were grouped in such a way that we could gossip easily. I was delighted to see Eileen Atkins there. She is a very down-to-earth person, and I respect her work.

One wet afternoon I was mooching around waiting for my scene. A man in a green suit began to talk to me. I liked him and we talked easily. I found myself telling him about the great sense of belonging I experienced when I went back to Australia. It turned out he was a priest who had just returned from years of missionary work abroad, and was happy to be in a small town in Ireland. We parted, having enjoyed the conversation, and the next day he sent someone round with the present of a book and an accompanying letter. It often happens to me, an immediate rapport with a stranger. I have met many such people in my life and they remain like beacons of warmth in my memory. I also went to visit my old friend Gordon Thomas, who was still living near Wicklow. He and his wife Edith made me very welcome. There is something about old friends. You may not see them for a while but when you do meet up again it is easy to pick up where you left off. We spent the whole day catching up on all our news.

Chapter Twenty-one

1999–2001

~

BY THE TIME I had finished work on *David Copperfield* I was incredibly tired but I was booked straightaway on to another film for Hallmark, *Mary, Mother of Jesus*, to play the innkeeper's wife. It was to be made in Budapest. As I was involved in only a few scenes and would have quite a bit of free time, I decided to go. I was put into a beautiful hotel, built on the eastern, Pest side of the city, with a balcony overlooking the River Danube. On the other side of the river rose the hills of Buda. The first day was spent being fitted for my outfits and make-up checks. Geraldine Chapman was being fitted as well so she and I were able to catch up with news about people we knew. It was good to see her again.

The Hungarians have a great film history and are thrilled to be using their studios again. They treat their actors wonderfully well, bringing you little cakes and endless hot or cold drinks while you sit around on location waiting for the cameras. The same Hungarian cameraman I worked with on *David Copperfield* was with us and he knew I worked fast. My first scene was negotiating some stone steps with a lighted candle while a wind machine blew full blast. I had to shout all my dialogue to a famous Hungarian actor who was playing the innkeeper, then talk to Mary and Joseph and usher them into the stables, keeping the candle alight at all times. I did it, much to the amazement of the crew. In another scene we performed with due reverence and sense of wonderment at the child's birth. The shepherds and the innkeeper and his wife were kneeling in the hay, paying homage to the 'Holy Family'; and so were the animals.

The camera was behind them and slightly raised, so the picture must have looked quite beautiful. We actors had to put up with the animals' bored faces and their less than holy behaviour, and keep our faces full of wonderment throughout the dialogue. The nearest goat sneezed, leaving a pile of snot dangling from its nose; one donkey peed long and hard, forcing the focus puller to hop over the resultant river; another donkey farted and then dumped a pile of poo; but the sheep behaved remarkably well. At the end of the take we all exploded with yells of 'uuuggghhh' and someone wiped the goat's nose.

I had a whole day free, and decided to take my son's advice to visit the Gellert thermal baths. These are the oldest baths in Budapest and are part of the famous Hungarian Spa Hotel. I queued for my ticket for a locker, bath towel and a massage, then slipped into the beautifully hot spring waters. There were a lot of really big Hungarian women soaking in the two baths. Some of them made me feel as thin as Twiggy, and that takes some doing.

Then I queued for my massage. The masseuses were great strapping women lathering all the female bodies that were lined up on soap-covered slabs, and then massaging with some strength. There were a lot of slapping sounds. As I lay on my back, I could see a long row of soap-covered pubic hairs reaching for the ceiling. I wondered what would happen if the masseuse squeezed too hard. Would I shoot out like a bar of soap knocking all the other soapy bodies off their slabs? After being lathered and pummelled until my skin tingled, I was helped off the slab and headed for the showers and the baths again. I have never felt so clean in all my life, except perhaps at the spring pools near Auckland in New Zealand.

When I returned home I was still feeling tired, which surprised me – the working schedule in Budapest had hardly been hectic. I was booked to play Greengrass's sister Isobella for an episode of *Heartbeat* for YTV. It was an outrageous part to play and good fun. My old friend from repertory days, Derek Fowlds, was a regular in the series and it was good to see him again.

When I travelled back home via London I met up with Gail Wiltshire from Brisbane who was in London on business. John, Gail and I went to the theatre and then out to dinner and I assured her that I would come back to Australia to do another play. I asked that next time perhaps I could play a smaller part so I would not feel so shattered at the end of each performance. She said she would see what she could find for me.

The day after I had seen Gail I was incredibly tired and just wanted to sleep all the time. Fortunately my annual medical check-up was due, and a clever nurse spotted diabetes and told my doctor. So there was an immediate series of blood tests. Sure enough I had type two diabetes. I could not understand why I had developed it. There was no diabetes in the family. Four of us from *Keeping Up Appearances* developed type two diabetes; all of us from different backgrounds, different age groups and none of us with diabetes in the family. I wondered what the common factor could be: overwork and stress?

In Brighton, we are very fortunate in having first-class national health facilities for diabetics. I found out everything there was to know, attended classes given by diabetic experts, had my eyes checked for any damage done by the disease, and my feet exam-ined. My doctor told me to lose weight and to eat a minimum of five servings of vegetables and fruit a day. It worked. Since being diagnosed, I have lost weight and exercised more. I have totally changed my eating habits and tried to remove myself from any stress, which is not easy. A telephone call to an office with a list of push-button options to cope with is taxing; listening to tinny taped music while being left waiting on the phone drives me berserk; talking to someone in Bangalore to get a telephone number in London is beyond comprehension. Stress starts the moment you get out of bed.

As soon as I had reduced my weight and got used to the med-ication, John and I decided to fly to New York and meet our son there for a pre-Christmas week. New York before Christmas is quite wonderful with all the spectacular decorations. We visited every-thing from the Metropolitan Museum of Art to the Statue of Liberty. I am not good with great heights but at the top of the twin towers of the World Trade Center, I was able to hold on to the chrome bar by the window and look down at the New York traffic moving along below. It struck me then that I was standing inside a building built by people belonging to the richest and most powerful nation in the world. I thought what a great responsibility it was for the American people, to have such a huge influence in the world. We had our picture taken at the top, a place never to be revisited.

On New Year's Eve, after returning home from a party, we watched the nations celebrate the dawn of the new millennium. I was so proud of the Australians. They celebrated with such style and such confidence. The less said about London and the Dome, the better.

~

MY NEXT BIRTHDAY was going to be my sixtieth. Remembering how dreadfully both my mother and mother-in-law behaved when they reached sixty, and not forgetting the traditional lies actresses tell about their ages, I decided to celebrate my birthday in style. I would rather be known as a reasonable sixty- than a decrepit fifty-year-old. John threw a dinner party for me in the Milne Room at the Garrick Club. It was a wonderful evening spent with friends. I was thrilled at being sixty. All those years of paying national insurance stamps and taxes, and now I was going to have a pension, to be paid for doing nothing. Everyone got on well at the party, though it started dramatically. James Herbert, the horror writer, and his wife Eileen were dropped off at the club. The car, however, was towed away when the chauffeur went for a pee. He had to get a taxi back to the club to ask Jim for money to pay all the charges to reclaim the car. Poor Jim and Eileen had no money on them but a whip-round among our friends produced nearly two hundred pounds in cash to cover the costs. Much hilarity followed that little incident.

Brian Murphy gave a wonderfully funny speech on behalf of the guests and raucous laughter echoed through the night. One of my favourite presents came from Nigel Ellacott and Peter Robbins. It was a remote-controlled fart machine, from which I have derived endless pleasure, especially during a dinner party in danger of becoming a bit pompous.

In 2000 I did a lot of radio. I was also offered the part of Mother Cuxsom in the film *The Mayor of Casterbridge* from the book by

Thomas Hardy. I had to learn the old West Country dialect, which I managed quite well, but – as the director, David Thacker, joked – when we all spoke the dialect correctly, we could have been speaking Serbo-Croat for all the sense it made to today's viewers. It was a very good adaptation by Ted Whitehead and I was working with Tony Haygarth again, whom I had not seen since we were together on *December Rose*. The company was friendly, and because I warned them about my being diabetic, they never let me go too long without having some fruit. When journeying back to Brighton, I had to make a point of stopping for snacks.

Most of my best scenes went on to the cutting-room floor. David was most apologetic and I was distraught. However, when I saw the final production it really did not need them; it would have taken away from the power of the younger people's excellent performances.

Then Central Television got in touch with me about playing Josie in *The Wrong Side of the Rainbow*. A group of writers had written individual soliloquies – based on real case histories – representing different cases of homeless people. Lavinia Murray had written the one that they wanted me to portray. It was beautiful writing and I loved the character. When the series was transmitted, money would be raised to provide food and shelter for people who, for one reason or other, were without a roof over their heads.

Fiona Oates was the documentary producer in charge of my filming. I was given a dog, who took one look at my dishevelled, dirty appearance and turned up his nose in disgust. I think if he could have spoken, he would have said, 'I'm really not with this person.' I was being filmed on a broken-down bench, surrounded by litter, in a park with some of the most beautiful rose bushes I have ever seen.

A group of tramps hurled abuse and tin cans at me when I walked over with the production team to the bench. We found out that they thought I was a tramp from another area who had strayed into their territory and was getting paid for something to do with television. When they were told what was really happening, they sat quietly on the bench opposite to watch my performance. When

I started to rant and shout, the dog walked off in disgust and the tramps cheered and joined in the shouting, which was great for the scene. We shot the whole thing in a day and a half and I loved every moment of it.

Just before the programme went out on air, there was a party where all the social workers who had been working with the homeless people came to a showing of our work. I received the greatest compliment from the real-life Josie's social worker, who asked me how I had managed to sound and act just like her. I said Lavinia's great writing had helped me to find the character.

I also had a request to perform the role of Josie at the Donmar Warehouse Theatre run by Sam Mendes. A young director, Josie Rorke, who was sponsored by Carlton, was putting the now critically acclaimed television production *The Wrong Side of the Rainbow* on stage for a gala Sunday performance. The funds raised would be given to the London Connection, a day centre for young, homeless people, based in Covent Garden. Everyone she asked agreed to take part – Art Malik, Charles Dance, Cherie Lunghi, Emilia Fox, David Calder and Roger Sloman. We all turned up for rehearsals and worked free of charge to support the Carlton Homeless campaign.

~

MEANWHILE I WAS still writing my novel, which was set in the new millennium, and already the synchronicities were beginning again. Events I was dreaming up for the book were beginning to happen in the daily news stories.

Our ruby wedding anniversary was on 18 December 2000. We talked about having a party but decided not to. Instead we celebrated quietly, on our own, by walking along Brighton Palace Pier where we had first met. The pier has changed considerably since John first introduced himself to me. We wandered round our old haunts and sat having morning coffee together. In the evening we went out for a Chinese meal.

We had a quiet Christmas with friends. I was feeling quite proud of myself because I had managed to get my blood sugar levels right down so I was able to come off tablets. I was now on diet control instead of rattling with pills.

By January 2001 I was feeling quite fit again and was looking forward to working at the Donmar. Young Josie Rorke was full of wonderful ideas. The theatre was packed and after only two days' rehearsal and, feeling quite nervous, we put on a really great show. We would watch each other from the wings and cheer each other on. I was proud to be a part of it. Afterwards, Carlton threw a party at the Ivy Restaurant, where we all let our hair down.

The previous year, Brian Murphy had sent me a play written by his friend Ron Aldridge, called *You're Only Young Twice*. Brian wanted to tour the play but wanted to work with chums he knew would all get on well together. There is nothing worse than getting stuck on a tour with people you loathe. I can survive it, and have done so, but it is no fun. I liked the script and the role of Rose so agreed to take part. The producers decided we could rehearse and open at Eastbourne. The playwright, Ron Aldridge, who was also directing us, had cast my friends Victor Spinetti and Carmen Silvera in the other roles. So it looked as if we were going to have a lot of fun together. I was also pleased because it meant that for the first few weeks, I could live at home in Brighton and drive to Eastbourne every day.

Just after the dates were set for the play, the producers of Public Service Broadcasting in America wanted to arrange a series of chat shows for me as part of their annual PBS appeal. It would mean flying out to Dallas at the beginning of December. I talked it over with John and we agreed it was a lovely excuse to stay on for Christmas and spend the time with Edward in California.

During rehearsals at Eastbourne, we had a press photo call where the Eastbourne Heads of Entertainment introduced the four of us as 'national treasures'. I whispered to Victor, 'When they start calling you a national treasure, you know you're getting old.'

Then, one day, while getting ready to drive from my home to the Devonshire Park Theatre in Eastbourne, where we were playing, I glanced into the sitting room and saw what I presumed was a Bruce Willis film on television. I was saying to John how clever production companies were getting with digitalization work, when

I realized this was not a film. I was watching the news, and a plane had just flown into the World Trade Center. I was shocked. Then another plane flew into its second tower. John and I could not believe what was happening. Our son telephoned from America. 'I'm looking at the picture of the three of us standing at the top of the Twin Towers,' he said. 'Isn't this terrible?' There were several jokes in our play about the fear of flying. We cut them out from that performance until the end of the run.

Planning where to stay when on tour is quite an adventure. Victor and I swapped names of hotels. I thought I had found a very good cheap deal with a hotel in Crewe. Victor joined me while Carmen found her own hotel. Ours turned out to be a knocking shop. Large bundles of sheets went out each day and yet there were only two tables disturbed by breakfast, Victor's and mine. From then on Victor, Carmen and I decided we would pay more for comfort. As 'national treasures', we reckoned we should look after ourselves.

Carmen and I often dined together after the show. I enjoyed her company and we had a lot in common. She had spent much of her youth in Canada, and felt the same way about it as I did about Australia. It was while we were walking back to the hotel that I noticed Carmen was having trouble with her breathing. I became quite worried for her and suggested she went to a doctor to sort the problem out. It was then she confessed to me that during the following year she would celebrate her eightieth birthday. I, as a mere sixty-one-year-old, thought she was incredible.

The Christmas lights were decorating the shops in Guildford when the tour finished. The cast all promised to keep in touch and they wished me luck with my trip to America and all the US TV stations.

Chapter Twenty-two

2002–2004

~

IN JANUARY 2002 I began work on the old play *Ghost Train*. I had met the producer, Ian Dickens, while touring the previous year and found that he shared the same philosophy as the late Anthony Quayle. He wanted to present first-class plays on tour to encourage people back to the regional theatre. I liked this young man and I immediately had faith in him, so I agreed to tour for twelve weeks before leaving for Australia to work with Gail at the Twelfth Night Theatre again.

We were rehearsing in Felixstowe for a few weeks, where the first person I saw was Henry McGee, who was playing the station master and whom I had worked with on the Feydeau farces and then with Charlie Drake. After the warmth of California, the aching cold of the English east coast was a real challenge to the survival of humour. We were all booked into the same hotel. I had a room with a sea view and plenty of space to prowl around while learning my lines. Each morning I would stride out along the seafront on the way to the theatre. After rehearsals, several of us would brave the wind and cold to walk briskly back to the hotel.

Ghost Train was written by Arnold Ridley, who was a well-known character actor and played Private Charles Godfrey in the situation comedy *Dad's Army*. The play is set in 1925 and takes place in the waiting room at Fal-Vale, a wayside station on the South Cornwall Joint Railway, during a winter evening. I was playing Miss Bourne, an old spinster with a parrot in a cage. Having alighted from a train, the passengers are stranded in the station waiting room for the night, and are subjected to a host of ghostly happenings. Miss Bourne is offered a sip of brandy from a flask to calm her fears, drinks the lot and spends the rest of the time sleeping it off on a table in the corner of the waiting room. Then she says the last line of the play.

This was a seriously dangerous part for me to play, because I only have to lie down, and I really do go to sleep. I was warm, I knew all the words, and the next thing I knew I was having my shoulders gently shaken by one of the younger actresses. My snores could just about be heard by the audience! Luckily for me the snores went with Miss Bourne's character; Stanislavski would have approved. They were a really great bunch of actors. Knowing I might drop off to sleep, they would every so often gently tap me on the foot as they passed. In the blackouts, however, it was a free for all and two of the young men would either pinch my bum or tickle me – so much for respect. The last line of the play being mine, I would receive several tweaks of the feet to make sure I could pretend to wake up on time.

It was a fabulous show, brilliantly directed by Ian Dickens, and it was wonderful to hear the gasps of fright from the audience when they heard the sounds of the approaching ghost train. The effects were incredible. When I signed autographs at the stage door, it was gratifying to see *Keeping Up Appearances* fans had enjoyed this theatrical experience, and wanted to return to the theatre again.

As the tour progressed, and we all felt at ease with the text, my naughtiness welled up inside me. During a blackout, when the gas lights had all gone out, one young actor, Christopher Hackett, suddenly had to say, 'I smell gas!' This meant they could all light the lamps again. By now I had my remote-control fart machine with me and I had placed the little speaker close to where he would stand as he said his line. It was just a matter of timing the noise properly. The blackout came, I waited a few seconds and then pressed the remote control. The most dreadful noise came out of the box. To give Chris his due, he did not pause for one second, he just continued with the dialogue as if nothing had happened. Only one person came apart at the seams – me. The younger actors told me they could see my tummy shaking as I lay on the table. I had

to bury my face inside my coat to stop myself yelling with laughter. The audience were unaware of what was going on, and
thankfully Ian was not there, otherwise he would have killed me.

As we toured all the different towns and cities, I carried with
me the memories of past tours with different companies. In each
venue, come Friday and Saturday night, the yob culture dominated
the place. Drunken youths roamed in packs and we would all have
to be careful as we made our way back to our hotels. Taxis were a
must, even for short journeys. The same shopping malls with the
same chains of shops dominated most towns. Waste bins were not
emptied so refuse was drifting around the streets. Spotting a policeman was like trying to find a unicorn. I thought of all the years I
had spent on committees for preventative education, the endless
warnings from those committees that the cost of national drunkenness would soon outstrip their tax gains from the sales of alcohol.
As I listened to the defiant shouting, the obscene screaming from
drunken young girls who could hardly walk, saw the blood on
sleeves and the vomiting in the streets, I despaired. It was going to
take at least a couple of generations before any changes could be
made to the yob culture. And it would work only if the government
started action now.

Many places had spent a great deal of money on their theatres.
Local people were getting together and improving their old buildings. Some, however, thought that the building itself was far more
important than the show that would bring people into the theatres.
In Winchester, where I had never performed before, and will never
perform again, I was told they had spent a million pounds refur-
bishing the theatre, creating a modern restaurant in front, but they
had turned the dressing rooms into offices for administrators. Just
two dressing rooms, beautifully painted, were left for the performers, one for the men and one for the women; not very big ones
either. The manager came strutting up to me. 'Well, Miss Cornwell,
what do you think of all our improvements? We've spent a million
pounds on our theatre.'

'Who took the decision to turn all the dressing rooms into
offices?' I enquired.

'The committee,' he replied. 'Well, what do you think?'

'I think that the committee should be lined up against the wall and shot,' I said. He was very surprised at my reaction.

My final date with the *Ghost Train* was at Crewe, when Maggie Ashcroft, who had been with me in *You're Only Young Twice*, was rehearsing to take over from me when I left for Australia. I was sad to say goodbye to all the company and Ian said he hoped I would come back and work with him again – I felt a great loyalty to him.

∼

JOHN WAS TRAVELLING with me to Australia. This time, instead of flying straight to Brisbane, we decided to break the journey at Singapore and rest for a couple of days before travelling on. I loved Singapore. From the moment we landed at the well-run, scrupulously clean airport, I could see this was an efficient and orderly country. The people were charming and friendly; the streets were immaculately clean, possibly because at that time chewing gum was banned. Since then the World Trade Organization has insisted that chewing gum be allowed into Singapore. I hope they do not have the gum-marked pavements now that Britain has in every city. Our brief stay gave us time to recover from the long flight so that we arrived in Brisbane reasonably bright and alert.

Gail and her husband, Ken, met us at the airport at 6.30 a.m. and took us to our apartment by the river. The read-through was at ten o'clock so I had a couple of hours' rest before joining the rest of the cast.

Peter Farago, a director from England, was at the read-through. He was born a Hungarian, but had been brought up and educated in Britain. Before we started he told me how much he liked my work and was looking forward to working with me. Despite the seven-hour flight from Singapore, I was as bright as a button at the read-through.

It was a Ray Cooney play called *It Runs in the Family*. Gordon Kaye was playing Dr David Mortimore, the leading male part. I had already met him before when I was touring with Carmen Silvera and he had come to see her. He and Carmen had worked together for years on the situation comedy *'Allo 'Allo*. I was playing Matron in the Ray Cooney play.

During the coffee break I got to know the Australian actors. Some were British who now lived in Australia, like Katy Manning. Robert Colby, who was playing Dr Bonney, was also British and, like me, had been brought out to Australia as a child, returned to Britain with his parents, but had been yearning to return. At the first opportunity, he and his wife settled back in Australia. He understood exactly how I felt about returning to Queensland. Brian Cahill, who was playing Bill, remembered talking down the line to my father at station 4GY in Gympie when Brian was a young radio newsreader. Brian and his wife, Denise, have become close friends since.

By the afternoon, the jet lag hit me so Peter Farago let me go back to my apartment to sleep it off. For the rest of the rehearsals, I had a great time working on all the comedy business. John came to the opening night and laughed a lot. Although I was on and off the stage most of the time, I did not have to do as much as I had during the Ayckbourn play, so I could join in more and go to the functions organized by the theatre. In the play, as I crawled along the back of a window sill and apparently fell off, it was rewarding to hear the horrified gasp from the audience. When I was upside down in a wheelchair, showing my bloomers, it did occur to me that I was not ageing gracefully, but disgracefully. Here I was at sixty-two, showing my knickers, with naughty Gordon Kaye whispering out of the side of his mouth, 'I hope you haven't been eating any mung beans today,' and trying not to laugh in case I slipped off the wheelchair.

My old school friends got in touch with me. They organized a lunch party at the Gympie golf club and I drove up to see them on my free day. As before, on my last trip to Australia, I felt overwhelmed by the sense of belonging to this country. I talked it over with Robert Colby and he told me how the same emotions hit him when he returned to Australia. He thought of himself as Australian even when he had returned to England. John too revelled in the Australian way of life but soon had to return to England for his work as a columnist.

Next the company was due to travel to Perth. Kevin Palmer phoned me and invited me to Sydney to his retirement party. So I went to Perth via Sydney and joined in Kevin's celebrations, a wild party over a pub. After the party I returned to his house, where his partner, Bruce, had cooked dinner for a few of us. Kevin said to me, 'When are you coming back home to Oz, Jude? You know you belong here. You're a Gympie girl.'

In Perth, Lisa Broadby collected me from the airport. She was in charge of us as Gail was staying back in Brisbane. I was in the same apartment block as Gordon Kaye. He was very upset because he had heard that Carmen Silvera was in hospital, dying of cancer. Her eightieth birthday was near and her friends hoped to have her in her own home for the day. We phoned her on her birthday and she was thrilled to hear from us. While we were in Perth, Gordon wanted to know what to buy her as a present. He was desperate to see her before she died. We went out and found a beautifully delicate cocktail hat she could wear when receiving visitors; also a really good red lipstick.

While we were playing the theatre in Perth, we all drove down to Fremantle to see the market and the harbour. I remembered arriving in Fremantle as a child, when the family first reached Australia. The memory was so clear that I could even remember the women's conversations. They had been so excited about seeing all the food on display.

There were many British people who had settled in Perth. They came up to me all the time wanting to tell me how much they had enjoyed my work. A few of us drove out into the bush to see the great rock wave. The land spoke to the core of one's being. The smell of sandalwood permeated the country air. Even though I enjoyed being in Western Australia, I was still glad to return to Brisbane and Queensland. It was here that I felt most at home and I was glad that we were playing for a few more weeks at the Twelfth Night Theatre.

Several of my old school friends lived in Brisbane and we met up and talked for hours. There was an immediate cultural cohesion. We spoke a shorthand of understanding.

At the end of the run there was a farewell party. I stayed on in Brisbane for a while. My novel was beginning to speak to me once more and I began to write again. I flew down to Sydney to see

Kevin and Bruce and to meet Gary La Rocca, who was taking over Kevin's agency. Another school friend who lived in Sydney took me to the Sydney State Theatre. The standard of acting was exceptional, the young actors quite brilliant. I met the director afterwards who asked me whether I wanted to work in Sydney. I told Gary and he said, 'Come back to Oz, Judy. There'll be plenty of work for you here.'

I left Sydney on 1 August. As the plane circled before heading for Singapore, I looked down at the vast stretches of the city, the coastline and the land and felt a great pull towards the country I was leaving yet again.

~

THEN CUNARD CONTACTED me and wanted to know whether I could give a talk on the *Caronia*, which was leaving Southampton on 23 September for Cadiz, Barcelona and Civitavecchia, where we would leave the ship and fly back to England from Rome. John and I agreed to stay in Rome for a few days before flying back. The thought of travelling on the *Caronia* again made us laugh. We had been invited with many other guests to the launch of the *Caronia* in December 1999 after it had had a massive refit at Liverpool. We then sailed down the Irish Sea to Southampton where we transferred to the *QE2* for a lunch. The official launch of the *Caronia* took place in drizzling rain, on the Liverpool dockside. All the guests waving little Union Jacks stood patiently while Michael Buerk introduced Larry Pimentel, the president and chief executive of Cunard Line Ltd, and John Prescott, who was going to thank him for bringing the refit contract to Liverpool. Unfortunately John Prescott found the name 'Pimentel' difficult to remember. First he called the American Mr Pimento, and at the end of his speech of thanks he called him Mr Pimpernel. Michael Buerk looked as if he had swallowed a lemon. Hardened journalists were hysterical with laughter, and we all waved our flags frantically as if to cover up Prescott's gaffes. After a huge display of fireworks we sailed in a force-nine gale all the way to Southampton. I have never ever felt so ill on a journey.

So, with some apprehension, John and I set off again on the

Caronia. We had a wonderful time and finally laid to rest the memory of the stormy voyage from Liverpool.

I returned from Rome on 4 October in time to attend Carmen Silvera's memorial at St Paul's Church in Covent Garden. With many of her friends who spoke about Carmen and her life, I read some poetry. We all went on to the Garrick Club for drinks and canapés afterwards.

The memorial made me thoughtful. I had been to too many memorials over the years. So many of my friends had died. While I did not feel morbid about it, I now felt that the precious time left should not be squandered endlessly on work as an actress but on living. I still wanted to write because I can write anywhere, but I wanted to spend more time with my husband, doing all the things we wanted to do together. I also needed to spend more time in Australia.

So, we booked our flights to return to Brisbane. Ed said he would join us there for Christmas. I was leaving first, to arrange everything. This time I decided to break the journey twice, in Dubai and Singapore, before continuing to Australia. I reached Brisbane in late October and drove through a haze of blue spring blossom on the way to the apartment. Just breathing the air was filling my blood with energy. The sense of space returned. I felt alive. I was in my other homeland.

This was the first time in Brisbane that I had not been in a rush to accomplish something, or needing to learn lines, or having my inner time clock warning me to prepare for a performance in the theatre. I sat on the veranda drinking a cold Diet Coke, watching the movements on the river and generally luxuriating in the pleasure of living in the moment.

Someone once said to me that one is never truly a grown-up until both parents are dead. I was now a real grown-up jelly baby, with time to think and explore this beautiful country for myself. I explored the parks, the wonderful university complex, the city, the beaches, and spent endless hours going up and down the river on the City Cats. My mind was free to roam through the parallel lives I could have lived, and to imagine how different my life might have been if I had been allowed to return to Australia sooner.

When my son arrived from California he brought the fast pace of thought and speech with him. His energy was phenomenal. Over the following week, while we caught up on all our news, visited friends and shared our time together, he relaxed into the Australian rhythm. By the time John arrived and we were the family of three again, Christmas came and we celebrated Australian-style. Ed was the first to leave, returning at the end of December to Los Angeles. John and I welcomed in 2003 among all the Queenslanders who had turned up to see the great firework display on the South Bank.

In early January John had to return to England. I stayed on longer, visiting Sydney again to meet up with friends before leaving for England. I had an invitation from my friends in Gympie to attend the huge centenary celebrations for the schools in the town the following year. I said I would do my best to be there. Kevin had told me there was to be a memorial for Joan Littlewood at the Theatre Royal Stratford East, and he and Bruce were returning to England to attend. We arranged to meet there. Then I reluctantly boarded the plane at Sydney airport.

~

ON 2 FEBRUARY, all the old Theatre Workshop crowd turned up for the memorial. As I talked to them, I was remembering them as they had once been, when we had all worked together in *Oh, What a Lovely War*. The theatre was no longer the rather run-down, shabby affair of those days; now it was smart, well decorated and efficiently run.

My agent sent me a script to appear in an episode of *The Royal*. I agreed to play the part of Martha Hook, housekeeper to a priest. The wardrobe fittings were to be at the beginning of April and the read-through in the middle of April, starting the filming two days later.

While working on *The Royal* I had a scene with Robert Dawes, who had played my young son in the series *There Comes a Time*. Robert beamed with pleasure when we were working together, saying how lovely it was to work with me again because it felt so easy and natural. I accepted the compliment by assuring him that

I had enjoyed the scene too. Robert was playing a middle-aged doctor. In fact, as I watched a lot of television programmes, all the young men who had once played my sons in plays were now playing middle-aged parts. Perhaps it was time to write my autobiography I decided. I was most certainly old enough now.

~

IT HAS BEEN a strange experience reliving all the years. Patterns and cycles have emerged in my life. Who has influenced me? Because my grandmother had our family tree, which reached back to the twelfth century, I know from which ancestors I have inherited various characteristics. It seems as if I have often relived their lives with my own interests. I have followed the natures of warriors, adventurers, writers, magistrates and the performer. I have also upheld my father's family motto, 'Perseverance and faith'.

As a child I loved to parade my achievements before my father. He shared with me the idealism to which he aspired. His praise was akin to approval from the gods.

In my teens and older years, my mother was the person to whom I could boast about my conquests – both romantic and professional. She was the one who heard my wails of disappointment and was ready to kill anyone who hurt me. From her I learned about loyalty. She was the one I always phoned just to regurgitate old conversations.

I had two mentors, Sybil and Musi. Sybil gave me the confidence to become an actress and Musi inspired my imagination, the exploration of philosophies, the love of books and creative writing.

In choosing and loving my husband, John, I found all I had ever needed from anyone. He is my other half. Everything anyone had ever shared with me, he gave me all of that and more. He is my best friend as well as my husband and will always tell me the truth.

From my son I have learned what it is to love unconditionally. He is someone I will always be able to rely on, who is utterly loyal. He has shared the thoughts of his generation, insisting that I keep an open mind.

Then there is the entity I call my guardian angel. This power has taught me that miracles do exist, and shown me the difference between revelation and self-delusion. It has shown me that one of reason's greatest achievements is to realize reason's limitation. During my lifetime it has increased my understanding and shown me a path to follow.

In November 2003, I returned to Australia and spent a lot of time working on this book in Brisbane. Watching the river and all the changing moods in the ebb and flow inspired me. After Christmas and New Year, John returned to England and left me to write.

On 21 February 2004, I returned to Gympie for the centenary celebrations. By chance, I found a room in a new motel which had been built in the same road where I once lived. The room had excellent air conditioning. I needed it. The temperature was forty-two centigrade. My friend Margaret Stallard collected me in her car, and we drove out to join the others who had flown in from all over Australia, New Zealand and other parts of the world. The party was held at the big stadium, where there were fans but no air conditioning. Ice for the drinks was greatly in demand. All my friends were there. My hair which had started out all freshly washed and fluffy was now like wet seaweed against my head; my blouse was wet. Everyone else was in exactly the same state; except for the oldest convent girl, who was one hundred and two, frail but straight-backed, and looking fine and cool. She was asked to cut the centenary cake. She stood dignified and poised as she waited to cut the first slice.

As part of the oldest group we were allowed to get our supper first. Everything was done considerately and in an orderly fashion. It was as if I had never been away when I caught up with all the boys and girls I had known in the past. They stood before me, older, as I was, but with their faces changed only by experiences of life. Confessions of childhood thoughts, concerns, and family problems were shared as they never had been when we were children and trying to survive the perplexities of the world around us. Everywhere I looked there were familiar faces with stories to tell; the expressions had warmth, understanding and love from the sense of belonging.

As the rivulets of perspiration dripped into every part of my clothes, I suddenly needed to be on my own and definitely in an air-conditioned room. Margaret felt the same and drove me back to my motel. I peeled off my wet clothes and fell on to the cold sheets letting the air conditioning bring down my blood pressure. At any moment, I thought, my body was going to explode with spontaneous combustion.

I slept heavily, a videotape of my life parading through my dreams. At three o'clock in the morning I woke and realized it was my birthday. I made myself a cup of tea and let myself out of the door into the hot night air, and sat on the small chair outside.

The scents were the scents I used to breathe when I lived in this street. The stars in the Southern Hemisphere were the stars that I used to gaze at from my back door steps. A warm breeze touched my cheek.

Sixty-four years ago, this jelly baby was born on her mother's birthday. I realized that I should never have blamed my mother for leaving Gympie. She had done what was right for her. She would have died young if she had put up with the heat of the summers in this climate. There had been no air conditioning then. I wished her happy birthday and told her she was right all along.

I also told my father that he was right to stay in Australia. It might have taken a long time but now, as a grown-up, I understood.

As I sipped my tea, I saw two little lights form and dance in circles. The lights grew stronger and larger, dancing together towards me. I put down my tea and gazed at them. My sense of reason told me they were probably fire ants. But there was always the chance that maybe, just maybe they were the souls of my father and mother, wishing the jelly baby a happy birthday.

Index

~

fortieth birthday 263
joins alcoholism charities 265, 287
tour of New Zealand 269, 271–4
meets namesake cousin 274
visits Australia 274–5
elected to executive committee of
  Equity 278
films in Ireland 278–81
films in Prague 281–5
at British Council of Churches
  conference 286
becomes magistrate 287, 292–3, 306
Santa Claus premieres 295–8
silver wedding 298
films in Zimbabwe 301–5
home hit by hurricane 306–8
repertory in Belfast 309–10
visits Egypt 313–17
Keeping Up Appearances see sub-
  heading below
Christmas at health farm 329–30
problems with son's court case and
  mother's mental health 319,
  334–40, 341–2
mother's death 346
visits Grenada 340, 341
cruise to New York 347
breaks arm 351–2, 353
resigns from committees and as
  magistrate 356
Australian tour 350, 356–60
visits son in Los Angeles 360
films in Dublin 362–5
films in Budapest 366–7
in Australia again 367–8
sixtieth birthday 369
ruby wedding 371
diabetes diagnosed 368, 371
regional tour 374–7
Australian tour 377–80
gives talk on cruise ship 380–1
Australian visits 381–2, 384–5

films
  Country Dance (Brotherly Love)
    195–7, 200, 207
  Cry Freedom 301–3
  Cry Wolf 191
  David Copperfield 361, 362–5, 366
  *Every Home Should Have One (Think
    Dirty)* 197, 200–2, 207
  *Gingerbread House (Whoever Slew
    Auntie Roo?)* 210, 212–14
  Hieronymous Merkin . . . 186–7
  Mary, Mother of Jesus 366–7
  Mayor of Casterbridge, The 369–70
  Paddy 191, 297
  Rocket to the Moon 171
  Santa Claus the Movie 289–92, 295–7
  Two for the Road 166–9
  Wild Racers, The 175
  Wuthering Heights 205–6, 211, 212,
    232
radio 276–7, 349, 356
  Flight 230
  My Beautiful Career 336
television
  Anniversary 202
  Bergerac 299–300
  Bill, The 361–2
  Bonanza 80
  Bonus, The 207–8
  Boon 318
  Brothers Grimm 253–4
  Cakes and Ale 235–7, 263
  Call Me Daddy 178, 181, 188, 192,
    196, 207
  Call My Bluff 349
  Can Do show 95–7
  Charlie Drake Show 165
  Chinese Prime Minister, The 215
  Coronation Street 153
  Cranford 247
  December Rose 293–5
  Devil's Lieutenant, The 281–2